The Dark Stuff

Nick Kent was born and brought up in London. After making a name for himself as a contributor to the self-styled British underground press while still at Bedford College, he was asked to do the same by the *New Musical Express*. There followed a long period of collaboration that stretched through the 1970s, during which time Kent also enjoyed a career as a musician working with the Sex Pistols and recording with his own group the Subterraneans. In the 1980s he wrote for *The Face*, *Arena*, the *Sunday Times*, *Spin*, *Vox* and numerous other periodicals. In the 1990s he moved to France, where he still lives with his girlfriend, writer and TV personality Laurence Romance, and their son, James. In 2002 he was presented with the NME/Brats 'God-like genius' award for his thirty-year career as a rock writer, and he is currently a contributor to the *Guardian*, *Mojo* and France's *Libération*.

The Dark Stuff

Selected writings on rock music

NICK KENT

faber and faber

First published in 1994 by Penguin

First published in the United States by Da Capo in 1995

This new updated edition first published in the UK in 2007
by Faber and Faber Limited
74-77 Great Russell Sreet London WC1B 3DA

Photoset by RefineCatch Limited, Bungay, Suffolk
Printed in the UK by CPI Bookmarque, Croydon, CR0 4TD

A CIP record for this book is available from the British Library

ISBN 978-0-571-23271-0

10 9 8 7 6 5 4 3

Contents

Sources and Acknowledgements

'The Last Beach Movie Revisited' was written in the spring of 1993. The first two chapters use many quotes and describe incidents that were first featured in 'The Last Beach Movie', a 30,000 word text that the *NME* ran in three parts on 21 June, 28 June and 12 July 1975. The third part is based on an encounter first written up in an *NME*, 19 April 1980, feature entitled 'High and Bri', and the fourth comes largely courtesy of a French writer, Michka Assayas, whose remarkable interview with Wilson, conducted in the summer of 1992, takes up much of the text. I want to thank him here for so graciously allowing me full permission to quote from it.

'The Killer in Aspic' was first published in *The Face* in May 1989, under the title 'Man on Fire'.

'The Bewildering Universe of Roky Erickson and His Two-headed Dog' first saw the light of day as 'I Talked with a Zombie' in the *NME*, 30 August 1980.

'The Cracked Ballad of Syd Barrett', as it appears here, was written in the winter of 1992 but sections still correspond to the article of the same title that first appeared in the *NME*, 13 April, 1974. A couple of new quotes come from Jonathan Green's *Days in the Life: Voices from the English Underground 1961–1971* (Heinemann, 1988). Nicholas Schaffner's *Saucerful of Secrets* (Harmony, 1991) was also helpful.

'Brian Jones, Tortured Narcissus' first ran in *20/20* magazine, September 1989.

'Twilight in Babylon' was written in the summer of 1993. The piece fleetingly quotes from some of the many features I've written on the Stones, most notably 'Melodrama in Munich' (*NME*, 24 December 1974), 'Jagger Hits Out at Everything in Sight' (*NME*, 15 October 1977) and 'Back to Zero' (*Spin*, April 1986). The Glyn Johns quotes first appeared in a *Musician*, December 1988, interview with Bill Flanagan.

'All Dressed Up, Got No Place to Go' begins with a feature, 'Dead-End Kids on the Champs-Elysées', first printed in the *NME*, 26 January 1974. The coda was written in the autumn of 1993.

'Lou Reed: The Wasted Years' begins with an extended quote from John Cale taken from 'A Welshman in New York' (*NME*, 13 April 1974), followed by a shorter quote from Nico, from 'I was a Hausfrau from Hanover Until I Discovered Heroin'. The Lou Reed quote after that is taken from an interview written up by Tom Hibbert and run in *Q Magazine*, February 1989. The piece that follows originally appeared as 'A Walk on the Dull Side' in the *NME*, 9 March 1974.

'Sid Vicious – the Exploding Dim-Wit' first appeared in *The Face*, August 1986, under the title 'The Scum Also Rises'. Belated apologies to Hunter S. Thompson.

'Horn-rims from Hell' began life as 'The Man Who Would Be King', which ran in the *NME*, 27 August 1977. The coda is based around a summer 1991 encounter I later wrote up for the French journal *Libération*.

'Morrissey, the Majesty of Melancholia and the Light That Never Goes Out in Smiths-dom' is loosely based on several pieces I've previously written, chiefly 'Dreamer in a Modern World' (*The Face*, May 1985) and a piece on the Smiths in *Les Inrockuptibles* – a French quarterly – in June 1989. A couple of quotes also come from 'The Deep End', my final encounter with Morrissey (*The Face*, March 1990).

'The Moon, the Gutter and Shane McGowan' is the unedited original of what ultimately became printed as 'The Agony and the Ecstasy', the clumsily edited feature that appeared in *20/20*, August 1989.

'The Daze of Guns'N'Roses' is the unadulterated original of an article that first appeared in *The Face* in January 1990.

'The Mancunian Candidates' is the unadulterated original of an article that first appeared in *The Face* in January 1990.

'The Four Ages of a Man Named Pop' is another new piece of writing from the early winter of 1993, and quotes liberally from many articles I've written on Iggy Pop, chiefly 'Iggy Pop vs the Chilling Hand of Blight: A Fight to the Finish' (*NME*, 3 May 1975), 'Dr Iggy and Mr Pop' (*NME*, 24 March 1979) and 'Goodbye Cool World' (*The Face*, December 1986).

'Lightening Up with the Prince of Darkness' first appeared as 'Prince of Darkness' in *The Face*, October 1986. Thanks to Paul Rambali for his sterling editing job on the original.

'God's Got His Plans and I've Got Mine' first gained exposure as 'His Master's Voice' (*The Face*, 1989).

'Neil Young and the Haphazard Highway That Leads to Unconditional Love' was written in the summer of 1993. I'm indebted to Scott Young's book *Neil and Me* (Seal, 1975) for helping me to comprehend the breadth of his son's odyssey. I'm even more greatly indebted to Young himself, who allowed himself to be interviewed at length in the winters of 1989 and 1990 and the late autumn of 1992. The Elliot Roberts and David Geffen quotes come from *Long Time Gone* (Doubleday, 1988) by David Crosby and Carl Gottlieb. The Dylan quote stems from an interview conducted by Scott Cohen and run in *Spin* magazine (1986).

'Kurt Cobain, 1967–1994' first came out in *Mojo*, May 1994.

'Iggy Pop: The Innocent' was first published in the September 1999 issue of British *GQ* magazine.

'Prince Is a Champion Too' originally appeared in shortened form in a December 1999 edition of the French daily newspaper *Libération*.

'The Conflicted Cool of Johnny Cash' was first seen in the September 2000 edition of British *GQ*.

'Eminem's Rage in a Cage' originally appeared in the January 20/February 5, 2001 issue of the French magazine *Les Inrockuptibles*.

'Sly Stone's Evil Ways' was first printed in the September 2001 issue of France *Rock & Folk*. I'm indebted to Joel Selvin whose remarkable book on Sly & the Family Stone provided many of the quotes featured in this chapter.

'A Portrait of Serge Gainsbourg' was first printed in the Saturday April 15, 2006 edition of the *Guardian*.

'Phil Spector's Long Fall From Grace' was originally published in the April 2001 edition of *Rock & Folk*. Mark Ribowsky's excellent *He's a Rebel* (Dutton Press) was an invaluable source of information and quotes relating to Spector's glory years in the early sixties.

'Self-destruction in Rock and Elsewhere' is a piece that the Scottish group Franz Ferdinand asked me to contribute when the group guest-edited an issue of the *Guardian* in 2004.

I would like to thank James Osterberg, Angus Cargill, Lee Brackstone, Richard Thomas, Jonathan Riley, Christian Eudeline, Michel Vidal, Neil Young and Nick Logan.

Extra special thanks to my beloved Laurence Romance without whom this book probably would never have materialized.

The Dark Stuff is dedicated to the memories of Lester Bangs, Pete Erskine, Ian MacDonald and all the 'death or glory' boys gone too soon.

Foreword

I read this nasty book with an unusual degree of interest. I found it to have a kind of feverish effect. By the end of each chapter I experienced an exhausted, depressed feeling, coupled with a desire to relisten to the music of the subject/artist.

Such, I suppose, is the strange relationship between the repulsive and attractive poles of human beings. I love you, I hate you, you disappoint me, you elevate me.

It needs to be mentioned that Mr Kent has a side to his history as sordid and generally unsavory and sometimes downright hilarious as anyone described in this book.

An unlikely, ungainly figure, well over six feet tall, unsteadily negotiating the sidewalks of London and LA like a great palsied mantis, dressed in the same tattered black-leather and velvet guitar-slinger garb regardless of season or the passing of time, hospital-thin, with a perpetually dripping bright red nose caused by an equally perpetual drug shortage, all brought to life by a wrist-waving, head-flung-back Keith Richards effect, and an abiding interest in all dirt. That's Nick Kent for you in the seventies and eighties. In short, a true rock'n'roller: someone who cared.

Which brings us to the end. It's hard to care anymore. The 'music industry' is fat and satisfied. They can buy anything, and turn anyone into a spiritual eunuch. That means no balls.

Yet, reading this creepy book, I wanted to hear the music again. I was interested. As for 'today's music industry' and its bed-mate 'music journalism', I just don't care anymore. How could I?

Iggy Pop, November 1993

Preface

When I first started writing professionally, right at the end of 1971 – I was nineteen going on twenty – it was as if the whole London scene I'd inherited was still in the last sorry stages of denial that the sixties had really ended. I began penning stuff for a self-styled 'underground' journal called *Frendz* – I just walked in off the rainy Portobello Old Street and offered my services. To my eternal gratitude, the young man seated on a beanbag with what appeared to be herpes sores on his upper lip told me I could join up there and then. The place turned out to be a breeding ground for sixties dreamers who couldn't wake up to the fact that the dream really was dead – to the point that it was starting to kill them one by one. One guy – who was like the journal's pet mascot – fell from a section of drainage suspended along the third floor of the paper's offices one night while his judgment was impaired from too many tranquilizers. I met Syd Barrett there too. Less than five years earlier, I'd stood transfixed, watching him in all his retina-scorching, dandified splendor as he'd performed with his group the Pink Floyd, silently praying that one day I might be just like him. Now, as he stood before me with his haunted eyes and fractured countenance, I was having second thoughts. I asked him about his current musical project (a short-lived trio called Stars, briefly managed by *Frendz*'s accountant) as his eyes quietly burned a hole through one of the four walls surrounding us with a stare so ominous it could strip the paint off the bonnet of a brand new car. 'I had eggs and bacon for breakfast,' he then intoned solemnly, as if reciting a distantly remembered mantra. I repeated my original question quizzically. 'I'm sorry! I don't speak French,' he finally replied.

That encounter helped crystallize in my mind the fixations I'd return to over and over throughout my decades of writing about musicians. As a teenager – moving around the country at the behest of my father's work locations, feeling shy and awkward and experiencing few solid friendships along the way – I developed fantasy relationships with my favorite rock and pop stars of the time. I'd read all the fan magazines and music comics of the day and came to cherish the most mundane details about my faves, crap that I still remember for God's sake even now, though I've forgotten most of the names and details of that era's day-to-day realities. I used to imagine their lives were perfect in every way. Then I rubbed up against the likes of Syd Barrett and realized that these were people who'd gotten what they wanted, only to find out that it was the last thing on earth they actually needed (adulation, creative lift-off) to maintain their own mental equilibrium. This meant something. I quickly realized these were the stories that needed to be addressed.

I was aided considerably in focusing on this often disturbing area of pop life by meeting the late rock writer Lester Bangs in early 1973. By that time I'd managed to get myself booted out of two of the world's most upstanding universities (Oxford and London) in slightly less than a year, a fact I'm still immaturely proud of. The English music weekly *New Musical Express* had offered me work during the early summer of 1972 and I was having a fantastic time interviewing everyone from Little Richard to Led Zeppelin, but I also knew in my heart that what I was writing wasn't good enough yet, that I was too young and inexperienced and needed to get better very quickly. So I made enough money to fly off to Detroit where *Creem* magazine, the best rock mag in the world at the time, was located. The night I got in, I took a taxi to the address in Birmingham, Michigan I'd been given. I didn't even phone in advance: that's how on fire I was. It was after midnight when *Creem*'s resident 'star' writers, Lester Bangs, Dave Marsh, and Ben Edmonds, let me in. I didn't make things easy for myself by taking two Quaaludes beforehand, so it's no small credit to the warmth of his enormous heart that when I mush-mouthedly asked Lester whether, as the greatest writer of his day, he could, if not teach me, then at least indicate to me how to achieve some vague approximation of his creative intensity, he good-naturedly replied, 'Sure.' For the following two months, I'd follow him around, but – most importantly – I listened intently to everything he had to say. With Lester, it was all about penetration, breaking on through to the other side. He was always questioning everything: 'So you like this music? Why? What do you mean, it's got a nice middle-eight and the cow-bell sounds cute on the finale? That's not good enough. What are these guys really trying to sell us here? What does this music say to your soul? Do these guys sound like they even have souls to you? What's really going on here? What's going on behind the masks?' The whole concept of punk rock was his too, even if Marsh actually came up with the phrase. The other thing he insisted upon was that in rock'n'roll it wasn't the winners but the losers who made for the most compelling stories. I soaked up everything he shared with me and returned to London in the spring of 1973 ready for practically anything fate could throw at me.

By this time, the *NME* was in the throes of a creative and commercial renaissance of its own. Back in the fifties it had been a respectful, cheery, reactionary pop sheet, featuring lots of 'exclusive chats' with Perry Como, much speculating on whether Glenn Miller and his unfortunate band were still alive, and inane editorials about whether or not Elvis Presley's 'wild' gyrations were harmful to youth.

This approach carried into the sixties when the *NME* latched onto the beat boom while its chief competitor *Melody Maker* ill-advisedly preferred to concentrate on the dreary old traditional jazz craze still holding sway throughout Great Britain. Instead of Perry Como, now there was Tom Jones or maybe Englebert Humperdinck, always talking exclusively about his new record, his new stage clothes, his new car. There'd be exclusive chat sessions with the Beatles, most of them in fact written by the group's publicists. The few staff writers they had back then seemed a funny lot in that they tended to judge a group's general worth not on the quality of their music but by the number of drinks members would stand for them in any given swinging London club.

The *NME* sold close to a quarter million copies a week during most of the sixties. However, this was not to last. Progressive rock was on the rise and suddenly young music-loving people everywhere wanted to read endless interviews with ego-besotted guitarists staring intently at the hash burns in their loon pants and talking about 'cosmic harmony' and 'musical oneness.' *Melody Maker*, who'd been such dummies for sticking with their tired old 'trad' jazz bores while the Beatles and Stones were first happening, were determined not to lose out again. Suddenly you could read interviews – with the likes of Alvin Lee, Leslie West, and even that idiot who shot himself from the group Chicago – that went on even longer than their guitar solos. The *NME* simply couldn't tackle this sort of stuff effectively – particularly when they printed reviews such as the one for the first Pink Floyd album where the group's bass player was referred to as Muddy, instead of Roger, Waters.

Finally, at the outset of 1972, after sales had plummeted to 60,000 and a review of guitar instrumentalist Duane Eddy had been printed which began with the immortal words 'On this, his 35th album, we find Duane in as good voice as ever,' the *NME* had been told to rethink its policies or die on the vine. The former was successfully attempted mostly at the instigation of assistant editor Nick Logan (he'd joined the paper at seventeen back in 1967 as cub reporter), who picked a number of young writers who'd been published only in England's self-styled 'underground' magazines like *Oz*, *International Times*, and *Frendz*. That's where he found me, anyway, along with a rotund frizzy-haired fellow who looked just like Rob Tyner of the MC5 named Charles Shaar Murray, and an owl-faced Cambridge graduate named Ian McDonald. Together we managed to double sales figures over a period of six months, trebling them by the beginning of 1973. The cozy superficial approach of former times was left in the dust. Writers were instead encouraged to speak out, criticize, make some noise – just don't be boring.

For a while there, it just kept getting bigger and bigger until, by 1974, we were the ones with the edge over everyone else in the radical-international-youth-mag sweepstakes. *Creem* had taken the torch from *Rolling Stone* as the essential rock read at the beginning of the seventies and it was still doing great work. But the *NME* had the power to tap into *Creem*'s best writers while cultivating their own champions. Julie Burchill, Chrissie Hynde, and Bob Geldof all got their start working for the paper during this time. Lester Bangs quickly became a considerable presence. Even the letters pages regularly harbored the names of future icons such as Pet Shop Boy Neil Tennant and one 'Steve' Morrissey, an obsessive New York Dolls fan later to front the Smiths.

As for me, well, I was right there in the thick of it all, propelled by an ultimately disastrous mixture of almost obscene arrogance and reckless intensity. Hard drugs were playing an increasingly important part in my day-to-day existence and people who knew me then often indicate the period of my working with the Rolling Stones in late '73 as the point at which I started to 'go wrong.' They will insinuate that the group somehow corrupted me. This is bullshit. Some men are born with an overwhelming desire to don women's clothing; my destiny impelled me just as irresistibly to use heroin and cocaine. Not a good idea. I was well and truly strung out by 1975, and it practically ruined my talent as a writer.

That's when I worked with the Sex Pistols, by the way. Maybe you'll wonder why I've kept from documenting my own experiences with the band in a special chapter. The answer is a simple one: they were all ungrateful, back-stabbing bastards. At first, they'd been known as the Swankers and had played old Small Faces songs alongside such unpunk and insipid old sixties pop numbers as 'Build Me Up Buttercup' and 'Everlasting Love.' I changed all that and got them into the Stooges and Modern Lovers. The leader was eighteen-year-old Steve Jones, a remarkable young cat burglar and all-purpose criminal. Steve lived at home with his mum and her fancy man – a retired boxer – but now, after years of being beaten up as a kid by this ersatz stepfather, Steve could beat *him* up, which he did often. Also – and this was one of the reasons he was so obsessive about his thieving – he prided himself on having all the good gear in the house stashed in his room. He had a big color telly in his bedroom while his mum and her prick boyfriend made do with a little portable black-and-white monstrosity. Another thing about Steve. He could neither read nor write. I'm telling you this so you'll understand where the real essence of the Sex Pistols stemmed from. It didn't miraculously emanate from Malcolm McLaren's crackpot art-college concepts. At heart, it was really the sound of Steve Jones finally expressing himself, annihilating his horrible stepdad with guitar riffs that struck home like pummeling fists to a winded gut.

John Lydon was the other key ingredient, of course. Far more so than poor old Sid. There's a chapter on Sid in this book that will endear few to his memory, and, with hindsight, I'm almost willing to voice a tinge of regret over the extreme terms in which I've portrayed him. But by the same token, he went to those extremes and died because of them. He had his charm, though. Sid's problems – in my view – boiled down to his mother's life style and the fact that she'd been an intravenous drug user during his pre-natal period. He wasn't retarded exactly, but he wasn't all there mentally, and drugs made him even more stupid. Everyone recognized that Sid was too stupid to live too long. McLaren exploited it for better or worse, just as he was the one who coaxed Sid into attacking

me with a rusty old bike chain while the future 'Jah' Wobble
held a knife one inch from my face. People talk to me about
the liberating force of '76–'77 UK punk rock sometimes and I
feel like I've been living on another planet. After the aforementioned knife-chain-Sid incident I became an ongoing victim of
mindless punk brutality throughout 1977. I was stabbed
repeatedly one night in an open field close by London's King
Cross by four youths clearly overwhelmed by the liberating
force of punk rock and their ardent desire to ape anything Sid
did. Another time I was attacked in the toilets of the fabled
Roxy by a guy with a knife. Fortunately, that time no real physical harm was done, but I can still distinctly remember staggering out of that privy with a great gash in my coat sleeve,
wondering to myself: Did Dave Marsh ever get to experience
this kind of shit from associating with Bruce Springsteen? Did
Greil Marcus get to find himself in such life-or-death situations
when out reviewing Randy Newman?

By the end of the seventies, sad to say, the *NME* had lost
most of its creative momentum. It was never the same after
Nick Logan left as editor. It was lucky for me that Nick went
on to found and edit *The Face*, a youth-oriented monthly.
During the eighties he encouraged me to write again, and
among the results are several pieces included herein. In 1988 I
finally managed to turn my back on drug addiction for good,
moved to Paris, and began working for television while still
writing for an array of magazines and daily journals. Penguin
Books in England wanted me to compile a 'best of' all my
published articles, a concept that appealed to me until I actually began reading through my old features. So much of what
I'd written grated on me now: the over-abundant stylistic flour-
ishes, the endless unwieldy sentences, the over-emphasis on
now redundant 'hip' jargon. And yet – lurking beneath the
stylistic debris – I still recognized the fact that compelling
stories were being told. Through an arduous process of editing
and rewriting I finally arrived at the contents of this book.

The first edition was published in April 1994 less than a month after Kurt Cobain had chosen to blow his brains out. It evidently hit a nerve because it received a ton of glowing reviews and even briefly found its way into the UK Top Ten literary best-sellers list in the late spring of that year. As the nineties progressed, the book also came out in America, France and Czechoslovakia. In early 2006 Faber and Faber contacted me about re-publishing the original work and we both agreed that some new chapters would be a welcome addition to the existing text. I'm particularly happy that I've managed to induct both Sly Stone and Phil Spector into my *Dark Stuff* hall of fame. Johnny Cash, too. Their troubled sagas give the book's central themes a deeper resonance.

On its most basic level, *The Dark Stuff* is a series of profiles of musicians about whom I've been asked the question 'What's he really like?' over and over again. This is my way of answering them as elaborately as I can. But there's something more going on in this book. Some people will tell you *The Dark Stuff* is all about rock stars taking too many drugs. They're wrong. It's all about 'character' – more specifically, the breed of person who gets marked out to play the big, bad, mad, and dangerous-to-know 'rock'n'roll star' in his day-to-day life. It's partly about the childhood experiences that formed these stars, but it's also about the terrible triumvirate of ego, drug abuse, and self-absorption that preys so relentlessly on the creative mind. Time and again, you'll find gifted individuals tormenting themselves with the question 'Am I really good at what I do or am I just lucky?' *The Dark Stuff* starts with a portrayal of encroaching madness and segues through some truly hellish scenarios before finding a sort of redemptive force in the final tales of those who've spent a few seasons in hell themselves but who've survived with some real wisdom to offer the world. I conceived it as a warts-and-all celebration of the driving essence that is rock'n'roll. I only hope it moves you in all the right ways.

Nick Kent, Directly from my heart to you

The Last Beach Movie Revisited: The Life of Brian Wilson

Part 1

'It was a childhood dream of mine: to make music that
made people feel loved' – *Brian Wilson, 1992*

It was another spectacular LA early evening in late '74 with the
sun still high in the sky and well, it just had to be said. The
Hills were alive with the sound of music: Beverly Hills, that is.
Or so imagined Paul McCartney as he glanced across to his
wife Linda driving the two of them to a special social
call/rendezvous with the ex-Beatle's most audaciously talented
musical rival from that era now commonly referred to as 'the
fabulous sixties' – the Beach Boys' reclusive mastermind, Brian
Wilson. As their car whizzed past one garden – right alongside
the sound of spinning hoses gushing out a gentle drizzle of
water across a long verdant lawn – the sound of Neil Sedaka
gushing ardently on about hearing 'laughter in the rain' was
making itself instantly apparent. In another, the bulbous boom
that is Barry White was serenading various species of pond-life.
From the next, two adolescent bathers were twisting on a
diving-board to the strains of the Eagles. And at the end of
the street a transistor radio blasting out Disco Tex and his
Sex-O-Lettes seemed to have temporarily petrified a small
kitten also playing on the lawn. Everywhere you turned, it
was as if the numb, throw-away sound of the seventies –
with its 'aural exciters', cocaine-addicted session musicians,

mellow vibrations, not to mention those inky-dinky, synthe-
sizer sounds cropping up everywhere on soundtracks for
TV/radio jingles – was seeping up through the landscape like
so much swamp-gas. And so McCartney temporarily cast his
mind back to better times, back to the last time . . . How long
had it been?

How long had it been? Five . . . six . . . no, it had been over
seven years since they'd last met, also in LA, in the early spring
right before the summer of love itself, when the world was still
full of promise and untapped cosmic possibilities. McCartney
had arrived at a Beach Boys recording session with Derek
Taylor, the suave Liverpudlian who was on both the Beatles'
and the Beach Boys' pay-rolls, two crazy guys sporting these
heavy-looking moustaches like they were students from
straight out of the Russian revolution. Of course Brian was in
control – fat, bashful, weird Brian with his pudgy fingers
forever fiddling with the ample bouffant fringe virtually
obscuring his glazed eyes and the room full of vegetables piled
up to further authenticate the vibrations that needed to flow
through the performance of this song called not unsurprisingly
'Vegetables'.

Paul, who was used to eccentric behaviour in the recording
studio, smiled indulgently and even nibbled a couple of carrots.
Come to think of it, they'd had a hell of a good time together,
even jammed out an eccentric version of 'On Top of Old
Smokey'. And at the end of a long evening – with good old
Derek doing the prompting – McCartney sat down at the
piano and played a new song of his entitled 'She's Leaving
Home' that floored everyone present, even moving Marilyn
Wilson, Brian's long-suffering wife, to a bout of unrestrained
weeping.

There were tears in the eyes of Marilyn Wilson during this
second encounter too, but they did not spring from joy; nor did
they spring from the sound of beautiful music being played. In
fact, there was to be no music whatsoever ringing from the

Wilsons' Spanish mansion that evening. Just the sound of a little dog's static barking from down some steps a few feet away from the little changing-hut that overlooked the pool out there in the garden, where Brian Wilson had pretty much taken up permanent residence. Around this make-shift construction, the ex-Beatle had gathered with his wife Linda, Marilyn and a couple of friends, gently pleading with the overweight composer to come out and show himself.

But Brian wasn't coming out. He stayed in there, petrified, all his guts clenched up, eyes shut tight, praying with all his might that all the tiny atoms of his body would somehow break down, so that he could simply evaporate into the thin smog-strained air surrounding him. It was all to do with something his brother Carl had told him not long before, something about Paul McCartney once claiming that Brian's song 'God Only Knows' was the greatest pop song ever written. And, in his mind, it had all become hopelessly twisted: 'Like, if "God Only Knows" is the greatest song ever written, then I'll never write anything as good again! And if I never write anything as good, then I'm finished. I'm a has-been and a wash-up, just like everyone keeps saying.'

Dark thoughts swooping down. Dark mutterings speaking up. Ugly voices screaming and cursing, 'It's over for you, motherfucker,' again and again.

He never came out until long after they'd all left. Someone said afterwards that you could just make out the sound of him inside that claustrophobic room, weeping softly to himself, like an unloved little boy who'd recently experienced a particularly savage beating.

'Why in Christ's name do you want to waste your time writing about Brian Wilson?' an LA music biz hot-shot asked me with a withering look and a weary alcoholic voice. 'It's 1975! Go out and do something on Bruce Springsteen, for Chrissakes! Wilson's all washed up. Bloated. Beached. Sure, he used to be great. Everybody knows that. *Now*, he's just another sad fuckin' case. Listen, I can't stand to be around the guy. I'm just being frank with you here. He's such a fuckin' loser. I was with a bunch of people one night, driving around, and somehow he ended up there in the back of the car too, screaming and carrying on. He was wearing pyjamas and a bathrobe and he smelled fuckin' awful. Later, we're in this bar and he made this embarrassing pass at a waitress and she looked just terrified, like a big grizzly bear was about to attack her. Finally we ended the evening by having to stop the car for him and, Jesus Christ, I just remember sitting there watching him puke his guts out on to some nice middle-aged Californian couple's front lawn at 3 o'clock in the morning.

'And this guy – less than ten years ago – he was the fuckin' king of California. The whole culture – the surfing, the hot-rods, the music, you name it – he was on top of it all. He ruled it all. All this' – he waves his hand, indicating all the palm trees and endless perfect gardens spread out before us across this golden state – 'all this was once his personal kingdom.'

The king of California, with madness in his eyes and vomit on his 'jammies': it was the Citizen Kane of all great rocky-horror stories, but for me it was more personal. I remember being twelve or thirteen years old and to escape from the ravages of adolescence I'd go into record shops to study Beach Boys album covers for what seemed like hours on end. They'd always be grinning a lot. There were always pretty girls surrounding them, with perfect blonde hair and 'fuck me' smiles. Surf was boldly cresting in the background. Weenies were often being heated up on a blazing beach fire under a big harvest moon. Everybody was happy and everybody was successful and clean and had great teeth and good hair (except Mike Love). 'Fun' wasn't a concept I was too personally attuned to at this point in my life and I can't begin to tell you how exciting it felt to stand there holding photographic proof that it actually existed somewhere – albeit thousands of miles away from the land-locked dumps I found myself inhabiting.

But that was nothing compared to the thrill of hearing the music itself. At the beginning, their records all sounded so intoxicatingly up-beat but there was also this aching feel creeping in, this pure tone of exquisite longing, that, when those voices got to harmonize over a set of sweetly melancholic chord changes, could just rip my heart out. However depressed I'd get, listening to the Beach Boys would always cause my moods to lift. I loved their music unconditionally and followed Brian Wilson's phenomenal progress as a composer with a religious fervour.

Then, in 1967, something happened and Wilson was never the same again. His music quickly lost all its focus and ambition while he himself seemed to vanish off the face of the earth, save for the occasional press-shot of a fat, ungainly figure with disturbed eyes and an unsightly growth of beard.

That's why I was currently resident in the ridiculous state of California, doing this equally ridiculous 'gumshoe' routine, tracking down and attempting detailed conversation with old alcoholic record execs, long-discarded song-writing partners, former image changers, self-styled scene-makers, Hollywood headcases, Sunset Strip scandal-mongers, hopeless drug cases and twisted mystics. I even went so far as to locate a female massage parlour employee he'd recently written a song about. It was a dirty job but someone had to do it. Looking back, I remember how the darker it got, the more my eyes lit up and the more I fantasized that I was Lou Harper, the private eye in Ross McDonald's *The Moving Target* swimming through the murky human debris of weird-assed LA to arrive ultimately at a deeper truth: I had to discover what really happened to the golden state's once-golden princeling, the sad young man with the pale blue eyes and the fragile heart who, as a youth, somehow managed to tune his one good ear to connect with the music of the spheres until the awesome intensity of its sound finally drove him to insanity.

'WE FIRST GOT . . . no, well . . . uh . . . my brother
Dennis came home from school one day and he said . . .
um . . . "Listen you guys, it looks like surfin's gonna be
the next big craze and . . . uh . . . you guys oughta write a
song about it." 'Cos at that time we were writing songs
for friends and . . . um . . . school assemblies.

'So it happened we wrote a song just due to Dennis's
suggestion and from there we just got on the surf wagon
'cos we figured . . . y'know . . . it'd be a hot craze. It's all
because of my brother though.

'And he didn't know . . . he didn't . . .

'It just happened.

'By chance.'

He was born Brian Douglas Wilson on 20 June 1942, at
Centinela Hospital in Inglewood, the first of three sons brought
into the world by Murray Wilson and his wife Audree, née
Korthof. The three brothers were brought up in the post-war
stucco community of Hawthorne, one of the utterly character-
less and culture-free Californian suburbs positioned some
thirty miles from the Pacific Ocean. The Wilson family was a
claustrophobic, profoundly dysfunctional experience, with a
broken, alcoholic mother, three terrified little boys and Murray,
the vicious ogre, at the head of it all. In his younger days,
Murray Wilson would have been referred to as a 'pistol', an
extrovert boisterous sort who never got out of the habit
of cracking terrible jokes and anticipating the response by
elbowing listeners in the ribs. The whole family lived comfortably owing to his moderately successful self-invested business
dealing in heavy machinery, but Murray's dream was to make
it as a songwriter in the music business.

If his talent as a composer was simply non-existent, his lack
of success as a father was to prove rather more significant. Put
simply, the man was a sadist and what he practised on his three
sons was child abuse of the most vicious kind. 'Murray was

always out of his depth,' a co-worker of his and the Beach Boys reminisced to me one day. 'He was just a hot-shot from the suburbs but he knocked his sons about emotionally to the point where they became the image he'd set up for them. Carl had to take so much weight, be so calm. Dennis had to be such a crackshot son. A daft man, really, but he certainly scared the hell out of his boys. Mike Love knew some great stories about him. I was always asking, "Tell me more stories about Murray, Mike."'

They were invariably sordid and mean-spirited little sagas. There was the one for instance about the numerous times Murray back-handed Brian across his head as a baby, the heavy blows more than likely sparking his continual deafness in one ear from the age of two onwards. Then there were the tales of Murray and his two glass eyes? (He'd lost one eye in an industrial accident some years earlier.) There was a normal-looking one for everyday use and a special blood-shot model for those mornings after he'd drunk too much. On one such morning, he awoke in state of considerable disrepair to discover that Dennis had stolen the blood-shot eye and taken it to school to show off to his little punk buddies. Dennis was never to forget the way Murray's belt stung his arms and legs when he'd come back home that evening. Murray was not only missing one eye, by the way: most of one ear was gone too, literally ripped off the side of his young head by his own stinking drunk of a father one night, a man reputed to be even more vicious than his own son.

Physical beatings and emotional brutality were virtually everyday occurrences in the Wilsons' bleak, white-bread household, and though all three sons (and even, on occasion, poor, petrified Audree) were mercilessly picked on, it was Brian who suffered the worst because first he was eldest but also he was easily the most sensitive. Little brother Dennis was such a tough little bastard, dumb as hell and shiftless too, but so cute-looking he could always get away with wild escapades his

ungainly elder brother would get nailed to a fence for perpe-
trating. The youngest of all, Carl, meanwhile seems to have
been viewed merely as an indifferent little blob by everyone in
his family (apart from Audree, who constantly spoilt him) at
this juncture of his life, partly owing to the fact that he spent
so much time hiding under his bed in fright while his brothers
were being beaten by their father.

Well over thirty years later, when Brian Wilson was only one
week shy of his fiftieth birthday, he would talk about his father
still in a tone of utter dread:

'You go through your childhood and you have a mean father
that brutalizes you, that terrorizes you – and Dennis and Carl
– many years ago with a double belt . . . He'd take his belt and
he would double it over and he'd have maximum control and
power and . . . Boom . . . boom . . . boom . . . boom [*imitates
sound of being whipped*] he'd knock the hell out of us. In fact,
I said to myself: "What in the hell was all that about?" A mean
father who turned us into egomaniacs, 'cos we felt so insecure
our egos just jumped up . . . It was such a scary feeling.'

Music quickly proved itself to be the one force able to still the
malevolent emotions coursing through the house whenever
Murray was playing king of the castle. There was a piano in the
living-room and he'd play it a lot, running through these silly
tin-pot serenades he'd compose in a misguided attempt to break
into the music business. Audree played too and Brian was only
six or seven when he started playing himself, mostly in an
attempt to impress his dad. He was always able to lose himself
in the sound of music but the first time he fell hopelessly in love
with it was the day at age fourteen when his mother bought him
a copy of *Four Freshmen and Five Trombones*, an album of the
renowned fifties harmony group's honey-coated hush-a-bye-
baby vocal stylings. The night he played it all the way through
he felt his skin prickle at the back of the neck, the hairs rising
all over his body and the white hot flush of communion with
something sacred and all-powerful.

At age sixteen he was given a tape recorder for Christmas. The previous year Carl had introduced him to R'n'B music on the local radio stations and he was already writing songs in his head that he sensed were as good as anything by the Del-Vikings or even Chuck 'crazy legs' Berry whose ringing guitar riffs Carl was starting to master on a cheap Rickenbaker guitar he'd got for Christmas. Then Mike Love – the Wilsons' odious extrovert of a cousin who thought he was just so cool, then got his girlfriend pregnant when he was seventeen, had to marry her and suddenly he wasn't so cool anymore – started coming round a lot. He was still a brash little egocentric prick but he sensed his only possible escape from a life of marital gloom and a numbing succession of straight jobs was to follow through on his half-baked musical ambitions. It didn't matter to him that he didn't have any musical talent: he knew gawky cousin Brian could play the piano and so he forged an alliance with him. Ambition, drive, a weedy voice and a capacity for extrovert behaviour that knew no bounds was what Love brought to the equation. He also managed the occasional set of asinine lyrics. Brian concentrated on the music as well as bringing in a fifth guy, an outsider called Al Jardine, to sing, basically because he'd accidentally broken one of Jardine's legs during a high-school football play-off not long before and wanted to make it up to him.

At first they were the Pendletones. Then they called them-selves Carl & the Passions before changing it yet again to Kenny & the Kasuals. Brian was Kenny. Then they recorded a single with a couple called Morgan who owned a little do-it-yourself local studio, funded by money Murray had given his sons to live on while he and Audree went on vacation. The long and short of it: they ended up cutting a song of Brian's called 'Surfin' inspired by Dennis's tall tales of riding the local waves; the Morgans stuck it out and, without consulting anyone, decided to credit them on the disc's centre as 'The Beach Boys'. The Wilson brothers and their two pals didn't like the new name at all but couldn't do much about it as their record starting selling in massive quantities all over the golden state and beyond almost immediately. As soon as he saw the reactions his boys were stirring among young record buyers, Murray wasted no time in asserting his awful omnipotence over everything he could. Never backward about coming forward, he immediately elected himself the Beach Boys' manager, producer and song publisher, after he'd bullied Brian into handing over control of all his songs to his father. Then they went big-time and signed to Capitol under the A&R guidance of Nick Venet, a young LA hot-shot who favoured camel-hair coats, hip slogans and the same slicked-back look of deadly efficiency favoured by *Hawaii Five-o*'s Jack Lord. Venet couldn't abide Murray: couldn't stand the demeaning way he treated his sons, couldn't stomach the clueless way he'd try to upstage Brian and the others in the recording studio, waltzing around like a puffed-up little Caesar screaming, 'Surge! Surge!' whenever he felt the tempo should quicken, which was practically all the time. But first of all he couldn't stand the hideous fuckin' promo shots Murray had taken of his three sons, Mike Love and a local replacement called David Marks (Al Jardine had decided to commit himself to the more exciting prospect of dentistry) looking like five little lost doomed rabbits in ill-fitting lumberjack shirts, being royally upstaged by the large wooden surf-board they awkwardly prop up. It took over a year of Murray's merciless and tactless bullying before the Beach Boys finally snapped. Mike Love challenged him to a fist-fight on some wretched night-ride back from a far-away gig before pinning him square in the gut, causing the old man's flabby weight to buckle before hitting the pavement with a resounding thud. They told him he was finished as their manager, the day after. Murray never forgave them, least of all Brian, and swore to get even, but by then it was too late. The son he'd terrorized and now envied with such a sickening ardour was taking control and single-handedly creating a whole new culture. As Nick Cohn observed in his book *Awopbopaloobop*: 'He [Wilson] worked a loose-limbed group sound and added his own falsetto. Then he stuck in some lazy twang guitar and rounded it all out with jumped-up Four Freshmen harmonies. No sweat, he'd created a bona fide surf music out of nothing. More, he had invented California.'

Brian had the whole surfing beach craze cased all by himself. In 1962 he took Chuck Berry's 'Sweet Little Sixteen' and transformed it into 'Surfin USA', again, in Cohn's words, 'the great surf anthem, the clincher: a hymn of unlimited praise'. In 1963 he even eclipsed his own fantasies for the Beach Boys when, with Jan Berry of Jan & Dean fame, he created 'Surf City', a virile all-American sunkissed Valhalla where the gender ratio was strictly 'two girls for every boy'. And who really cared if such fantasies were basically all pie-in-the-sky fantasy froth? Their very bug-eyed charm only helped compound the appeal further. Then just as the surfing craze was cresting to a peak, Wilson quickly expanded his range of topics to embrace the motor sports fad of the early sixties.

Already he was seeing other lyric-writers. First there'd been Gary Usher, a plucky little hustler five years Brian's senior, who turned up at the Wilsons' front door looking for an introduction. He and Brian had hit it off immediately and went on to write '409' and the immortal 'In My Room' before Murray's vicious meddling forced Usher unceremoniously out of the picture only a month or so after his introduction. Another brief collaborator was a jovial 'jock' named Bob Norberg, who even let Brian stay at his place when things between him and Murray got too out of control at the Wilson house. Bob also introduced Brian for the very first time to the unearthly sounds of Phil Spector and his special productions of sundry pop and R'n'B singers, an encounter so earth-shattering to Wilson that Spector's music would quickly become an all-absorbing obsession for him. Then came Roger Christian, who 'was really . . .

really a guiding light for me. I'd go over there, see . . . He'd get off at midnight, OK. He'd do a nightime radio show from nine to twelve every night and we'd go over to Otto's, order a hot fudge sundae and just . . . whew! talk and talk. We'd be writing lyrics . . . hustling, y'know. And all of a sudden we'd realize we'd just written fifteen songs.'

Christian's lyrics were the acorn all-American gospel: stout-hearted salutations to the competitive spirit littered with patri-otic references to 'daring young men playing dangerous games' and in-depth motor mechanic descriptions of stripped-down cherry corvettes. The most famous Wilson–Christian collabo-ration has to be the classic 'Don't Worry Baby', wherein Brian utilized a heart-melting set of chord changes and a feel already close to Spector's in order to underpin what at first seems a straightforward teen passion proclamation. It's only on closer inspection that the listener realizes the subject's angst is focused on Christian's protagonist having bragged his way into a potentially fatal car chase. Romance in Roger Christian's lyrics was always a strict second-runner to heavy machinery. Cohn again:

> There was by now no subject too soap-opera for him
> [Wilson/Christian] to take on. He churned out 'A Young
> Man is Gone', an ode to the departed James Dean, and
> 'Spirit of America' and 'Be True to Your School'. At the
> same time, he did some fine rejoicings, full of energy and
> imagination – 'Shut Down', '409', 'Little Deuce Coupe'.
> Fine rock'n'roll music but brought up to date, kept
> moving and not left to atrophy. Best of all was 'I Get
> Around'.
>
> What Brian Wilson was doing now was making
> genuine pop art. Not camp word plays on pop, but the
> real thing. He was taking the potential heroics that
> surrounded him and, not being arty, not being coy in the
> least, turning them into live music. Simply, he'd taken

high school and raised it to completely new levels. He'd
turned it into myth.

But oh, how exhausting it was, building up these myths and
then having to ceaselessly schlep all over the States promoting
them via hysteria-ridden live dates. For over three years, he
never stopped working, never slackened the pace for an
instant, never lost the cold metallic taste of nausea lurking deep
down in his guts. Then, one day, he started cracking up.

Brian became completely hysterical on a flight taking the
Beach Boys from LA to Houston for a show two days before
Christmas 1964. His face first went red as a beetroot and then
it turned deathly white and he started screaming he was going
to die, before breaking down and crying like a little baby. They
had to send him back to LA, where Audree met him at the
airport and attempted to nurse him back to normality. But
Brian's condition was so ragged he went on to suffer two more
nervous breakdowns in the following months. These traumas,
though, were providential in the sense that they were finally
able to extricate Wilson from all his touring commitments
with the Beach Boys, enabling him to concentrate solely on
composing and recording. In fact, the move was perfectly
timed. Brian could now concentrate on what he did best and
moreover be allowed the creative elbow-room to experiment a
little more, develop new formulae to combat the likes of those
pesky Beatles who had suddenly surpassed the Beach Boys'
sales and popularity in their own goddamn country that very
year. Brian Wilson, left to his own devices, could settle that
score easily enough. The other guys knew that. At that point,
they still trusted Brian's instincts implicitly.

Off the road and away from its attendant nightmares, Brian
remained at home, sleeping through the day, staying up all
night, smoking hash and listening intently to the songs of
Bacharach & David, when not obsessing about the competitive
nature of his work. And that meant getting wise to a few

things. Ego, for one: the unfettered thrill of pitting one's talents against all the other acts, bulleting up and down on the *Billboard* and *Cashbox* charts. This new band for example – the Rolling Stones – they weren't so damn hot!

The Beatles, mark you, were different. Brian dug the hell out of those albums. And that Paul? Boy, what a talented guy!

As for Bob Dylan . . . Well, Dylan actually scared Brian a little, made him uneasy. Brian was frightened in this almost child-like way: disturbed by something he couldn't quite fully comprehend, yet fascinated all the same. Brian was getting this funny vibe off of Dylan's whole sound. He confided to friends that he honestly believed Bob Dylan was out to destroy music with his genius.

Meanwhile Brian Wilson began getting all wrapped up in big complicated ideas like 'Art' and 'Civilization'. People would tell him the most commonplace facts about such-and-such a composer or painter and Brian would just flip right out: 'You mean to say Beethoven wrote some of these works when he was completely deaf? Boy, I bet . . . I bet this whole painting thing has been going on thousands of years, right?' A visitor would read a fragment from a volume of Omar Khayyám and Brian Wilson would leap up, his head just awash with all this magical dumb inspiration, screaming, 'Wow' and 'Too much' over and over again because he sensed right there and then that this guy had access to all the answers to the problems besetting our troubled universe.

At the same time, there was business to attend to. The first post-touring album turned out to be *The Beach Boys – Today* and it found Wilson both taking care of business with teen-beat bonanzas like 'Dance, Dance, Dance' and great high-school ra-ra romance rock ('Good to My Baby'), as well as extending his range in both production and composition. What Wilson was now aiming for, in terms of production at least, was to pick up on all that had made Phil Spector's records great – that majestic *presence* – and modify the very essentials to accommodate an almost self-effacingly 'clean' all-American white harmony combo sound. Less of that marvellously over-bearing Wagnerian pomp-and-circumstance stuff: more clarity, more fragility. Also, in songs like 'She Knows Me Too Well' and 'In the Back of My Mind', Wilson's dream lovers were suddenly no longer simple happy souls harmonizing their sun-kissed innocence and undying devotion to each other over a honey-coated backdrop of surf and sand. Instead they'd become highly vulnerable, slightly neurotic and riddled with telling insecurities.

What was really happening was that Brian's whole approach to romance was becoming more and more personalized, more honest in a distinctly autobiographical way. The innocence was still in there certainly. God, it had to be . . . for it remained the absolute deciding factor, the master-force that dictated to almost every aspect of his creativity. But everything was becoming more worldly now. The rigours of experience were beating relentlessly against his muse and Brian Wilson could no longer snugly dream on like before. To begin with, he'd somehow managed to get himself married. His wife's name was Marilyn and she was the younger daughter of Mae and Irving Rovell, a nice outgoing Jewish family, comfortable enough to be able to afford the elder of their offspring Diane the benefits of a good nose job. Marilyn was no beauty and at times her and Brian's relationship seemed more than a little strained. Also, it was becoming more and more apparent – even to the casual onlooker – that Wilson held the elder Rovell sister in slightly higher esteem. Maybe he was just a little infatuated with her. After all, she was prettier, with an aura about her that was a little more innocent.

Yet even with worldly temptation and a nagging wife to contend with, Brian Wilson's penchant for creating 'the great all-American teen anthem' hadn't deserted him yet awhile. In 1965 he went on to compose his greatest work in that effusive genre. 'California Girls' at once took all that was best in

Wilson's heroic myth-weaving patriotism and combined it with his new melodic and arranging sophistication. The results created an even more irresistible myth than the ones that had gone before. Twenty-seven years after he'd conceived it, it would become the one and only Beach Boys track Wilson could still get a jolt of pleasure listening to.

There were two more Beach Boys albums before the advent of *Pet Sounds* and both were, in their own sweet way, cop-outs or, more to the point, 'manufactured' product put out to placate Capitol. Both *Summer Days (and Summer Nights)* and *Beach Boys Party* were more easy-formula halcyon-days fare. The former was forced out by Capitol, though, such was Wilson's talent at this point, even these out-takes and unrelated tracks recorded at earlier sessions were of breath-taking quality, most notably the Beatles homage 'Girl Don't Tell Me' and the Bacharach-influenced majesty of 'Let Him Run Wild'. The latter album was a different horse altogether and seems almost symbolic in retrospect. A supposedly informal 'live' recording of a Beach Boys beach party (it was of course done in the studio), it featured lots of acappella singing, acoustic guitars strumming over the crackling of weenies, bongos, giggling babes ruining the choruses, everybody making much too merry. The whole album was very simple, very all-American and very dumb. Mike Love and Murray both thought it was a great piece of product, but you could hear Brian thinking to himself: 'OK, that's it now, you guys.' From that point on, fun – good, clean or otherwise – was to become a very secondary consideration to art in Brian Wilson and the Beach Boys' ever-expanding universe.

At the very end of 1965, Tony Asher had more or less settled into the routine at the office he was working at. The building housed a strictly nine-to-five breed: hack tune-smiths and instant slogan writers – straight-arrow dudes with mortgages and ulcers who concentrated their efforts on coming up with 'jingles, catch-phrases and the like for various advertising campaigns'. Asher had been allocated about five products, and was making a moderate success of things. The bosses thought his jingle for 'Gallo Wines' for example was particularly promising. 'And I've got to say it . . . I was really just interested in a regular income. Security y'know.' He laughs to himself, 'I am a pretty conservative guy.' So imagine Tony Asher's shock when, out of the blue, Brian Wilson of the Beach Boys – the leader of America's No. 1 top pop sensation – phoned him with a proposition.

Wilson had a problem. Capitol were once again on his back, breathing heavily and threatening possibly even to *sue* if a new Beach Boys album wasn't quickly delivered. And all he had were two unfinished tracks: one, this weird backing track, replete with piccolos and flutes, for a version of 'Sloop John B', the other an abortive new song called 'In My Childhood' which Wilson had decided he hated, scrapping both lyrics and melody-line. (The basic track would later be transformed into the Wilson–Asher 'You Still Believe in Me.' Assorted bicycle bells and horns, added to complement the theme of the song in its original 'Childhood' form, were never wiped off the mix and can be heard on the *Pet Sounds* take to this day.) In short, Wilson needed collaborative aid fast, though why he enlisted Asher remains a mystery – not least to the lyricist himself.

Tony Asher had known Wilson vaguely from a few chance meetings when, in his younger days, he'd hung out at recording sessions attempting to peddle songs he'd written. The aspiring lyricist was a relatively worldly individual for his age and Brian Wilson had struck him as an out-and-out hick, very dumb, barely able to express himself in company at all, though, at the same time, he'd also seemed very conscientious and extremely hard-working. Asher could remember finding him pleasant enough to be around, but ultimately rather insipid. He can't recall to this day whether, back then, he had mentioned to Brian the fact that he wrote lyrics but presumes he must have done.

So, anyway, here was the King of California with his oval face and his weird little voice at the very least offering Tony Asher the chance to pick up on a potential gold-mine in royalties. He told his boss he desperately needed three months' vacation and precisely one day later he was to be found settling down to work with his new-found collaborator in the living-room of the latter's garish mansion in opulent Bellagio.

Unbeknownst to both of them, *Pet Sounds* was to prove Brian's great musical 'breakthrough' and Asher's role – though the credits on the album suggest a strict division between lyrics and music – was soon to make itself obvious. Wilson knew what he wanted lyrically. Each song, each melody and arrangement, stated a mood and Tony Asher's job was simply to express that mood as eloquently as possible:

'It's fair to say that the general tenor of the lyrics was always his and the actual *choice* of words was usually mine. I was really just his interpreter. There were exceptions to the rule, mind you: as I recall, "Here Today" contains a little more of me both lyrically and melodically than Brian. Also I feel that I inspired "God Only Knows".

'I can even remember a discussion I had with Brian over that song because he was terribly worried that incorporating the word "God" into a song – into the title itself – might be considered blasphemous [*laughs*]. No, but it's true. He loved the idea but was terrified that all the radio stations would ban the song just because of the word "God". It took a lot of persuading.

'Brian was constantly looking for topics that kids could relate to. Even though he was dealing in the most advanced score-charts and arrangements, he was still incredibly conscious of this commercial thing. This absolute need to relate.'

To this effect, 'Wouldn't It Be Nice', the song that would lead off their finished creation, was little more than a sophisticated play-off on the old 'We're too young to get married' teen angst dialogue that Wilson had already zeroed in on in 'We'll Run Away', the song he'd written a year or so back with Gary

Usher, not to mention his recent plaintively fulsome reinterpretation of the Four Teens' vintage heartbreaker 'I'm So Young'. But this time Brian Wilson was out to eclipse these previous sonic soap operas, to transform the subject's sappy sentiments with a God-like grace so that the song would become a veritable pocket symphony: two minutes of limpid harps imitating teenage heart-strings in a tug of love, growling horns, joyous little bells, cascading strings, harmonies so complex they seemed to have more in common with a Catholic mass than any cocktail lounge acappella doo-wop – in short, a fantasy island of the most exquisite musical longing imaginable.

Brian knew the score, see. The beach wasn't where it was at anymore. It wasn't even as though he'd been actually *into* surfing. That was all Dennis's scene. He'd just interpreted his brother's enthusiasm, blending his own fantasies in to add a little extra flavouring. But this new music had a spiritual thing going for it. This was his music, the sound of his soul rising up, and as he leaned forward to embrace it Brian suddenly sensed that getting as close to the voice of God as possible was what was going to be truly happening for him, in the immediate future. At this point, he was out to move the very soul of teenage America, to create music so passionate, so majestic that when you turned on your radio – shazam – Instant Epiphany. And inspiration was everywhere.

'"Wouldn't It Be Nice" was definitely Brian's idea,' says Asher. 'The innocence of the situation – being too young to get married – seemed to be immensely appealing to him. I can remember being in restaurants with him and some young girl would inevitably walk in and he'd almost melt, y'know. He'd get all misty-eyed and just stare at her, muttering on and on about, "Oh wow, she's just so-o beautiful. Don't you think . . ."

'Also, there was his sister-in-law Diane and I don't . . . I don't think I'd be wrong in saying that he was definitely infatuated by her. Again, he was obsessed with this innocent aura she seemed to possess. Brian was really just *so* naive.

'I've got to be frank here, I guess. See, the only times I actually enjoyed myself or even got comfortable with Brian were when I was standing by the piano working with him. Otherwise, I felt hideous! First, there were the physical surroundings which exhibited the worst taste *imaginable*! I came over one time and he'd bought . . . God, my powers to describe these are just inadequate, but . . . They were two clockwork parrots sitting on a perch made out of feathers. And every feather was dyed some disgusting synthetic colour. These monstrosities cost him apparently something like 700 dollars and he thought they were just *the greatest* [laughs] . . .

'Concurrent with all this, Brian was also starting to cultivate an entourage – and the people that were surrounding him were inevitably rather more learned . . . more sophisticated, generally more *knowledgeable* than he was. There was a guy named Arnie Geller. He was really just a hanger-on who later became Brian's flunky ['a job', according to Derek Taylor, 'not even worthy of a dog']. And Terry Sachen, an ex-roadie who'd become another hanger-on. Plus a couple called Lauren and Judy Schwartz who had a great influence on Brian, I seem to recall. Lauren was heavily into mysticism. In fact, a couple of years later he changed his surname to "Darro" in order to spiritually balance the number of cyphers in his name [laughs].

'Anyway, Lauren was something of a Mephistophelian character. He was a real social manipulator and he turned Brian on to all this awful literature. Well, Brian just became over-awed by all this bullshit . . .'

Volumes like *The Little Prince*, the works of Kahlil Gibran, Krishna – 'the marshmallow mystics' as Asher calls them – were devoured ravenously. Herman Hesse was a firm favourite; Brian even descended to the likes of Rod McKuen and Walter Benton's *This Is My Beloved*. And each work was greeted as a further extension of the Word.

'Brian just got so hung-up on all this crap, this dumb mysticism. There was another thing too, a record made in 1958 called "How to Talk Hip" which was basically a humorous bohemian thing about smoking dope: "in" humour from the whole Dharma Bums era.

'Anyway, this junkie beatnik type says at one point after a long build-up, "And then we'll have world peace!" [*Laughs.*]

'Brian thought this was *so-o* amazing! . . . That was going to be the title of a song on *Pet Sounds* – "And Then We'll Have World Peace!"'

Lauren Schwartz, it transpires, also turned Wilson on to his first acid trip *and* introduced him to this whispery-voiced little bohemian guy with funny-looking glasses who wrote songs and was something of an intellectual – a poet too – and an avid user of amphetamines. His name was Van Dyke Parks, and he was going to take over the chore of writing Brian Wilson's lyrics just as soon as Tony Asher had stepped out of the clique.

Listening to *Pet Sounds* nowadays, it's all too tempting to imagine Wilson and Asher feverishly pounding out these remarkable songs as though their lives depended upon it. The lyricist doesn't remember it quite like that, however:

'I wish I could say Brian was totally committed. Let's say he was . . . um, very *concerned*. But the thing is, Brian Wilson has to be the single most irresponsible person I've ever met in my life. You just wouldn't believe the extent of this absolute lack of responsibility he constantly maintained.

'I mean, there were always documents to be signed, appointments that were never kept. Christ, Capitol would even phone me as kind of a last resort and say, "Listen, we hear you're seeing a lot of Brian. Would it be possible to get him to sign this?" I mean, I can even remember seeing this 125,000 dollar cheque that he needed to endorse, just laying around the house.

'He had this obsession with sleeping, for example. He'd sleep all through the daytime – only get up when it was dark. He was smoking an awful lot of dope then. He just used to get these incredibly intense depressions. He'd just started taking acid too.

'You asked me if he ever showed flashes of lunacy, right? I'd have to say . . . Well, he had fits of this just *uncontrollable* anger. Then he'd fall apart and start crying during play-backs of certain tracks.

'He was constantly being buffeted between these two emotional extremes. From elation to depression and back again. It's like . . . yeah, you could say he was doomed in a way. He was just so damn self-destructive! It wasn't the acid, so much. It was more things like the way he seemed to surround himself constantly with bad people and bad situations.

'That whole claustrophobic scene with his family for example was so blatantly obvious to me. It was like this dumb guy saying to himself, "Aw, gee, I don't deserve all this success. I'd better surround myself with all these jerks to make up for my good fortune."

'First there was the weird relationship he maintained with Marilyn, his wife. It was this constant interplay of Brian just acting in this utterly belittling way toward her and Marilyn retaliating by storming off into another room yelling back something quite inane. It was always very caveman-like, like something out of *The Flintstones*. Personally, I could never understand why he'd married her in the first place. I don't know, maybe he actually loved her!'

The Beach Boys had been out on an extensive tour of foreign countries while Wilson and Asher were beavering away on the music for *Pet Sounds*. In fact, they'd just returned from a highly successful sojourn in Japan when they were allowed to hear what big brother had been up to in their absence. From the get-go they didn't like it.

Here they were back from a highly lucrative tour of Europe, where in England they'd been voted as suddenly more popular than the Beatles themselves, having fucked anything and everything wearing a short skirt and packing a pulse-rate, and Brian had been back home all along wasting his time with this Asher guy – whom no one knew – on this high-falutin' un-American pansy-assed 'ego music'. Asher still recalls their reaction and personalities vividly:

'Well, I always thought Al Jardine was kind of an underrated force in that band. I felt he was genuinely impressed by some of the music we were making. He'd take me aside sometimes and tell me how good it was.

'But Dennis . . . oh God, Dennis wasn't bewildered by anything! He just wanted to get the hell out of the studio and get back on the beach [*laughs*].

'And Carl . . . well, I always felt Carl was playing a part, y'know. He wasn't so much a hypocrite as . . . well, he seemed to be totally into promoting this role of himself as calm, loving, serene. He was always stroking his wife's hair, for example, acting the Fat Buddha.'

Then there was Mike Love, who couldn't conceal the fact that he was utterly pissed off by the whole set-up. Love's main concerns were success, money and pussy in no particular order; art and self-expression did not appeal to his set of values in any way whatsoever. So he acted morose and wouldn't say much in front of Asher or Brian except to throw in the occasional barbed 'Well, it sure sounds different to the old stuff' wise-crack. And if that wasn't enough, there was always good old Murray Wilson, by now completely out of his depth, but still desperately determined to make his daunting presence felt. According to Asher:

'Murray was so strange. I've got to say that he came across to me as a really sick man. Pathetically so, in fact, but sick none the less. There were times, for example, when he'd be saying to me, "Oh! All I'm trying to do is to help Brian. He hates me, he hates me." Or, "Why are the other guys giving Brian such a hard time? Can't you talk to them, make them see . . ."

'And then, behind Brian's back, he'd be talking to the other guys . . . in the bathroom, say, just stirring it up. His whole thing it seemed to me was to get the guys at each other's throats constantly so he could establish himself as the one solid figure. He wasn't the leader though – Brian was – and Christ, you wouldn't believe how Murray secretly resented him for that. His own father!

'And the other guys . . . listen, the Beach Boys would have gladly ganged up on Brian if they conceivably could've but they were powerless. No one really challenged . . . no one could challenge Brian, for Chrissakes! Because they weren't talented enough to take over. God knows, they've proved that since.

'I mean, even then they were trying to do things off their own bat and it was just pathetic really.

'As far as I'm concerned, the Beach Boys had become absolutely expendable to Brian Wilson's music. Absolutely, yes. No question about it. I mean, they were getting to be an impediment to him even in the areas they should have helped. There used to be incredible rows – fist-fights, everything.

'They were all allocated certain vocal parts, OK, and they wouldn't be doing 'em right so Brian would just explode and start screaming, "Goddam it, you assholes, we've been here for three hours and you can't even do this simple thing!"

'Brian could have done it all by himself. The Beach Boys didn't play a single note on the album, either. It was all session musicians – Hal Blaine, Larry Knechtal, Ray Pullman and Billy Strange as well as the Sid Sharpe Strings.'

On the second side of *Pet Sounds* one of the tracks featured is a number called 'I Know There's an Answer', featuring lyrics written not by Tony Asher but by Terry Sachen, the ex-roadie/hanger-on at the Brian Wilson homestead who'd go on to chauffeur the composer haphazardly around in a black Rolls-Royce with tinted windows. The original title of the song, however, was 'Hang On to Your Ego' and when the Beach Boys discovered this, they just couldn't handle it. Hang on to your ego? No way were they going to participate in a song with a title like that. Asher was there to observe Brian cave in to his nagging in-laws on this issue:

'You see, all the time Brian was having these nagging fears that the music was maybe going a little *too far out*. He knew it was great in a way, but he was out on his own, out on a limb with his brothers and cousins – his whole family set-up – undermining his confidence. There was this constant inner conflict going on.'

Brian Wilson suddenly backed down. The 'Hang On to Your Ego' title was axed, the decision becoming the very first in a tragic series of paranoid freak-outs that eventually were to destroy the whole experimental fabric of his 'new' music.

It's possible that Brian Wilson was also seriously considering launching a solo career. Certainly he was trying to establish himself as a separate entity from the Beach Boys in the media. In one interview conducted while *Pet Sounds* was being mixed he even spoke critically of other members. Mike Love 'couldn't stand being alone long enough to write something creative', while baby brother Dennis 'is the most messed-up person I know . . . If you want him to sit still for a second, he's yelling and screaming and ranting and raving . . . I think he'd fall apart if the girls stopped screaming for him . . . I pray for Dennis a lot.' More tellingly, he chose to put out a solo single just prior to the release of *Pet Sounds* – a track from the album itself called 'Caroline No'. The song meant a lot to Brian. Many years later he'd claim it referred directly to the first girl ever to break his heart back in high school, one Carole Mountain. But Bruce Johnston, Brian's touring replacement, felt it went deeper than that: 'There is no such person as Caroline . . . there never was. That song was directly about Brian himself and the death of a quality within him that was so vital: his innocence. He knows it too.'

The album, though Asher denies that such a policy was consciously activated, is in many respects the first concept work ever in rock. Beginning with 'Wouldn't It Be Nice' and its glorification of the two young lovers' star-crossed longings, the album documents the male participant's attempts at coming to terms with himself and the world about him. Each song pinpoints a crisis of faith in love and life: confusion ('That's Not Me'), disorientation (the staggeringly beautiful 'I Just Wasn't Made for These Times'), recognition of love's capricious impermanence ('Here Today') and finally, the grand betrayal of innocence featured in 'Caroline No'.

Then again, bearing in mind this conceptual bent, there are certain incongruous factors about the album's construction. The main one is the inclusion of the hit single 'Sloop John B', as well as of two short instrumental pieces, at least one of which ('Let's Go Away for a While') Tony Asher had in fact written lyrics for. The reason for this, is that Capitol had gone far beyond simply demanding, issuing ultimatums and stipulating deadlines that they knew fell on deaf ears – they confiscated the tapes to Brian Wilson's masterpiece just before it had reached completion and released it as it stood.

A cover shot was taken at a zoo in the LA district just prior to the group being banned from the place for 'mistreating the animals' (the incident made the small columns of the *LA Times*; Dennis had apparently been the ringleader).

The Beach Boys singles 'God Only Knows' and 'Wouldn't It Be Nice' were issued and both sold in spectacular quantities, but over in America the album itself was, ironically, to live up to the barbed prophecies of the 'guys', Murray and Capitol itself. It bombed.

1966 was evidently not a good year for 'visionary pop music' taking off in America. Even Phil Spector's orgasmic 'River Deep Mountain High' nose-dived away from the US charts almost as spectacularly as it was taken into the hearts and homes of the more astute British consumer, prompting the increasingly demented producer to retire altogether from the studio for several years. The Beach Boys' new-found mass audience in Britain – presumably the very same breed that had discovered the group via the incomparably banal 'Barbara

Ann', their first large-scale hit in the country some months earlier – bought the album in droves, causing it to gloriously transcend even its expected cult acceptance.

Brian's own 'Caroline No', one of the most beautiful songs he has ever written, however, failed to activate sales *anywhere*. Even after dear old Murray had allocated himself the final say by commandeering the final track and speeding it up from the key of G to the key of A 'in order to make Brian sound younger'.

Tony Asher meanwhile had disappeared back to his secure post at the advertising department: 'That was the nature of my personality then. To be able to depend on a regular income. And I found Brian's lifestyle so damn repugnant. I mean, for every four hours we'd spend writing songs, there'd be about forty-eight hours of these dopey conversations about some dumb book he'd just read.

'Or else he'd just go on and on about girls. His feelings about this girl or that girl. It was just embarrassing as well as exhibiting this awful, awful taste. His choice of movies, say, was invariably terrible. TV programmes . . . Everything. Plus he was starting to get pretty weird.'

Asher still doesn't regret disassociating himself from Wilson and the Beach Boys:

'I do believe Brian is a musical genius. Absolutely. Whatever I thought about him personally was almost always overridden by my feelings of awe at what he was creating. I mean, he was able to create such extraordinary melodies . . .

'God knows where he discovered those chords, those ideas for arranging a certain song. Maybe he'd had some formal training, though I seriously doubt it. I can vividly remember, for example, the first time he played me his finished track for "Don't Talk (Put Your Head on My Shoulder)". I was literally speechless. Let's just say it was a great joy making music with him but that any other relationship with Brian was a great chore. I just felt, see, that the guy was going to go . . .'

Over the top, so to speak?

'Yeah, but that there was nothing I could possibly do to prevent it happening. That whatever was causing his problems had been predestined inside of him from the age of nine, say. I'd try to talk with him about it and every time it just fell on deaf ears. He'd say, "Oh, I can't handle this" or use some other useless catch-phrase.'

And now?

'The stories I've heard about this untogetherness these days would seem to figure. It could easily have happened, really: the irresponsibility . . . the inability to get himself together would ultimately just have had to affect his music. His occasional "conditions" must have transformed themselves into a total life style.

'It's so weird though. I mean, you were talking to me just now about *Pet Sounds* being a masterpiece. Neither of us at the time thought that . . . at least, I . . . I don't know. I was more impressed by the production, really.

'To me it was just a great album, and nothing more. I remember Brian was always saying during play-backs, "Boy, for the first time ever Beach Boys songs are going to get lots of cover versions."

'As far as I was concerned, it was just a chance to show some people, like my parents, and the guys at the advertising company, that rock music could be . . . a mature medium. That's about as far as it went for me.

'Brian, though, was looking for acceptance. I mean, "God Only Knows" . . . Mantovani could have easily made a cover version of that song. Lawrence Welk, too. But before . . . well, Andy Williams would never have covered something like "Little Deuce Coupe".

'It's a shame, really – what's happened since. I suppose I must hold the same view as most everyone else. I haven't heard anything particular stirring from Brian or the Beach Boys. That track "Sail On Sailor" is just dandy, but otherwise it's been down to just isolated brilliant flashes.

'It's tragic actually – 'cos it's obviously still there, but it's no longer in any usable form.

'But that's Brian, maybe, for you.

'A genius musician but an amateur human being.'

Part 2

'We were doing witchcraft, trying to make witchcraft music.'

'The "Brian Wilson is a genius" thing? Yes, I started that off,' confesses Derek Taylor, a laconic acid-era Ronald Coleman-type with a gentle scouse burr to his voice and a remarkably agile memory for one who fried his senses so ferociously throughout the late sixties. 'It was my line: "Brian Wilson is a genius, I think." I seem to recall it all came about because Brian told me that he thought he was better than most other people believed him to be. So I put this idea to myself and went around town proposing it to people like Van Dyke and Danny Hutton and they all said, "Oh, yes, definitely, Brian Wilson is a genius." Then I thought, "Well, if that's so, why doesn't anyone outside think so?" Then I started putting it around, making almost a campaign out of it.

'And I still believe it. Absolutely, Brian Wilson is most certainly a genius. It was something that I felt had to be established.'

Pet Sounds was about to be released when Taylor was taken on the Beach Boys' pay-roll, receiving a handsome 750 dollars a month for renovating the group's public image. Strategically, it was an extremely canny move – instigated, naturally enough, by Brian, who saw Taylor as a vital factor in establishing credibility for the Beach Boys' image and his own new music. Derek Taylor was at that time the single most prestigious figure with whom to have one's name linked in matters of promotion. He was very witty, very dry, a kindly soul, and also a Liverpudlian then resident in a city still totally besotted with folk of said nationality. Most decisively, he knew the Beatles and had actually worked with them and Brian Epstein. There could be no more spectacular recommendation. Once enlisted into the ranks, Taylor worked fast. The candy-striped shirts that had for so long symbolized the Beach Boys' image were conveniently 'lost', while marriages – all had been wed for some time now, unbeknownst to their fans – were immediately made public knowledge.

Next came the grand initiation ceremony afforded the release of *Pet Sounds*. Taylor convened a reception in a suite at the London Hilton, where England's most prestigious pop pen-pushers were given a preview of the album. Self-styled LA 'freak out' specialist Kim Fowley was unofficial master-of-ceremonies at the unveiling. Marianne Faithful hovered fetchingly, while guests of honour Paul McCartney and John Lennon sat, their ears cupped against the speakers, listening intently to a music that represented the most formidable threat to their own aesthetic dictatorship of rock in the year 1966.

According to Fowley, after the record had finished Lennon and McCartney left the suite, returning immediately to the latter's St John's Wood home, where, under the heady spell of Brian Wilson's 'new music', some hashish and a couple of amphetamine pills, they went on to compose 'Here There and Everywhere' that same evening. For Brian, information like this was music to his ears. Moreover, that George Harrison had spent hours phoning acquaintances to rave over the album's merits or that Andrew Loog Oldham had, upon being handed a test-pressing, pontificated that the work be labelled the 'Scheherazade of pop' – this was precisely the kind of effusive reaction Brian Wilson was after.

'By this time Brian had become very, very competitive,' confirms Taylor. 'So much so that it was no longer that healthy sort of competitive spirit thing. It was a mad possessive battle against the Stones and particularly the Beatles, an absurdly maniacal "Who's the fairest in the land?" campaign, really. And I was in the middle of all this because . . . Well, firstly, he liked me because I was English and different. My life style certainly seemed to appeal to him greatly.

'But also there was the problem about my other connections. He'd constantly be testing the strength of my devotion to his cause. For example, he'd play me a new song and immediately start this thoroughly insistent psychological arm-twisting tactic, making statements like "Better than the Stones, yeah?" Then he'd put on . . . oh, "Paperback Writer", say, and keep saying in this deliberately cute, precociously taxing way – actually he'd sound just like Tony Hancock when he indulged in these sessions – "Is that any good? I ask you. Is that really *any good*?" And I'd have to say very deliberately, "Yes, Brian, *it is very good*"! He was never satisfied though. Never.

'It's strange, too, because the fact that *Pet Sounds* hadn't sold at all well didn't affect him in the least. I doubt, in fact, whether it even registered with him. He was only interested in these "Who is the best?" heats.

'The Beatles . . . now, the Beatles were hot enough not to be over-concerned about anybody else, but they did think the Beach Boys were good. In fact, they'd arrived at that conclusion long before I had.

'Brian . . . of course, at that time Brian was very hot. He was always talking about a new plateau. All the time: "The next record will create a new plateau for the Beach Boys in terms of creativity and acceptance." Always these grand statements.

'He was constantly making changes with his collaborators too. Tony Asher had left the picture by that time and Van Dyke [Parks], who was also as hot as hell right then, was brought in to deal with the lyrics. I mean, Van Dyke was mad too, but it was a constant thing, and on that level anyone with the appropriate sensitivity could relate to it. Brian on the contrary . . . Well, one day he'd be coherent, bright, and the next he'd be so damnably illogical and strange. He was scary quite frankly.

'Brian was taking acid, smoking a hell of a lot of grass and generally enjoying a new-found freedom that he would ultimately cut himself off from during one of those totally illogical frenzied brain-storms of his that would inevitably wreak havoc over everything.

'In terms of an era, this was all pretty much pre-acid, mind. I seem to recall only Brian and Dennis were turning on at this time. The rest certainly weren't.

'The *other* Beach Boys? Oh, it was always something of a pleasure touring with them because they were professional, you know . . . good company. They were very concerned about Brian too. All the time they'd be asking, "How is Brian? What does he think?" and so on. I never really heard a single disparaging word in all that time. Maybe a few jokes about his eccentricities, but always basically affectionate.

'Mike Love by then was tough as hell and was taking care of things. A worldly fellow, Mike. Marriages, and all that. There was no God in his life then, I can tell you!

'Then came Al Jardine who was . . . amusing. He possessed a very dry sense of humour did Al. Bruce [Johnston] was very business-like, very diplomatic.

'Dennis was . . . oh, I could never make up my mind whether Dennis was actually *childish* or *child-like*. Maybe more of the former. He was pretty wild, certainly. Irresponsible, too. Though I didn't find him to be much of a problem.

'Carl was so sweet and young I found him difficult to relate to really. I just felt too damn worldly next to Carl's innocence. I was frightened I might taint him in some respect [*laughs*].

'I didn't really have too much contact with Murray, which was probably just as well. I remember one half-hour when he rushed into my office. The first thing he said was, "Am I coming on too strong?" I immediately replied, "Yes."

'He wanted photographs, so I gave him some new shots with the boys' hair protruding over the ears and touching the collar and he tossed them away: "Never mind that, I want them looking like Americans. It's for a six-foot . . . no, make that an eighteen-foot stain-glass window. Just imagine this – the boys *looking like Americans*, and 'Sea-of-Tunes' [the name of his publishing company] inscribed underneath."

'He just kept throwing these photographs around then suddenly leapt up and ran out of the office. He never really intimidated me. Though I wouldn't have liked to have been one of his sons. Brian hated him from time to time. And, of course, Murray hated the new music, which didn't help matters.

'I also recall having – oh God, I still can't believe this one! – a conversation with Brian and Dennis about the Beach Boys never having written surf music or songs about cars; that the Beach Boys had never been involved *in any way* with the surf and drag fads.

'I was told this one afternoon and I kept saying, "Listen, how can . . . I mean, how dare you give me this nonsense about you never having been involved in all this? I have the proof right here."

'But no, they would not concede. I just felt it sad that they should be so determined to disown their past. The Beatles went through that – at about the same time, as it happens.

'That all-American tag that Murray was still attempting to yoke them on to had done them a hell of a lot of damage. Brian, in particular, suffered. I mean, to begin with, it was really nothing new to Hollywood that people were strange, lived vampire-like existences, had bizarre whims. It was just that Brian Wilson was not supposed to be strange. And even then, with Brian . . . it's weird actually, because Brian would only do things in fits and starts as if they had just been invented.

'He was definitely a man of whims. Fanatical . . . illogical whims at that! Religions were one thing. He'd be into Subud one minute, then on to something else without bothering to really absorb any of it.

'And also there were his food fads. Oh God, yes, his food fads! [*Laughs*.] I did most of my business down at the Gaiety Delicatessen, a restaurant in Hollywood . . . basically because I was something of a heavy drinker at that time. Brian seemed rather fascinated by this semi-alcoholic existence because it had never seemed a really strong Californian trait to drink a lot. Anyway, he'd be sitting with me in this restaurant going on and on about this supposedly strict vegetarian diet of his, preaching vegetarianism at me while at the very same moment he'd be whacking down some massive hamburger.

'It was such ridiculous hypocrisy and I'd turn on him and say, "Look, do you realize what you're doing? Here you are preaching on about dieting and stuff and you're stuffing back this massive hamburger." And he'd just fix me with this cunning look of his, signifying, I suppose, that the joke was really on me.

'Also . . . God [*laughs*], Brian was telling everyone that the next album would be recorded in a gymnasium and that he wanted me to coordinate the transformation of his recording studio into a gym.

'It was, again, all so bloody absurd because the man couldn't even pick a bar-bell up! He was driving us all crackers by that time because, well, God, he was so temporary, it was awful. And I'd dread the phone call at 4 a.m. demanding that I come over because I knew he needed me. We had a terrible falling-out that lasted about three weeks.

'I couldn't stand the fact that Brian didn't want me to like any other artist but himself. I could never stand bands competing over me. It was never a problem with the Byrds, mind. But Brian . . .

'Mind you, he *was* making some amazing music at that time. I mean, even when I couldn't face him, even when I couldn't handle his mad competitiveness or his temporary whims, he could win me over with his music. He could manipulate people, could Brian. He was very cunning, very clever, even though there was a naivety there. Part of him was this terribly shy young man whom you could tell the most mundane things to and he'd express just sheer amazement . . .

'But despite his strangeness, how could you deny him when he was creating something like, well, "Surf's Up"?'

Taylor was hardly alone in his role as Brian's trusted confidant. Jules Siegel was a journalist with furtive eyes and a near fatal fondness for LSD who had been one of Brian's special little gang, one of the stellar crew bent on making Brian Wilson's new spiritual music as cataclysmic a multi-media event as humanly possible. He was present at session after session, watching the madness pile up, hearing extraordinary music being played and recorded only to discover that most of it would never see the light of day, and that he too would be banished from the gang just as suddenly and inexplicably as he'd been taken in in the first place. Siegel was a pal of David Anderle's, a noted LA hipster/businessman who'd recently left MGM having almost succeeded in wooing Bob Dylan to the label in mid-'66. But all that was in the recent past, as, Anderle was now hanging out and working with America's other great white rock genius on all sorts of creative projects, the pre-eminent one being the establishment of a Beach Boys record label all their very own, named Brother Records. But there were all these other amazing ideas just buzzing around, particularly on those crazy nights when Anderle and Brian would be spread out by the pool with the lava lamps a-glowing and that big telescope you could focus in on all the stars and planets with, lost in great mind-scrambling sessions boosted by amphetamines and pot wherein both parties would space out and giddily theorize about the imminence of a better world beginning with a bigger bolder style of life bereft of borders and limitations.

Van Dyke Parks liked those little black speed pills too. He was a bookish-looking fellow with owlish little glasses and a personality that was more flamboyant than maybe burly guys like the rest of the Beach Boys could comfortably relate to. His self-penned LA music hustler's biography of the time – entitled 'Van Dyke Parks is real, valid, and twenty-two!' – claimed, among other things, that 'at nineteen he slipped from parts in TV dramas to Carnegie Institute where musical oceans deluged his mind . . . Returning to the ocean, he contemplated the meanings and considered the lilies. He wrote a song, a pop-art version of Beethoven's ninth symphony, and called it simply "Number Nine". He is undoubtedly where it's at.' He'd also been a session organist for the Byrds, had created some musical waves of his own around LA and now he was into his self-styled 'American gothic' period of lyric writing, a sort of 'Rock-Rock-Roll-Plymouth Rock-Roll-Over' type of abstract thing. Brian would play Parks these little musical pieces – 'feels' he'd called them – and the lyricist would conjure forth these self-conscious artsy splurges of imagery. Sometimes it was pretentious gibberish but there were other times when something was created like the fantasia of 'Surf's Up' or the eerie simplicity of 'Wind Chimes' or the homely surrealism of a 'Cabinessence', and it was all at once blindingly clear that something of extraordinary cultural importance was taking place, because everyone in the room would gasp and rise as one, exploding with spontaneous applause. Anderle and his protégé, singer Danny Hutton, Siegel, another writer, Paul Robbins with the satanic beard, worldly Liverpudlian Derek Taylor, Michael Vosse, Anderle's assistant, with the thin moustache and the omnipresent white panama hat – they'd all be on their feet, glowing because here they were in the presence of America's very own baby Mozart, playing the midwife and helping him nurture this latest in an ongoing series of break throughs in contemporary popular music for a brave new world.

Hearing *Pet Sounds* (as well as meeting Brian round at dope dealer Lauren Schwartz's) was what had tripped them all out in the first place. That was the first breakthrough, and Brian had got straight on to the second stage that very autumn with this wild track he'd first written with Tony Asher called 'Good, Good Vibrations'. It was even short-listed as track fourteen on *Pet Sounds* by a Capitol A&R guy for a while before getting dropped, and Brian had ended up devoting session after session as well as tens of thousands of dollars to finding the sound that best represented the acid-dazed tones now ringing around in his head. The song itself could already boast a long and bizarre history, as David Anderle takes up the story:

'When I really got in with Brian, it was right around the time of the fourth attempt at "Good Vibrations". I heard it, and it knocked me out, and I said, "Uh, oh there's something happening here that is unbelievable." And the next time I came up, it was quite different again. And *then* I came up one evening, and Brian said that he'd decided to totally scrap "Good Vibrations". He was just not going to put it out. The track was going to be sold to Warner Bros. to be put out as an R'n'B record, sung by a coloured group.

'Originally, see, it had been a lot shorter . . . tighter rhythmically and melodically much simpler. It was much more of a commercial ditty.

'Anyway, I told Danny this and he said, "Well, let's see if I can't record the song myself and have Brian produce and finish the basic track." So I called Brian back the next day and made him the proposition – which I don't personally think prompted him to decide to finish . . . though maybe. Well, anyway, he went ahead and finished it.'

And 'Good Vibrations', with its vocal arrangement and that innovative use of the theremin went on to become the Beach Boys' biggest-selling single ever, totally undermining – at least temporarily – the prophecies of such as Murray Wilson who'd seen 'all this progressive stuff' as dealing out the veritable death-blow to the popularity of his boys.

'Good Vibrations', then, was the Brian Wilson master-plan in second gear. Reports had it that the third stage would next be achieved via the follow-up single – a Wilson Van Dyke Parks collaboration, 'Heroes and Villains', of purportedly epic proportions. Finally, there would be the unveiling of the biggest jewel in the Beach Boys' crown, a whole album laden with Parks Wilson gems, a breathtaking masterpiece that would leave all supposed competitors reeling in their tracks.

This project already had a title. At first it was supposed to be *Dumb Angel*, but that was quickly changed. Finally it was decided: the next Beach Boys album would be entitled – simply – *Smile*.

A cover had even been conceived for it: a primitive child-like drawing of a 'Smile Shop', and by December 1966, there was also a full track listing. Side one was to begin with a track entitled 'Do You Like Worms?', while the final track of side two was another unreleased piece called 'The Old Master-Painter'. Sandwiched between these cuts were the titles 'Vegetables' (spelt 'Vega-Tables'), 'Surf's Up', 'Wind Chimes', 'Cabinessence' (again spelt 'Cabin Essence'), 'Who Ran the Iron Horse', 'The Grand Coolee Dam', 'The Elementals Suite', 'Our Prayer', 'Heroes and Villains', 'Good Vibrations', 'Bicycle Rider', 'Wonderful' and 'Child is the Father to the Man'.

And where is it now?

In his piece 'Goodbye Surfing, Hello God' Siegel refers constantly to music bound by 'entire sequences of extraordinary power and beauty' that were ultimately to be 'sacrifices to the same strange combination of superstitious fear and the God-like conviction of his [Wilson's] own power he displayed when he destroyed the Fire Music sequence of the "Elementals Suite".'

Michael Vosse is more explicit about the actual form that *Smile* was trying to take in the mind of its increasingly demented creator: 'I would say without a doubt that *Smile*, had it been completed, would have been basically a Southern

California non-country-oriented gospel album – on a very sophisticated level. Because that's what Brian was doing: his own form of revival music.

'Also, Brian's other preoccupation was the need for humour . . . which is almost the key to his whole scene. He told me that he felt laughter as one of the highest forms of divinity and that when someone was laughing, their connection with the thing that was making them laugh made them more open than they could be at just about any other time.

'You can find that in all art forms: the minute you inspire laughter you also make that person vulnerable, which means either you can shock them, make them laugh more, or, at that moment, you can be totally honest with them. And Brian felt that it was time to do a humour album.'

On the one hand, Wilson was about to expose his audience to the gargantuan heaviness of the Van Dyke Parks collaborations, and on the other he wanted the project to weigh in with this new concept of his: *Smile* as the great cosmic humour album. The guy was always biting off more than even he could chew.

Let's see, there was Brian's healthfood fetish demanding to be eulogized on the album, plus the whole health kick which set Wilson to blubbering orders to Taylor, Vosse and Anderle about building sauna baths and a gymnasium in the recording studio. Next, business meetings started being held in the swimming-pool. Brian's theory here, according to Vosse, being that 'if you take a bunch of businessmen and put them in a swimming-pool with their heads bobbing out of the water, then they really get down to fundamentals. Because nobody can bullshit when they're in the water.' If they *did*, Brian would dunk them. And if it got boring, he would just start splashing about. Then came the sand-box. Vosse again:

'In what had been his dining-room Brian had a guy build a partition about four feet off the ground into a box shape. Then he put his grand piano in it and filled it with sand up to about two feet, so he could play the piano with his shoes off in the sand. And then he got into having meetings in the sand-box because you could roll around and cover yourself up to *here*.

'He would bring these things up at meetings at the office. He would come in and everybody would sit around a table – and have lists . . . Brian was always making lists. And they were just classic . . . like, you'd look and see "Monday March 23rd. – Vitamins/Studio Time at Western/Sand-box". "Ah the sand-box. We have to start meeting more in the sand-box."'

Everything started spinning much too fast at around this point. Wilson had also discovered that Capitol were trying to stymie the band with an outdated clause known as the 'breakages' amendment. And so he immediately sued the company, an act destined to throw the forthcoming release of his ongoing masterpiece into serious jeopardy. According to Derek Taylor:

'Ah yes, this was all concurrent with Brian's spectacular eccentricities, wasn't it? He decided that Capitol were ripping him off and instigated a whole campaign against them. He'd employ people just to audit Capitol, sue Capitol . . . hate Capitol.

'The breakages area dated back to 78 rpm records . . . it was simply a redundant clause that Capitol were using to extort more money from the band. Brian actually employed a young lawyer guy – Grillo, Nick Grillo – as the overseer to this campaign and was spurring him on every-which-way.

'Actually I always thought that Capitol took pretty good care of the Beach Boys. That was only my own opinion though.'

Probably the high-point of the whole *Smile* era was reached around November 1966 when CBS set about filming a TV documentary on Brian Wilson and his new music. This was not going to be just another dumb pop show: the programme was to be introduced by Leonard Bernstein and be overseen by

David Oppenheim, a middle-aged director of high-brow documentaries who'd recently filmed an award-winning documentary on the composer Stravinsky. Brian naturally saw this as being 'very heavy' and full of portent.

The show's actual peak occurred after a frankly disastrous Beach Boys recording session when the young composer performed a live preview of 'Surf's Up' on the piano in his living-room – and it sounded quite perfect. So perfect, in fact, that Bernstein himself broke down afterwards and made some ecstatic claim that the song was the most brilliant piece of contemporary music he'd ever heard. Bernstein's frenzied gushing really moved Brian. It horrified him.

Of course, Brian should have been over the moon but he wasn't. He broke down there and then. Freaked right out and ended up phoning his astrologer, a woman named Genevlyn, who told him to beware hostile vibrations. So he stayed in bed for five days, eating candy bars, smoking pot and brooding to the sound of his wind chimes.

There was always something wrong now, something not quite right. There was dog shit in the sand-box. Marilyn was getting hysterical more and more often. Brian would still stand in front of mirrors for hours at a time, playing with his hair, but it never looked good anymore, and he felt suddenly old, fat and kinda washed out. Even his precious Rolls-Royce with the cooky smoke-screen windows had been broken into. Brian sensed it was all the work of 'mind-gangsters' plotting against him. 'This new music I'm making is going to scare a lot of people,' he'd keep claiming in his most puffed-up, ego'd-out moments. But those moments were getting few and far between now. Meanwhile this new music was really starting to scare him more than anyone else. The drugs he'd been relying on to give him all that limitless energy and creative vision now only gave him cold sweats, stomach cramps and chronic paranoia. Worst of all, the 'Boys' were back from Europe, and once again, there were fist-fights in the studio.

The guys – and in particular Mike Love – all mistrusted and resented Van Dyke Parks and his 'weird' druggy lyrics, and Parks was consequently to be the first of Brian's new allies to be ousted from the new gang. According to Vosse:

'What ultimately happened was that Warner Bros. made him an offer for his services as a solo artiste that he couldn't refuse, and the day Van Dyke signed, he put his head back into his own music again and became less and less available to Brian. And Brian suddenly became less and less sure of what he was doing with the album.

'You see, where I had always seen a musical co-operation going on was definitely in the studio, and particularly when they were cutting tracks. In the studio together, they had a very happy relationship going ... That's where Van Dyke had this great respect for Brian. And for his part, Brian wanted him there *all the time* and when problems developed, he would call him; and the two of them together in the studio was just a joy.

'Without the other guys, that is. And I think that while the Beach Boys were in England touring and while Brian was doing the tracks for the album, *Smile* was a totally conceived entity.'

Or, as David Anderle would bitterly observe only a year after *Smile's* cancellation:

'I think the major problem from *Pet Sounds* onwards has been the Beach Boys themselves. The Beach Boys as a musical instrument and the Beach Boys always being negative towards Brian's experimentation. They were generally very aware of the commercial market when Brian really wanted to space out and take off ...

'He'd have to go through a tremendous amount of paranoia before he would get into the studio, knowing he was going to have to face an argument. He would come into the studio uptight, he would give a part to one of the fellas or to a group of the fellas, say, "This is what I would like to have done," and there would be instant resistance.

'And it just wouldn't be happening. And so there'd be endless takes and then he would just junk it. And then, maybe after they left to go on tour, he would come back in and do it himself. All their parts. But it was very taxing and it was extremely painful to watch. Because it was like a great wall had been put down in front of creativity.'

In the midst of the Beach Boys' latest punk rebellion there were all the other little breakdowns occurring, cutting him down, pricking into his once mighty ego bubble. He was totally at the mercy of these utterly vicious mood swings now, jerking him back and forth from giddy elation to frantic sobbing sometimes in the space of a single minute. He was getting these scary acid flash-backs too, as well as these voices inside his head. They weren't saying anything too distinct yet, just making this dark, ghostly murmuring sound back there in the lower recesses of his brain. At one session for 'Heroes and Villains' he'd tried to capture this latest ghoulish sound taking up squatter's rights in his head by taking a tape of some acappella Beach Boys vocal horse-play and slowing it down until it was just this vast swamp-like groan of terror. It was the scariest sound of anything he created for *Smile*, but it wasn't as scary as what the voices in his head were starting to insinuate. Jules Siegel chronicled one chilling outburst:

'Van Dyke Parks had left and come back and would leave again, tired of being constantly dominated by Brian. Marilyn Wilson was having headaches and Dennis Wilson was leaving his wife. Session after session was cancelled.

'One night a studio full of violonists waited while Brian tried to decide whether or not the vibrations were friendly or hostile. The answer was hostile and the session was cancelled at a cost of 3,000 dollars.

'Brian seemed to be filled with secret fear. One night at the house it began to surface. Marilyn sat nervously painting her fingernails as Brian stalked up and down, his face tight and his eyes small and red.

'"What's the matter, Brian? You're really strung out," a friend asked.

'"Yeah, I'm really strung out. Look, I mean, I really feel strange. A really strange thing happened to me tonight. Did you see this movie, *Seconds*?"

'"No, but I know what it's about."

'"Look, come into the kitchen; I really have to talk about this."

'In the kitchen they sat down in the black-and-white houndstooth-check wall-papered dinette area. A striped window-shade clashed with the checks and the whole room vibrated like some kind of op-art painting. Normally Brian wouldn't sit for more than a minute in it, but now he seemed to be unaware of anything except what he wanted to say.

'"I walked into that movie," he said in a tense, high-pitched voice, "and the first thing that happened was a voice from the screen that said, 'Hello, Mr Wilson.' It completely blew my mind. You've got to admit that's pretty spooky, right?"

'"Maybe."

'"That's not all. Then the whole thing was there. I mean my whole life. Birth and death and rebirth. The whole thing. Even the beach was in it, a whole thing about the beach. It was my whole life right there on the screen."

'"It's just a coincidence, man. What are you getting so uptight for?"

'"It's Spector . . . Phil Spector . . . I mean he has shares in movies, right? He's behind these things, right? I think he's after me, I mean, I think he set that whole thing up – really. He's out to get me. I mean he's uptight about the way I took his sound and . . . It's no coincidence, man. Spector's out to get me. *He set it all up*."'

'Oh God, the Spector thing,' laughs Derek Taylor. 'Yes, indeed, there *was* a time when Brian thought Spector actually had people following him, therefore he had people following Spector. Then Murray was having Brian tailed and so Brian got someone to tail Murray and it just went on and on. All of it complete insanity.

'By that time . . . well, it was just all hell breaking loose. It was tapes being lost, ideas being junked – Brian thinking, "I'm no good," then, "I'm too good" – then, "I can't sing! I can't get those voices anymore."

'There was even a time back then when there hardly seemed to be a Beach Boys at all.'

The venerable scouse publicist visited his mind-blown employer one final time towards the end of April 1967 and wrote about it for a teenage magazine shortly afterwards:

'Up at Brian's house there is considerable reconstruction . . . the place is becoming a structural symphony western in origin with eastern overtones.

'Come in through the front door and you are welcomed by a four-track recording studio with wrestling mats and a vibrating table. Close by, Wilson has a sauna bath and, a few feet away from that, he has his room of sand . . . a room within a room, with a grand piano set in the sand.

'"The sandroom has got to go," Brian says sadly. "There's sand everywhere, in the food, in the bed, in our clothes. The dogs have scattered it all over the house. I can't stand it."

'But there are still compensations, for the gold and scarlet meditation tent remains and so does the office lined with purple drapes.

'Inside the tent, Brian, the Beach Boys, their wives and friends sit on pillows, eat carrots, and think about things and talk and occasionally laugh and sometimes spray each other with chocolate cream and frosting from aerosol cans.'

By that time *Smile* was well and truly jinxed to death. All of Brian's gang had been exiled from their master's presence for paranoid, frankly insane, reasons. Meanwhile, the key problem blocking the album from being completed was that Brian had forgotten how all the pieces – all these weird 'feels' he'd recorded – actually fitted together. There were seven different versions of 'Heroes and Villains' for example, with numerous little orchestrated motifs of the main theme also recorded and given separate titles, but where they were all supposed to go, Brian simply couldn't remember anymore.

The vocal sessions with the Beach Boys had proved so disastrous, most of the *Smile* vocal tracks weren't complete while many contained half-finished run-throughs often ruined by the vocalists exploding into crude giggling fits for no apparent reason. There were some dazzling sections too, of course. There was an almost-completed 'Surf's Up' with Brian providing a remarkable lead vocal, 'Cabin Essence' with its eerie Aaron Copland-like segues into 'Who Ran the Iron Horse' and the Zen-like 'Have You Seen the Grand Coolee Dam' sections and a version of 'Wind Chimes' with just the sound of two vibraphones and electric piano and Brian's aching soprano navigating the gorgeous melody-line, that overwhelmed the few fortunate enough to hear them. There were some mellow healing chants and a special Beach Boys prayer too, but there was also all this weird spooky music stuff, like this long atonal extract from 'Heroes and Villains' where it sounds like Brian's mind is being ripped apart, or the dark, booming reverb-drenched blur of sound that was 'Mrs O'Leary's Cow' a.k.a. 'The Fire Suite'. Even Brian's Swiss-cheese memory would be able to recall the facts surrounding that piece of music and its place in causing the untimely cancellation of *Smile*, a full twenty-six years after they'd happened:

'At the session I brought a bucket of firewood and put it right in the middle of the room, and I said, "This is supposed to get you guys in the mood."

'We were all messed up on drugs. We were doing witchcraft, trying to make witchcraft music. I was stoned on hashish and grass and I got a little too much into this one tape called "Fire". Then, a place down the street burned down the same day we did the song. And I said to myself, "Somehow we must have burned that building down." And I threw the tape away and erased all the tapes, except . . . I erased "Fire". All the rest that we kept, they were just like twenty-second little pieces, trying to imitate Phil Spector, and not getting anywhere near him. I was crazy then, I was a crazy person.'

By May, Taylor had terminated his employment with the Beach Boys, to take on the organization of the now legendary Monterey pop festival held that same year, but he was still to cross paths with the group in circumstances once more to be highlighted by Brian's infuriatingly erratic behaviour:

'The Beach Boys cancelling Monterey at the very last minute undoubtedly set the band in a very bad light. They were certainly very heavily criticized at the time for it. It seemed rather like an admission of defeat. And well, yes, I presume it had to be down to Brian. Those sorts of decision were always his, really. I know, for example, he'd said "Yes". And so he must have have said "No" as well. It was certainly very much in keeping with his character at the time.

'Also, you've got to remember by this time he was completely out of circulation. He'd vanished seemingly off the face of the earth. In fact he didn't re-emerge or come back into circulation again until long after I'd left LA. It got very depressing at times – after I'd returned to London – hearing the stories about him being in some wretched club in some equally wretched condition.'

In September 1967 a two-week series of recording sessions involving the Beach Boys and Wilson that had taken place in the latter's new Spanish Mission estate in Bel-Air using make-shift home recording equipment two months earlier were edited down and released by Capitol as an album trading under the title of *Smiley Smile*. There were several *Smile* compositions featured but all in versions that undersold their worth considerably. There was a lot of silly shit as well: dumb pot-head skits, so-called healing chants and even some weird 'loony tunes' items straight out of a cut-rate Walt Disney soundtrack.

Twenty-five years after its release it would become regarded as a top-rate 'chill-out' album for those looking for something a bit spooky and otherwordly to float down from, after a long lysergic exploration of the senses. At the time of its release, though, it appeared like the single most underwhelming musical statement of the sixties, the work of a bunch of doo-wop singing acid casualties. What was it that Murray had screamed at Brian that day back in early '66 when he'd stormed into the house and thrown his son's secret pot stash all over that hideously coloured carpet in the living-room?

'Y'know, Brian, the one thing God gave you was a brain. If you play with it and destroy it, you're dead, you're a vegetable . . . There are going to be people killed and people in sanatoriums and insane asylums because they played with God.'

In January 1968 the Beach Boys released another new set of Brian Wilson tunes, *Wild Honey*, this time with the ever-winning Mike Love providing the lyrics. The songs were simple, homey and a bit eccentric with squeaky, righteous harmonies and big chunky chord changes that reflected Brian's love of Motown-styled rhythm'n'blues. Several of the best ones he hadn't even written for the Beach Boys. He'd written them for Danny Hutton, the promising young singer that David Anderle managed, and these two other guys – great singers, all three of them. But Mike had somehow hijacked the whole project and here he was, back at square one, banging out these chirpy ditties with the guys again. But the whole reason he'd written them was as a favour to Danny. In fact, Danny would go on to return the favour to Brian very quickly; he would introduce him to cocaine. The first time Brian snorted some he felt he was kissing God, just like he had on his first acid trip. But as the weeks spun by, the more he snorted, the less the melodies appeared. Only the voices in his head increased in volume.

In 1969, after more consecutive flops, the Beach Boys released *Friends*, their first album in which they pretty much went it alone creatively speaking. First of all Mike Love had tried to become the leader, pushing transcendental meditation down the other members' throats and organizing an elaborate tour of the States with the Maharishi so sparsely attended it almost bankrupted the group. Mike got so into the whole meditation trip he'd go out to the desert and fast for weeks at a time, until he was having all sorts of godawful visions. Just like his cousin, he'd gone completely crazy at one point and had had to be hospitalized.

Meanwhile Dennis was starting to write songs and, though they weren't anywhere near his brother's, they weren't too bad either, offering a refreshingly sensitive counterpoint to such an otherwise thoughtless, rough-neck exterior. What was it Mike had told that limey journalist in an unguarded moment back in late 1968 about the drummer? 'The first thing you've got to understand about Dennis is that Dennis doesn't understand.' This was after Dennis started blabbing to the guy about this new discovery he'd found, this creepy little guy with a herd of syphilitic-hippie girls to do his bidding for him. *Rave* magazine, a British fashion monthly, went on to print his remarks:

'Fear is nothing but awareness. I was only frightened as a child because I didn't understand fear – the dark, being lost . . . It all came from within. Sometimes "the Wizard" frightens me. The Wizard is Charlie Manson who is a friend of mine who thinks he is God and the Devil. He sings, plays and writes poetry and may be another artist for Brother records.'

They even wrote a song together – 'Cease to Exist' – that the Beach Boys recorded and released on their follow-up to *Friends* – 20–20.

Dennis's connection with Manson went on to earn him death threats and a front-page profile straight after the Wizard masterminded a murder massacre at Sharon Tate's mansion during the early summer of 1969. When reports of Manson's and Dennis's socializing hit the evening news after the former's arrest, Carl became so frightened he drove the wife and kids over to stay at Audree's the night the news broke for fear of reprisals from the Manson 'family'. 'I don't know why you brought them here, son,' whispered his mother through a dull whisky haze. 'Those Manson people are bound to know our address too.'

1969 was also the year good old Murray decided to drive yet another knife into his eldest son's back. Reckoning it was all over for the Beach Boys, he sold Sea of Tunes, the publishing company that owned all of Brian Wilson's timeless songs. In his ghosted autobiography Wilson now claims he was practically destroyed by the news, but Tony Asher remembers it another way:

'Chuck Kay, who runs A&M publishing, phoned me up one day clear out of the blue. He sounded pretty concerned and straight off he says:

'"Listen, I'll be frank with you, Tony, I don't know if our buying up all the Beach Boys publishing off the old man was really such a good idea. I mean, some of the melodies are great, sure – but take this song 'Don't Worry Baby', for example. A great set of changes, but I just checked out the words and I suddenly discover that there's all this shit about hot-rod racing in there. I mean, how can we get an artiste – an established artiste, someone like Wayne Newton, say – to cover a song with dumb lyrics like that? We've got a real problem here, Tony. Anyway I was wondering whether you'd consider perhaps rewriting the lyrics to some of the songs all over again so they wouldn't sound so . . . dumb."

'Well, first of all, I said, "OK. Sure," y'know. It sounded like easy money. And then I got to thinking, "Why the hell would I want to be rewriting something like 'Surfer Girl' all over again? I mean, what's the point?" So I declined the offer.

'But the really weird thing was Chuck actually had got in touch with Brian beforehand – very apprehensively, mind you – to kinda check out whether he'd mind too much if the lyrics to his songs were rewritten . . . made more sophisticated, if you like. I mean, I would have thought Brian would have gotten really upset at the very idea of his songs being altered in any way but no, he just went ahead and said, "Sure" – y'know – "Do whatever you want." Chuck said it was like Brian just couldn't give a shit about it either way. He'd just given up on his music at that point altogether.'

Just as the sixties turned to the seventies it became Carl's turn to take the helm. In 1970 they'd left Capitol and signed to Warner Bros., but the first album – *Sunflower*, more 'olde worlde' Beach Boys pop – sold wretchedly. This prompted the youngest Wilson, whose former youth and puppy fat were now hidden behind an ample beard and the perpetual look of a disoriented monk, to bring in a manager called Jack Rieley, a terrible old fraud who got them to go political and address 'contemporary issues' in their songs. Mike and Al went for this 'awareness' shit in a big way and scribbled out some atrocious texts to order but Brian skulked even further back inside his bearpit of a bedroom. Finally Dennis came to tell him the big news. After Warners had rejected the original track listing and title (*Landlocked*), the next album was going to be called *Surf's Up* and Rieley and the guys had dug up the old *Smile* track and just touched it up here and there. Brian's bloated open-shirted frame was hunched on a child's swing when he heard the news and he doubled over, sobbing frantically. He couldn't bear the idea of that bedevilled *Smile* music being let out of the vault to haunt him and send him spinning back to those god-forsaken times when everything seemed like it was on fire. He pleaded for hours that the track should not come out. But to no avail. As a result of this act of fraternal treachery, the Beach Boys started selling records again.

But not for long. The next one, *Carl and the Passions*, was a real loser and Brian's big contribution to that was this bizarre song – 'Marcella' – about a masseuse he knew who worked at a parlour just off the strip called Circus Maximus, who treated him nice and who'd let him stay and talk to her even though she was aware most of what he said was crazy bullshit. Brian felt close to her because, in most of the other sex joints he'd wander into, something weird would always happen. He'd start acting clumsy and a girl would turn real cold on him and, the next thing he'd know, some guy with muscles on his muscles and hot sweaty palms would be all over him, dragging him out of the building and on to the hard, grey sidewalk. Once or twice he wondered to himself if Phil Spector ever let himself get into that kind of situation. Then the thought would swerve from his mind like an auto accident about to take place, leaving him to pick himself up from the cold concrete and shuffle off into the uncertain night.

Then there was . . . oh god, this clown Rieley somehow persuaded the Beach Boys to decamp to Holland in order to make their album for 1973 and the whole endeavour quickly turned into a very costly disaster indeed. They returned with their album but Warners refused it yet again and despatched Van Dyke Parks – a company man himself – over to Brian's lair to coax a song out of him. He returned the next day to the office with a cassette tape which began with the sound of Wilson screaming to Parks, 'Tell me I'm not crazy, Van Dyke! Hypnotize me! Hypnotize me into thinking I'm not crazy so I can write a song.' Parks keeps telling Wilson to 'cut the crap' until finally the Beach Boys' troubled genius's hands start playing these rolling portentous chords that quickly slide into sublime changes as the melody motions from verse to chorus. The finished song 'Sail On Sailor' – as recorded for the album *Holland* – turned out to be a brief return to earlier glories but it also bore composer credits from three other sources, one of whom, a little-known LA songwriter called Ray Kennedy, still claims he wrote the whole thing alone.

Something else happened that year, something that mother Audree would recall in heart-rending detail to a journalist from *Rolling Stone* three years later:

'I went into the kitchen to make cereal for him, and all of a sudden I heard him yelling for me. I started dashing down this long hallway. He was in the bathroom, sitting on the toilet. And he said, "Nitroglycerin," so I grabbed it and said, "Put it under your tongue." But he just sat there, very pale . . . I realized he was really in bad trouble. By that time his face looked very flushed and his eyes . . . I knew he didn't see me, because I went like this [*pats her cheek*] and said, "Baby, baby." All I said to him was, "Baby, baby, I love you." I ran into the bedroom and called the fire department. I never went back in that bathroom.'

Murray was gone, leaving three numb, emotionally stunted boys to grieve in their own respective ways. Carl was the first to let the tears and sorrow overwhelm him. Dennis brooded: he and the old man had got strangely close in the last few years – truth to tell, their excessive volatility made them a lot alike – and his father's death made him even angrier, more irrational and more driven to get fucked up on drink and drugs. Brian just stayed in his bed with his dazed largactyl eyes and that thick knot of fear twisting ceaselessly around his bloated intestines. He didn't go to the funeral and, apart from a couple of flat-out screaming sessions berating his father, it was hard to tell exactly how his parting had registered with him. But then again, what with all the voices in his head now interrupting his thoughts like static on an ill-tuned radio forever muttering, 'You're finished, you're washed up! You've lost the plot, asshole, and you've lost your mind! You played with God and messed with forces that can only destroy you' throughout most of his waking hours, it's not as though he'd escaped the stinging taint of his father's presence and influence.

Now it was 1975 and Warner Bros. were at their wits' end. 'The Beach Boys hate us,' said Dave Berson, the troubled soul whose job it was to mediate between the two enterprises. Every record they'd handed in had been initially rejected. Berson could go on for hours about the obnoxiousness of Mike Love and Al Jardine, the selfishness of Carl Wilson, the shiftlessness of Dennis. And the heartbreak of trying to connect with Brian Wilson. That's why Berson had taken this godless assignment. He wanted to work with Brian Wilson. And what does he get? Mostly an evasive silence, punctuated only by the other Beach Boys and their ego-bullshit. But every now and then there'd be these phone calls. Like the one late last year when Brian phoned excitedly to tell Berson he'd written and recorded a special new Christmas song called 'A Child for Winter' he wanted to release as soon as possible. There was only one slight problem. It was already mid-December and far too late to capitalize on releasing such a record. Actually there were two problems. It was a lousy track, badly recorded and worryingly bereft of a decent melody, but Warners were so happy to have any kind of product from Brian they went ahead and released it anyway in a very limited run on 27 December 1974. Berson thought putting it out might shake something more palatable out of Wilson's on-going creative fog. But it had not proven to be so and now he and his staff were grasping at straws in their search for the stimulant that would finally restore Brian Wilson to some semblance of his former creative grace.

Finally, over in Warner Bros.' London HQ, Derek Taylor has a chance to stretch back on the office couch. His wife has just rung off – 'Listen dear,' he'd just asked her, 'I'm talking about Brian . . . Brian Wilson. Do you remember anything? Ah yes! Always demanding too much. He was, wasn't he?' Downstairs maybe five people are waiting to see him. His secretary keeps appearing with these memos. A final tug on the old memory wires, then. Another cigarette is lit.

'I could never deliver what Brian wanted, really. Personally I was frightened of him. He made me nervous and uncomfortable. I didn't know if he wanted criticism. Criticism was hell for him because you can only say it's great one more time and he'd never leave you in peace. He was like another Brian, come to think of it. Brian Epstein. Another man of whims, surges, arrogance, manic depressions and long periods of silence. Another man who was always demanding too much.

'Bloody good company when he was all right, mind. But there was always this terrible need of people. And it all turned against him. He couldn't go all the way with his genius, because there were all these people he had to look out for.

'There was a family to look after. A mother he adored, and a father he periodically hated. Two brothers. Two cousins. His wife's good Jewish family. All the friends and hangers-on.

'It's funny because only a couple of weeks ago he phoned me up for the first time in years. I was frankly astonished because naturally I'd heard all the stories. But there he was, Brian Wilson, telling me he wanted to come to England for a holiday and if he did, would he be welcomed. And I immediately said, "Of course you'll be welcomed, Brian. You're Brian Wilson, for God's sake. Everybody loves your music here." But it wasn't enough. And he started getting this strange petulant quality to his voice, like a little boy who can't decide what to do.

'There was always that sense of regret, you see. "Am I in too deep? Tell me I'm not in too deep? I can't do this. Make me!"

'He may, in very simple terms, just be completely crackers.'

Part 3
'When you work in my business, it's all scary.'

One day in the summer of 1980 I awoke from a deep disorienting dream to hear my letter-box rattling. Through it had been placed a telegram on which the following message was written. Epic records' publicity department had received word from the Beach Boys' new manager, Jerry Schilling, that Brian Wilson was very much on a personality upsurge, had rid himself of the various quirks and kinks previously bedevilling his troubled temperament and was ready to talk at length about himself, his music and his problems. The interview would take place at Wilson's home where intimacy was assured. Was I interested in firing the questions? Yes, of course . . . I suppose.

It had been almost five years to the day since I'd last set foot in Los Angeles, back in 1975, determined to turn the city upside down in order to find out what really happened to Brian Wilson. What I discovered wasn't pretty. Banished from his sprawling mansion to live in a small changing-hut by the pool because his degenerate behaviour was having too negative an effect on his two daughters, Wendy and Carnie, Wilson would spend his nights snorting cocaine, sometimes mixing it with heroin, as well as boozing to horrific excess. Wilson's family had finally to freeze his bank account in order to curtail his drug-spending. Consequently he took to wandering the streets of LA, spending much of his time getting thrown out of massage parlours, when he wasn't closeting himself away with drug-buddies.

When allowed in his own house he would stay in his room for days on end, lying in a huge bed surrounded by pornography and junk food. He'd reached the point where music no longer held any interest for him. Though he would fitfully work up scraps of melodies on the piano, he'd almost always fail to complete them. Then in '76 the protective wall around Brian Wilson was suddenly demolished. The previous year the Beach Boys' career had suddenly encountered a dramatic lift-off owing to the success of a compilation album of oldies released by Capitol (the label they'd left five years ago so they could instigate what subsequently became a stormy liaison with Warner Bros.). *Endless Summer* sprinted to the top of the US charts and scored platinum sales on the strength of four sides of classic sixties Brian Wilson songs finding favour with a new generation of American teenagers. An EMI compilation, *20 Golden Greats*, released in Britain at the same time was similarly successful. The Beach Boys' commercial renaissance was finally coming to pass. Yet all those new-found converts wanted to know just one thing: where was Brian Wilson?

In other words, the Beach Boys needed Wilson to truly cement this rediscovered fervour. To this end a psychiatrist was employed to draw him out of his shell and get him back to the piano, where it was presumed he would again bash out new compositions as if all those years lost in some psychic twilight zone had never really existed. This psychiatrist, Eugene Landy by name, thought he'd achieve all this by instigating a programme of bullying tactics. He bullied Wilson into acting the role of 'responsible member of society'; bullied him into writing songs; bullied him into going on stage with the group (even though Wilson's natural shyness of live shows had originally triggered the first of a number of nervous break-downs); and bullied him even into performing humiliating solo performances on network US television. To get full mileage out of this specious ploy, Brian was also made to do interviews. Most of them were farcical.

One of the most revealing appeared in *Oui*, where Wilson – who is nothing if not candid – stated, 'Today I want to go places – but I can't because of the doctor [Landy]. I feel like a prisoner and I don't know where it's going to end . . . he would put the police on me if I took off and he'd put me in the funny farm . . . I'm just waiting it out, playing along. That's what I'm doing. [*Pause.*] Do you have any uppers?' (In most of these interviews Wilson would deliver maybe twenty minutes of badly remembered facts before asking his interrogator for cocaine or speed and then suddenly claim to be feeling ill before skulking back to his room.) His presence on stage with the Beach Boys was equally painful to behold. Terrified, he couldn't sing properly and his piano playing and occasional bass work were rarely in sync with the song. The band simply and corruptly *used* their extremely confused former leader in order to make themselves more money.

The public was briefly fooled into going along with this whole sick charade, but soon enough it back-fired on the group. *15 Big Ones*, the album around which the whole 'Brian's Back' campaign was constructed, went gold but was such a wretched piece of product it turned innumerable Beach Boys fans – old and new – against this shoddy, over-promoted soap opera of a group. Utterly uninspired and weary-sounding, the album was clearly intended only as therapy for Wilson's long-dormant production talents. Through pressure and greed it was released, resulting in both Carl and Dennis publicly airing their grievances and criticisms.

The superior 1977 follow-up, *The Beach Boys Love You*, was what the record should have been in that it actually contained twelve new Brian Wilson songs. Unfortunately, bad feeling within the group meant that Brian Wilson and Carl were the only two Beach Boys featured on the record at all; and to compound misfortune, the group's plan to leave Warners and go with Epic/CBS was discovered just before the release of *Love You* and so the record consequently got negligible exposure, condemning it to meagre sales.

The group's inner relationship quickly deteriorated into two rival factions: Mike Love and Al Jardine versus the increasingly spaced-out Carl and Dennis with the hapless Brian as prized pawn in the middle. This back-stabbing antipathy reached its climax in '78 when Love and Jardine tried to sack Dennis and so make Carl's clout within the group ineffectual. Somehow a compromise was reached, but the dreadful *M.I.U. Album* – the band's final Warners release – was instigated by Love and Jardine. Both critics and the record-buying public alike ignored the product's pitiful contents.

In 1979 there was an uneasy truce with the release of the *LA Album* beginning the band's contract for Epic. With this record Bruce Johnston returned, having been ousted eight years earlier, and took on the producer's mantle to juggle together a collection of songs spotlighting all five members in equal portions. In other words, it was more mediocre pop, even including two extended disco re-jigs of 'Wild Honey' and 'Here Comes the Night' that the group felt obliged to apologize for whenever they performed them live.

After the group had experienced the terrible wrath of CBS president Walter Yetnikoff ('Gentlemen, I think I've just been fucked' was his opening remark to them at the meeting), they went in to record *Keepin' Summer Alive*, another album mostly given over to new Brian Wilson songs, but the critics had become so irritated by the group and their constant, tacky bickering that most reviews slammed it more out of instinct than anything else.

At least Schilling and the record company seemed finally to be facing up to all these prejudices. Consequently a vigorous promotional push had begun, with everything from Carl Wilson's earnest claims in *Rolling Stone* ('Remember that slogan, "Brian's back"? Well, Brian wasn't back then. But now he's *really* back!') to a TV special entitled *Going Platinum*, a grotesque and fawning documentary of the *Keepin' Summer Alive* sessions about to be broadcast all across America. Needing to attract an audience for several huge concerts set for Britain that autumn, Schilling was craving some serious column inches in the UK media. That's where I came into the picture.

Not that I was feeling too comfortable with any aspect of the up-coming journey. Back in 1975 I'd written a 30,000 word profile of Brian Wilson for the *NME*, using much of the information and many of the quotes gathered in these preceding pages. The Beach Boys had hated it and had instigated a long drawn-out communication breakdown with the paper lasting a number of years. Bruce Johnston even went so far as to state in a rival music paper that Brian Wilson had read the articles in question and had become suicidally depressed as a direct result. So did the group know *I* was coming over to do this interview, or was it some sort of set-up?

I finally boarded the plane to Los Angeles a day late (but that's another story). Fifteen arduous hours later I was just checking into the hotel when the English press officer approached me with bad news to report. Two other writers had already done interviews, not at Brian's house, but at the Beach Boys' offices. There, a wild-eyed and anxious-looking Wilson had been surrounded by brother Carl, manager Schilling and about five other record-company people silently scrutinizing his every nervous twitch. One guy from a British Sunday paper got twenty minutes of halting, stammered quotes punctuated by an array of embarrassing silences. Another from a music journal got maybe five minutes, most of them catatonic, before Wilson jumped up and ran out of the room, never to return. Both journalists still claimed to be fans of his music, but both were quite adamant they never wanted to find themselves in the same room as Brian Wilson again for as long as they lived.

Now the press officer was apologetically explaining that it was looking unlikely that Wilson would in fact do that promised 'definitive' interview with me. As I'd suspected, Bruce Johnston had not been alerted to my arrival until the very last minute and was now apparently in hysterics, berating manager Schilling with terrible warnings about the possible consequences of my encountering Wilson. So what was I supposed to do? Well, first thing tomorrow there was to be a screening of a new Beach Boys promotional film. And then, later in the day, I too was to be 'screened'.

'Hey, honey, do you remember the time that guy at the airport said to Brian, "Don't you get tired of being referred to as a genius?" Brian just stared at him, shrugged his shoulders and said "No."' Carl Wilson looks at his girlfriend for confirmation. 'Oh yeah,' she laughs back. 'Uh, didn't he say, "Nah, it doesn't bother me"? Something like that anyway.'

At four in the afternoon Carl Wilson has been talking for – well, goodness gracious, it's been almost two hours, about the

Beach Boys. Just one hour later singer Mike Love will storm into the office and scream in a very loud voice to Schilling and the girl at the switchboard (who's actually Priscilla Presley's younger sister and who can't tell one Beach Boy from another – 'It's the beards,' she tells me) that, goddammit, let the press get a good look at all the group's dirty linen. Hell, let them see for themselves that Brian's a vegetable, that Dennis is a drugged-out no-talent parasite (who we've sacked) and that the only guys on the ball here are clean-living talent-free Al Jardine. And Mike of course. But this kind of outburst . . . Well, it's just not Carl's style at all. Dubbed 'the Henry Kissinger of the group' by Schilling, he understands the power of diplomacy. In fact, he's a master at the art of the inscrutable understatement. Most of the time he fields questions – some innocuous, some rather more weighty – using his natural technique of 'Gee, yeah. I can see your point but you've got to understand I'm just an easy-going kinda guy and hey, that's just the way it is' self-effacement. Very occasionally he lets the mask slip a little and an utterly cynical chuckle slices through the veneer.

Carl and I are playing a game called 'tactics', or more specifically 'How do I prove myself inoffensive enough to get a shot at interviewing Brian Wilson?' The judge is Jerry Schilling, who sits quietly at his desk just a few feet away, well within earshot. Both he and Carl exercise that precious right of access to the eldest Wilson brother who, although officially 'suffering from a bug . . . he's pretty sick', will be wheeled out if the conditions prove conducive enough. I play my role close to the chest with three fairly innocuous questions to one actual 'relevant' query. The latter category involves thorny issues like the uneasy truce 'twixt the two Love/Jardine and Wilson factions, the reasons for Dennis Wilson's current absence (too much cocaine, but Carl doesn't tell me that) and, of course, the subject of Brian Wilson.

The dialogue always returns to Brian. The recent *Rolling Stone* quote regarding his eldest brother's full creative resurgence with the music on *Keepin' Summer Alive* is mentioned, along with a reference to the dreaded Dr Landy. Carl dodges the latter topic altogether, remarking with a certain strained nonchalance that 'Back then [1976] maybe it should have read "Brian's almost back".' He smiles to himself, then quickly adds, 'No, but Brian's real well now. I mean, he's totally into playing live. Don't you recall' – he turns to his girlfriend again – 'Brian saying, "Being on the road is my real home. It's my whole life now"?'

She nods. 'Yeah, *right*! Brian's *so* into touring. He's always there in the office asking Jerry when we're playing.'

Had this new attitude towards touring come about because of Brian's recent separation from his wife Marilyn? After fifteen years the marriage had just recently collapsed, with his former spouse filing for divorce and taking their two daughters with her.

Carl simply evades the issue yet again. 'It's hard to say just how that's affected Brian, y'know. But Marilyn brought Wendy and Carnie to a gig in San Diego not long ago.'

Talking about what's emphatically known as 'Brian's problem', Carl continues, 'He's coping much, much better. I don't know. Maybe it was a bad acid trip he took that caused all this inner turmoil. That's what I figure, y'know. But, like I said, he's so much better now. He's back into his music and he's . . . he's on this big health kick. He's got these hot tubs in his new house, a jacuzzi, sauna . . . you name it.'

Finally, our two hours have passed. 'Wow, that went really fast. Enjoyed talking to you,' Carl remarks, ever Mr Sincerity. Schilling hovers and I request a short interview. And so he talks in a somewhat disconcerting whisper mainly about himself. Previously he worked for Elvis Presley, first as a stuntman and stand-in when Elvis couldn't make it on to the set and later working for Presley's manager, Colonel Tom Parker. He remarks that Parker and he are still close – that the latter's offices are a mere two doors away.

'I figured when Elvis died that the Beach Boys were the next biggest legend in American music,' he opines. And he talks about re-establishing the Beach Boys 'as a real contemporary American music phenomenon . . . I think the Colonel's mistake was to keep Elvis too cloistered away from his audience.'

Also, there's the idea of movies. Schilling is really into film production and is currently working with Parker on an Elvis tribute. The final touch comes when Schilling mentions that he also wants to do a film of the Beach Boys. Even now a script is being written by the same guy who wrote the Elvis film.

'Nothing's certain yet but we were thinking of maybe getting Jeff Bridges to play Brian.'

Fade. Cut.

We leave the Beach Boys' office at five in the afternoon. I've played every wild card I can pull out of my sleeve. Schilling just nods silently. He'll see what he can do, he promises. Two hours later I'm informed that we'll be driving over to Brian Wilson's house in half an hour. Schilling simply asked to keep the interview short as Brian needs to get to bed early to be fresh for a business meeting the next day.

In the final years of the hellzapoppin' sixties, when he was the hermit recluse living in Bel-Air with his sand-box and purple meditation tent, Brian Wilson wrote and recorded an absurd little song entitled 'Busy Doin' Nothing' in which he gave the listener exact directions to his house: just drive down Santa Monica, take a left on Sunset, a few more detours and there he'd be, waiting for you standing by the gates of his mansion. Times and locations change. It takes us an hour to find Wilson's new house. An emergency stop at a country club up in the hills finally gives us the right direction and we duly arrive at a small, unimpressive two-bedroom Spanish-style building located well off the beaten track out past Santa Monica.

From the car you could already make out Brian Wilson's bulky silhouette through the bay windows. A black woman with fiery eyes opens the door to us (us being the press officer, a photographer and myself) and we walk into a totally unfurnished living-room. Right away, something is very wrong here. Wilson, who must weigh at least 280 pounds, is eating a vegetarian salad, a fork in one hand and a cigarette in the other. He awkwardly begins trying to play the genial host. He apologizes for the starkness of the house and clumsily goes around shaking hands. Obviously ill at ease, his discomfort is instantly contagious.

'Uh . . . yeah, now who's doin' the interview? Oh, you! Oh! [*Laughs self-consciously.*] OK, man . . . uh [*he stops to look at me*]. Say, how old are you? Twenty-eight . . . Wow, I'm thirty-seven. Maybe I should interview you. You look more like a rock star than me.' He lets forth a disconcerting bellow, then checks himself.

For my part, at this precise juncture I'm willing to strike up any sort of rapport with Wilson, whose sense of discomfort is becoming ever more imposing. I remark that Carl just mentioned that this new house is fitted out with hot tubs, a health spa and a . . . (I start stammering out the word) jacuzzi.

'*Jacuzzi?*' The word seems to totally unnerve him for an instant.

'*Jacuzzi??*' He looks first mystified, then quite horrified.

'*Jacuzzi???*' Then suddenly he leaps up off the couch on which he's been slumped. He is a very, very big man.

'Hey! I'll show ya something really great about this place. Wanna see it?' He immediately motions towards the large bay windows. 'This is really neat,' he says, sounding like an excitable little kid about to show his parents a brand new party trick. Then he simply opens the windows and gestures out at the night.

'See? Air! Fresh air! Ummm! Healthy!! Let's keep 'em open, yeah?' He breathes in and out, vigorously. 'Ummmmm . . . Neat! Outasight! . . . Healthy!'

Brian slumps back on to the couch, and it's only then that I suddenly notice the presence of a third party in the room.

'Oh . . . this is Diane,' he mutters by way of an introduction to his blonde companion, who looks about sixteen. Actually, her real name is Debbie, but I won't find that out tonight because she won't bother to correct Brian, so absorbed is she in maintaining this vacant, bedazzled grin on her face, even during those excruciating moments when her beloved Brian's own face is contorted with pain. She looks exactly like a Robert Altman version of an acid-casualty waitress working in a health-food restaurant, except Altman would probably end up naming her Starchild or Munchkin. This vision of inane serenity – all teeth and cut-off jeans – beams forth throughout the interview. I find myself wondering just what she and Wilson must talk about when they're alone, and then shudder at the thought.

'OK, fire away.' Another awkward chuckle.

So I start by asking him about some of the songs he wrote just prior to *Pet Sounds*, but, before I get the first sentence out, Wilson is looking pained. Then he speaks.

'Hey, emotional! Wow, all those are so emotional! Maybe too . . . No, I forget . . . Yeah, when you make music that emotional it can really get to you, y'know.'

Before I can ask another question, he starts going off on weird tangents. First, he wants to know all about Paul McCartney's recent drug-bust in Japan, suddenly seguing into comments like, 'Say, what's the weather like over in England? Boy, I'm lookin' forward to comin' over. I haven't been to London since . . . oh, wow . . . 1964! Yeah, wow! Long time.' (I don't bother to remind him that he and the Beach Boys played London in 1977 at a CBS convention.)

With a small transistor radio placed next to the couch – the only sign of music in this desolate room – blaring out some anonymous AM hit as we speak, I ask Wilson if he listens to the radio a lot. Does he check out new sounds?

'No, I've only been listening to the radio for a week,' he replies, sounding suddenly very melancholy. 'Ever since the new album's been out. Haven't heard it played much.

Don't know why! Seems like we're going through a real bad spell.'

Wilson keeps referring to 'we' constantly, presumably meaning the Beach Boys. Considering that he spent much of the seventies in exile from the group and at one point tried to break all ties with them, I enquire whether he still views his musical career in any terms beyond those of the Beach Boys. Once again he looks pained, then pensive.

'No, not at all. It's all I've got, y'know. The group.'

So what gives him the most pleasure in life?

'Well, I'll tell ya one thing,' he blurts out aggressively. 'I'm not into women anymore.' Then he pauses. 'Music probably. Yeah, definitely. I like to sit down at the piano, y'know. Playing those chords. I love the way they look.

'Plus playing live . . . that's the biggest thrill. It's real spiritual.'

When I ask him to define the term 'spiritual' a little better, he looks at me as if I'm completely crazy. By now the pauses are getting longer and the photographer's camera clicking is causing Wilson to flinch automatically as if torturous electric shocks were being triggered through his central nervous system. He keeps struggling to articulate himself but at the same time it's so obvious he is in terrible psychic pain. Certain references to his past suddenly make him visibly shudder. I name a song from the new album that I particularly like and he literally screams.

'I hate that song! I hate that song!'

So why did you put it on the record?

'I didn't,' he stammers. 'Bruce . . .'

This is becoming steadily more and more horrific. So we talk about ego – something Wilson once had in excess and now claims to be utterly devoid of.

'Yeah, I used to be real *competitive*,' he shudders. 'Not anymore, though. Ego can be dangerous. All that drive can destroy you. It almost killed me. It almost drove me insane.'

Wilson is now chain-smoking, flicking the ash into his half-eaten salad. Occasionally he digs a fork into the mess of chopped vegetables and cigarette ash and puts it in his mouth. When he is coherent, he talks like a man drowning in all the sorrow that this world can visit on one lost and sorry soul. This is what he has to say:

'I don't see my mother much. She doesn't like the Beach Boys. Not since father died . . . My father and I, we never got on. He used to come down really hard on me. We used to fight all the time . . . No, I don't see anything for me beyond the Beach Boys. It's like they're all I got, y'know . . . No, I don't want to make a solo record. I just don't see myself making music as strong as most of the old stuff ever again.'

Why, I keep asking back.

'Why? I don't know why. You dry up, I guess. It's like . . .'

Suddenly he shudders again, this time buckling over as if about to vomit violently. But nothing comes out. So instead he leaps up from the couch as though on fire and starts to stammer out an apology.

'I-I-I . . . I'm sorry. I-I . . . I feel real tired. It's late and I-I've got to see my psychiatrist real early tomorrow. M-maybe we can talk some more then.'

So, finally, I've got my Brian Wilson interview. All thirty minutes of it. Feeling numb, somewhat nauseous myself and desperate for fresh air, I walk straight out of the house to the waiting car. As I look back, I see the press officer standing staring at the house. He is quite speechless and will remain that way for the rest of the night. Meanwhile, the equally stunned photographer can't stop himself taking useless shots of the empty living-room from the outside of the house. Seated in the back seat for the return journey, I start feeling like an utter parasite for having intruded upon Brian Wilson's private hell. Then I snap out of it, go back to the hotel and start to write this story.

Part 4

'That's life: a constant challenge to perform, to punch in, and to have control over yourself. It's a constant struggle to do that, and I do it all the time. I do it twenty-four hours a day.'

If you close your eyes and listen hard enough, you can almost feel the salty air gently tickling the hairs in your nostrils. For behold the mighty Pacific ocean gleaming in the morning mist under a tall and cloudless sky, splashing shiny white sprays of foam against a deserted stretch of beach, each wave undulating with the stoic grace of a classic Beach Boys harmony-line sung in perfect unison. That's where Dennis was now: just a dusty speck on the water's endless silvery surface. They'd buried him out at sea back in 1983, after he'd bottomed out on drugs and alcohol so badly he'd made himself homeless and penniless, the substance-abuse equivalent of a washed-up punch-drunk old boxer. In his final months he'd got so grotesquely angry at everything and everyone: at all the dealers who no longer fronted him endless grams of dope, at all the dumb girls who wouldn't fuck him anymore because he was losing his looks, at his dead sick father who he was forever cursing out and at the rest of the Beach Boys because they'd exiled him from the group he'd helped start. But, most of all, he was mad at the world because it seemed to have suddenly stopped turning as fast and as thoughtlessly as he always had. The fallen idol drowned accidentally while diving for some remnants of his squandered rock star past supposedly lying on the ocean's bed.

Now, nine years later, Dennis's eldest brother could also be sighted, casting his own slightly stooped 6 foot 2 inch shadow across the same liquid landscape. But there was one crucial difference, for Brian Wilson was not decomposing in a body-bag covered with starfish and surrounded by all manner of deep-sea dwellers. He was alive and jogging and, what is more, he no longer resembled the deranged Grizzly Adams look-alike who once terrified waitresses the length and breadth of Hollywood Boulevard. No, this was a different creature altogether. To begin with, all excessive weight and unsightly hair had been stripped from his body, as if by a miracle. Where once there had been only cushion-like layers of flab, there were now ample muscles. His face even boasted cheekbones and a rugged looking cleft chin. In fact, if you stood back just far enough so you couldn't distinguish his various facial eccentricities, like the nervous tics, the look of stark terror occasionally penetrating his otherwise distracted blue eyes and the unsettling way his mouth sometimes drooped at the sides, you could imagine this suave-looking individual in one of his custom-made Armani suits meriting a passing resemblance to an old movie matinée idol like, say, Cary Grant or Rock Hudson.

'I have my fiftieth birthday coming up on the twentieth of this month. Ah, that's embarrassing. Now, what am I going to tell these girls? I've got a young face but they say, "How old are you?" – "I'm fifty!" That'll ruin it! "I don't wanna be with you, you're too old . . .!" In a sense, it is a set-back. It's not really the best point for a person that gets to the age of fifty and who still can relate to young music and young people, and all the young ideas that crop up in the recording industry. But I can't do it. I don't think I can handle my age.'

It's funny too, because Rock Hudson was the star of that film *Seconds*, the one that caused Brian to freak out and think Phil Spector was after him when he viewed it back in late 1966. The plot centred on a dull middle-aged banker who gets the chance to start a whole new life by entering into a Faustian pact with a diabolical organization that arranges for people to be 'reborn' via plastic surgery. The banker returns as the elegant, dashing Hudson but doesn't have the first idea of how to fit into his new image and lifestyle. Actually, when you think about it, it's not too hard to draw a rather telling parallel between that scenario and what happened to Brian Wilson in the 1980s.

Once that hideous decade was unleashed, the rest of the Beach Boys wasted no time in forcing their 340 lb liability of a composer to return to the ministrations of Dr Eugene Landy, the flamboyant ego-smitten psychiatrist whose constant bullying and complex mind games had managed to get Wilson away from drugs, losing weight and even writing songs briefly in the mid-seventies. Landy was duly given total control of Brian Wilson, who effectively became his prisoner, and positive changes started once again occurring. Wilson exercised and lost weight, he ate healthily, was unable to get near drugs (although Landy decided to issue him with 'mood-altering' drugs of his own prescribing, a move that was ultimately to lose him his medical licence in the State of California).

By the mid-eighties Wilson was back in the Beach Boys, playing nostalgia fests for the Reagan Nation and looking better than he had in almost twenty years. However, Landy had achieved all this by insinuating his own rather sleazy personality into Wilson's fragile psyche, bamboozling him with his specious therapy jargon and generally overwhelming his senses with a whole new thought-system. Also, the irritating little shrink's ego endlessly delighted in exhibiting the hapless musician as some freakish Frankenstein-like invention of his. In due course, one by one, the Beach Boys and Wilson's mother, ex-wife and daughters would all turn against Landy, ultimately banding together to denounce him publicly for taking unfair advantage of their troubled relative.

Still, the psychiatrist's results clearly weren't all negative, for by 1987 a rejuvenated-looking Brian Wilson had landed a lucrative solo album deal with Sire and Warner Bros. The heads of the company loved Brian's old music so much they even got personally involved in a never-ending production job on his first solo endeavour which wound up costing over a million dollars. It turned out to be an unpleasant and largely thankless ordeal for all of them, too, because of Landy, whose greed, egomania (he was now writing Wilson's lyrics with his girlfriend, Alexandra Morgan, and taking 50 per cent of all Wilson's earnings) and parasitical craving to control every aspect of his patient's life – and then shamelessly to take most of the credit for whatever music he created – had them absolutely sickened. However, they were unable to do anything to get rid of the wretch because, without him standing over there doing his 'Little Hitler' act in the studio, Brian would just go blank and be unable to function.

One of the many fine composers brought in to collaborate on the album was a guy very much like Brian had once been, a shy brooding Californian with a sensitive heart and a remarkable talent for squeezing out heart-rendingly successful pop music from the most disparate of personalities. His name was Lindsey Buckingham and he'd masterminded Fleetwood Mac's whole sound through their golden years in the seventies much as Brian had done with the Beach Boys in the sixties. He'd always idolized Wilson's music too, and was over the moon about the prospect of working with his hero. Until they actually got down to work.

'It was a very unsettling situation. If Landy wasn't there, he'd have these two little surf Nazis who would not let Brian out of their sight. I know Landy did him a lot of good in the beginning with his radical techniques, but in my opinion there was a role reversal where Landy glommed on to Brian as his ticket to a glamorous world. Brian was not happy, and there was no way he'd grow into a full adult in this situation. Musically, Landy was keeping him doing this "Baby, let's ride to heaven in my car" kinda stuff, when he really should have been getting into something a little more experimental, or adult at least. That was a little heartbreaking to watch.'

Anyway, the album flopped. It had got rave reviews and cover stories and God knows what else, but the general public generally preferred to keep their distance. It's tempting to think they intuitively sensed Landy's perverted puppet-master presence over everything and found the whole scenario too sordid to warrant further investigation. But maybe it's simpler than that; for Wilson's Beach Boys music has always epitomized only virile, healthy emotions for the mainstream nostalgia market who still teem to the group's concerts. That kind of audience probably just found all the stuff about Wilson's mental problems, solo projects and Beach Boys rivalries easier to ignore, mainly because it interfered too much with their cherished myths of endless summers, bronzed, wanton beach-babes boogalooing on burnished surf-boards and Ronald Reagan as the Great Provider.

They didn't even get a chance to ignore the follow-up, another Landy–Wilson collaboration entitled *Sweet Insanity*. It sounded so embarrassing that Warner Bros. simply refused to release it. Landy next coaxed Wilson into putting his name to a ghosted autobiography, *Wouldn't It Be Nice*, written in the first person and forever employing words and phrases its subject was simply too unsophisticated to fully comprehend. Most of his memories came from other sources too, be they Al Jardine, Van Dyke Parks or Danny Hutton, but the most disturbing aspect of the text was the way Brian's story was suddenly hijacked in the middle and turned into an unsolicited testimonial to the miraculous healing powers and all-round good-guy qualities of flat-out genius Eugene Landy. David Felton, one of the older guys at *Rolling Stone*, got it right on the money when he wrote that 'the autobiography reads like some slick parody of the end of *Psycho*, with the psychiatrist telling the police: "Brian was never all Brian, but he was often only Landy. Now the Landy half has taken over. Probably for all time."'

Finally, Landy's hold on Wilson seemed to slacken when the psychiatrist was forced to sign a separation order initiated by the composer's relatives and former band mates, forbidding him from 'talking to, seeing or interacting with the musician'.

Carnie Wilson, Brian Wilson's outward-going daughter, who'd recently enjoyed a number one album of her own alongside her sister Wendy and friend Chynna, daughter of John and Michelle Phillips of the Mamas and Papas, was particularly radiant about the outcome. 'Finally, the rat has fallen into the trap,' she gleefully remarked to a journalist, indicating Landy.

But in the July of 1992 the spectre of Landy and his string-pulling tactics still hung heavily over Wilson's stooped shoulders. For example, there was this great dumb lunk of a human being with a stern, curiously immobile face and the physique of a heavy metal Rambo wanna-be watching over him all the time. His name was Kevin Leslie, but he was better known to the international media as the 'Surf Nazi', a term they'd employed with tireless zeal whenever referring to the narcissistic young man who'd long been Eugene Landy's most cherished henchman. Every day Landy was getting up-to-the-minute reports on Brian via Leslie's telephone calls and could monitor everything from his own little hidey-hole. And even when he was all alone, Wilson still talked about Landy with such sickening reverence it was hard to discount claims made by his family of the psychiatrist having brain-washed his former patient in some way. Wilson continually referred to Landy as 'my master', even adding at one numbing instant, 'and a good dog always waits for his master'! He was also riddled with Landy's therapy talk, suddenly blurting out these dopey buzz-words or else using corny lines about 'life being a positive experience but we have what is known as "road-blocks".'

Yet even with all the mental interference going on, it wasn't hard to make out the various psychic remnants of the old pre-Landy Brian Wilson. For there were still the frightened child, the eccentric compulsive innocent, even the ego-besotted pop competitor still lost in an imaginary war with his old rivals of three decades past, Phil Spector and Paul McCartney, all lurking just below that dazed surface, bursting to come out.

'Music was an obsession, because the Phil Spector regime was so powerful in my mind that I had to do something in order to amount to . . . anything! Generally I was a perfectionist that went into the studio with a certain amount of panic in my chest. If I failed, I'd have to feel real bad about it. The fear of being rejected drove me on to be doing something which was pretty good. It was just that I had felt so many outside influences, like the Spector regime, Paul McCartney and the Beatles. We felt a little bit . . . squashed by all that. Those Beatles guys totally stole the limelight. They stole the show in the recording business, and with the public . . . If Paul McCartney heard this interview, he'd be on the piano right now, trying to outdo us!

'I think the sixties were a heyday for the music recording industry, as far as creating big music, great music. Like I said, I constantly refer back to Spector's music as a way to understand what else is going on. My music . . . I don't know, I never really realized what it was, I couldn't tell if people really liked it a lot. I know that the introduction of "California Girls" is a good sound. It's got a good sound, but I don't know who liked it, you know what I mean? Phil Spector makes this record, everybody likes it! It's not enough . . . We were his messengers, in a sense . . .

'Gold Star studios burned down. That's where Spector used to record, and I worked there too. I felt really bad about that 'cos I really thought I could do something there again, but I don't know . . . I guess . . . [*sighs*] I guess you've got to take it on the chin. The Wall of Sound . . . I enjoy it, but I still don't enjoy it when someone tells me I can't do it . . . Then I get a little upset! [*Laughs*.] Hey, how come the Beach Boys don't sound as good as Phil Spector? [*Almost screams*] I don't know! I just live here!'

In truth he lives in Malibu, in a discreet little house, a kind of glorified chalet built from slats of dark timber overlooking a landscape of rock and sand forever being buffeted by the foamy surf of the Pacific Ocean. There's a yellow Corvette parked out front – exactly the same model and colour of car that Landy drives – and a weird Japanese 'fish' mobile hanging by the front door. Inside it's all very spartan. There's a small kitchen with over twenty bottles of vitamins littering the draining board. In the living-room can be located a stereo system, a collection of approximatively fifty CDs, a few black-and-white photos framed to the walls alongside a poster from a museum, a chest of drawers and a modest couch. In the garden below stands a jacuzzi, while a small terrace offers a breath-taking view of the pulsing sea.

He now keeps the piano in his special office, the quiet room where he goes to plan out his next musical assignment, another solo album to be produced by Don Was containing half new material and half rearrangements of his old Beach Boys classics.

'Not "Good Vibrations" though. Fffftt . . . out the window! Too arty for me! Too arty and edited! I'm doing "California Girls", that's our anthem . . . I'm putting the key right and I'll sing the high notes without sounding like I'm trying to pass a gall-stone at the same time!

'I compose every . . . month. I don't compose as much, I'm not in a composing period right now, I'm more or less on arranging and co-production with Don Was. I go to work to my office. I play and sing a little bit of "Proud Mary" and then I'll go do a couple of other things. And I jump off the piano, and I'll pull back, and it's enough for the day. So I say, "Look, you gotta know when to leave, you gotta know when to stop." So I play for a while and say "Bang! That's it! Time to stop!"

'Sometimes you sit there, and it comes right to you. Other times you search round the keys, and you do this [*hits his finger on the table*] and TAHH! Now, wait a minute! [*imitates a beat*] Doo-be-doo/be-doo/be-doo . . . That's a beat, right? OK, now, I take that beat [*sings*]. It's all like that against the beat, see? First, I always go for the key, then I go for the rhythm, then I go for the melody, then I go for the lyrics, OK? That's how I do it.

'You get to the song, right? And then, of course, you start doing the arrangement: first, the rhythm, then the chord pattern, then the melody, then the voices. We got the harmonies through my thinking about the guys, and really relating to how Al would sing, or Carl would sing, or Dennis would sing, or Mike would sing, or I would sing. I give them the parts, right? I rule them out for the piano, then we go to the studio, and I give the Beach Boys the parts, for some of it . . . 'cos they never could learn parts more than just a little at a time . . . like, maybe eight bars at a time, OK? So, now, I give them eight bars of harmony, right? We get there around the microphone, and I oversee the vocal, the overall sound of it, but I do it unconsciously. I don't try to make the sound better. Trying is not the way to do it. The way to do it is to find a medium by which you can create a sound through these other guys and myself by that medium. When I did the guys' background parts, there was no doubt in the world that I was in control of those sessions. The guys knew. So I would try to get the sound down there on the microphone in a cohesive and harmonic medium that started up here in my head.

'I find that search on every song we've ever made: that search for a lost sound. "Do It Again" was a record that I thought was the perfect example of how our vocals spread. We don't have a real piercing masculine sound, right? The Beach Boys were basically feminine, except for Mike who was a very masculine singer. I was a more feminine singer.

'See, I think the job we did on *Pet Sounds* was in some ways meant to help people understand that love is not . . . a word. What we did was . . . what I did, anyway, 'cos that was really my album, in that I wanted to impart something that I had. It was a childhood dream of mine, to make music that made people feel loved, OK? And I have a thing for making people cry. So, I took on that kind of karma for a while . . . But I couldn't get that out of my blood. It was a very loving album, and a source of embarrassment for me. My masculine side had to take a bow, like a little hiatus, to get *Pet Sounds* to happen. But I did it. I did it 'cos I needed to. They say, "What about these high feminine parts, Brian?" – Well, that's how I felt, man. I wanted to be a girl in my voice, so I did. I wanted to sing like a girl. Not consciously, but it was all figured out in my brain, waiting for me to do it. So I went in there, put some beautiful music on tape . . . That "Don't Talk (Put Your Head on My Shoulder)" . . . That's a lovely, lovely record.'

It seems incredible, but somehow relationships between Brian Wilson and the Beach Boys reached an even lower ebb in the nineties than they had in the deeply acrimonious eighties. While Brian's solo album was bombing on the charts, his old group managed to score a freak number one hit with a catchy retro-pop confection entitled 'Kokomo' primarily because it was the most featured song in the soundtrack to a smash Tom Cruise movie called *Cocktail*. As a result, Brian's competitive side took a particularly vicious hammering and the whole experience seemed to have left him more paranoid than ever before.

'Every now and then I'll play maybe three or four concerts a year with the Beach Boys. Mike Love growled at me, like an animal. I said, "Can I borrow your mike? I'll be doing the lead on this next song." He said [*snarling*], "Get your own mike!" And when we start playing, I swear to God my instrument is not even loud enough to hear. I feel the whole time I'm up there saying things like, "Carl doesn't like me . . . Mike's mad at me . . . Carl's pissed off . . . Al Jardine's mad at me . . ." It's obvious the guys are mad at me, it's obvious. It's all turned to anger now; the whole deal is anger. They feel I intrude on their peace of mind by creating such a monster. I created a monster called the Beach Boys, but amongst the Beach Boys, it's an extremely hostile and cold relation that we have.

'But, even in the midst of the fact I don't like the Beach Boys, I have to make sure they're OK. That job was invented by me, to keep things cool with the group, and I thought, "Oh my God, what a job! What a thankless job!" And I said, "No, no, the reward is in the giving, you don't have to worry about rewards. The rewards are old-fashioned, it's all in the giving . . ." That's basically something I had to learn, because all of my life, I've been reward-conscious. It was always, "Hey! Good one, Brian! Good track!" And I had to do it to myself. But that's OK, 'cos I've seen a lot of people totally vulnerable. There's a vulnerability I had towards the Beach Boys.

'They're like little birds with their mouths open for a worm. They get that way, sometimes. They get insecure and they call me, and they want me to produce an album. But I didn't respond, 'cos I was mad at them. I can't understand where they're coming from. They're all so groovy, they're real good at music, but they also know how to really fuck me over. Mike, Carl and Al are the three guys that stomped my head in. Over the years they managed to stomp my brains out. They knew the secret formula as how to fuck Brian Wilson over. And they still do it.'

And now Mike Love was finally suing his own cousin, claiming he was owed back-royalties for having helped write many of the Beach Boys' classic songs. Brian had recently won something like ten million dollars from A&M publishing after his lawyers had succesfully shown that Murray's sale of his son's songs twenty years before had been fundamentally illegal, and Mike needed some of that cash to cover all those alimony payments he'd been building up over the years. As usual, he was fighting as dirtily and publicly as he could.

'Because he is classified as a paranoid schizophrenic, Brian is scared of almost everything and doesn't really internalize reality like an ordinary person would,' Love tartly informed a British journalist in the summer of 1993. 'He interprets things. He hears voices and imagines situations. Because he stole money and credit from me for all these years, he feels guilty. Until that is resolved and he feels absolved of guilt, he cannot engage in any meaningful act with the group.'

Where would it end? Two years before, it had been the turn of Love's repugnant brother Stan to instigate a law-suit trying to wrest control of Brian, his affairs and, most of all, his money from Landy's clammy grip. The whole demeaning process made the composer feel like a piece of cold meat on a slab being bartered over by a bunch of heartless scum-bags.

'I've lived a life of scare. I've known some nice scares in my life. Some of them weren't so nice though. It was like . . . I used to lay there, eating in bed and I could feel people grabbing my ankles. I could feel this . . . feeling! It was a fantasy. In fantasy, everything's possible; you can slip out of reality into a fantasy.

'It's a satisfying feeling to withdraw, what can I say? I live inside my own head, so my head contains a lot of memories and a lot of ingeniousness. I consider myself to be a creative genius and the child in me, of course, tries to get away though the world around me keeps me from going too far. But the child is basically the expression of the ego, and I think this is why I want to be a child; because you can express ego, but, at the same time, you can be innocent . . .

'The voices in my head've been happening for twenty years now. I couldn't do anything. I didn't trust anybody. It's just a crazy notion but . . . I have a lot of heroes and villains in my life – a lot of villains, unfortunately. A villain walks in and destroys something. Unfortunately, the same people who are heroes are villains to me. And it's hard for me, it's very difficult. It's been rough, too. I always thought, "Wow! Gee! Maybe we can resolve it." But it doesn't seem to resolve so good. Things have been going on like that for twenty-five years! If I told who I thought I was, you might print it and I can't take a chance on that!'

Yet there were times when it seemed strangely worthwhile, this confounded 'struggling on' business. There'd be moments for instance, like sometimes at dusk, when the ocean breeze would rustle in from the open terrace window and suddenly it was like the waves below were singing one of his songs – only better, fuller-sounding and without those squeaky falsettos messing everything up – and he'd see God slowly rising up before him with his hand outstretched, pointing at him, indicating for him to have no fear. And deep in his heart he would sense that it was all OK, that all the pain and suffering had been just part of a higher design and that all he needed to do was breathe in deeply, relax and rejoice in the sounds he had already created.

'Basically what I have done is I have freed myself, I've liberated myself into a position where I can talk to people and not have to worry about what I'm saying. I never was sure of what I was doing to people. I think an artist will have to know that the reward is in the giving. That's where it's at: it's called "unconditional love". You can tell when things are cool and when they're not. You say, "Waah! I think I'm going overboard! Aaah! I don't think I want to make any more music, I quit!" You do that for a while: "Fuck music! Fuck people!" And then you come back all around . . . People are what I need, I need to make music for people instead of saying, "Fuck people!" I used to say that, but not anymore. You love the people. You give to people. You create music for people to hear, so that they can say, "Hey, yeah, that's real . . ."'

'I used to go through things, and I wondered whether things were real or not. [*Softly*] I guess it's just another stage of development, but I do hear and see magical trips that I can turn on and off. Most people don't understand that. They say, "Why can't you do something about it?" I don't know! Because I took those drugs that made me search my soul, and try to see what I was all about . . . But the drugs back-fired. I took acid, and it squashed my ego down a little bit, and it hurt my feelings that I didn't have what someone else might have had. When you go through too much of that, it's like an attack you have inside your head. You won't accept it like that. I want it to be perfect! Music is perfect!

'But I never ever quit. See, I'm not a quitter. People say to me, "Brian, you're not a loser, you're a winner. There's a difference between a winner and a loser. You're a winner. You make good music." If you put music out that's spiritual, that has spiritual vibes in it, people are gonna hear it. But I don't push my power around because, see, whatever happens, I know I'll always have a spiritual power in this world.'

The Killer in Aspic: Going to Hell with Jerry Lee Lewis in Hollywood

He was trying to be courteous but you could tell almost at once that being courteous wasn't really part of his basic nature. 'Wahl, ah looks at it this-away, Kill-uh,' he slurred. 'There's only two they done it to this-away. There's your Al Jolson, they done 'im when he wuz still alive, and there's me, Jerry Lee Lewis, they doin' me now whilst ah'm still alive. So there's your two of us, yer two bona fide livin' legends o' all time! Now Adam, he was tellin' me t'other day somethin' about someone else [*he pauses, snorts*], some damn woman [*second pause*], Loretta Lynn or someone like that! . . . Hell she don't count!'

Throughout the world he alone was known as 'The Killer', but he called me and anyone else he was addressing by that title ('Howya doin', Kill-uh', 'Hangin' in there, Kill-uh' *ad infinitum*). It turned out to be his only affectionate term of endearment, infinitely preferable to the stern censorious 'son' or the Tennessee Williams-ominous, booming and hostile 'boy'.

What I remember most is how you had to stare directly into his eyes because if you lost his gaze, even for a second, you lost him too. And he'd be off and reeling, focus all shot to hell, raving on, both splendid and quite pitiful. He looked haggard, gaunt, and though his face bore the tell-tale signs of a heavy make-up job, he still looked hard and malevolent. But when the mad sparkle that rejuvenated his manner ceased to glow in his eyes, his whole character seemed to shrivel before me, becoming old and bone-dry. He muttered about 'wanting to get next to a whole new generation o' young people' and it sounded utterly obscene, yet he was only innocuously talking about his 'comeback' and about attracting the young people to buy his records and make him 'the biggest damn star I can hope to be'. And of course at this point I had to ask myself: is this man strictly for real?

But then, oh foolish query, this is Jerry Lee Lewis, large as life and five times as daunting, the last of the true primitives and a man so for real he's positively surreal. I mean, everybody knows about the Killer on some level: be it as 'wizened rock legend', 'the only real rival Elvis ever had', 'the most genuinely psychotic entertainer in show business history' or, in my perception, as the greatest living one-man soap opera in the entire history of glorious *National Enquirer*-era America. Take your pick. Anyway, come early autumn, that living legend will be unveiling itself anew at a cinema near you, immortalized for celluloid by Dennis Quaid.

Why a Jerry Lee Lewis biopic, you ask? Well why not? These are godless times we're living through and this man's story to date should stand as a terrible example to us all. More to the point, his is an odyssey so extravagant it mocks the very concept of fiction. It has everything: madness, bigamy, religious mania, tragedy, psychotic arrogance, epic violence and debauchery, drugs of every shape and substance, an ocean of alcohol, wealth, corruption, damnation, probably even murder.

Adam Fields, thirty-two, *Great Balls of Fire*'s producer, is more than cognizant of all these facets: 'His life is so hugely textured and consistently eventful it seemed out of the question to attempt covering it all. I mean, we're only tackling eighteen months of his life . . . Jerry Lee and Jimmy Swaggart – these two guys just keep on making history and you can never count them out. For me, Jerry Lee is the last great American original to be immortalized on celluloid . . . I think this will be just the first of a whole number of films dealing with aspects of his life. There has to be at least a sequel.'

The eighteen months covered in *Great Balls of Fire* focuses on the period – around 1958 – that witnessed the first extraordinary rise and fall of Jerry Lee Lewis, at age twenty-one, a period when, as Fields points out, 'he went from making $100 a week to $10,000 and right back again. And I don't think he's ever understood why.'

In that year and a half he went from playing piano in 'the evilest, baddest, lowest fightin'-and-killingest place on earth', a Memphis juke-joint called Haney's, to recording for Sam Phillips and Sun Records and selling a staggering 31 million records as a consequence. This coincided with Elvis Presley being railroaded into the army, and so mercurial was his ascent, so audacious was his demeanour, that Jerry Lee was really the only one who ever genuinely threatened to dislodge the King from his throne. Arrogance was his undoing however; for it was blinding arrogance and a fervent crazy sense of recognizing God's will or none at all that drove him to show off his thirteen-year-old bride on a trip to England. The press, discovering her true age, dug deeper and found Jerry Lee Lewis to have been married twice before – a multi-bigamist no less – and his disgrace came fast and furious.

The fruits of this jarring episode – the music he made for Sun Records – are known to everyone: as time goes by they just sound better and better, harking as they do back to a time when rock'n'roll was the sound of young men taking wild glorious risks, staring the whole world down. Director Jim MacBride (who has already paid extensive homage to Lewis in his albeit ill-conceived remake of Godard's *Breathless*) only becomes truly animated when he talks about that music: 'The most intense expression of young emotions . . . it appeals to all the restless excitement and raw energy that young people have.'

Maybe so, but now more than ever it sounds like the gleeful mad abandon of a man throwing coals into the furnace of a runaway train that's dragging him straight to hell. It survives as the most vivid and extreme music of its era and genre because it makes no differentiation between 'fun' and 'sin', between 'soft sex' and hard venal lust, between 'getting really gone' and flat-out dementia.

'Elvis was the greatest but I'm the best,' Lewis, immodest as ever, once stated and here at least he has a point. For though Elvis was the most obviously charismatic, Jerry Lee was the most dangerous and it's this sense of danger that envelops him to this day, that has him torn between 'fame' on the one hand and 'infamy' on the other, ricocheting helplessly and ceaselessly betwixt the two. In the brilliant *Hellfire*, Nick Tosches, Lewis's premier biographer, chronicles the extraordinary patterns that seem to control the destiny of an individual as undefeatable as he is utterly self-destructive. When Jerry Lee enters a room you feel the earth shuddering on its axis, the ground beneath him moving and shaking ever so slightly. You also get a terrible insight into what it can be like to find yourself in intimate contact with such a volatile force.

Throughout Tosches's accounts on Lewis havoc inevitably reigns: in-laws go mad or become accident statistics, offspring die horrible, mangled deaths, wives drown or suffer inexplicable fatal overdoses, band members also overdose a lot or end up drug-addicted, penniless and in jail (or, in one case, get shot point-blank in the chest by a 'Killer' too stoned to think better of such an action). Record people are terrorized, audiences verbally and physically attacked, promoters bankrupted, journalists threatened with broken bottles for no sane reason . . . On Jerry Lee Lewis's dark highway of a life everybody else seems to fall by the wayside while the Killer just keeps on rocking, shining ever brighter while everything around him turns to shit.

'Let's say it's made for a very interesting chemistry,' says MacBride – not without some measure of irony, one feels – when asked about Jerry Lee Lewis's spectral presence as technical adviser over the making of *Great Balls of Fire*.

'But I've personally kinda shied away from him . . . I haven't had much to do with Jerry Lee at all. See, I started my film career doing documentaries – *cinéma vérité* stuff – and I realized early that in that medium you can't really avoid betraying your subject in some form or another. And so this time I felt I should preserve myself from Jerry Lee himself in order to tell his story as best I can. I don't want to disappoint him, but maybe by placating him I'd end up disappointing myself, which would be worse.'

MacBride might have other, less aesthetic, reasons for keeping a wide berth from the Killer. The filming of *Great Balls of Fire* has been long, costly and arduous, as well as plagued by illness and inclement weather, but even these natural catastrophes seem secondary to the contagiously destructive presence that Jerry Lee Lewis himself may be exerting on the film set. Stories have already circulated claiming Lewis had pulled a gun several times on Fields during more delicate production negotiations. Fields denies this. 'There was a story that the Memphis hot-wire picked up stating Jerry pulled a gun and threatened to kill me if I didn't pay him $50,000 and that I had to escape through a bathroom window. There was another claiming I pulled a gun on him, which is ridiculous. I don't know where these stories came from. But they make great copy.'

Fields does admit that 'keeping Jerry Lee happy is a full-time job. He's had a lot of influence but it's been hard as well because . . . Jerry remembers the past one way, and Myra will remember it all completely differently. Then Sam Phillips's [another technical adviser] recollections are different again. He can be very difficult too.'

It doesn't help that Lewis openly despises the text the screenplay is partly taken from: former child bride Myra Lewis's *Great Balls of Fire*. (His most famous ex-wife Jerry Lee Lewis now refers to as 'a very, very mixed-up young woman' – a definition of mind-boggling implications from him – 'tryin' to poison mah daughter's mind against me with a bunch o' spiteful shit! I saw her just a few days ago. I says to her, "Myra, that damn book o' yours – that weren't no *Great Balls of Fire* you wrote. You shoulda called it *Great Buncha Balls* instead, darlin', 'cos that's all it is.'''')

But that is as nothing compared to the thorny matter of documenting the Killer's religious obsessions on celluloid for posterity. 'That's where the real problems have occurred,' says Fields. 'Jerry's tormented by his religious influences. He sees himself as forever torn between doing God's work and singing the Devil's music. It's a very personal thing with him, something he lives with and something he feels uncomfortable about having splashed over a cinema screen, I guess.' The Killer took greatest exception, according to Fields, to a scene in the film where, during an Assembly of God church service, one of the congregation is portrayed as speaking in tongues. 'He was shocked we'd even consider such a thing because he stated that speaking in tongues is the most serious and intimate thing that can happen to a human being. And that it was the greatest sin in the world to mock that state by acting it out.'

To give Lewis's religious side a more resonant context, the script also utilizes the character of Jimmy Swaggart, Lewis's equally notorious double first cousin and, up until early 1988, America's most outspoken, influential (and, many would add, most genuinely diabolical) TV evangelist.

'Jimmy's the only person who's still alive that we haven't contacted in order to get his side of the story,' confesses Fields. 'Since last year's scandals' – when the holier-than-holy Swaggart was reportedly caught slumming in New Orleans's most sordid red-light district, paying to photograph $10-an-hour prostitutes in pornographic poses while masturbating himself – 'he's sort of kept himself in hiding. He's basically a recluse right now. We don't know what to expect from him. He'll either bless us or damn the whole thing to hell, I suppose. But he and Jerry Lee are incredible, a contemporary Cain and Abel if you like. Only you're never quite sure which is which.'

Certainly, as Swaggart's own arrogance and self-destructive weirdness were last year being broadcast in every tabloid throughout America, so the same journals would point to his cousin the Killer and his rise once again – with this film's advent – from yet another yawning abyss of a career slump. Four years earlier Jerry Lee Lewis's notoriety quotient had reached a new and chilling peak: *Rolling Stone* printed a devastating exposé of his life of middle-aged craziness, drug addiction and corruption, baldly accusing him of brutally murdering his fifth wife, a former cocktail waitress from Michigan named Shawn, some thirty days into their marriage. After that, everyone was just waiting for him to drop dead, and Lewis certainly seemed to spend a lot of time bouncing in and out of detoxification clinics. Now once again a married man – he informed me that his current wife, Kerrie McCarver, is 'the only one I never done cheated on . . . that'll tell ya something right there' – he is also a father again, to a son named (what else?) Jerry Lee Lewis III.

When not consorting with Lisa Marie Presley (another media sensation: mother Priscilla was understandably 'very concerned') the Killer was re-recording his old repertoire with producer T-Bone Burnette, the man who'd done so much to revitalize Roy Orbison's career just before the latter's death, for the *Great Balls of Fire* soundtrack, receiving in the process 'major record offers, the likes o' which you wouldn't believe'. The whole experience has been 'a lesson well learned and a blessing well earned,' he told me. 'I'm ready to do business again.'

'You know what Jerry recently told me,' Fields finally confides. 'In all seriousness that he sees this film as his salvation, that's he's been "risen again by the Lord" and that its success would lead him finally to the Promised Land. I just said to him, "Hey Jerry, do I look like Charlton Heston?"'

*

'Dennis? I like 'im well enough, Kill-uh, but he's always talkin' a bunch o' crap . . . I'll tell ya this tho'. He was born to play me. And playin' me in this film is gonna make him into one hell of a damn star.'

But Dennis Quaid is already one hell of a damn star. 'Right now he's enormous,' says Fields. And that enormity is the key reason that this whole project is finally off the ground after eight years of being just another script doing the rounds . . . Quaid and MacBride scored heavily as a team with *The Big Easy* and the success of their relationship – 'There's a very lively chemistry between us,' says Quaid. 'We're either screaming at each other or we're like brothers' – has made *Great Balls of Fire* not merely bankable but the property on which Orion Pictures appear to have their highest hopes riding. A clip is already being shown in cinemas across America – a three-minute trailer for a film that isn't finished – and watching it you can see just how much pressure there is on Quaid to deliver the goods, for the success or failure of *Great Balls of Fire* will ultimately hang on his gangly Texan shoulders. Actually it's a disappointing showcase. Quaid looks weird and defiant but lacks the true-made arrogance.

That said, the Dennis Quaid who allowed one perfunctory interview during the three weeks of filming in London seemed to have achieved an impressive, if slightly unsettling, synthesis with the character's firmly primal instincts. His manner was authentically wild, flamingly arrogant, but also slightly comic, full of piss and vinegar. He looked very thin and extremely handsome in a disturbed sort of way, his hair dyed blond and swept into a pompadour so preposterous his head at times resembled an exploding field of corn. If this Jerry Lee Lewis madness is as contagious as the facts of his life purport it to be, then the 34-year-old Quaid was quite firmly in its grip. For the next half-hour you couldn't tell the two of them apart.

'This is a hell of an experience,' he began, his Texas drawl already merging with Lewis's Memphian cadences of punch-drunk bluster. 'A larger-than-life experience. It's been a big challenge. When I played Gordo Cooper in *The Right Stuff* he was a real person, but nothing's gonna prepare you for playing the part of Jerry Lee Lewis. For starters, we're talking about a man who is the ultimate extrovert on the face of this earth . . .

'He's like a goldmine, that's how I see it. He's also pretty scary. You have to take a big chance to really get near to what's goin' on in his heart. When we first met he was very, very wary of me. He'd start talkin' about the old days, then he'd clam up, just glare at me and say, "Ah ain't gonna tell you mah secrets, son." Stuff like that. He's a tough nut to crack and that's the truth. You'll be talkin' and you'll see him driftin' off there. But I've learnt now never to underestimate his powers. He's dumb like a fox that Jerry Lee Lewis! He's always surprisin' me.

'Basically he's been three different people in his life. The first's the guy I'm playin' right now. The second was this rather wild bein', the one they call the Killer, and the third is the person he is right now, this person who's kind of popped out the other side of madness. Actually I find him very reasonable most of the time.

'His obsession with goin' to hell? Well let's just say Jerry Lee Lewis has a very close personal relationship with God. I mean, haven't you ever felt that you were damned? I've felt that way. Man, I feel that way right now.'

The lady press officer was sympathetic. 'Today, he's being lovely,' she offered. Yesterday had been different though. 'He has a problem with women journalists,' she began, before admitting that yesterday he'd had a problem with almost everyone. In short he'd been surly, monosyllabic, disdainful and hostile. 'He just kept murmuring to one poor girl, "I don't like you, I don't like you."'

Downstairs a camera crew was filming an interview with the Killer. The press officer had a point, I suppose. He sounded as polite as any man in an advanced state of stupefaction probably can hope to be. But lovely? He didn't sound lovely to me. The TV interviewer – a plummy-voiced Brit from the old school of broadcasting – started a question about the fact that the character of Jimmy Swaggart was part of this film, but Jerry Lee misheard him or wasn't listening and the rest was deranged calamity.

'Jimmy? In mah movie? Are you sayin' Jimmy's in mah movie? [*Explodes*.] Well, what's he doin' in it, Kill-uh? Shit, they don't tell me nothing, these damn movie people! Always the last t'know! They still callin' it *Great Balls of Fire*? Shit, I don't know! If Jimmy's in this damn film, I'll probably end up with third billin'! To hell with it!'

Finally it was my turn and I got my first full glimpse of him. I was admitted to a large banquet room where ten, maybe fifteen individuals were standing in servile attendance, religiously savouring Jerry Lee Lewis's every slurred syllable. There were fan club presidents present, press people, film people, cameramen. But they all seemed invisible to me, like Scotch mist. All eyes fell fixedly on Jerry Lee Lewis. The Killer held the whole focus of that room right there in the hollow of his hand.

A young man from a Swedish magazine was asking him a question but he wasn't really paying attention. He was looking away from his inquisitor, one hand hiding the whole right side of his gaunt face and his left eye brimming with diffident disdain. Sometimes his mouth would flash a snarl and he'd look just like one of those evil old Alsatian dogs one occasionally encounters in squalid provincial drinking-houses – the kind no one seems to own but there they always are, crouched in a corner, immovable and authentically alarming, snarling at everyone within the general vicinity of their fangs. Even wearing a white ski jersey with gambolling red reindeer knitted on to the chest (hardly suitable apparel for such a professed homophobe), he still looked like Murder Incorporated. He was the Killer right enough. I offered up my firmest handshake and sat facing him.

For the next half an hour he seemed by turns heroic, pathetic, comic and dangerous. To quote Marlene Dietrich in *A Touch of Evil*, 'He was some kind of man.'

You once did Shakespeare, I began. You played Iago in *Othello*.

'That's right, Kill-uh. And it was the hardest six weeks o' my life. But I did it. It was rock'n'roll Shakespeare but I learnt all the lines in the damn play. Did it up pretty good. I kept askin' Jack Good, I says, "Why you got me playin' this cat Iago anyway?" "'Cos you were born to it," he tol' me. "'Cos you're the only one I know as evil as he is." Hell, I reckon ol' Jack had me pegged pretty good, doncha think?'

Did the location of both this hotel and the film's reconstruction of the child-bride gigs that brought about your first controversial fall from favour jar any strong recollections after thirty years? The Killer looked old and vacant.

'Can't say as they do, no. Memory's not what it used to be.'

Nothing at all?

'It's all vague, pretty vague. Even this hotel . . . I 'membered it as a big ol' place, twelve-storey high, and there ain't but three floors to it. Wouldn't a done no good me throwing Myra out the windows o' this place, Kill-uh? [*Weird laughter*.] Wouldna left a mark on 'er!

'The gig? There weren't no damn carry-cot wheeled onstage . . . Leastways I nevah saw one. Few tomaytas flyin' past. Coupla eggs maybe . . . but . . .'

He paused and his eyes looked glazed and faraway as though a heavy patch of brain-fog was suddenly crowding out his every thought process. And for a split second he looked incredibly old and frail, almost pathetic. Then just as spontaneously his whole personality shifted gear: his eyes regained their focus, only more so, becoming younger, somehow bigger, and his whole manner became charged, unsettlingly expansive.

'What I 'member most, though, is that in the audience there was a helluva a lot of good-lookin' women!'

He suddenly paused and burst out laughing.

'A lotta good-lookin' women! Man, ain't that just the kind o' shit you'd expect t' come out of the mouth of Jerry Lee Lewis?'

He laughed uproariously then just as suddenly stopped, becoming intense once more.

'But there was, Kill-uh. Lotta good-lookin' women! Hell, there was a lot of good-lookin' young men there too. I'm not queer or anythin', y'understand. It's just a fact: good-lookin' young people o' both sexes come to my shows. It's always been that way. Jerry Lee Lewis has always attracted the best-lookin' crowd o' people y'all can find packed inside o' four walls.'

I'm surprised you're doing any interviews at all, I continued. The press have almost destroyed your career in the past with their interference, revelations and accusations. Don't you hold the media in some contempt?

'Not really, Kill-uh. No, I think y'all done treated me pretty fair when all's said and done. I think most of the writers are decent fair-minded people and that I've always got pretty much what I deserved.'

Even with *Rolling Stone* insinuating you killed your last wife?

'Well maybe they did, Kill-uh, I don't know . . .' He paused, as though suppressing something distant and uncomfortable. Then he was once more suddenly transformed, animated, the grand extrovert, a Southern Baptist W.C. Fields.

'One time, the press – I had 'em all of one accord facin' me in one big ol' room. And I tol' em, I says, "Boys, I hear y'all bin doin' a lot o' writing about me and I can't say as ah blame ya. And I want y'all to know ah don't give a damn what ya write about me, but if one o' yous evah spells mah name wrong, ah'm gonna find 'im and come kill 'is ass!"'

His voice here receded into a low, treacherous-sounding growl.

'And they ain't nev-ah did that! 'Cos they know anyone messes with me, ah'll kill 'm! Everybody knows that.'

You're renowned for being mean.

'What's that shit? Mean? I'm not mean. Strict, yes, but I'm not mean. Hell, what kinda "mean" ya talkin' about?'

Mean as in ruthless and wild.

'Oh! Well then, ah'm mean!'

He fired it out like a punchline, ending the statement with a stranglehold laugh.

You've often been quoted as saying you consider yourself unquestionably the greatest talent in rock'n'roll. Is there anyone you view as being even close to you, talentwise?

More low snarling.

'Nah. There ain't never bin no one as good as me.'

Never ever?

'Nev-ah ev-ah.' Pause. He stared at me, eyes burning with a venal arrogance. 'There ain't never bin a one could cut me, boy. Are you shittin' me? Are you shittin' me? Listen, son, I'm fifty-three years o' age and I haven't yet ever bee-gun to reach mah peak or t'sell as many damn records as I can and be just as big a damn star as I wanna be. The rest of 'em . . . I already done buried the rest of 'em. And they were the only ones who were any damn good. Hell, there ain't nothin' on th' horizon that's got me breakin' sweat, boy. Are you shittin' me?

'Johnny Cash? He's history man. One damn word. Chuck Berry? History! Little Richard? You shittin' me? History! Plus he's queer! Is that it? That's all o' em? Right well, I reckon we just wrapped 'em all up, Kill-uh. Mopped 'em all up.'

Your relationship with Jimmy Swaggart is legendary, I began. The Killer was now squinting, myopic and sinister.

'Who?' he muttered querulously.

Jimmy Swaggart, your first cousin.

'Oh Jimmy!'

The brain-fog started slowly parting.

'What's that shit yo' just said?'

He's your first cousin.

'Double first cousin.'

He paused, shot me a killing glance, then coldly muttered, 'Well, what about 'im?'

What do you think of his current fall from grace?

Here Jerry Lee Lewis could contain himself no longer. 'Boy how can you be fallin' from grace for just wantin' to beat your meat?' he exploded. 'Shit, that's stupid. Let's not get too down on Jimmy now. Hell, he's a human bein' same as the rest of us. We all got our urges. He's picked hisself a pretty hard row to hoe.'

But he's a hypocrite, something you've never been accused of.

'True, Kill-uh, true, I have never been a hypocrite. Shit, I ain't got nothin' to hide. Never tol' a lie in my whole life. 'Cos my life has always bin an open book. Don't believe in lyin' and hidin' and damn secrets. Anyone as does, they've got big problems. You can call me any damn name you want but I ain't no hypocrite and no one can call me one.'

Is the subject of religion something you feel comfortable talking about?

'I feel comfortable talkin' about religion 'cos I don't believe in it. Shit no! I believe in salvation. Salvation and sanctification. The rest is just a bunch o' wrong-headed bullshit.'

You've been quoted as saying you're going straight to hell . . .

'Well I probably will if'n I don't change my way of livin'. I don't want to think about it too much but it's probably a fact.'

And here he started laughing, at first sardonically.

'Hell where d'you think I'd go? You think ol' St Peter's gonna swing open them pearly gates for a crazy old rock'n'rollin' cat like me?'

His hysterical laughter rang out loud and long for several seconds.

But doesn't it worry you?

'Does it worry me?' There were almost tears of laughter in his wild eyes now. 'You're damn right it worries me. Shit, yes. Are you shittin' me?'

But you've tried to join the ministry several times . . .

'I've tried. Tried and tried and tried.' Suddenly his mood became sober and bleakly reflective. 'I tried once for three long years. Just couldn't do it. Had to back off. It's just not in me an' I can't live a lie . . . See, it's like, Satan, he's got power next to God.

'He's second in command, seated right next to 'im. Satan, he's the Archangel, he's like the Programme Director or somethin' . . . Anyway, seems like the two o' them are always playing some damn game against each other, using me as their pawn. That's what it feels like anyways.'

And this feeling of being damned is something you live with constantly?

'It's somethin' I live with every damned minute of every damned day and night o' my life! You're absolutely right, son.'

Moving right along here, is it true you've been teaching Lisa Marie Presley how to play piano?

'What?'

Suddenly his whole manner seems under attack from waves of random hostility, like static on the radio. I repeat the question.

'No, she taught me. You don't teach a lady nuttin' in this life, son. Shit, don't you know that?'

Has she inherited much of her father's talent?

'Oh . . . Yes . . . I think . . . Ah . . . She . . .'

(Suddenly reception is getting very vague again.)

'. . . Yes . . . I do believe she probably has. If'n it's in her and that's what she really wants to do. It's early days for that little lady, Killuh. Just a babe in arms. She ain't but a chile. Good people but a chile all the same. Just a chile livin' in a world o' greed 'n' trouble! [*Nods sagely.*] Them Mormons and that other son o' bitch Parker – them type o' people can give a little girl a rough ole ride.'

Talking of rough rides, how does it feel to file bankruptcy with debts of three million? Do you ever see yourself getting over your financial difficulties?

'Shit, yes. I'll get out under it if not over it, anyways. Same as I've done all my damn life. Are you shittin' me? Hell, it ain't nothin'. Just a damned formality. See, filin' bankruptcy's just a form of business you go through just so's you can get a bunch of motherfuckin' leeches off your damn back. That's all it is. Doin' it legal. Man, where I come from, if you got honest debts t' pay you go to jail. I just got a load o' people who placed these judgements agin me. And not a one of 'em showed up in court! Nossir! Not one of dem debt-seeking motherfuckers showed 'is face . . .'

Maybe they're frightened of you . . .

'Hell no, son, frightened ain't nothin' to do with it. Theys just lyin' sons of bitches is all! Goddamned sons o' bitches at that! [*Almost screams*] Goddamned sons o' bitches!'

He was snarling and steaming now, his eyes looking every bit as cold and mean as his legend could hope to suggest, and for a split second I sensed that I'd overstepped the bounds of reasonable provocation here, for he was staring right through me, his left hand clenched into a fist, his right hand pointing a remonstrative finger directly at me.

'They ain't evah gonna take nothin' from me, boy! Print that! Shit, I got one of the most beautiful homes you could ev-ah imagine! Got eighty damn acres o' the prettiest land! Two big ole lakes runnin' thru' . . . Ten miles outside o' Memphis. Had it sixteen years. They ain't takin' nothin' from me.

'Enough o' this talkin'! I've had enough anyway. All this talkin' bullshit! Like to make a man lose his sex drive! Ah've said mah piece. Now ah aim to abide by mah word. Gonna cut more hit records – that's mah first love. Bein' in the studio, cuttin' hits. Gonna keep playin' live, hell yes. I'd play a hundred damn shows a month if'n they could stack 'em all up for me. Keeps me in shape. It's when I'm not working things get weird. Start dragging around the damn house, your attention gets side-tracked. It can easily happen, son. Hell, for damn years mah attention was wanderin' everywhichway. I was strung out all over the damn universe. I didn't know what the hell wuz goin' on.

'I'm coming back. Now, I've said it, it's for me to prove it. That's my job. Never get thru' provin' yourself in this life, son. And if'n you do, you're dead. But I'm only still doin' it 'cos I can and 'cos I want to. Don't have to prove nuttin' to nobody! I just likes to kick ass is all.'

The Bewildering Universe of Roky Erickson and His Two-headed Dog

At 4.20 on a Tuesday afternoon, in a room steeped in humidity, I am waiting my turn to interview Roky Erickson. No one seems to know what exactly is going on. The location appears to have mysteriously changed from CBS records UK headquarters in London's Soho Square – where I am – to the Portobello Hotel, where Erickson is. Queries as to the whys and wherefores of the move are met with a vagueness that becomes increasingly irksome to have to confront. Finally a call from the Portobello fills me in as to the strategy afoot. A timid-voiced PR addresses the matter at hand: 'Ah . . . we decided that doing interviews here would be more conducive. You see, Roky is a . . . um . . . very sensitive person and uh . . . very *shy*. It would be wise, Nick, if you were . . . um, *patient* and a bit tactful when talking to him. The flight over has probably . . . *disorientated* him somewhat.'

The Roky Erickson interview. Extract 1

NK: Though you were raised in Texas, apparently you're currently living in San Francisco, isn't that so?

RE: [*Long pause.*] Uh . . . it's a secret. Ah don't give out mah address to anyone.

NK: Why is that?

RE: [*Even longer pause.*] Beg pardon? Could you repeat that question again?

NK: Why do you keep your current base of operations a secret?
RE: Well . . . it's a . . . [*a pause of approximately sixty-five seconds' duration*] it's a secret.
NK: [*Changing subject*] Your songs, the lyrics, are constantly referring to 'demons' and demonic forces. How do these creatures manifest themselves to you?
RE: [*After an absurdly long pause*] In secret.

If this was the nineties, Roky Erickson would probably be termed 'an alternative rock performer'. But as it's only 1980, he gets to be called a cult-hero instead. Which is to say, he doesn't sell many records – in fact he doesn't get to make many – but those few he does manage to release end up being bought by the most influential kind of people. Just don't try asking him why that is, though.

He was born in 1947, the eldest of five criminal-minded brothers and his upbringing within the lower-middle-class confines of Austin, Texas, was shaped principally by a domineering mother, who'd once been an opera singer only to become a fervent Bible Belt fundamentalist. Throughout his formative years Erickson the eldest was constantly being force-fed a sensory diet of hellfire-and-brimstone religious dogma. Meanwhile, his own fixation with trashy fifties horror comics and the vintage black-and-white ghoul B-movies that appeared on late-night TV made for a queasy mix of instant culture shock.

The Roky Erickson Interview. Extract 2

NK: What was the first music you recall hearing?
RE: Uh . . . ah . . . ah don't . . . [*Complete blank-out for some forty seconds.*]
NK: Well, when did you first play the guitar?
RE: Ah . . . uh . . . ah . . . didn't play the guitar *first*. Ah played the piano *first*. Picked up t' guitar when ah was ten years. But ah played piano first.

NK: What sort of music did you play on the piano then? Were you classically trained or did you try and play like, say, Little Richard?

RE: [*Obligatory long pause.*] Nooo, ah didn't play like Little Richard. T' way ah played piano was, uh, ah'd put a razor-blade between the keys so when anybody . . . y'know – [*lethargically demonstrates a hand running over the eighty-eight keys*] – their fingers'd be cut off. [*He smiles at this, then his eyes return to their frozen droop. He lights another cigarette.*]

Inspired by British Invasion bands like the Kinks, Yardbirds, Who, Rolling Stones, etc., at fifteen years of age the diminutive Erickson formed his first group, the Spades. As lead singer and guitarist, Erickson also began song-writing, with the result that a local Austin label – International Artists – signed the group and released a single, 'You're Gonna Miss Me', composed by him. A fervent garage-band stab at the kind of white R'n'B that Them and Rolling Stones themselves were waxing at the time, it became a local hit before accelerating into a national Top 40 smash. During this time the Spades suddenly metamorphosed into the Thirteenth Floor Elevators.

The name change came about when Erickson and his collaborators were approached by one Tommy Hall, a self-appointed Svengali-type several years their senior and a teacher in sociology around the Austin area. While the early acid experiments instigated by Ken Kesey on the West Coast were being immortalized by Tom Wolfe, similar less-publicized forays into the world of hallucinogenics were being undertaken by a clique of young Austin students who'd discovered mescaline and other intoxicants growing in the fields around their home state. Hall was among the first to discover the potency of 'psychedelic' drugs, and introduced his findings to Erickson and Co., also electing to become the group's ersatz guru, lyricist and – oh yes – jug-player.

The Thirteenth Floor Elevators' short, erratic history is a quintessential odyssey of the so-called psychedelic life-style run ragged, of utopian ideals duly dashed into the dirt by the very drugs that set the whole thing in motion in the first place.

Basically the group weren't that startling. They made sniggering references to the virtues of taking psychedelics in their rather silly lyrics, while the music was a curious grab-bag of folk rock, jug band and rhythm'n'blues that occasionally sparked to an inspired consequence but just as often sounded stodgy and self-indulgent. Of the original members, one has since been murdered, another has found Scientology, another is a junkie . . . And then there was Roky.

He'd already become addicted to methedrine during a ruinous stay in San Francisco during 1967 that had forced the whole band to return glumly to Austin. Once back in the Lone Star State, Erickson quickly became marked by the authorities as a subversive influence on the state's youth owing to his band's overt promoting of hallucinogenics. Soon enough he got busted for a small amount of hashish. Faced with the choice of jail or mental hospital, he chose the latter without fully comprehending the consequences of his decision. Once incarcerated, he escaped and was eventually caught again – in possession of some opiate though it could've been a frame-up – with the result that he was sentenced to stay in Shoal Creek Mental Institution for an indefinite period. Erickson remained there, subjected to thorazine and electro-shock therapy, for three long years, until certain acquaintances enlisted the aid of a lawyer to help get him out again.

The Roky Erickson interview. Extract 3

NK: The period you spent in the, uh, hospital – did you feel that you had been used as a scapegoat?

RE: No.

NK: What do you feel about the three years you spent there? How did it affect you?

RE: [*Long pause.*] Beg pardon? Could you repeat the question again?

NK: The mental hospital – your stay in the hospital . . .

RE: Uh . . . we-e-ell, that was propaganda.

NK: What was?

RE: [*Pause.*] The hospital, yup.

NK: Are you saying that you didn't get locked away in a mental hospital, a sanatorium, for three years?

RE: Uh [*long pause*] . . . no, ah have to say ah didn't. Oh, will you excuse me for a second!

Once released, Erickson found himself getting involved in flirtations with heroin and methedrine. Back in Austin he met up with Doug Sahm, whose Sir Douglas Quintet had been Austin's other mid-sixties rock band of consequence, albeit purveying a Tex-Mex sound totally at odds with the Elevators' rambling psychedelia. With a budget of exactly one hundred dollars Sahm took Erickson into the studio.

The result was four tracks, including a single, 'Red Temple Prayer' – also known as 'Two Headed Dog' – which was released on the little-known Mars label in 1976. Credited to Erickson and 'Blieb Alien', the cut was a quite extraordinary piece of music, commencing with what sounded like twenty out-of-tune Fender Jaguars imitating the sound of Hitchcock's *The Birds* descending in full flight on a lone Volkswagen. Then Erickson opened his lips and commenced his deranged howlings, bemoaning the fact that he'd 'been working in the Kremlin with a two-headed dog'. The cumulative effect was something else again, not dissimilar to Captain Beefheart in terms of undermining conventions, although the basic chord structure was stock three-chord hard rock. The components, though – Erickson's crazed vocals, the disorientating clash of rock guitar and electric autoharp, the fractured splurge of images that somehow conspired to mould together a vision of psychotic dread – created a record of quite unique mood and power.

Then just as the Erickson single appeared, so the Thirteenth Floor Elevators suddenly became a hip name to drop. First Television's Tom Verlaine and Richard Hell raved about the group, even going so far as to perform 'Fire Engine', an Elevators original, as a kind of homage. Then Patti Smith, who always knew a good bandwagon when she jumped on one, immediately cited the group as 'inspirational'. Cleveland's Pere Ubu did likewise. All of a sudden, old long-deleted Elevators albums (there are four in all) were changing hands in London record stores for twenty pounds or more.

Erickson meanwhile was recording demos of new songs – he boasted of there being some three hundred to choose from – with titles like 'Creature with the Atom Brain', 'I Walked with a Zombie', 'Mine Mine Mind', 'Bloody Hammer Dr Chane', 'Night of the Vampire', 'Don't Shake Me Lucifer', 'I Think of Demons' and 'Bo Diddley was a Headhunter'. Tapes circulated around proved conclusively that the perverse brilliance of 'Two Headed Dog' was not a one-off. Like Syd Barrett's, Erickson's music expressed a state of sanity dangerously at odds with convention. While the likes of David Byrne and Richard Hell attempted to articulate the psychotic mentality through the craft of study and theatrical assimilation, Erickson was quite simply the real thing running rampant.

So how does a special kind o' guy like Roky get to land a major record deal with CBS when he's clearly several bricks shy of a full hod? Well, this is actually all the province of a young A&R man named Howard Thompson who single-handedly battled to sign his idol up for one album, even when the American parent company would have nothing to do with the scheme. As a result, an album, Erickson's first ever, entitled *Five Symbols*, is getting released. Unfortunately, where previous demo-tapes still sound alive with a menacing magnificence, *Symbols* removes all that edge, rendering the music as nothing more than average heavy-metal amp-ups. The production makes Erickson sound like a side-show freak spewing forth

Hammer-horror mind-scrambles. Where Erickson's music once was disturbing and rabidly radical, *Five Symbols* conspires to make it sound tame and rather insignificant.

To make matters worse, Thompson gets granted a three and a half thousand pound promo budget, insufficient funds to bring Erickson's band over here to play gigs (Erickson is generally considered a forceful live performer 'when the mood is right'). Instead, he gets flown in for a series of interviews with the music press spanning several days. Even though he is accompanied by his newly wedded bride, Holly (a former waitress whom he met at a club), plus managers Bruce King and Craig Luckin, Erickson appears to be a virtual zombie. Of course, the interview turns out to be a fiasco. Looking like a heavily sedated midget Rasputin with long crow-black hair and a lank beard to match, Erickson is barely capable of articulating more than two syllables every five minutes. The lights may be half on, but there is absolutely no one home. In fact, during an hour-long attempt at communication, Erickson only 'awakens' once. His eyes suddenly come alive, certain words catch his thus-far dormant brain-waves and he suddenly mutters, 'Hey, yeah, positive love! That's right! Hey, this is a good interview. Let me get another coffee, OK!' (He's already poured down five steaming black cups in less than half an hour.)

As he waddles off, his wife turns to me. 'I'd advise you to ask all your questions again,' she says evenly. 'He's woken up.'

Are his communication lapses something of a put-on then, I innocently enquire?

'Oh no, not at all,' she shrugs. 'He's like that all the time.'

'The Devil . . . no, ah'm not afraid of the Devil. Why should I be? It's mah religion.'

Welcome to my second Roky Erickson encounter. Apparently he tends to liven up a bit once it gets dark. It's 10 p.m. Same location, two days on. Of course, he fails to recognize me.

(Poor old Howard Thompson, who's been with him all week, arrives later laden with presents – books on Stonehenge – for Roky. Roky doesn't recognize him either.)

'See, the Devil will punish you if you are bad.'

Each word is masticated over in an irksome Texan drawl that heightens the somnambulistic effect even further. 'He stands at the gates of Hell and if you're bay-ad he'll send you down there. Ah know all this, see. Ah know 'cos the Devil is like mah friend. Ah am his, uh, chosen one. Out of all the people in the world he came to me and said, "Roky, you are mah . . . human" . . .? Ah don't know just the right word for it. Maybe you do?'

Mouthpiece?

'Uh . . . no. There's this word, though. Like ah'm his "chosen one". He chose me to do his biddin', see.'

I'm sorry. Let me get this straight. You are the Devil's chosen one . . .

'Yup.'

The Devil being the very incarnation of Evil itself.

'Well, ah wouldn't say that! He punishes you if you are bayad. He'll send you straight to Hell.'

And what, precisely is Hell?

'Whew boy, it's a . . . *terrible* place to be. Believe you me, it's lahk all fiery and full o' sinners. And you're in there for ever.

'No-oo, ah'm not frightened of goin' to Hell. The Devil, see . . . he's mah friend. Just as long as ah'm good, ah'll be all right. See, them at the hospital, they tried to keep me in there but they didn't realize mah power. How could they?

'Poor fools! Them doctors and nurses, whew, they're all crazy! They couldn't hold me in! They couldn't mess with the Devil's chosen one! How could they?'

Quite. But back to the Devil himself.

'Well, I'll tell you one thing about the Devil. He don't wanna rule the world. [*Pause.*] But then again maybe he does! [*Longer pause.*] I guess I'll have to figure that one out!

'See, the Devil has chosen *me* on his, uh . . . own – but I've got to have mahself a good time at the same time. Now how do you figure that?'

Roky Erickson fiddles with what look like dried-up food particles festooned in his beard, squints and ponders this pressing dilemma awhile. You can literally see the eyes beginning to fog over again: a strange chemical mist descending around the retinas. In three minutes he'll be back in the land of the living dead. ('Ah kinda liked that film. Ah love to see them zombies dance.') I meanwhile will be silently praying the much-predicted psychedelic revival gets postponed just a little while longer.

The Cracked Ballad of Syd Barrett

First came the Floyd. Then came the void. And sometimes in between this tragic passage the omens were there for all to see that something terribly wrong was happening to their golden boy but everyone was being too cool and 'laissez-faire' to accept them for what they were. Like that night, just as the summer of love was starting to crest into autumnal green, backstage at a London club where his group were about to take the stage, when Syd Barrett could be espied quietly blowing his mind to tiny psychedelic smithereens. His kohl-encircled eyes were glazed and sunken and his hair looked even worse, bursting from his skull like a badly orchestrated explosion. All evening he'd been impossible to communicate with. Instead, he stayed slumped in a chair, hallucinating at an image of himself from a long grubby mirror while the others busied themselves, tugging a stray thread from their latest fop-hippie fashion accessory or tuning up their guitars. Actually, it was down to Rick Wright, the keyboard player, to tune up the guitars. Roger Waters, the bass player, was unfortunately tone-deaf and, by this stage, well, let's just say Syd was about as enamoured with the idea of maintaining concert tuning as he was with employing 'chord progressions' or – God forbid – 'coherent guitar solos'. Which is to say, not at all. As anarchy came screaming through his psyche, so the sound it made overwhelmed his muse and its music.

The rest of the group were actually all three standing on the stage, ready to begin, when Barrett finally awoke from his numb narcissistic reverie in front of the dressing-room mirror. First he roused himself to action by emptying a bottle of strong tranquillizers known as 'Mandrax' of its contents and breaking the pills into tiny fragments on a nearby table. He then produced a large bottle of Brylcream, an extremely greasy form of British hair gel, and emptied the whole jar on to the pills. Next, taking the main residue of this gunk in both hands, he lifted it aloft, dumping the whole filthy mess on top of his head, letting it slowly seep on to his scalp and duly down his neck. Then he turned, picked up his white Telecaster with the groovy mirrored discs reflecting out, and stepped uncertainly towards the stage.

A quarter of an hour later, as the tom-toms were thumping their way into trance-time, the bass began booming out low ominous frequencies and the organ arched off into a tentative solo full of spicy Eastern clichés. But anyone could tell that Syd, once the leader, was no longer inhabiting the same planet as the other three. Sometimes he'd twang a few desultory notes, sometimes he'd run his slide up and down the strings but everything sounded so random and fragmented now that nothing he did really connected with the overall sound. Meanwhile the lighting had grown hot enough for Barrett's acid-casualty hair remedy to start running amok in several grotesque oily streams down his neck and forehead while the residue of the broken pills was being deposited all over his face. It was then that everyone could see how desperately things were going wrong, for he looked like some grotesque waxwork of himself on fire, a blurred effigy of melting flesh and brain tissue coming apart in front of his peers, his fans and his followers.

There is a photograph of Syd Barrett which sometimes appears that was taken well before the darkness descended. He's sweet sixteen and sitting cross-legged in the garden of his mother's delightful house in Cambridge, playing with a kitten. The image it conveys is the very epitome of rising sixties affluence.

His clothes are casual, his hair is neither long nor short, but already he's got the air of someone from the first ranks of England's 'You've-never-had-it-so-good' generation who knows he possesses both good looks and easy charm, someone beamingly confident about his place in the future scheme of things. Why, there's even an 'I can't help it if I'm lucky' twinkle in his eye, an impish grin that's almost impossible not to be a little seduced by. It's an image worth studying long and hard, because in only a matter of two years, maybe a little less, the twinkle in those eyes and the glow in those cheeks would be cruelly snuffed out, perhaps for ever. Also, the picture indicates the nature of Syd Barrett's roots. Nice. Genteel. Upper middle class. Cambridge. It was into this rarefied atmosphere that Barrett was born, one of five children, to Dr Max Barrett, a police pathologist (and leading British authority on infant mortality), and his wife. He was always a popular, conscientious student, gifted artistically, and girls found him attractive.

Storm Thorgeson, another Cambridge lad who went on to enjoy a long creative relationship with the Pink Floyd as their sleeve designer, remembers Barrett as a 'bright, extrovert kid. By 1962 we were all into Jimmy Smith. Then 1963 brought dope and rock. Syd was one of the first to get into the Beatles and the Stones. He smoked dope, pulled chicks – the usual thing. He had no problems on the surface. He was no introvert as far as I could tell back then.'

The same year he was caught merrily posing with his kitten he'd already joined his first group, Geoff Mott and the Mottoes, a timid-sounding youth club ensemble, fond of strumming out Cliff Richard and the Shadows numbers in the dens of their parents' houses. Barrett would soon leave his childhood chums to secure a short tenure as bassist in a fledgeling R'n'B outfit known as the Hollering Blues. At roughly the same time he began strumming an acoustic guitar at one of the city's local folk clubs, notably a place called the Mill. He could be found mostly wherever attractive young people gathered together to play Beatles songs on village greens and smoke the odd stick of 'pot'.

Then came the Architectural Abdabs, or the T-Set, as they were also sometimes known. They were a five-piece, anyway, consisting of three aspiring student architects, a jazz guitarist called Bob Close and – the youngest member – recently moved to London as an art student, Roger Keith Barrett. (Barrett, like most other kids, had been landed with a nickname – 'Syd' – which somehow remained long after his schooldays had been completed.) Of the three would-be architects, the most notable was Roger Waters, a Cambridge acquaintance of Barrett and a haughty youth over six feet tall who inwardly despised the druggy scene and sensibility his group became quickly bonded to. Waters seethed with a terrible inner rage and his main obsession in life was to take control of everything he ever got involved with. His main ally was fellow student and London-based drummer Nick Mason, born into a life of luxury and fast sports cars, and more of a boozy 'hooray-Harry' type than a hippie. Rounding out the line-up was another Londoner, Richard Wright, a likeable flake who attended the same college as Waters and Mason, smoked dope, listened to a bit of jazz and noodled around on the keyboards. The band, it was generally considered, were pretty dire – but, as two of them emanated from the hip élitist circles of fruity old Cambridge, they were respected after a fashion, at least in their own area.

Before the advent of the Pink Floyd, Barrett had three brooding interests in life – music, painting and religion. A number of Barrett's seniors in Cambridge were starting to get involved in an obscure form of Eastern mysticism known as 'Sant Mat' or 'The Path of the Masters', which involved heavy bouts of meditation, much contemplation of purity and the inner light, and the dispensing of wisdom by means of cosmic riddles. Syd attempted to involve himself in the faith, but was turned down for being 'too young' (he was nineteen at the time). The rejection was said to have troubled him deeply. 'Syd has always had this big phobia about his age,' states Pete Barnes, who became involved in the labyrinthine complexities of Barrett's affairs and general psyche after the Floyd split. 'I mean, when we would try to get him back into the studio to record he would get very defensive and say, "I'm only twenty-four, I'm still young. I've got time." That thing with religion could have been partly responsible for it.'

At any rate, Barrett lost all interest in spiritualism after the incident and soon enough he'd be giving up his painting too. This was unfortunate as he'd been a good enough artist to land a scholarship at the prestigious Camberwell Art School in the London suburb of Peckham. Both Dave Gilmour and Storm claim that Barrett's painting showed exceptional promise: 'Syd was a great artist. I loved his work, but he just stopped. First it was the religion, then the painting. He was starting to shut himself off slowly even then.'

Music, still, remained. The Ab-Dabs . . . well, let's forget about them and examine the 'Pink Floyd Sound' instead, which was really just the old band but minus Bob Close, who 'never quite fitted in'. The Pink Floyd Sound name came from Syd, after a blues record he owned which featured two bluesmen from Georgia, Pink Anderson and Floyd Council. The two Christian names meshed together nicely so . . . Anyway, the band was still none too inspiring – no original material, but long, anarchic versions of 'Louie Louie' and 'Road Runner' into which would be interspersed liberal dosages of staccato freak-out guitar white-noise and snake charmer's organ solos. 'Freak-out' was happening in the States at the time – the time being late 1966, the year of 'Happening Ten Years Time Ago', the Mothers of Invention and the first lysergic croaks from the West Coast. Not to mention *Revolver* and 'Eight Miles High'. The future looked so 'day-glo' bright, in six months' time everyone would be having to sport little wire-rimmed dark glasses and pretend to be in the grip of some intense spiritual awakening. But the Pink Floyd Sound weren't exactly looking to the future at this juncture. Peter Jenner, a lecturer at the London School of Economics, and John 'Hoppy' Hopkins, two of the London sixties counterculture's more dynamic figures, were in the audience for one of their first London gigs and were impressed enough to offer them some sort of management deal there and then. Admits Jenner:

'It was one of the first rock events I'd seen. I didn't know anything about rock really.' (Jenner and Hopkins had in fact made one offer prior to the Floyd – to a band they'd heard on advance tape from New York called the Velvet Underground.) 'Actually the Floyd then were barely semi-pro standard, now I think about it. But I was so impressed by the electric guitar sound. The band was just at the point of breaking up then. It was weird. They just thought, "Oh, well, might as well pack it all in." But as we came along, they decided to change their minds.'

The first underground coup involved adding a light show and setting up the UFO concerts. Jenner and Hopkins were leading emissaries of London's alternative-underground network, and by allying themselves with this pair the Floyd became automatically the flagship band for the English underground movement. The next was activating a policy of playing only original compositions.

This is where Syd Barrett came into his own. Barrett hadn't really composed tunes before this. He'd come up with a nonsense song called 'Effervescing Elephant' when he was maybe sixteen and he'd once put music to a poem, to be found in James Joyce's *Ulysses*, called 'Golden Hair', but that's all he had to show when he first started the Floyd.

'Syd was really amazing though,' says Jenner. 'I mean, his inventiveness was quite astounding. All those songs from that whole Pink Floyd phase were written in no more than six months. He just started and took it from there.'

The first manifestation of Barrett's songwriting talents was a bizarre opus entitled 'Arnold Layne' which dealt with a male cross-dresser stealing women's underclothing from suburban washing lines. (Barrett had drawn the lyrics from real-life observations around Cambridge.) It was weird, it was highly controversial and it was incredibly hip with its Fellini organ, bizarre subject matter and Barrett's dead-pan quintessentially English monotone of a voice guiding the whole thing quaintly along.

The Floyd were by now big stuff around Swinging London. Looking back on those early days, it was all very frivolous but the music already had a depth and a sense of mystery. Certainly, enough for prestigious folk like Brian Epstein to mouth off rhapsodies of praise on French radio and all the 'chic' mags to throw in the token mention. There were even TV shows – good late-night avant-garde programmes for Hampstead trendies like *Look of the Week* on which the Floyd played 'Pow R. Toc H'. Jenner remembers:

'Syd's influences were very much the Stones, the Beatles, the Byrds and Love. The Stones were the prominent ones, he wore out his copy of *Between the Buttons* very quickly. Love's first album too. In fact, I was once trying to tell him about this Arthur Lee song I couldn't remember the title of, so I just hummed the main riff. Syd picked up his guitar and followed what I was humming chord-wise. The chord pattern he worked out he went on to use as the main riff for "Interstellar Overdrive".'

As for his guitar playing: 'He had this technique that I found very pleasing. Not that he was what you'd call a guitar hero. He wasn't remotely in the class of Page or Clapton, say.'

The Floyd cult was growing as Barrett's creativity was beginning to hit its stride. This creativity set the stage in Barrett's songwriting for what can only be described as the quintessential marriage of the two ideal forms of English psychedelia – musical rococo freak-outs joining together with Barrett's sudden ascent into the lyrical realms of ye olde English whimsical loone, wherein dwelt the likes of Edward Lear and Kenneth Grahame.

Pervy old Lewis Carroll, of course, presided at the very head of the tea-party. And so Arnold Layne and washing lines gave way to the whole Games-for-May ceremony and 'See Emily Play'. 'I was sleeping in the woods one night after a gig we'd played somewhere, when I saw this girl appear before me. That girl is Emily.' Thus spoke Syd Barrett in the May of '67, obviously high as a kite lost in spring.

It was glorious for a while. *Piper at the Gates of Dawn* was being recorded at the same time as *Sergeant Pepper* over in Abbey Road and the two bands would occasionally meet up to check out each other's latest masterpiece. Paul McCartney would sometimes step out to share a joint and bestow his papal blessing on *Piper*, a record that manages to capture Barrett's blinding spurt of acid creativity in its perfect ascendant. There are songs about hallucinating felines, the I-Ching, about strange exotic fables and the spirit of Albion suddenly transformed into spaced age day-glo. It's a breath-taking record and things only start to cloud over at the very end, with 'Bike', which augurs things to come, reeking as it does of warped crazy basements and Barrett's eccentricities beginning to go the way of the warped.

For, concurrent with all this mind-blowing music-making, strange things were starting to happen to the Floyd but more particularly to Barrett himself. 'See Emily Play' went Top Five, which enabled Barrett to live out his pop star infatuation number to the hilt. The Hendrix curls, kaftans from 'Granny's', snakeskin boots and Fender Telecasters were now all his for the asking. But there were also all these new unstabilizing elements to take into account. First came the ego problems and slight prima donna fits, but gradually the Floyd, Jenner and all, realized that something deeper was going on. Take the Floyd's three *Top of the Pops* appearances for 'Emily'. 'The first time,' says Jenner, 'Syd dressed up like a pop star. The second time he came on in his straight-forward, fairly scruffy clothes, looking rather unshaven. The third time he came to the studio in his pop star clothes and then changed into complete rags for the actual TV spot.' It was all something to do with the fact that John Lennon had stated publicly he wouldn't appear on *Top of the Pops*. Syd seemed to envisage Lennon as some sort of yardstick by which to measure his own situation as a pop star. 'Syd was always complaining that John Lennon owned a house while he only had a flat,' states Peter Barnes.

But there were darker manifestations. Barrett was at that point involved in a relationship with an attractive model named Lynsey Horner – an affair which took an ugly turn for the worse when the lady appeared on Peter Jenner's doorstep fairly savagely beaten up. 'I couldn't believe it at the time. I had this firm picture of Syd as this really gentle guy, which is what he was basically.' (In fact there are numerous fairly unpleasant tales about this particular affair, including one that claims Barrett locked the girl in a room for a solid week, pushing water-biscuits under the door so she wouldn't starve.) To make matters worse Syd's eyes were starting to cement themselves into a foreboding, nay, quite terrifying stare which *really* started to put the frighteners on anyone in his company. The head would tilt back slightly, the eyes would get misty and bloated. Then they would stare right at you and right through you at the same time. Perhaps it was just the drugs. He was subjected to a frightening amount of the stuff and seems to have been 'tripping' constantly throughout 1967. Even when he wasn't dosing himself, sundry flat-mates – among them the aptly named 'Mad Sue' and 'Mad Jack' – would be slipping it into his tea, unbeknownst to him.

Such activity can, of course, lead to severe mental disorientation, but I fear one has to stride manfully blindfolded into a rather more Freudian landscape to understand what essentially went wrong with Syd Barrett. Many of the people I talked to claimed that Barrett's dilemma was triggered by certain childhood traumas: the youngest of a large family, Syd was heavily affected by the sudden death of his father when he was only twelve years old, and was spoilt by a strong-willed mother who may or may not have imposed a strange distinction between the dictates of fantasy and reality. Each contention forms its own patchwork quilt of insinuations and potential cause-and-effect mechanisms. 'Everyone is supposed to have fun when they're young – I don't know why, but I never did,' said Barrett in an interview to *Rolling Stone*, in autumn 1971.

According to Peter Jenner: 'I think we tended to underrate the extent of his problem. I mean, I thought that I could act as a mediator – y'know, having been a sociology teacher at the LSE and all that guff . . . I think, though . . . one thing I regret now was that I made demands on Syd. He'd written "See Emily Play" and suddenly everything had to be seen in commercial terms. I think we may have pressurized him into a state of paranoia about having to come up with another hit single. Also we may have been the darlings of London, but out in the suburbs it was fairly terrible. Before "Emily" we'd have things thrown at us onstage. After "Emily" it was screaming girls wanting to hear our hit song.'

So the Floyd hit the ballroom circuit and Syd was starting to play up. An American tour was then set up in November – three dates at the Fillmore West in San Francisco and an engagement at LA's Cheetah Club. Barrett's dishevelled psyche started truly manifesting itself though when the Floyd were forced on to some TV shows. *Dick Clark's Bandstand* was disastrous because it needed a miming job on the band's part and 'Syd wasn't into moving his lips that day'. The *Pat Boone Show* was even more surreal: Boone actually tried to interview Barrett on screen, asking him several inane questions and getting a truly classic catatonic stare for an answer. 'Eventually we cancelled out on *Beach Party*,' recalls Jenner's partner and tour manager, Andrew King, wincing slightly at the memory. So then they returned to England, and the rest of the Floyd, or at least Waters and Mason, had made the decision. On the one hand, Barrett was the songwriter and central figure; on the other, his 'out-there'-ness was simply too irksome to tolerate any further.

But not before a final studio session at De Lane Lea took place – a mad anarchic affair which spawned three of Barrett's truly vital twilight rantings. Unfortunately only one has ever been released. 'Jugband Blues', the only Barrett vocal and composition to appear on the Pink Floyd's *Saucerful of Secrets*, is as good an explanation as any for Syd not appearing on the rest of the album. 'Y'see, even at that point, Syd actually knew what was happening to him,' claims Jenner. 'I mean, "Jugband Blues" is the ultimate self-diagnosis on a state of schizophrenia.' Barrett even had a Salvation Army band troop in during the middle of the number, much to everyone else's utter shock. Of the two unreleased one is a masterful splurge of blood-curdling lunacy, 'Scream Your Last Scream', the other, 'Vegetable Man', a crazy sing-along. 'Syd,' recalls Jenner, 'was around at my house just before he had to go to record and, because a song was needed, he just wrote a description of what he was wearing at the time. Then he just threw in a chorus that went "Vegetable Man – where are you?"'

A nationwide tour of Great Britain followed – Jimi Hendrix, the Move, the Nice and the Floyd all on one bill – but it didn't help matters at all. Syd often wouldn't turn up on time, sometimes didn't play at all, and always sat by himself on the tour coach, looked estranged while the rest of the Floyd socialized with the Nice (guitarist David O'List played with the band when Barrett was incapable). Apparently Hendrix used to refer to the Floyd leader – somewhat ironically – as 'Laughing Syd Barrett'. But surely these two uncrowned kings of acid rock must have socialized in some capacity? 'Not really,' states Jenner. 'Hendrix had his own limousine. Syd didn't really talk to anyone. I mean, by now he was going onstage and playing one chord throughout the set. He was into this thing of total anarchistic experiment and never really considered the other members of the band.'

There was also this thing with Syd that the Floyd were 'my band'. Enter Dave Gilmour, not long back from working with various groups in France – an old mate and an able guitarist. The implications were obvious. Jenner recalls: 'At the time Dave was doing very effective take-offs of Hendrix-style guitar-playing. So the band said, "Play like Syd Barrett."' But surely Dave Gilmour had his own style – the slide and echo sound? 'That's *Syd* onstage. Syd used to play with slide and a bunch of echo-boxes.' (Gilmour begs to differ on this point, claiming it was he who first introduced Barrett to this particular technique.)

The Floyd played maybe four gigs as a five-piece and then Barrett was ousted. The final outrage had been a rehearsal in which Syd had forced them through an excruciating new composition which kept changing chords, timing and lyrics. The only constant was the chorus which had Barrett shouting, 'Have you got it yet?' (the song's apparent title) and the others having to chant back at him, 'No, no, no.' It took them over three hours to realize it was Barrett's way of saying 'Fuck you, you stupid bourgeois wankers.' But then again, maybe he thought what they'd played had been truly brilliant. It was impossible to tell anymore. The next day, on their way to a gig, Roger Waters forbade the others in the car to pick Barrett up and that was the last time he ever played as a member of the Pink Floyd. In one sense it was a courageous move – in another it was very ruthless. But everyone else thought it rather justi-fied. Except Syd. 'Yeah, Syd does resent the Floyd,' claims Jenner. 'I don't know – he may *still* call them "my band" for all I know.'

So Barrett loped off into the stoned hinterlands of Earls Court to sink back into some full-time freak-flag flying, but not before he'd stayed over at South Kensington awhile with Storm Thorgeson:

'Syd was well into his "orbiting" phase by then. He was trav-elling very fast in his own private sphere and I thought I could be a mediator of some sort. Y'see, I think you're going to have to make the point that Syd's madness was not caused by any linear progression of events, but more a circular haze of situations that meshed together on top of themselves and Syd. His stay didn't last long and didn't end nicely. I just couldn't handle those stares anymore.'

By this time the Floyd and Blackhill Enterprises had parted company, with Jenner choosing Barrett as a brighter hope. What happened to the Floyd is now history: they survived and flourished with mighty concept albums often reflecting on their fallen leader's mental condition in their lyrics. Meanwhile Syd most certainly did not flourish. *The Madcap Laughs*, Barrett's first solo album, took a sporadic but none the less laborious year to complete. Production credits constantly changed hands – from Peter Jenner to Malcolm Jones (who gave up half-way through), finally to Dave Gilmour and Roger Waters. By this time Barrett's creative processes refused to mesh properly and so the results were often jagged and unapproachable. Basically they were exercises in distance – the Madcap waving whimsically out from the haze. Or maybe he was drowning.

Many of the tracks, though, like 'Terrapin', almost just lay there, scratching themselves in front of you. They exist completely inside their own little world, like weird insects or exotic fish, the listener looking inside the tank at the activity. 'I think Syd was in good shape when he made *Madcap*,' Jenner offers. 'He was still writing good songs, probably in the same state as he was during "Jugband Blues".'

Others beg to differ – Thorgeson, for example: 'The thing was that all those guys had to cope with Syd out of his head on Mandrax half the time. He got so mandied up on those sessions, his hand would slip through the strings and he'd fall off the stool.'

June Bolan, ex-wife of Marc and one-time secretary of Peter Jenner, has even worse recollections:

'I went to all Syd's acid breakdowns. He used to come round to my house at five in the morning covered in mud from Holland Park when he'd freaked out. He used to go to the Youth Hostel in Holland Park, climb up on the roof and get wrecked and spaced, and he'd walk all the way to Shepherd's Bush, where I was living.

'He was extraordinary . . . Like a candle that was about to be snuffed out at any minute. Really, all illuminations. He took a lot of acid. Lots of people can take some acid and cope with it in their lives, but if you take three or four trips in a day and you do that every day . . . And then, because it was the hip drug, you go around somebody's house for a cup of tea and they'd spike you. People did that a lot to Syd.'

Barrett, the second album, was recorded in a much shorter space of time. Dave Gilmour was called in to produce, and brought in Rick Wright and Jerry Shirley, Humble Pie's drummer, to help:

'We had basically three alternatives at that point, working with Syd,' says Gilmour. 'One, we could actually work with him in the studio, playing along as he put down his tracks – which was almost impossible, though we succeeded on "Gigolo Aunt". The second was laying down some kind of track before and then having him play over it. The third was him putting his basic ideas down with just guitar and vocals and then we'd try and make something out of it all. It was mostly a case of me saying, "Well, what have you got then, Syd?" and he'd search around and eventually work something out.'

The Barrett disintegration process continued throughout this album, giving it a feel more akin to that of a one-off demo. Occasionally songs would be shot through with sustained glimpses of Barrett's poetic sensibility at its most vivid, like 'Wolfpack', or 'Rats', with menacing double-edged nonsense rhymes. 'Dominoes' is probably the album's most arresting track, as well as being the only real pointer to what the Floyd might have sounded like had Barrett been more in control of his 'orbiting'. The song is rather exquisite – reflecting a classic kind of lazy English summer afternoon ambiance which spirals up and almost defies time and space, before drifting into an archetypal Floyd minor-chord refrain straight out of *More*. Gilmour says: 'The song just ended after Syd had finished singing and I wanted a gradual fade so I added that section myself. I even ended up playing the drums on that.'

Most intimates claim Gilmour by this time had become perhaps the only person around who could communicate effectively with Barrett: 'Oh, I don't think *anyone* can communicate with Syd. I did those albums because I like the songs, not, as I suppose some might think, because I felt guilty taking his place in the Floyd. I was concerned that he wouldn't fall completely apart. The final re-mix on *Madcap* was all mine as well.'

In between the two solo albums EMI Harvest or Morrison had decided to set up a bunch of press interviews for Barrett, whose style of conversation was scarcely suited to the tailor-made requirements of the media. Most couldn't make any sense whatsoever out of his verbal ramblings, others suspected something was seriously wrong and warily pinpointed the Barrett malady in their pieces. Peter Barnes did one of the interviews:

'It was fairly ludicrous on the surface. I mean, you just had to go along with it all – Syd would say something completely incongruous one minute like, "It's getting heavy, innit," and you'd just have to say, "Yeah, Syd, it's getting heavy," and the conversation would dwell on *that* for five minutes. Actually, listening to the tape afterwards you could work out that there was some kind of logic there – except that Syd would suddenly be answering a question you'd asked him ten minutes ago while you were off on a different topic altogether!'

Another Syd quirk had always been his obsessive tampering with the fine head of black hair that rested firmly on the Barrett cranium. Somewhere along the line, our hero had decided to shave it all down to a sparse grizzle, known appropriately as the 'Borstal crop'. 'I can't really comment too accurately,' states Jenner, 'but I'm rather tempted to view it as a symbolic gesture. Y'know – goodbye to being a pop-star, and all that.' Barrett, by this time, was well slumped into his real twilight period, living in the cellar of his mother's house in Cambridge. And this is where the story gets singularly depressing. An interview with *Rolling Stone* at Christmas 1971 showed Barrett to be living out his life with a certain whimsical self-reliance. At one point in the conversation, he declared, 'I'm really totally together, I even think I should be.'

Almost exactly a year later, out of the sheer torment of his own inertia, Barrett went temporarily completely haywire and smashed his head through the basement ceiling. In between these two dates, he went back into the studio to attempt another record. 'It was an abortion,' claims Barnes. 'He just kept overdubbing guitar part on guitar part until it was just a total chaotic mess. He also wouldn't show anyone his lyrics – I fear actually because he hadn't written any.' Jenner was also present: 'It was horribly frustrating because there were sporadic glimpses of the old Syd coming through, and then it would all get horribly distorted again.' Nothing remains from the sessions.

And then there was Stars, a band formed by Twink, ex-drummer of Tomorrow, Pretty Things and Pink Fairies. Twink was another native of Cambridge, had previously known Barrett marginally well, and somehow dragged the Madcap into forming a band including himself and a bass player called Jack Monck. The main Stars gig occurred at the Corn Exchange in Cambridge where they were second-billed to the MC5. It was an exercise in total musical cacophony and, after half an hour or so, Barrett simply unplugged his guitar and sauntered off the stage to return once again to his mother and his basement. Since that time Syd Barrett may or may not have worked in a factory for a week or so/worked as a gardener/tried to enrol as an architectural student/grown mushrooms in his basement/been a tramp/spent two weeks in New York busking/tried to become a Pink Floyd roadie.

All the above are stories told to me by various semi-authentic sources. More than likely, most of them are total fabrications. One thing though appears to be clear: Syd Barrett is unable to write songs anymore. ('Either that or he writes songs and won't show them to anyone,' says Jenner.) In the meantime, Barrett has been elevated into the position of perhaps the leading mysterioso figure in the whole of rock. Arthur Lee and Brian Wilson are the only others who loom anywhere near as large in that bizarre twilight zone of notoriety and myth-weaving. In countries as diverse as France, the USA and Japan, Barrett is still a source of fanatical concern. Throughout the seventies there was even a Syd Barrett International Appreciation Society centred in Britain which put out magazines, T-shirts and buttons.

'I mentioned the Society to Syd once,' states Peter Barnes. 'He just said it was OK, y'know. He's really not interested in any of it. It's ironic, I suppose – he's much bigger now as the silent cult-figure doing nothing than he was when he was functioning. It's strange also because apparently he still talks about making a third album. I don't know – I think Dave is the only one who could pull it off. There seems to be a relationship there.'

Dave Gilmour is decidedly less convinced about the strength of his relationship with Syd Barrett, however:

'First of all, I don't know what Syd thinks or *how* he thinks. Still, I think, of all the people you've spoken to probably only Storm and I really know the whole story and can see it all in the right focus. I mean, Syd was a strange guy even back in Cambridge. He was a very respected figure back there in his own way. In my opinion, it's a family situation that's at the root of it all. His father's death affected him very heavily and his mother always pampered him, almost made him out to be a genius of sorts. I remember I really started to get worried when I went along to the session for "See Emily Play". He was strange even then. That terrifying stare of his was already starting to appear.

'Yeah, it was fairly obvious that I was brought in to take over from him, at least on stage. But it was absolutely impossible to gauge his feelings about it. I honestly don't think Syd has opinions as such. He functions on a totally different plain of logic, and some people will claim, "Well yeah man he's on a higher cosmic level," but basically there's something drastically wrong. It wasn't just the drugs. We'd both done acid before the whole Floyd thing. It's just a mental foible which grew out of all proportion. I remember all sorts of strange things happening. At one point he was wearing lipstick, dressing in high heels and believing he had homosexual tendencies. We all felt he should have gone to see a psychiatrist, though someone in fact played an interview he did to R. D. Laing, and Laing claimed he was incurable. What can you do? We did a couple of his songs live on *Ummagumma*. We used "Jugband Blues" for no ulterior motive. It was just a good song. I mean, that *Nice Pair* collection will see him doing all right for a couple of years. All of which only postpones the day of judgement, I suppose. Sometimes I think that maybe, if he was left to his own devices, he might just get it together. But it is a tragedy – a terrible tragedy because the guy was a real innovator. One of the three or four greats along with Dylan. I know though that something is terribly wrong because Syd isn't happy, and that really is the criterion, isn't it? But then I suppose it's all part and parcel of being a legend in your own lifetime.'

Brian Jones, Tortured Narcissus

To any of the countless prolific dreamers of my generation – those of us who were adolescents in the sixties – Brian Jones meant something, and from the moment we made contact with his perfect blond impudence it was weird love at first sight. When I first saw him live with the Rolling Stones it was early 1964, I was twelve, they were only weeks away from being the biggest thing to hit England since the bubonic plague – and, oh, I will never forget it. They looked simply out of this world, like a new delinquent aristocracy, and they played music of a stunning arrogance and unbridled potency. And they had Brian Jones, who really appeared like their leader that night, with his china-cat smile of contagious evil assurance. He looked to me like a young man who had everything – charm, beauty, grace, success, infamy – every wondrous virtue this world could hope to offer, and for a long time afterwards his vision epitomized everything I in turn could hope to aspire to.

The next time I saw the Rolling Stones live five years hence, Brian Jones was there but not in the flesh. He was just a huge cardboard cut-out representation at the side of a stage. He was five days dead and the Rolling Stones, cool and disengaged as ever, were playing at his wake. The strange thing again was how little genuine sorrow there was emanating from the 250,000 plus crowd gathered at Hyde Park. A sense of loss, perhaps, but not sorrow. In a *Rolling Stone* obituary already circulating that afternoon Greil Marcus stated how when he'd heard that Jones was dead he'd felt no sense of shock, only that this was the most natural thing to hear happening to this tormented narcissus. It was true: the way Brian Jones lived his life he had nowhere to fall but into the grave.

He was born on 28 February 1942 in Cheltenham, and it was genteel, conservative Cheltenham as much as drugs, stardom or notoriety that was to prove his undoing. Certainly Keith Richards has strong views on this:

'Brian was from Cheltenham, a very genteel town full of old ladies. It's a Regency thing, you know, Beau Brummel and all that. Just a seedy place full of aspirations to be an aristocratic town. It rubs off on anyone who comes from there . . . He [Brian] had to conquer London first, that was his big thing. He felt happy when we'd made it in London, when we were the hip band in London. For me and Mick, it didn't mean a thing, because it was just our town.'

His mother was a rather prim, religiously finicky woman. His father, a small Welshman from whom his son gained some of his singular looks, was quiet and deferential, inwardly seething with terrible anger. He had an older sister, whom a psychiatric report, one of many in his last years alive, would identify as a source of intense childhood jealousy on Brian Jones's side. 'He never truly felt loved,' concluded the report.

He was obviously a prolific dreamer, and a prolific hustler too. From a very early age Brian Jones must have learnt just how contagiously precociously charming he could be and how by using this easy charm he could go a long way to getting whatever he wanted. Apparently excellent scholastically, he none the less bucked that system by staging a mini-revolt at school and getting turfed out as a result. If there was ever a turning-point in his life, it was probably here, but it's hard to tell. After all, he was always a pretty audacious guy: already a girl was pregnant, the family shamed and he didn't really seem to care. He let that easy charm grease his path away from the spectre of provincial ruination time and time again. Meanwhile he was being audaciously awful as a saxophone player in a

Duane Eddy-styled combo, the Ramrods, but as a guitarist and harmonica player he started showing weird promise. He became a rhythm'n'blues obsessive – and as his best instrumental contributions to Rolling Stones records will later readily attest, this was the music that he had the most feel for. He aped old blues stylists like Jimmy Reed and Elmore James and planned on changing his name to Elmo Lewis, moving to London and becoming a big wheel. In 1961, in a tiny Cheltenham club, Alexis Korner, performing with Chris Barber's Jazz Band, was accosted by an extremely intense young man who also was extremely inebriated: 'It was Brian, of course. He was accompanied by a mate of his, I seem to recall, who said nothing. Not that anyone else could, because Brian was this pent-up ball of obsessive energy, talking away thirteen-to-the-dozen in an incredibly intense manner.'

That's how people talk when they reminisce about Brian Jones. 'I vividly recall the first time I met Brian but I can't for the life of me remember where I first met Mick,' Korner once told me, and he was being honest not bitchy because already Brian Jones had reinvented himself, he was larger than life and on fire for acclaim. And of course he was always hustling, stealing and petty pilfering. More often than not, he appears to have been caught, yet each time he slipped through with only a caution. This happened also in London just after he'd moved down: sacked from a record shop for having his hand in the till.

But by then he'd encountered Mick – then Mike – Jagger and Keith Richards after an impromptu performance sitting in with Alexis Korner and Cyril Davis. His ability to duplicate 'Dust My Blues' live with all the slide guitar embellishments had the pair royally gob-smacked, and they were even more impressed, if a little shocked probably, by Jones's casual disclosure that he had two illegitimate children by different girls and the second one was living with him now there in London, but he was just living off her money, man, you know what I mean. Actually

Jagger and Richards were much less worldly and didn't know what exactly he meant but they nodded because they got the gist right enough and because they definitely wanted in. From that moment on the Rolling Stones were born and the sixties started really swinging.

To the vital Rolling Stones equation Jones brought with him a brawny Glaswegian straight-looking geezer-type, Ian Stewart, a hard worker who played strong piano and whom Brian Jones would soon enough back-stab and betray. Together this fourpiece (with Jagger moonlighting at the LSE) rehearsed, and, with Keith and Brian living in now mythic squalor over in Chelsea's Edith Grove, a sound was formed: Keith Richards's primordial gut riffing – the very churn of sedition itself – over which Brian Jones's guitar carelessly agitated, investing the blend with a seething malicious energy that was his and his alone. This and the sheer maniacally assertive force of his personality made him the leader of the Rolling Stones at this time and it was a position he was to connive his way into steadfastly maintaining until the other members could be bothered to dispute it. He did himself no favours here because, as the others, Jagger, Richards, stone-faced Charlie Watts and Bill Wyman – the bassist they engaged simply because they needed his amp-power – were soon to discover, behind the easy charm and china-cat precocity lay a shallow, maladjusted temperament. As a leader he was just hopeless, playing one off against another ceaselessly. When he went behind the others' backs to demand an extra £5 per gig for himself the jig was well and truly up, but it was over anyway the minute sixties megaspiv Andrew Oldham, nineteen, laid eyes on the Stones.

That Oldham and Jones never got on is a little ironic because the hype that Oldham successfully sold the world – the Rolling Stones-are-not-just-another-group-they're-a-way-of-life – was totally dependent on the infuriating dimension that Brian Jones gave the whole endeavour: because the fans instinctively guessed that the 'way of life' they intimated at was the one Brian Jones more than any other appeared to be leading on a day-to-day basis. Anyway, although they initially conspired together (Ian Stewart's expulsion was their first piece of smarmy manoeuvring), they hated each other, and Oldham wanted Jones out before 'Satisfaction' even, probably pretty much from day one. For, reckless and beautiful Jones may have been, but Oldham's showbiz instincts told him that there was no staying power in a Brian Jones. He was too much of a pain in the arse, one big problem. If he could have written songs, if he could have focused and articulated his torment instead of letting it turn him into a self-indulgent brattish malcontent, then things might have been different. But when Oldham successfully elicited Rolling Stones original material from the hardworking and more disciplined Jagger and Richards, Brian Jones's careerist and artistic pipe-dreams of controlling the Stones framework evaporated before him.

In things that really mattered, Jones was always his own worst enemy anyway. His natural talents he squandered, as simple as that. After the beginning of 1965 he rarely if ever played guitar on a Rolling Stones record again, forcing Keith Richards ceaselessly to double-track in the studio because Jones was too out of it, or because he was ill and just didn't feel like turning up. On the ceaseless treadmill of a gruelling world tour schedule through 1965 and 1966 Brian Jones was always the weak link. It didn't matter so much that he couldn't – or wouldn't (he'd defiantly vamp the riff to 'Popeye the Sailorman' during 'Satisfaction', for example) – play his prescribed parts because at Rolling Stones concerts in the sixties all definition was lost under a sulphurous wall of frantic strumming and screaming anyway. But when he physically couldn't make it onstage – he was always being hospitalized for nervous breakdowns, for taking too many drugs or because he'd broken his hand beating up a girlfriend – the other four hated and resented him. Not without reason, one feels.

Also, he was always hanging out with the rivals. He was a bit of a groupie really in that way, though they all treated him as an equal. The Beatles regarded him with genuine affection (they even recorded with him), Warhol thought he was just fabulous, and Dylan was fascinated by him. 'How's yer paranoia meter runnin'',' he'd ask Jones, a twisted mass of helpless charm but always delightfully turned out. And though he'd agonize about his increasing isolation from the other Stones, who'd inevitably be working while he was out partying with his peers, he was secure, whether he knew it or not, in his capacity for being the kind of star who just has to 'be there' in order to generate the very mystique that culminates in a force like the Rolling Stones transforming itself from an irritant to a national outrage. In his finest photos (and until 1968 there was no such thing as a bad photo of Brian Jones) he looks like a little prince, just exquisite. Quite simply, he was the quintessential beautiful damned face of the sweet, sick sixties. And he was also the sixties' baddest dandy. This was understood everywhere, it seems. All the big wheels stepped back when Brian Jones walked into a club, stoned of course, particularly when Anita Pallenberg was in tow. She was 'the only one he ever really loved', say his friends, and certainly she got inside him, tormented him like no other woman he ever got to know, because Anita Pallenberg, a North Italian actress, model and full-time swinger, was as reckless, abandoned and amoral as him but much tougher. He couldn't stand to be without her for a minute, but when he was with her he couldn't stand not to hit her. They looked like twins – eerily beautiful together – and were an item for one sexy ruinous year between the fall of '66 and the spring of '67. It was a hell of a fling. And it could only get worse when Pallenberg left Jones in Tangier to take off with Keith Richards.

He'd been 'behaving disgustingly', according to the latter. 'I just said, "Baby, we're getting out of here."' Another source now opines:

'Anita was no fool. She first thought that the real power of the Rolling Stones lay with Brian, but after a while she found him to be weak . . . She found him pathetic in many ways. Her timing was perfect: she intuitively knew that the real power base in the Stones – the one strong man – was Keith and she latched on to him. Keith couldn't believe his luck.'

With that it was game, set and match to Jagger–Richards in the psychic war over who meant the most in the Rolling Stones, the war that Brian Jones had obsessively instigated against them in the first place. He had every excuse now to get even more fucked up and did so with a terrible abandon. He'd always taken too many drugs but now his consumption rocketed alarmingly, as he chased after numbing stupefaction with a vengeance. 'I'll never make it to thirty,' he'd once confided to Richards, just before their flimsy comradeship was destroyed once and for all by Pallenberg's 'betrayal', and now it was just a matter of time before he fulfilled his own prophecy. When Alexis Korner spotted him at some London 'happening' in the late summer of '67, three months after the break-up with Anita, he was 'already starting to look hideous . . . Like a debauched vision of Louis XIV on acid, gone to seed. It was then that I suddenly realized there could be such a thing as an acid casualty.' Not that it was just acid. Tony Sanchez, a minder and dealer for the Stones who divided his time and loyalties between Richards and Jones, once described to me the typical start to a day for Brian Jones in 1967 through 1968:

'He'd wake up in the morning, take leapers [speed], cocaine, some morphine, a few tabs of acid and maybe some mandrax. Then he'd try to get dressed and end up with, like, a lizard-skin boot on one foot and a pink shoe on the other. Then he'd find he couldn't stand up.'

Keith Richards now maintains that Jones's chief drug problem was barbiturates: 'He had an obsession about piercing the capsules so that they'd get into his bloodstream quicker. He knew all these junkie tricks!' Barbs and alcohol combine to cause an often fatal wooziness. Jones was once spotted in this habitually warped condition attempting to shepherd a similarly blotto Judy Garland out of a club – talk about the blind leading the blind! He'd been an alcoholic anyway since late '64. Back then Charlie Watts, to his credit, had cared enough to try and help him, but it was all to no avail. Brian Jones never seemed to grasp simple common sense. When he entered a clinic to come to terms with 'stress' and 'nervous fatigue', he took with him all the drugs that had helped put him there in the first place.

This was the essence of his pitiful nature: he'd plough through the dolly birds with a rapacious, again often malicious, zeal and then agonize fretfully about the loveless life he led, the fact that none of his countless conquests really 'loved him'. Suki Poitier, the girl he picked up with briefly after Pallenberg absconded from his life another doomed blonde sixties beauty, once confided that Brian's problem was that 'he basically thought of himself as an utterly useless member of society', and it's this one line that ultimately says more about him than all the reams of psychiatric reports and surveys he underwent in 1968, only to have their contents leaked before he had even been afforded a decent burial. For though he harboured all the flaming arrogant vanity of a peacock, he possessed the sense of self-worth of a hopeless psychic cripple. Self-love and self-loathing were always in conflict, the latter getting stronger as each blurry barbiturate minute of his life ticked away.

The Stones, meanwhile, were off being industrious. They were survivors after all, and Brian Jones was not. After the psychedelic folly of 1967's *Satanic Majesties Request* they were back playing their lascivious pagan music again, only it was even darker now, more malevolent and assured. Their big comeback, the 1968 *Beggar's Banquet*, redefined them perfectly. They became 'the greatest rock'n'roll band in the world' instead of 'more than a group, a way of life'. The way of life Brian Jones had represented was being abandoned. He was out of step, out of time, but most of all he was just out of it.

During the *Beggar's Banquet* sessions, if he turned up at all, Brian Jones would roll up in a feeble, intoxicated state, incapable of being even remotely productive. Pallenberg and Richards were always together now, as thick as thieves, and that must have stung deeply. His paranoia meter – 'He was so paranoid by that time he was too scared to go into a shop to buy cigarettes even, because he thought anyone behind the counter had to be a plain-clothes cop' (Sanchez again) – also received a terrible caning from Jagger. 'What can I play?' Jones timidly asked the singer during one session. 'I don't know, Brian,' Jagger had replied icily, 'what *can* you play?'

'Actually,' says Alexis Korner, 'I thought Mick and Keith were very patient with Brian, particularly him being in the state he was in. They didn't broadcast his problems to anyone else, they didn't put him down publicly. They were concerned in their way. And they waited a long time to see if he could recover before starting to consider replacing him.'

By 1969, facing a crippling tax bill, the Stones wanted and needed to tour again. This was the principal reason now for Brian's exclusion because even in the last months of his life, when he seemed more settled, less desperate and drugged, he was incapable of physically sustaining a tour. After narrowly missing imprisonment for two drugs offences, the second of which all the facts seem to point to being a set-up, in '68 he'd eased up, moved out of London to take up active residence in A. A. Milne's old house. It was a gorgeous place apparently, and acquaintances remember Brian in the last weeks and months of his life pottering around the grounds like Milne's Pooh Bear, quite hopeless but helplessly charming all the same. The most poignant image in Korner's observation of Brian spending hours crouched excitedly rummaging through wardrobes and trunks full of golden trinkets which he'd try on, finest silks and velvets that he'd stroke, all the sprawling booty of his past peacock finery. When Jagger, Richards and Charlie Watts came down to tell him that they already had young Mick Taylor, a new guitar hero, waiting in the wings, Jones accepted the news graciously. Only when they departed did he break down, crying softly. A month later, five days after his departure had been made public to the world, he died – death by misadventure, the coroner stated. Late one evening, his mood buoyed by the mixture of amphetamines, barbs and alcohol he still found himself hopelessly dependent upon, he went swimming in his pool and drowned. There are still several nagging questions hanging over the circumstances of his death – a disquieting feeling that all has still not quite been revealed. For a time conspiracy theories were running riot all over the place but they've never amounted to much under scrutiny. Alexis Korner again:

'It's true that a lot of people hated Brian and some of them may have wanted him killed. But I genuinely believe it didn't happen that way. Everyone was just waiting for him to do it to himself anyway.'

Dying when he did – frankly that was the best thing that could have happened to Brian Jones. For friends and fans alike, as sick as it sounds, it was a blessing because he was getting fat, losing his looks fast, and the image of a fat ugly Brian Jones was simply intolerable. For his girlfriends, in a way, it was good too, for now they could dream about his perfect doomed sexiness without having to confront its often vicious reality. For the Stones, of course, it was perfect because the dimension no replacement could ever hope to cover was suddenly filled up by his ghost. I mean, everyone knew the Stones were *bad* but now they were so bad one of them was holding up a tombstone.

For him, too, it was the right time. He was certainly intelligent enough to understand that he could never hope to match the impact he'd had as a Rolling Stone, that without their active context he was a has-been. And he died a martyr of sorts – the first major rock death of the sixties superstar era, a whole year before Hendrix and Joplin. At his funeral a letter written from Jones to his parents during the chaos of his drug busts was read out and its plaintive plea, 'Don't judge me too hardly', became his epitaph and was duly respected for a while.

But his absence hasn't made many hearts any the fonder of his memory. 'Quite honestly, you won't find many people who genuinely liked Brian,' stated Keith Richards in 1988 before launching into a blistering put-down of his former partner-in-crime. Well, yes, of course Brian Jones must have been a constant pain to work with, but now, twenty years after his death, it's the infamous conduct and outrageous narcissism that he's regarded for, the stuff that takes up the lion's share of all those weighty Stones biographies. People duly point to his musical legacy, to little flashpoints of inspiration like the slide guitar on 'Little Red Rooster' (his own favourite) and the percussive modal malignancy of his sitar-playing on 'Paint It Black', but really they don't amount to much. What he gave to the Stones was the full force of authentically damned youth. What he lived informed Jagger and Richards's best songs, and when he died they were robbed of a whole third dimension of meaning, really, becoming first the greatest rock'n'roll band in the world, then 'it's only rock'n'roll', then . . . Well, let's face it, it's been downhill ever since and leave it like that.

'He was all right, y'know, when he wasn't too out of it or in one of his states,' a friend once told me. 'Brian's real problem . . . He couldn't feel love, he wasn't capable of feeling real love *ever*, not even for Anita really. That's why he was such a mess.'

That's it. Poor baby Brian Jones, so twisted, lost and loveless: the spirit that Jim Morrison and Patti Smith have eulogized in public verse, the image that stares out provocatively, disdainfully from all those timeless sixties photographs. He will never grow old.

Who loves you, baby?

Twilight in Babylon: The Rolling Stones after the Sixties

The first thing you need to know about my adventures with the Rolling Stones is that they pretty much all took place once the basic thrill had gone out of the group and their music. Mick Jagger himself would admit as much many years later when he informed an interviewer, 'To use a cliché, the sixties never really ended until later on in the seventies. I sort of remember the album *Exile on Main Street* being done in France and also in the United States, and after that going on tour and becoming complacent, and thinking, "It's '72. Fuck it. We've done it." We still tried after that, but I don't think the results were ever that wonderful.'

Still, back in 1973 no one wanted to believe that just yet awhile. After all, back in the sixties the Stones, the Beatles and Bob Dylan had formed rock's sparkling holy trinity but, three years into a new decade, the Beatles were no more and Bob Dylan was still locked away somewhere in the same state of confused semi-retirement he'd entered back in 1966. By contrast the Stones just seemed to go from strength to strength, reaching an all-time creative peak only the previous year with the aforementioned *Exile on Main Street* double album. The accompanying tour of America had also sprung them on to a new level of success. More fans than ever passed through the turnstiles to witness them, whilst backstage an extraordinary media circus had built up populated by Truman Capote and other bored upper-crust luminaries of an older generation. Capote finally hadn't managed to write a word on the group he'd been following around at such great expense, but a *Rolling Stone* stringer named Robert Greenfield was supposed to be releasing a book on that tour with some seriously compromising incidents of a sexual and pharmaceutical nature prominent in the text. More alarmingly, all those incidents and more had been filmed by a Canadian called Robert Frank and he'd edited them together into a frankly mind-boggling piece of *cinéma vérité* he'd entitled *Cocksucker Blues*.

I mention this as a possible explanation for why, in the autumn of 1973, I was suddenly commissioned by the Rolling Stones office to write a short 'up-beat' official account of the group's European tour that season. I just assumed they intended whatever I croaked up to counteract the murky revelations of these other projects. (In actual fact the Stones owned the rights to the Frank film so its availability wasn't even an issue, but there was another book to beware of: Bob Dylan's biographer, Tony Scaduto, was now doing a volume on Mick Jagger and had let the singer know personally that it would be anything but a puff-piece.)

Still, enough with the 'context'; let's cut to the chase. After *Exile* and the US tour, the Stones had decamped to Jamaica and duly concocted a set of tracks that ended up being released under the title *Goat's Head Soup*. However, there was something very unexciting about the music on the record, for it had been frustratingly hard to locate Keith Richard's guiding presence during the sessions.

Jagger and Richards had suddenly started calling themselves the Glimmer Twins on this new album's credits. They ruled the roost of course, or at least Jagger did, as Keith seemed content generally to exert himself less and less. Those two were a regular case-book study in contrasts. In the flesh Jagger looked smaller and less impressive than one might imagine, so he had to work any room he entered. Which is to say he had to flit around ceaselessly, wave his hands expressively a lot, wiggle his bum a bit, chat with certain people while pointedly ignoring others. He was constantly on the move, his body language like that of an over-indulged eleven-year-old allowed to stay up late and show off at his parents' dinner party.

He had this other peculiar habit of adopting the dialect and accent of anyone he was talking to, just as he was talking to them. On one occasion I found myself in a room with him, a white guy from the American South, a black guy from Los Angeles and someone from the North of England; and everyone stood quietly aghast as the singer's voice weaved a reckless path away from his usual *faux* Cockney intonations to attempt a 'y'all' drenched drawl straight out of a particularly arch Tennessee Williams production before slipping into 'soul brother' black speak somewhat in the over-excited cadence of Little Richard. When he finally started talking like a Manchester bus conductor, everyone in the room looked utterly mystified because the whole performance was frankly ridiculous to begin with and you couldn't really tell if Jagger consciously realized he was even doing it or not. But ultimately it didn't matter because it got him what he wanted, which was to be the centre of attention.

But he'd only stay the centre of attention until Keith Richards walked in the room. At which time all eyes would shift towards the guitarist and pretty much stay that way for the rest of the evening. Keith wasn't what you'd call a 'mingler'. He'd lope into a room, often accompanied by a couple of unsavoury individuals who seemed destined to have their faces turning up on some FBI 'Wanted' posters in the not-too-distant future, slump down on a chair, turn his back to the milling throng and glower a lot. Talk about drop-dead cool! I thought he was just like Lee Marvin in *The Commancheros*, only with better hair and a bad-ass pirate earring too. There was also this doomed poetic quality about him that Marianne Faithful pegged nicely when she talked about 'how if you're an over-imaginative schoolgirl who's read her Shelley and Byron, well that's what Keith Richards is. This perfect vision of damned youth. Even though he's turning more and more into Count Dracula.'

Of course, Keith had one over-riding passion at this point in his life. He consumed drugs like other humans consume air, which is to say, unceasingly. OK, it's true, he slept, but only in brief spasms and only after days and nights of running his body down with endless shots of heroin and snorts of cocaine. His concept of bed-rest seemed to be a couple of hours of being splayed out unconscious on some ratty old sofa and then he was good to go for another three or four days and nights of non-stop carousing. There was talk in the camp that he might indeed be possessed of super-human faculties. Roadies whispered in hushed tones about Keith's latest hedonistic marathon and several firmly believed he was blessed with two livers. On the matter of his sleeping habits, Ian Stewart told me an instructive tale about the Stones travelling through the Midlands at dead of night in a cramped little transit van, back in 1964, when the vehicle swerved and crashed, sending a large amplifier on wheels that Keith Richards happened to be passed out on flying through the back doors and down a long winding hill. After searching the hedgerows in vain for almost an hour, the other members eventually located the young guitarist still asleep atop the amplifier which had somehow fallen into a deep ditch. Keith hadn't noticed a thing.

It was always so much fun hearing and collecting these tales of wanton foolishness that it became easier and easier to ignore the other side of the issue, which was that drug addiction was slowly but surely destroying Richards's talent as a musician. Night after night I'd watch him on stage, and for most of the time he was just coasting, only half there. Dope was making him slow and clumsy too. He'd fall over his guitar lead from time to time and step on the wrong 'effects' pedal too often for it to be funny. On a good night he could still be magnificent: he was the group's motor after all, and whatever flame they were still cooking with, he was its keeper. But hard drugs – particularly in the amounts he was consuming – can only end up blunting creative instinct and stealing all natural reserves of energy and that's what was happening to him. Watching him on stage, it was like he was lost in this deep dense fog, but there was something so poignant about seeing him still standing because there was always a very real possibility that it could be the last time. But it was also kind of sordid seeing him stumble through his signature tune, 'Happy', missing half the lyrics and having Jagger conclude the thing by adopting his most sarcastic voice to remark, 'Uh, thank you, Keith, that was really amazing!' As in 'not'.

Although I remember being in seventh heaven for almost the whole duration of the two-month tour, looking back on it now, most of the images that stand out are distinctly ugly ones. For example, there was the evening in Manchester when Richards and Bobby Keyes sat at the hotel bar having just heard the news that one of their biggest musical allies and drug-buddies, Gram Parsons, had died from a morphine overdose in some cheesy motel outside LA with only some half-witted groupie for company. Their manner was sombre and the muscles in their faces were tensed like a couple of old western hombres who'd just come back from burying one of their gang out by the old corral. Behind the stoned fog they constantly inhabited I could still see they were deeply, deeply shocked and more than a little frightened too, though they'd probably never have admitted it. But it was only natural, really. After all, the thing that had killed Parsons in such an ugly, senseless way was the exact same distraction Richards and Keyes loved to partake in more than anything else in life.

Keyes, at least, should have paid the circumstances of Parsons' demise closer attention, for only a few days later in Germany his dazed, inert carcass was taken and put in a taxi cab by a Rolling Stones assistant who accompanied him to the nearest airport and placed him on the first available flight back to the States. His big old body had suddenly just packed in on him and it meant he'd also let the Stones down badly in the middle of an important tour. It would be many humiliating years before he'd be allowed to work with them again, years spent adjusting to the fact of having to play half-empty road-houses in the back of beyond for beer money, billing himself as 'Mr Brown Sugar'.

Then there was the lovely Bianca Jagger, or 'Bianca the Wanker' as she was known to the road crew whom she treated despicably at all times. This mutual disdain extended to group members also, principally to Richards, who loathed her with a vengeance. It was all about 'appearances' with Bianca: looking beautiful, making the right entrance, being seen with the richest and most elegant people and exploiting any and every circumstance for maximum publicity value. She always cultivated this expression somewhere between haughty disdain and utter uninterest, and looked at people as though she was mentally adding up the cost of the clothes they had on their backs to see if they were worthy of communicating with or not. One time she actually smiled at me and it was almost terrifying to see the blinding whites of her teeth, like Scott Fitzgerald's description of Daisy in *The Great Gatsby* whose smile was like an old cash register ringing up a particularly costly sale.

On a more positive note, one of the undisputed highlights of the trek for me was the continued presence of a joyful lunatic from Arkansas called Newman Jones III, who was Keith's guitar roadie and personal guitar-maker at the time. Apart from his employer Jones, or 'Ted' as he was constantly referred to for a reason that always escaped me, was the most genuinely fascinating guy to be around on that tour. He was a wild young kid from the South with blond hair and almost Scandinavian good looks who always wore a beat-up stetson topped off by an eye-catching snakeskin hat-band. If he liked you enough to talk to you in the first place, Ted would always get around to telling you how he'd killed that snake. In great detail. He was amazing, too, because though he worked for Richards he hadn't got sucked into the drug dependency vortex that others coming into close contact with the guitarist inevitably succumbed to. In fact, he appeared to be virtually drug-free, a condition both Jagger and tour manager Peter Rudge would sometimes silently pray be rectified with a sharp injection of tranquillizers whenever they saw the hyperactive Jones – a self-confessed 'genius with wood' – taking out his large Bowie knife at chic European restaurants catering for the band after shows and carving up another expensive dining table in his search for the perfect material for a possible fretboard he was designing.

Ian Stewart, the group's old road manager, was the other sweetheart in the pack. He was the conscience of the Rolling Stones – the conscience its principals all too often lost in a haze of drugs and ego – and pretty much what was left of the group's heart as well, even though he knew it was all slowly slipping into a long decline. He told me he thought *Goat's Head Soup* was 'too bloody insipid' and that Keith's drug problem was turning him into 'a walking bloody tragedy . . . a terrible waste of a talent'. He knew that Jagger was becoming increasingly remote and hard to communicate with, that Mick Taylor was dissatisfied and toying with heroin too, that Wyman was thinking of quitting he felt so frustated with his role, and that Charlie . . . well, Charlie would just shrug and live with it all but that that wasn't going to change anything, was it now.

He'd been there all along – since they'd kicked him out of the group itself for not looking unconventional enough – and he'd had to witness every dirty deceitful deed the group had ever pulled on one of their own since then. He'd watched Jagger and Richards also become particularly cold and mean in their business dealings with the outside world after the pair had realized most of the money they'd made in the sixties – over 14 million dollars by some accounts – had been pocketed by former manager Allen Klein, who also held the rights to all their music from that era. Yet Stewart still hung in there, dressed like a suburban family man fresh from twelve rounds of golf with his big benign bulldog face and his gruff old voice trying to create a bit of 'order' and 'focus', gently pricking 'ego' bubbles floating above certain members' heads and – lest we forget – lending his own singular touch to the ivories of a grand piano located discreetly behind Billy Preston from whence honky-tonk trills and arpeggios would ring throughout several numbers per show.

That's why he was there, of course: for that twenty minutes or so when he could hide behind the PA and hunch over the piano slapping out the kind of strident runs pioneered by Chuck Berry's accompanist Johnny Johnson and commune awhile with the greatest rock'n'roll band in the world. They could still justifiably refer to themselves by that high-handed title in 1973 even though on record they'd suddenly turned a bit flaccid and irrelevant. Live, though, they could still bring the house down even if there were just as many nights when the music sounded stiff and impersonal and the audience looked on the verge of becoming ever so slightly bored. I can remember two or three extraordinary concerts, shows where Keith Richards would suddenly find his bearings and start driving the rhythm along, pushing and pulling it with every motion of his body, shoulders hunched, eyes staring dead at Charlie Watts as the pair locked into yet another murderous groove. This was always the cue for the rest of the band to straighten up and fly right, musically speaking. Mick Taylor would suddenly coax more lethal solos from his guitar, the horns would play with a punchier attack and even Billy Preston would stop his odious Uncle Tom grinning and shuffling to concentrate on just playing his keyboards effectively. It also afforded Jagger the opportunity to stop flouncing complacently around the stage and to start delivering the kind of inspired performance he was capable of. At those moments the Rolling Stones were still something to behold with genuine awe, for the music seemed to drip from their fingers like dark honey. It all seemed so effortless and yet so all-consuming in its intensity. And Jagger knew all about this music, how to inhabit its sharp angles and bleak crevices, how to caress it with his voice and how to ride its terrible momentum like a surfer on a perfect wave to hell. Just such a gig occurred at – of all things – an afternoon concert the band played in Birmingham and also at the last concert of all, in West Berlin, the latter providing yet another study in lurid contrasts.

That was the evening I got to have my first real conversation with Charlie Watts, a frail but lovable soul who dealt with being a Rolling Stone by putting up with as much as he could stomach and trying hazily to ignore the rest. He spoke with the guileless quality of a slightly dazed child and talked incessantly about how he really loved jazz and that rock to him was all a bit . . . well, silly, really. Not the music itself – at least not the Stones' music, he'd quickly add – just all the brouhaha surrounding rock, all the earnest *Rolling Stone* reviews, all the sociological guff, all the hype and the bullshit. All . . . this! And he gestured meekly out at the crowd of two hundred or so rich bored-looking Germans who'd come to gawk at the Stones and celebrate the end of their tour in this classy, old, decidedly decadent-looking Berlin hotel the group were all booked into. The music was raging into the early hours of the morning. Mick Jagger flitted around the room imperiously, Keith Richards looked indescribably stoned and glowered at a lot of people, and Newman Jones destroyed yet another perfectly good dining-table in his quest for the perfect guitar frame. At about 3 a.m. the music being played through the sound system came over all Eastern and a bunch of professional dancers duly arrived to perform a soft-core erotic routine for the assembled throng. Once they'd departed, a dark-haired woman entered in a fur coat and performed a strip-tease to some strange Turkish music. Then another woman appeared, also stripped, and the two of them commenced to simulate sexual intercourse on the former's fur coat laid out on the floor. As the love-making grew more intense, someone from Billy Preston's backing group decided to register his contempt for the spectacle by tossing a lit candelabra on to the coat, which quickly caught fire. Flames were spurting out but the women were too wrapped up in their performance to notice at first. But what was really shocking was that no one out of over one hundred people grouped around watching jumped forward to alert them. Or even toss a handy beaker of water over the conflagration. Instead, all heads turned to Jagger and Richards, who were seated in two throne-like chairs right at the head of the party. But they weren't moving one muscle. Instead, they continued to watch with cold, dead eyes as the flames increased until they finally began burning the women's flesh. They leaped up, screaming hysterically. After what seemed like an eternity, someone proffered some water and the fire was extinguished. Then one of the women – naked and humiliated – turned and stalked right up to the two Stones. For a second it looked as though she might hit one of them but instead she stood only a matter of inches away from them both and spat out a series of vicious-sounding German curses directly in their faces. Yet there was no sign of shock. In fact, none of it seemed to register with the pair in the slightest. They just sat there, radiating this numb, burned-out cool, this 'you-can-never-reach-me' sense of otherness. Not a pretty sight. It was like their souls had taken up permanent residence in the sentiments of the most sublimely loveless song ever written, immortalized by Peggy Lee, Leiber-Stoller's 'Is That All There Is?'

Let's face it, even though they were kings of the hill, lords of all they surveyed, the hideous spiral of fame they'd both been riding rough-shod over had fucked with their souls badly. As smitten as I was by Richards's bad-assed buccaneering image even I could see that behind the evil reputation and the sullen scowls there hung a shy, introverted soul whose life, family and talent were steadily turning to shit in front of him, because he was too weak to walk away from the drugs that he loved to take so much for the way they made him feel invincible and helped perpetuate this image he also loved, that of 'big, bad Keith Richards, Mr "So tough he doesn't have to prove it"'.

As for Jagger . . . well, anyone who's ever known him will tell you what an interesting bunch of guys Mick Jagger can be. During that tour I'd seen him turn into the leering hedonist, the repellent aristocrat, the working-class 'oik' with a social edge, the concerned family man, the life and soul of the party, the 'don't approach me' prima-donna, the narcissistic old queen, the ruthless businessman, the loving husband, the rapacious adulterer. There was really no limit to the masks he'd don. Yet in his ceaseless quest always to stay one step ahead of everyone else he'd somehow lost contact with his own humanity, or at least some interconnecting essence that threw all the mystifying contrasts in his personality into some sympathetic relief.

The book, meanwhile, got written but under such circumstances that little of any lasting merit could seep into the text. At first they wanted only 9,000 words to be included with a possible live album the group were thinking of compiling from the European tour, but that project got axed when the Stones returned to the studio later that winter and recorded what turned out to be the backing tracks to a whole new project, an album that would see the light of day late the following year entitled *It's Only Rock'n'Roll*. By the time my project was completed it had simply become old news. I was paid well for my efforts but the text never got to see the light of day. It was no great loss to the world.

So then we were into 1974 and suddenly I found myself running with a faster crowd consisting mainly of these young narcissistic scene-makers with loads of ready cash, easy charm and drug connections. Almost all of them had luxury flats in Chelsea and they were well-connected, somewhat spoilt individuals who'd had a little bit too much of a good time during the latter years of the sixties, and now that the general mood was clouding over somewhat they'd kind of sulked off and taken up sanctuary in their well-appointed dimly lit living-rooms hung with drapes and enchanting little Eastern nick-nacks where they'd snort lines of heroin and cocaine one after the other and stare silently at the big colour TV screen sucking up all the energy from the room. These guys had several things in common, but the one common factor they all shared that had me most interested was that they all knew Keith Richards in some capacity. In fact, most of them lived less than a stone's throw from his Cheyne Walk townhouse and were always brimming with news of the guitarist's latest escapade. Actually, come to think of it, they tended to talk more about Anita Pallenberg, his girlfriend, and her increasingly skittish moods, but I'd sit there and soak it all up excitedly like some big moon-struck calf-eyed girl at her first disco.

You're probably wondering at this point why someone like myself, a successful young guy with everything to live for, who's already claimed he could see through the guitarist's exotic image, would still bother to walk so closely in his shadow. That's not so easy to answer. Let's just say I was free, white and twenty-one and over the past two years my life had turned into some great adventure I wanted to take to its absolute limits. I knew he was going to hell. But it just looked so cool down here that I wanted to check it out for myself. Famous last words. Several years later I was talking to Marianne Faithful about the Stones and I asked her if they'd really 'corrupted' poor old Gram Parsons, as certain sources had maintained. She looked at me as though I was being utterly ridiculous:

'Listen,' she said, 'they didn't have to corrupt Gram Parsons! Don't you understand Gram Parsons was already ripe for the picking? He was ready for absolutely anything! He was ripe, just like I was ripe and just like you yourself were ripe for the whole experience. It's just like what happens when an apple gets too ripe to hang on a tree! Who knows how far it's going to fall?'

Who, indeed! Somewhere in the late fall of the year, I finally got to . . . y'know, hang out with the guy, just the two of us, *mano a mano*, so to speak. I'd met him first at a record-company office where he was in the process of ingesting enough drugs and whisky to fell an entire herd of water-buffalo. I partook of only one line of some pharmaceutical concoction he was endlessly fashioning on a nearby table, and was so overwhelmed by the consequent sensation that my head was about to explode, I had to grab hold of the sides of my chair so as not to start levitating on the spot. In due course he invited me to accompany him to an interview he was doing with *The Old Grey Whistle Test*, a BBC TV 'rock' programme. That's when I found out that being the passenger in a high-speed Ferrari sports car driven by Keith Richards is a thrill second only to joy-riding down a steep winding hill with Ray Charles at the wheel. Keith didn't have his own licence. Keith never actually took a driving test. Keith lived a lot in foreign countries and was so stoned all the time he'd always forget what side of the road he had to drive on. But that didn't stop him from gunning up the motor to between 70 and 90 miles an hour and never letting it drop. Particularly when he was making corners on small provincial roads. I learnt a lot about Keith Richards that night just from watching him drive in this almost unthinkably self-destructive fashion of his. Talk about bravado: it was all about him against the rest of the world and bugger the consequences. I'd see it in his face at clubs and restaurants too, where he'd openly snort lines of cocaine from dinner tables until other customers and waiters couldn't help but start staring at him. At which point he'd fix them all with this cold, disdainful glare, as if to say, 'Yeah, that's right! I take drugs. In fact, I'm a fully qualified drug-abuser. Now what exactly are you going to do about it?'

It was a routine he pulled that night too, after the TV inter-view, which went unspectacularly but well, considering he'd actually nodded out in the toilet ten minutes before its live transmission was due to commence. His voice had shrunken to a husky croak now and he'd occasionally slip into a state of unconsciousness from which he'd suddenly snap back a full minute later. But he'd eaten some first-rate Chinese food so it was time to move the excitement over to Keith's current base of operations – a humble servant's quarters in Richmond. Yes, I was a bit underwhelmed by the location, too, initially, but Keith had to lie low from the Chelsea police force, who seemed to view him and his drug-taking as a constant target for busts and bribery. That's why he'd vacated Cheyne Walk and was living in a modest two-storey building in the grounds of his new pal Faces guitarist Ron Wood's opulent estate. Once inside, the place looked as dysfunctional as its occupant, which is to say that nothing really worked apart from the heating and the light fittings. Keith had brought me back specifically to play me some music but the record player didn't seem to work. Neither did the cassette player. 'Oh dear!' said Keith, who promptly sent out 'Frank', his well-built straight-looking minder who was in fact nothing more than a layabout and a scrounging 'ne'er-do-well', to fetch some functioning audio equipment from Cheyne Walk. Frank never returned. So we sat and talked for a long time – most of it about either the Stones or drugs. Or both. He started talking about the old days and Brian Jones, and he made no bid to disguise his loathing for the guy. Jagger he chose to criticize mainly for his choice of wife: Bianca, according to Keith, had been the ruination of Jagger. He'd 'never been able to handle chicks' and this one was walking all over him, making him take on all these phoney airs and graces, making him lose touch with who he really was. As for the heroin, well, like all good junkies, Keith was seriously into 'denial'. He was fiercely critical of a number of mutual acquaintances who'd become addicted to the drug but seemed to think he'd be spared the sorry end he foresaw for all of them. He said he thought that one could never get truly addicted to the drug simply by snorting it, only by fixing, which I was already experienced enough to know was a bunch of bullshit. He also claimed not to be injecting anymore, but an hour after stating this he accidentally overturned a Kleenex box full of syringes and looked ever-so-slightly guilty, before slumping into one of those temporary states of unconsciousness I've referred to earlier. Only this one wasn't so temporary. Instead his head lolled back, his mouth fell open and his face lost all trace of its natural colour, turning instead cold and grey with tinges of blue forming around the mouth and under the eyelids. In other words, it looked like he was over-dosing and I was the only one round to do anything about it. I cradled his head in my arms and slapped him gently several times. I picked him up and tried to drag him around the room on my shoulders. I asked him to tell me his name over and over again to no avail. After what seemed like an eternity – but which was probably more like eight minutes – he came to long enough to register the fact that he wasn't actually in a coma and that this was absolutely nothing out of the ordinary, before falling back into his stupor. He had the sweetest little smile on his face as I held his head in my hands while searching for a cushion to lay it on. Once I could tell he was breathing properly, I left him and passed out in an adjacent bedroom.

The next morning I was awoken by my stomach running out of the room I'd been sleeping in in search of anything resembling a toilet. Finding none readily available, I galloped to the front door and opened it just in time to hurl violently all over the quaintly designed 'welcome' mat lying at the entrance of the house. I felt Keith Richards saunter up behind me. 'That's a charming way to show your appreciation for last night, isn't it?' he remarked with a certain dead-pan breeziness. He looked remarkably chipper for a man I'd thought to be splayed across death's very threshold a few hours before. And then he turned all wistful and looked forlornly across to some fields laid to the west over which some crows were swooping. It was then that he told me the strange saga of the kilo sacks of raw opium he'd buried in a barn overlooking those very same fields only a short while ago. He'd left them there for safekeeping, but when he'd returned, the barn had been demolished and his drug stash had disappeared with it. He'd searched and searched but no signs were forthcoming. The story clearly still saddened him greatly, and I could see by the way he coldly eyed those crows he felt the ugly black birds might actually have masterminded the heist. The sun was rising in the distance, I was wiping my mouth with the back of my hand and Keith was silently seething at a bunch of crows in a nearby field. Memories are made of this.

But not far from this scene of pastoral bonding Mick Taylor could be found stewing glumly over his situation within the group. I'd seen him a few days earlier and he'd spoken excitedly about some songs he'd written with Jagger and Richards that were to appear on *It's Only Rock'n'Roll*. When I told him that I'd seen a finished sleeve with the song-writing credits and that his name wasn't featured, he went silent for a second before muttering a curt 'We'll see about that!' almost under his breath. Actually he sounded more resigned than anything and that was maybe the real problem. He was too frightened to confront either Jagger or Richards directly, so he fumed in private about the miseries of being a junior partner in the Rolling Stones until he'd persuaded himself he ought to leave the group altogether. This did not please the rest of the group, who were all set to fly to Munich for more recording when the news of his defection came through.

I was in Munich when I finally got to see them work in a record studio, albeit as a quartet with old pal Nicky Hopkins back on the piano to round out the sound. Keith had splashed out on a new set of teeth, but his face had become so haggard-looking and his skin so translucent they didn't really help him look any better than before, when his mouth had resembled a run-down graveyard. The very wretched Bill Wyman was moaning away in a corner putting everybody else down. God, what a deeply unattractive mean-spirited little man he was! And then there was dear old Charlie, who was starting to go bald and had taken to sporting a particularly brutal-looking skinhead crop. 'So 'ow's the Prisoner of the Isle de Ré, then?' Mick Jagger would keep asking Charlie, who looked more and more pissed off whenever he heard the remark, probably because he didn't know who the fuck Jagger was talking about. Jagger had just come back from Paris, where he'd been swanning around the clubs with Rudolf Nureyev, and so he'd arrived in Munich sporting a large Russian Cossack hat and a more gauchely 'camp' exterior than usual. When they finally started making music together, Jagger strapped on a guitar and strummed out a chord progression not dissimilar to the one dominating Martha and the Vandellas' 'Heatwave'. Richards played it back alone over and over again for maybe twenty minutes, giving it different punctuation points, shifting the dynamic to his own specifications. Then Watts and Wyman were summoned, along with Hopkins, and the musical spade-work commenced. Soon enough, a backing track was rolling along with Jagger also on piano, providing a guide-vocal by grunting and chanting a vague melodic pattern bereft of intelligible meaning. Then they'd do it again. And again and again. And each time it would get a bit faster until no one seemed to know what on earth was going on anymore. Glyn Johns, their old engineer/producer, was manning the desk and at the time spoke glowingly about 'how it felt like the good old days again'. But some years later, in an interview with *Musician*, he gave a more accurate verbal representation of his frustrations regarding those Munich sessions:

'I must be honest with you, I don't think Mick and Keith have a clue how to make records. I don't think they've really ever had that much of a clue, if you really want to know. They were enormously frustrating to work with. To me the Rolling Stones was unequivocally the best rock'n'roll rhythm section I've ever been in a room with. And to take something as natural as that and work it to death until it deteriorates into something in my opinion quite bland – to take the amazing adrenalin rush that they got together when they were playing well and just dissipate it by flogging it to death the way they did and be so very critical about it – I never understood it, they left me behind. I found it really frustrating. I've watched these guys who I knew were just wonderful playing worse and worse until Keith would come in and say, "That's the take!" For some reason better known to the Lord than anybody else!'

Numerous guitarists were auditioned, but you didn't need a crystal ball to see that Ronnie Wood was ultimately going to get the gig. He got on well socially with both Jagger and Richards and had an infectious energetic quality about him that both Watts and Wyman found stimulating to be around. He had a good thing going with the Faces but he'd lived in awe of the Stones for so long that when he was offered a job in the group he just didn't know how to say no. So, in 1975, Wood filled in on another riotous American tour with them as well as keeping up his Faces duties, but when Rod Stewart flounced out of the latter combo that winter to go solo, the die was well and truly cast for the guitarist with the profile of a kindly jackdaw. Celebrating his new role as foil for Jagger and Richards at his Richmond home that Christmas, Wood waxed effusive to an interviewer about how 'I think the Rolling Stones bring out the best in me'. However, in a matter of only a few years, everyone who'd ever known Wood before he made the choice would shake their heads sadly when considering how the change had turned out for him. One of these was Glyn Johns, who'd produced for both the Stones and the Faces:

'Ron Wood was probably the worst choice they could have made, in my view. I thought it was absurd. I'm sure he got the gig more on his wonderful personality and his friendship and all the rest of it. It was an easy transition for them. But musically I don't think he fits with the Stones at all. I don't think the band has benefited from having him and he's not benefited from being in. He might have benefited financially, he may well have enjoyed being in the band for other reasons, but to me the man was an extraordinary musician and he's being completely wasted. I don't think he's been given an opportunity to grow. He might tell you differently. The guy was wonderful, he had a very individual style. Woody seems to me like the court jester somehow. I think that's unnecessary and it's degrading.'

Anyway they put out their weakest album thus far – a bunch of half-assed jams performed while auditioning various guitarists, padded out with a couple of make-weight ballads – entitled *Black and Blue* in the late spring of 1976 just as they were setting out on another tour of Europe. I caught up with the tour in Paris, where everything was really starting to fall apart for Keith Richards. The level of drug traffic and general drug abuse in and around that tour was very, very intense indeed, and the guitarist was more than ably abetted in the consumption of these pharmaceuticals by both Jagger and Wood, the latter fast becoming like Richards' second shadow. Everywhere, backstage at Les Abattoirs where they played for three nights, you'd find heroin and cocaine dealers with special laminated passes on their jackets embossed with Keith Richards' own signature. Even the roadies were scoring off them. The tour manager, Pete Rudge, was going completely haywire trying to keep all this illegal activity under guard, but the more he'd try to impose some kind of order and sanity, the more Richards would work to undermine it. Jagger didn't even seem to care anymore; in fact, all the group's principals appeared to believe they were quite simply beyond the law. The shows meanwhile were terrible. There was no mystery and no momentum anymore; just an ill-focused blur of a sound buffeted by Wood and Richards's frankly clumsy guitar inter-play and fronted by Jagger content merely to pose and primp coyly around the stage, utilizing grotesque gimmicks like a giant inflatable penis for cheap effect.

Let's be honest about it, they were all just coasting along, smug as lords, lost in this vast bubble of dope-fuelled invincibility. Then tragedy struck. Anita Pallenberg had recently given birth to a third child by Richards after a 'difficult' pregnancy, but after only two months alive, the infant – a little boy the parents had named Tara after Tara Browne, a doomed aristocratic chum from the sixties – expired in his crib over at the couple's rented home in Switzerland. The grieving mother flew over to be with the guitarist for the final show in Paris and I'll never forget seeing the couple leaving the venue afterwards. Anita was crying and seemed to be having difficulty moving, Keith was shepherding her along but he was crying too and looked all of a sudden to be impossibly fragile, like a stiff breeze could send him spinning to the ground. No longer the Scott and Zelda of the rock'n'roll age, they looked like some tragic shell-shocked couple leading each other out of a concentration camp. I honestly never thought I'd see them alive again. In a way, it was a blessing what happened to them in Toronto only a matter of months after that.

The facts are all a matter of public record now. The group moved to the Canadian city to record several live shows at a club there in February of 1977 only to have the Mounties catch Richards and Pallenberg red-handed in a hotel suite with more than two ounces of both heroin and cocaine in their possession. It was all very ugly indeed: Keith strung out all alone in Canada, facing the possibility of life imprisonment and being abandoned by his jittery pals Jagger and Wood. But it was also rather inevitable.

'Are you askin' if I knew it was gonna happen, like . . . sooner or later?' Mick Jagger remarked to me with a forced expression of naivety exactly seven months to the day after Keith's fateful meeting with the Mounties. We were seated in a Vietnamese restaurant in Soho doing yet another interview. 'Well, yeah of course! Christ, Keith fuckin' gets busted every year.'

Yeah but it keeps getting more and more serious . . .

'Until it reaches a head. That's what you're saying. Yeah, sure. And then you've got to do something about it. But I'm not judge and jury. I can't morally . . . I can't go into those sort of details. Christ, I can tell you what I *think* of the case but I can't . . . I mean, it's not even my case. I don't know how many needles they found lyin' around. I didn't have anything to do with it all. I never even went to see the cops.'

But how did you really feel about watching him decline like this?

'Listen, we shouldn't be talking about this. Really, I mean, he's in too much trouble as it is. Afterwards sure . . . but . . . right now anything we say could somehow go against him. I could say right now, "yeah, it was irresponsible, and what happened was totally inevitable," but what good would that do? It's not worth it at all and anyway the fact is that I simply can't and don't blame anyone for the bust.'

While I had him a bit on the defensive, I thought I'd give it my best shot and pop the only truly relevant question worth asking the guy in the first place, which is, 'Why the fuck does someone as purportedly rock-solid and all-powerful as Mick Jagger feel this insatiable need to inhabit all these different, often unappealing personalities as often as he possibly can?'

'I just enjoy changing personality,' he replied after a moment of silent deliberation. 'Honestly, I feel I've got to be very . . . uh . . . chameleon-like just to preserve my own identity. You have to do it sometimes . . .'

But doesn't it reach a point where you lose contact with yourself?

'Hmmm, maybe that's true, but I don't feel threatened by that possible eventuality. I don't want to have just one front. I feel like I need at least two just to carry on doing what I'm doing comfortably. It's acting, sure it is . . . that's what it obviously comes down to. It just gives me the facility to do practically anything I want, see. And even then the most drastic changes of personality don't really affect me 'cos I never feel the need to do 'em that often. It's all part of being a rock'n'roll star, after all.'

At another moment his face twisted itself into a suitably condescending smirk as he witnessed my personal shortcomings at mastering the art of eating with chop-sticks. 'Get a fork instead, mate. You're too shaky anyway.' It was his way of saying 'However sharp you think you are you're never going to pin me down.' Mick Jagger was always a little too tricky for me. He and Richards both had it: this total sense of self-possession. If you locked eyes with them, you'd always be the first to be lowering your gaze because theirs was always so steady and intense it just ultimately seemed to bore through you. That's why these guys were going to survive even this hideous drug Waterloo with Keith and go on to prosper into old age as rock'n'rollers, whereas a walking casualty like Elvis – a punk loser who never fully comprehended the vast charisma and talent the good Lord entrusted in him and so was led by fools and flatterers – would fall into a drug-fuelled demise straight down to the grave with half his life still ahead of him. They were just too damn strong and too damn hip.

'Who's dead this week then?' he sneered finally. 'Roy Orbison? Hard to tell these days, innit! Pop stars! They're droppin' like flies! Droppin' all over the place, mate!

'I was in Turkey when Elvis choked it by the way. They started playing all his records one after the other on the radio in some bar I was in and after three or four hours I sussed the logical thing. He'd snuffed it, the poor bastard!'

Of course, everybody knows Keith finally got virtually pardoned for his transgressions, even though any other junkie would have gone down for many long years for holding such large quantities of two grade A drugs. The Toronto trial reeked of a set-up and there was intense talk of some colossal pay-off – 3 million dollars 'filtered through to the right people' was the sum being referred to in most of the rumours circulating at the time. However, by then, the group had managed to record and release their last 'significant' album to date, *Some Girls*, a raw rebuttal to the then-current punk icons' accusations of the Stones' debauched redundancy. There were a couple of lumpy three-chord thrashers created by Mick Jagger in the style of Lou Reed, an ersatz disco rocker written for the woman he'd finally left Bianca for, Texan model Jerry Hall, that went on to sell millions as a single entitled 'Miss You', a surreal country honker with Jagger singing like some straw-sucking Bakersfield bumpkin called 'Faraway Eyes', and two fine Keith Richards songs. 'Before They Make Me Run' was a hearty two-fingered 'fuck you' to all those who wished him dead or behind bars, but the real highlight was 'Beast of Burden', the last Stones ballad to be able to stand gracefully alongside something as timeless as 'Wild Horses' or any other of the Stones' truly finest tender moments. I've always imagined it as Richards's tired but determined plea to partner Anita Pallenberg not to drag him down any further with her into the lowest depths of substance abuse and border-line insanity.

After Toronto it was pretty much all over for Keith and Anita. Couples committed to drug treatments are often kept apart, and certainly the powers-that-be in the Rolling Stones' business empire felt that Pallenberg was perhaps the more destructive influence in the whole issue of drug abuse involving the pair. Anyway, she wasn't around on the 1978 American tour they played to promote the *Some Girls* album, a disastrous and much criticized series of dates which still stand as the all-time low point of the group's considerable live career. After that, the group continued to coast as though nothing could shake their tree. They'd recorded enough tracks in Paris back in 1977 to fill out at least two more records, but returned in 1979 for further sessions that would amount to the contents of the 1980 release, *Emotional Rescue*, and its immediate successor, *Tattoo You*, in 1981. The latter sported a punchy rocker called 'Start Me Up' and a couple of other lively items, but, like *Emotional Rescue*, there was too little creative sparkle and too much raunch-by-rote for any kind of long-term satisfying listening experience.

None the less, the tour of the States they underwent to promote *Tattoo You* proved they'd not lost their vitality for the millions who avidly flocked to see them. One of the big reasons for the improvement in their live sound was Keith Richards back on form – now heroin-free and looking almost robust.

The following year the tour hit Europe and I got to spend a long evening with Richards just prior to the group's two London shows, and it was the nicest time I ever got to have with the guy. He was in love again, with a beautiful blonde model named Patti Hansen with a seemingly warm and vivacious personality, and so he'd straightened up a lot or at least cut down on his intake of cocaine drastically. Still, there were three large black bottles of Rebel Yell on the table in front of him; one was already empty and he wasn't backward about reaching out to the second for further liquid refreshment. He was still staying up three or four nights at a time and had outdone himself with his choice of 'personal assistant', this time employing a dubious specimen of humanity known as Sven, an individual so wretchedly seedy-looking I could only imagine him as having been a professional grave-robber in some previous incarnation. And then there was the usual circus surrounding Keith, the bashful musicians who wanted to jam and get high, the huddle of roadies and dealers who prostrated themselves in front of him to get his attention. One big fat guy almost literally had a heart attack that night, he was hyperventilating so much from finding himself suddenly so close to 'the living embodiment of rock'n'roll itself', as he kept referring to the unimpressed guitarist. To his credit, Keith played the whole room like a harp, sitting back strumming an acoustic guitar and running through an eclectic blend of songs predating the sixties. Only a day earlier he'd reconnected with his long-alien-ated father Bert and now the sweet old bloke was sitting here among this motley parade of all-purpose rock'n'roll flotsam and jetsam, puffing on a pipe and chuffing back lagers with a happy smile on his big red face. Thus Keith would choose songs that his dear old dad could relate to. Unfortunately he could find only one – 'Danny Boy' – but played it sombrely and reverently several times, an act that seemed otherwise to confuse those present who'd come expecting raucous rhythms, dancing girls and silver syringes bursting out of any corner of the hotel suite we were all holed up in.

But these were also dark days for the Stones, for while Richards's hedonistic nature was on a more even keel, Ron Wood had fallen into serious problems with 'free-base' cocaine and was getting sloppy and stupid. He even fell asleep on stage during one of the London shows and Richards had to wake him up with a sharp punch in the face. Jagger and Richards meanwhile were no longer seeing eye-to-eye on anything and so there was this huge ego battle going on, spilling out on to the stage. Half the fun of watching these shows – for insiders – was in seeing the withering glances this odd couple would shoot at each other or the way Jagger would try to hurry songs up only to have Keith slow them down even more. It got so bad that on one show Richards hijacked this cherry picker that Jagger was using to haul himself over the crowd and stood suspended over the masses playing a twenty-minute guitar solo while Jagger stood seething behind the amps.

Once the tour had wound down, the Stones recorded yet another album, *Undercover*, which attempted to return to the dark world view of *Exile* but only ended up sounding like a tacky comic book version of the original. After that the group moved from Atlantic, their US record base since the beginning of the seventies, to Columbia, where Mick Jagger shamelessly courted the attention of the record company's odiously flam-boyant president, Walter Yetnikoff, getting himself signed to a major solo deal to the same label as a direct consequence. This is when the big problems occurred. Jagger wanted to distance himself from his old group because he saw them getting old and obsolete and because he was sickeningly obsessed with staying as young and on top of the trends as he possibly could. He'd become obsessed by other solo acts gaining great international acclaim at the time (like David Bowie and Prince) and wanted to duplicate their success without having the other Stones around to share the spotlight and all that lovely money. Jagger had also been deeply stung by some statements John Lennon had uttered to *Playboy* at the very beginning of the decade just a few weeks before his untimely death:

'You know they're congratulating the Stones on being together 112 years. Whoopee! At least Charlie's still got his family. In the eighties they'll be asking: "Why are these guys still together? Can't they hack it on their own? Why do they have to be surrounded by a gang? Is the little leader frightened someone's gonna knife him in the back?" That's gonna be the question. They're gonna look at the Beatles and Stones and all those guys as relics . . . They'll be showing pictures of the guy with lipstick wriggling his ass and the four guys with the evil black make-up on their eyes trying to look raunchy. That's gonna be the joke in the future . . . See, being in a gang . . . it's great when you're at a certain age. But when you're in your forties and you're still in one, it just means that you're still "eighteen" in the head.'

Right in the middle of a decade remarkable only for its sustained levels of gross ambition and back-stabbing greed, Jagger put out his solo record *She's the Boss* and went into complete overdrive in his zest to force it right down the general public's throat. He employed the hottest producers and session players and even bank-rolled a ninety-minute comedy film based around the album's songs and starring himself and Jerry Hall as a jaded narcissistic rock star couple separated by a ludicrous series of misfortunes. There was only one problem:

the record was a lousy lifeless piece of work causing the film to become a foolish exercise in over-the-top vanity. Which meant that his solo career started out a bit of a flop, though you'd have been forgiven for thinking otherwise, had you viewed him in mid-'85 looking like a stick insect all dressed up in canary yellow and belting through a lively five-song set that ranked among the most exciting performances of an already star-studded show-down of rock talent otherwise known as Live Aid. With virtually every other major rock band for the two shows taking place in London and Philadelphia, it was typical of the Rolling Stones' innate perversity to do exactly the opposite thing, for straight after Jagger's exhilarating twenty minutes, the actor Jack Nicholson introduced the final performer of the event – the only one deemed capable of topping this monumental bill – Bob Dylan accompanied by two mystery guests. The increasingly eccentric singer/songwriter had joined forces with Ron Wood and Keith Richards, the latter particularly savouring the possibility of up-staging his infuriating lead singer. They'd apparently rehearsed together but then, just as they started to walk towards the stage, Dylan turned to Wood and muttered something about first performing 'The Ballad of Hollis Brown', a song that hadn't been rehearsed by the trio and which Wood himself wasn't even familiar with. 'Hollis Brown?' the guitarist offered back hopefully. 'Isn't that the name of a cough syrup?' It was downhill from there, which is to say that Bob Dylan performed like he'd just been beamed down from another planet while Richards and Wood made themselves look ridiculous and not a little obsolete with their slovenly ill-focused accompaniment and self-satisfied smirking in the background.

Meanwhile, the turmoil that resulted from the making of *Dirty Work*, the first Stones project for Columbia that got recorded while Mick Jagger was simultaneously preoccupied with promoting his solo career, has resulted in some fine old tales that have been part of public domain for over six years now. There's the one about Charlie punching Jagger full in the face after the singer had referred to him condescendingly as 'my drummer' during a drunken altercation. There's the one about how Keith got so pissed off by Jagger's absences and bitching behaviour he started calling him 'Brenda' around the studio. And there's the one about how the album really wasn't a proper Rolling Stones album in the first place because Charlie's only on half of it, because Bill's also absent from several tracks and because it was recorded with Keith's little nucleus of players – he, Wood and session drummer Steve Jordan called themselves the Biff Hitler Trio – and then Jagger who'd stomp in separately and record his vocals as quickly as possible before returning to plug his solo career ever more relentlessly. By the same token, Jagger didn't like being around all the drinking and doping anymore, spending numbingly long hours waiting until everyone's heads were in the right place and the groove was right, and he deeply resented Richards for trying to take total musical control of the band, not to mention poking his ill-informed nose into matters of business and general administration. He'd grown tired of Wood's cocaine excesses and aimless rock star stupidity, Wyman he'd never been able to stomach, and poor old Charlie, his biggest pal, suddenly seemed to be going off the rails a bit from the old evil influences that had gutted others in the band back in the seventies.

Fate, then, provided the crowning blow to the Rolling Stones' crumbling identity, when at the end of 1985 Ian Stewart suddenly dropped dead in his doctor's waiting room from a heart attack brought on by severe respiratory pains. He was forty-seven years old and the last one connected to the Stones name and legacy anyone expected to die from anything but natural causes at a ripe old age. 'I thought he'd be the one to hold the shovel, the one to bury all of us,' stated Keith Richards. 'What a hole he's left, such an obvious gap. He would always be there to comment on things and sometimes you'd think he was crazy. But then you'd go and realize he was right all along.'

They were all there at his funeral – alongside other old stalwarts like Eric Clapton and Glyn Johns – held down in Surrey just before Christmas 1985, and the photographs taken that day of them crying and holding on to one another with dazed and frightened expressions on their faces are among the most haunting Stones shots that exist anywhere.

Anyway, just as *Dirty Work* was being released at the beginning of 1986, Jagger told Richards he didn't want to tour with the Stones to support the record and that effectively broke up the group for almost the next three years. I'd ended up being the bearer of the bad tidings after I'd spotted Charlie in the street next to the group's West End office and he'd hazily told me as much. ('Touring with the Stones again? I can't imagine it,' he'd muttered with a weary old look straining down on his face. 'I always have this image of me when playing with the Stones and there are all these sixteen-year-old girls in the front screaming at us. I mean, my daughter's actually older than them now! I just find it all rather embarrassing!') I put all the dirt in too, and the consequent article – published in *Spin* that spring – scarcely endeared me to the group's principals and their organization. To me, the issue was simple: the Rolling Stones were falling apart and someone needed to tell the public what was going on, even though I knew that whoever did it was bound to be excommunicated from the inner sanctum for his efforts.

But then Jagger's career *really* flopped with the release of his second useless solo album and his girlfriend Jerry Hall left him for the umpteenth time over the compulsive philandering he'd become hopelessly addicted to as he grew older, even going so far as to refer to him as 'that wizened old man' in public places. What it all added up to was that after an eternity of being always the winner in everything he attempted, the singer suddenly felt the cruel sting of being perceived as a loser and he didn't like it one bit. Worse still, there was his son of a bitch nemesis Keith Richards slagging him all over the popular press, calling him an 'ageing victim of a Peter Pan complex', 'a wimp', a 'back-stabbing cunt' and all-purpose betrayer of the primal essence that was the Rolling Stones. In fact, this was the way Keith chose to promote *his* début solo album, a pleasant collection of chunky jams with two or three meaty songs thrown in for added sustenance entitled *Talk is Cheap* that garnered respectful reviews but limited sales. Meanwhile, from all corners of the globe, offers were pouring in to get the group back together with sums like 100 million dollars being thrown around as the kind of revenue to anticipate. Of course, they finally swallowed their pride and embraced anew in 1989, banging out a reasonable album in the process which Jagger entitled *Steel Wheels*, and then off they went on a financial megablitz of a tour that broke all established box-office records all across America.

Of course, I went when the tour hit Paris even though I'd been warned about Jagger's theatrical bullshit and the pre-recorded samples littering certain items. I was expecting the worst anyway and so was consequently truly taken aback by the force and focus with which they played and the sheer magnificence and unstoppable vitality of Mick Jagger's work as a front man and vocalist. Sure, the show was aimed to placate both the tourists and the purists who'd gathered in this 70,000 capacity outdoor swamp to ogle at the hardy old legends, but to anyone who'd seen them play live from the very beginning there was no doubting that they'd ascended to a new peak of musical interplay, dynamism and non-stop visual magnetism.

Later, in a nearby bar, a couple of French journalists came over and started commiserating about how soulless it had been and the next minute they were evoking the memory of Brian Jones: I had to tell them to disappear. The Stones had been great, goddammit, and to hell with all the clod-headed nostalgianiks who couldn't see past their own blind reverence for the cherished past of their long-departed youth.

I guess I should take this particular opportunity to temper all the less-than-joyous-reminiscenses I've been spinning out here and tell you about the good things I experienced from getting so close to the Rolling Stones. Because when I actually stop to think about it now, I realize I learnt so much from being around them and that they influenced my life in so many ways, some good, some less good. If there has been one constant message coursing through the group's music from the beginning right up to the present day, it's been that the world is a strange and ruthless place and that if you want to make a mark on it in your own terms without getting martyred, robbed blind or endlessly stabbed in the back, you've got to be even more ruthless in your own dealings. So if touring with Led Zeppelin was like travelling around with Ghengis Khan and his boys on a particularly lurid rampage of some foreign dominion, and working with the Sex Pistols was like blending into some late-twentieth-century update of Charles Dickens's portrayal of Fagin, the Artful Dodger and that wretched den of teenaged thieves out of the pages of *Oliver Twist*, then being around the Stones was rather like finding yourself in the company of something like a cross between a stuffy old English gentlemen's club and the Mafia. Little was stated outright, most things were only intimated and if you didn't read the signs or got too sloppy – or worse still, too uncool – you were treated like you simply didn't exist. But if you could stay on the wild kicking horse long enough to assimilate all the tumultuous ups and downs, you were off on the best and baddest ride of an adventure you could ever hope to handle. I wouldn't have missed it for the world.

All Dressed Up, Got No Place to Go: The Troubled Splendour of the New York Dolls

'Now John Lennon . . . Y'know, that song "Gimme The Truth"?' The Dolls' David Johansen's cracked Brooklyn drawl appears from the left side of his mouth while a cigarette is coyly dangled directly to the right, so as to give the impression that he's seen too many Humphrey Bogart–Lauren Bacall movies and can never quite decide which one he wants to steal his poses from. 'I just want to throw the words to that right in his face to show him what an asshole hypocrite he really is! [*Shouts*] I'm a yellow-bellied-son-of-Tricky-Dicky . . . Oh my God! Do you know someone showed him a film of us performing, on a video machine, when he was in LA, and do you know what he called us? Faggots! He called *us* a bunch of fuckin' faggots.'

'Huh! So would I if I was that pussy-whipped!' cracks Johnny Thunders, perfectly on cue with a goofy grin sprawling across his amiably deranged features. He's thatched with a coiffure that might resemble Ronnie of the Ronettes, were a tree to have fallen on her.

'Pussy-whipped!' hiccups Johansen, seizing up with the giggles. 'Oh Johnny, how fabulous.'

Five minutes off the plane in Paris, walking up towards the airport entrance, and Johnny Thunders throws up. *Bl-a-a-a-g-g-h-h!* God knows how many photographers are there: *Paris Match, Stern* magazine, all the European rock press and the nationals. The record company folks have arranged a special welcome. *Bl-a-a-a-a-g-g-h-h!* The other members of the band start taking odds as to whether he might actually fall into his vomit. David Johansen, who's always one to inject a little humour into any given situation, pulls out his best German officer impersonation: 'Vee did not co-operate viv de Naz-ees.' David finds this very funny. The massed media minions look just a little bit more nervous. *Bl-a-a-a-a-g-g-h-h!*

The New York Dolls the toast of Paree? Oh honey! I remember these buckaroos when they were still playing dingy Manhattan clubs, sprawled out on minute stages and insulting their down trodden zombie audience between numbers by way of Johansen's charmingly condescending raps: 'We just luhv playing these places because we just think you kids are really [*sneer*] where it's at. Ha, ha!' Or posing down Max's Kansas City every night where Thunders would invariably be seen staggering around with the sexiest-looking babe in the joint and Johansen would be socializing with the right people as usual.

Meanwhile, Iggy Pop and his cronies are just lying fallow amid the accumulated debris of their past notoriety and gross untogetherness, with only true devotees still wagering that the Stooges can pull off their grand coup and destroy us like we'd all hoped they would from the beginning. Almost all the New York deca-rock bands are struggling away, hoping in vain for a record contract to pull them out of the tedious New York club circuit. The Modern Lovers, one of the few true originals of the whole schism, are reportedly splitting and re-forming with alarming regularity around the amazing Jonathan Richman, their vocalist (he's the one who looks like Dustin Hoffman's afterbirth), true romance idealist and writer of such nuggets as 'I'm Straight' and, more recently, 'Picasso Ain't No Ass-hole'. An album on Warner Bros., produced by Kim Fowley and John Cale, remains unreleased.

Of course, there's the Blue Oyster Cult, who are more mainstream heavy metal really; and Wayne County, who's signed with Mainman. 'Yeah, he's blown it now,' mutters Johnny Thunders cryptically, while Johansen recounts some extremely amusing tales of County's pre-transvestite days in the South, where he used to have buck-shot fired at his buttocks whenever he paraded around the streets in his Beatle suit jacket and Cuban heels, but . . . While others still search in the wilderness, the Dolls have strutted out to infinitely greener pastures, capturing the American spotlight more than any other pack of glowing up-and-comers in 1973. Notoriety was already guaranteed via advance flak, so is it any wonder that Johansen was busted onstage in Memphis, or that the Dolls were banned from two – two, mind you – hotels in LA. Or . . . the list continues.

Europe is a horse of a very different colour. The Dolls swooned into London, gave a chaotic but entertaining press conference (where, in between questions about their supposed ambiguities and debts to the Velvet Underground, Johansen got into a number of eminently quotable statements like, 'We attract only degenerates to our concerts,' and 'We want to be known as the tackiest boys in New York.' When asked for definition of 'tack' by one reporter, he free-associated, 'Oh . . . I think it's an arch-attitude towards a particular thing . . . It's like . . . it's just like that terrible jacket you're wearing. That's tack, if I ever saw it.' And he was right) and played a predictably controversial pair of gigs at trendy old Biba's restaurant – which failed to approximate the feeling one can get from any real Dolls performance when they are working within a suitably sleazy environment. 'Y'know, we were caught changing price-tags on the clothes at Biba. They were gonna get heavy, so Marty just came along and said, "I don't wanna hear anymore about this incident." They dropped it.'

Marty is Marty Thau, and Marty Thau is still the New York Dolls' acting manager and father-figure. (Even though the group are really managed by two early yuppie Jewish lawyer-types called Leber and Krebs.) The Dolls are His Boys. Period.

And nobody messes around with His Boys. No half-assed local record company is going to cop out on promotion with the New York Dolls. No petty faction of this industry is going to put the brakes on the New York Dolls' progress to the top, because the New York Dolls are the most important thing to hit rock music since they invented electricity, and if you don't think so, then go suck a brick, buster! Marty's got that kind of attitude. He's also got unique punk management credentials: a partner in Cameo-Parkway records, hall of fame for Terry Knight and the Pack and Question Mark and the Mysterians. The Lemon Pipers too. He even had Van Morrison signed up during his *Astral Weeks/Moondance* phase. But what about Question Mark, Marty? 'Yeah, his real name was Rudy Martinez. Didn't you know that? And his mother, this fat Mexican woman, owned Go-Go Records. The reason he wore those shades all the time is because he was cross-eyed.'

'Yeah,' butts in David Johansen, 'just like Ian Hunter, who has these terrible "piggy" eyes.' Johansen's rap on his touring experience with Mott is typically bitchy and libellous:

'They *used* us on that tour. I mean, the times when we were getting booed onstage, I'd say, "Listen, if you think we're bad, just wait'll you see Ian Hunter" [*howls of laughter*]. It was hysterical! And Hunter would bring out – what's his name – (guitarist Ariel Bender) into the audience when we were onstage and tell him to study how Johnny was moving. And all the times, after gigs we'd go up to their room, steal their drink, fuck their groupies and leave 'em wondering what happened [*more laughter*].

'I mean, all the Frenchies are so serious about these bands. They get so offended when I put down all their fave groups that I just go ahead and do it! Like someone asks me what I think of the Stooges and I say, "Yeah, well, they've done a coupla good things, y'know, but . . ." and when they ask me what I think of the Blue Oyster Cult, I say, "Oh, you mean the Blue Oyster 'Cunt' don't you?"'

The band have grouped around the bar of the Ambassador Hotel in readiness for their afternoon gig at the Olympia and are behaving in their usually invigoratingly boisterous manner. Sylvain Sylvain, ex-native of Paris, who also spent some time at Finch's pub down in good old Ladbroke Grove dealing dope, is going wild with a cap-gun. Drummer Jerry Nolan acts sullen and seems none too bright. Bassist Arthur Kane, a completely freakish character, dressed in a ballerina's pompom and looking to all intents and purposes like he'd just been run-over by a truck-load of valium, takes me aside for a moment.

'Hey. You know Stacia?' (Hawkwind's well-proportioned dancer). 'She's a nice girl, I met her in New York. She's kinda crazy. I like crazy girls but the last crazy girl I was with tied me up while I was asleep and tried to cut my thumb off.' He stops the dialogue – performed in a slow drizzle of a monotone – for a second to show off a slashed-up thumb. 'I'm worried she might come back and try to kill me,' he adds as an afterthought. Jeez, another death in the band and the Dolls could trade themselves off as the Allman Bros. of sleaze rock.

And then again, Johnny Thunders looks none too well. Also quintessential punk-kid stance with impeccable rocker credentials, his dialogue is hardly the kind to set a typewriter on fire while it's being transcribed into print but still pin-points his no-nonsense attitude. And those credentials? Eddie Cochran, early Who and the MC5 are Mr Thunders' cup of meat – while he's also living with fifteen-year-old legend, Sable Starr, in New York. His thoughts on his beloved are typically dynamic: 'We just . . . uh . . . livin' together, y'know . . . We ain't married, or nuttin' . . . She got out of the whole groupie scene. Changed a lot. When I first met her, she was really . . . I dunno . . . weird chick but kinda nice. She's crazy but . . . uh . . . she's cool . . . y'know?'

Thanks, John. So what about the new songs?

'Well, there's "Mystery Girl" and, uh, one that I wrote called "Jailbreak Opera". It's short, y'know – no longer than five minutes. I just like to grab everything I can, throw it all in and get out, y'know . . .'

'Also there's "Puss 'n' Boots", which is quite sensational,' interjects David. 'It's about shoe fetishism, or as Arthur observed, it's about "the woofers in relationship with the woofee". And then we have this ballad which isn't quite finalized yet, but it's the most beautiful song since the Drifters' "On Broadway". It's also the title of the next album.'

The conversation turns to the Olympia gig. 'I can't wait. I mean, when I think of all the great artists who have performed there . . .'

Like James Brown?

'No, like Edith Piaf.'

So, when you're ready to label Johansen as nothing more than some preening, precocious runt, he pulls out a pure New Yorker rap like:

'I've checked out all this "Paris-is-the-city-of-romance" thing. It's just because all the chicks have to get fucked at least five times a day or else they go crazy. And that's why the guys are such pricks. Hey, did you know I used to be a child porn-movie star? Uh-huh – well, let me tell you I was the biggest draw on 42nd Street. What films did I make? Oh, *Studs on Main Street, Bike Boy Goes Ape* – I was only sixteen when those were made and I was very naive. I was manipulated, so to speak. I wouldn't like those things to get out now. They might do my image great harm. My image? Well, I think I look more like Peter Noone or David Cassidy than Mick Jagger. I think Noone is very together as an artist and a person. It was wonderful meeting him, actually. And David Cassidy – who I also think is a great performer.

'Oh, I think the New York Dolls are very, very relevant. I see rock'n'roll as like a changing of the guard and this time around, we're it. All I know is that we have all these beautiful, magnificent songs which I believe to be all classics. I mean, our first album is marvellous even if Todd Rundgren . . . uh . . . I don't even want to put him down, because if I did, it might detract from the sales potential and I want everybody to hear that record because there are some wonderful songs.'

(Johnny Thunders is more blunt in his appraisal of Rundgren's efforts for the Dolls: 'He fucked up the mix really bad. Every time we go on the radio to do interviews we always dedicate "Your Mama Don't Dance and Your Daddy Don't Rock'n'Roll" – know that song? – to Todd.)

'No, I don't see myself as a rock'n'roll star. When I think of that term, I think of people like Jeff Beck or Stevie Winwood – that whole English invasion. Keith Richards? Oh c'mon now, Keith's past it. He's had his day! And Bob Dylan – I was around on the scene in '66 – I knew what was going on and it was laughable. I see myself as an artist who is now ready to entertain the people who were always a focal point of the scene – the people I acted for or danced for when I was a kid. It was a process of self-assertion, of saying I can do this and I want to perform it for you. That's how the Dolls started for me. Though I'm very, very different from, say, Johnny, who's pure rocker and has that total awareness.'

The Dolls troop on stage at the Paris Olympia at 3.30 p.m., suitably bedraggled. Johansen, decked out in bastardized evening dress with various badges and emblems strategically placed on his costume ('for political purposes, I mean the leftists will get off on my Mao button and . . .'), commandeers proceedings, but the band are immediately dogged by a PA failure which totals the electricity for over five minutes. Once underway the sound is distorted and falls like lead inside the hall, pinpointing the already cacophonous sound to a slightly less-than-comfortable degree. Then there are other problems. Johnny Thunders, for one, looks about as well as his guitar sounds in tune. He staggers around the stage in obvious discomfort, attempting to motivate himself and the band simultaneously and succeeding only in beating his instrument into an ever-more horrendous state of tunelessness. The sound reaches its nadir on 'Vietnamese Baby', when the guitar inter-play is so drastically off-balanced that it becomes quite grotesque to listen to. On the next number Thunder stops half-way through, puts down his guitar and moves behind the amplifiers to throw up for five minutes, 'Y'know in some ways Johnny is just a child,' Marty Thau will state later, with a dewy-eyed paternal concern.

B-l-l-a-a-a-a-g-g-h-h!!

After the gig Steve Leber, the real manager, approaches Johansen. 'Hey, David, y'know we almost blew it there, with Johnny. He was so out of tune on "Vietnamese Baby" it was painful.' 'Oh I thought it was great,' David rebounds. 'Who cares about the music when one has that sense of [*an obliga-tory hand gesture*] *drama*. I mean, *really*!'

Outside the dressing-room hordes of Parisian poseurs are piled up, desperately trying to osmose a kind of gauloise-and-gold-earring cool. Only Syl and Johnny Thunders are holed up in the bar frisking back the drinks, while David socializes with all and sundry, telling one journalist, 'Listen, you want a scoop? Whaddya mean, it's not a scoop 'cos I've been talking to someone else? I got something different to tell all you boys.'

The evening sets in and everyone goes to a restaurant down along the main drag. Thunders and Syl leave first with a couple of girls, intent on smoking dope and getting wrecked just like they did the night before – in fact ever since they were the kids who were always being kicked out of Nobody's. David Johansen has his mind set on other things, though. A young pretty girl is exhorting him to come back with her. 'Oh, David, I luhv you, Dah-vid.' Johansen smiles cutely in a non-committal way. I mean, the night is still young and there are other things to consider: like the party where actor Pierre Clementi is supposed to be appearing. And Nico, she of the Velvet Underground legend days, now a recluse in Paris, having had to leave New York '*très vite*' after gouging a broken bottle into the face of a girlfriend of the city's Black Panther leader down at Max's one night.

'Oh, now, Nico has a really great sense of humour,' Johansen states absent-mindedly in the car leaving the restaurant. He, too, is starting to look tired. The sound check, the gig, the social activity, no sleep the night before – it all builds up. Arthur Kane is already sprawled out unconscious with his minuscule Parisienne girlfriend. Hey David, what was the title of that song? Y'know, the new one which is the greatest ballad since 'On Broadway'? '"Too Much, Too Soon" – It's autobiographical, y'know,' he grins. Five minutes later he too has flaked out from exhaustion.

They were the cockiest bunch I *ever* encountered but God knows the New York Dolls were anything but the luckiest. They managed a second album but somehow conspired to get the thing produced by a full-blown alcoholic called 'Shadow' Morton whose main claim to fame had been his extraordinarily kitsch work for a sixties all-girl group, the Shangri-Las. Meanwhile, the lethal combination of reckless arrogance and even more reckless drug-taking had wiped them out as a feasible live act for the stadiums and arenas. By the end of 1974, their management, Leber–Krebs, shunted them aside in favour of a more resilient Boston-based Stones-clone act called Aerosmith who'd taken several telling cues from the Dolls' own image. This is where Malcolm McLaren stepped in to try and save them. He had the idea of dressing them up in red patent leather and making them pretend to be Marxists. They wrote a bunch of new songs too but the McLaren concept basically got them laughed out of every club they played in by the old New York cognoscenti who ordained them so 'hip' to begin with.

They broke up in early 1975 during a residency at a crummy little Miami club McLaren had booked them into. Thunders became increasingly irritated about being away from his New

York heroin connections and he'd had enough of McLaren's ideas and singer David Johansen's 'let's get professional' bullshit. He told them both exactly what he thought of them and then flew back to New York, leaving several contracted gigs still to be played.

After that, Johansen and Sylvain kept the name going for a while but couldn't get a record deal until the singer reverted to his own name. Johansen's début solo album was a fine piece of work which added to the Dolls' rather limited legacy but it didn't really sell, and the ones that followed were consistently less impressive. Then, for the eighties he metamorphosized into Buster Poindexter, a sort of cross between Cab Calloway and Fatty Arbuckle who enjoyed much critical kudos but – once again – unsatisfactory record sales. Even so, he managed to stay busy working in films and has fared decidedly better in his career choices than any of his cohorts. His old collaborator Sylvain Sylvain lost most of his hair, is apparently poverty-stricken and keeps struggling to get new bands together in Los Angeles. The hapless Arthur Kane – after numerous years of fighting chronic alcoholism and incipient bad luck – was recently mugged and beaten to a condition where approximately half his brain has now shut down on him.

Nolan and Thunders meanwhile went on to form the Heartbreakers in 1975 with Richard Hell, but conflicting drug schedules and rampant egomania from all quarters quickly put paid to that alliance before it'd had time to blossom. Then the pair debarked to London just as 'punk-rock' was taking off and actually did quite well for themselves until their heroin problems turned everything to shit again.

In view of our mutual recreational activities, it's hardly surprising that Thunders and I became fast friends for a while. He was always a lively guy to be around and he always had this genuinely classy way of carrying himself like he saw himself as the Prince of the Streets or something equally grand.

He was a fearless little motherfucker and he was never boring, but the guy was also self-centred and spoilt rotten and he made himself a loser by buying into the myth that if you're a rock'n'roll star you're automatically absolved of having to confront the consequences of your actions.

Johnny was and remains at the very least a remarkable source for mind-boggling tall tales and it's impossible for me not to think about him now without breaking into some sort of smile. But, oh, what a lost soul! He never once questioned the impossible, heedless lifestyle he'd rail-roaded himself into. I remember the last time I really spoke to him – it was some-time in 1986 – and he was heavy-lidded as usual and full of that whiny-voiced New York junkie attitude of his turned all the way up to 11. He started bragging to me about how in a Pennsylvania hotel some guy from 'Narcos Anonymous' had lately approached him and invited him to an NA meeting taking place just down the hall. Johnny told that guy just what he could do with his meeting. But the young man persisted, even offering him a book about challenging drug dependency and signed it 'To Johnny – a hero of mine. Maybe this book can save your life.' When Thunders read that dedication, he threw the book straight back into the poor guy's face. I mean, didn't this sap – this fuckin' walking waste of sperm and egg – realize that he – the great Johnny Thunders – wanted to stay exactly the way he was supposed to stay, living the life of an unregenerate, double-dealing junkie under-achiever. So what if he'd taken up permanent residency in hell! He liked it down there.

The last time I saw him though – Jesus Christ, I could hardly stand to look at John. You know in a bull-fight how when the decisive dagger has been plunged into the neck of the bull and basically it's all over for the poor creature and it goes limp and cross-eyed before sinking slowly into the saw-dust. Well, that's how Thunders looked on the night of New Year's Eve just as 1991 was being ushered in: limp and cross-eyed from all the torments he'd been visiting upon himself in the pursuit of maintaining his righteous rock'n'roll identity. A few weeks later he died in New Orleans in a lonely hotel room with only some bad cocaine, some prescription Methadone and two dope-dealing low-lifers whose names he probably didn't even know for company. *Que sera sera.*

But right now I'm not thinking about John's demise or about poor old Jerry, who died only a year after his old partner-in-crime from ailments directly connected to his drug problems. I'm trying to cast my mind back to a time when everything has a naive little sparkle about it – 1973. And suddenly I'm twenty-one again and terribly over-dressed but then so is everyone else who's come to be squeezed into this tiny little Manhattan club called Kenny Castaways to see the New York Dolls. 'This is a song for the twenty-first century when women will have taken over all the power and all the men will have to seek refuge for themselves in massage parlours . . .' dead-pans David Johansen in his flapper chic, perched in front of the microphone like a little girl trying to look coquettish in her mother's high-heels. To his immediate left Johnny Thunders is twisting up his goofy Italian face into the perfect cut-throat sneer, throwing his remarkable explosion of ink-black hair back and forth and playing the only guitar riff he knows over and over again, while to his left Sylvain Sylvain is strumming rudimentary chords on a big, slightly out-of-tune Gretsch guitar while making these little tottering steps back and forth and shaking his Raggedy Ann cork-screw curls unceasingly. Just behind these three the unfortunate Arthur Kane – dressed in a little tutu and little else – is playing crappy one-note bass and looking like the world's foremost ongoing accident statistic while Jerry Nolan with his shag-cut and that look on his face that always screamed, 'Duh!', is holding the music together with his power-house drumming. The music is raw and alive, played with reckless abandon until it becomes a joyous celebration of the whole 'be young, be foolish, be happy' school of thought. Believe me, the records don't even begin to capture the special magic of the Dolls on a good night playing in a pissy little club to their élite little crowd of mascara-daubed misfits and vagrant vamps. Misty glitzy memories of the way we were. So cute. So vital. So star-crossed.

Lou Reed: The Wasted Years

'I originally met Lou Reed at a party. I came with a friend, we both had long hair and some guy approached us and told us we looked very commercial and would we like to meet this band called the Primitives who had this terrible single out, called "Do the Ostrich". Lou was in the band, but he was bitter because they wouldn't let him do "Heroin". A relationship was struck up and we moved into an apartment together. I remember always noticing these faggy-looking types hanging around the apartment. It took me quite a while before I realized what was going on.

'Sterling [Morrison] had gone to Syracuse College with Lou, and Mo lived down the street from him. She was a button operator or something by day and in the evening she'd go home and play drums. We had so much trouble with drummers but Mo was good at being basic so she was brought in . . . Actually Lou was always saying, "Sterling can't play guitar," and that Mo couldn't play . . . He kept saying, "But man, she can't play . . ."

'My idea was to keep the sound simple, but by overlaying the instruments' simplistic pattern the accumulative effect of the sound would be incredibly powerful. I was highly intrigued by the whole Phil Spector wall-of-sound concept but obviously I had to modify it to a four-piece set-up. Actually I always found myself caught between playing the viola and playing bass. I never thought we made enough of the viola, which is a very powerful instrument.

'There were always conflicts and presumably always will be. Though we both basically agreed on that particular policy. Lou was the vocalist, front man and songwriter for the band. I was just taking it easy and generally having fun. Now I look back on it all, I wasn't particularly enamoured of the more garish aspects of, say, the whole Exploding Plastic Inevitable. But then, that's exactly what Lou was very into.

'Those guitar solos – they're all Lou's – and one of them, I think it's on "I Heard Her Call My Name," is really incredible. But that was his sound. Actually all those songs are so fast – I kept trying to get them down to a slightly slower pace, y'know.

'But then the break-up occurred. I'd just got married, which was one cause, I think. Also Lou was starting to act funny. He brought in this guy called Selznick – who I thought was a real snake – to be our manager and all this intrigue started to take place. Lou was calling us "his band" while Selznick was trying to get him to go solo. Maybe it was the drugs he was doing at the time. They certainly didn't help. I mean there was another time – an incident that Sterling can in fact witness to – where Lou played me this song he'd written and I immediately started adding an improvised viola part.

'Sterling muttered something about it being a good viola part and Lou turned around and said, "Yeah, I know. I wrote that song just for that viola part. Every single note of it I knew in advance!" It was sad in a way because there were still some great songs to be recorded like "Here Come the Waves" which later became "Ocean" on his first album and a bunch of others. I heard a bootleg tape of a concert we did at Columbus, Ohio, and all it sounded like was Lou constantly tuning his guitar up and down for ten minutes at a time. Also there was absolutely no applause.

'Actually, I'm amazed at just how different we were in our ideas, now I've heard everything Lou's done since that time. It all just sounds like a weak representation of tunes and nothing more. I mean, some of his songs in the Velvets really made a point, y'know. Now he just appears to be going around in circles, singing about transvestites and the like. The only thing I've heard him do since, where he put up a good performance, was on the song . . . uh . . . it's a girl's name . . . oh – "Sweet Jane".

'I think he might start writing some good songs again, were he to go back and live with his parents. That's where all his best work came from. His mother was some sort of ex-beauty queen and I think his father was a wealthy accountant. Anyway, they put him in a hospital where he received shock treatment as a kid. Apparently he was in Syracuse and was given this compulsory choice to either do gym or ROTC [a military service deal]. He claimed he couldn't do gym because he'd break his neck and when he went to ROTC he threatened to kill his instructor. Then he put his fist through a window or something and so he was put in this mental hospital. I don't know the full facts. Every time Lou told me about he'd change it slightly'

– John Cale, talking to the author, spring 1974.

'New York is so desperate. You have to be desperate to go there at all. Lou asked me and . . . Lou isn't my friend though. Because he wouldn't share his drugs with me. He was taking Octagell, which is the strongest form of speed. You know of it? It makes your teeth clench together [*she demonstrates*]. Also I had to leave his house because he was beating his girlfriend'

– Nico, talking to the author, summer 1974.

'I was really fucked up. And that's all there is to it. It's like I really encouraged it. I did a lot of things that were really stupid and I don't know how they could sit and listen seriously to that stuff. But I catered to it for a long time because I thought it was funny.

'It was such a big deal, a song called "Heroin" being on an album and I thought that was really stupid. I mean, they had it in the movies in the forties – *The Man with the Golden Arm*, for Chrissakes. So what was the big deal? It was like talking to pygmies. People were offended because we did a song called "Heroin" but there's plenty of stuff about that in literature and no one gives a shit but it's rock'n'roll so we must be pushing drugs or something. I thought after all that stuff about "Heroin", well . . . If you find that so shocking, take a look at this. It was a stupid, childish attitude I had but, you know, as long as they were going that way I thought, "Fuck it, I'll give it a little push that way, a little street theatre." Getting involved in all that was like going along with it, pandering to it. I don't think it brought out the most attractive features in me'

– a clean and sober Lou Reed talking about the seventies in Q Magazine, spring 1989.

Another predictable 'nothing-to-do' night in New York in the early spring of 1974 and a couple of friends and I decided to forestall yet another predictable lurch down to Max's Kansas City by paying a short visit to some 'nouveau-tack' disco/lounge-bar dive that someone from the record company had earlier handed me a free pass to, called (aye-aye-aye) The Twinkie Zone. The cab checked us out on 49th and Lexington and already, as we walked down to the entrance, there was some sort of a ruckus going on around the cloakroom area. Nothing to get too concerned about: just a bunch of negroes laughing and giving everyone 'high-fives' with their ample palms. Then I noticed the centre of attraction, huddled stooge-like within this morass of grinning black faces, and things start to get vaguely sinister. From a distance the character looked like just another sub-human Manhattan dementoid who must ... ah, but then I started getting closer and distinct physical characteristics started uncomfortably insinuating themselves on the vision.

He (She? It?) stood there looking to all the world like one of those mangy half-starved Mexican dogs (who always appear limping pathetically across the desolate stone landscape of a Sam Peckinpah movie just after the outlaw heroes have vamoosed across the border) but transformed by some hideous miscalculation of fate into human form. The hair was shaved as close to the head as possible, like Charles Manson's when he was graced with a prison cut, and went one step further, but mutilated even way beyond that by what appeared to be large random patches of diseased albino colouring. It was only when I got closer that I noticed these areas on the sides of the head were in fact specifically shaped like Nazi iron crosses. Then there was the face which possessed not only the most uniquely grey and decayed fleshly pallor I've yet to witness on any human visage but also a fixed glazed look to the eyes like several hundred watts of electricity were being fired through his central nervous system. The body was skinny and emaciated almost beyond belief. God, he looked awful!

My boot heels were already set to go a-wanderin' straight out the door again when one of the assembled company, a former Warholite as it happened, started chirping away in perplexed quasi-Brooklyn chipmunk tonalities.

'Lou! . . . Lou! . . . Lou? . . . LOU Reed? . . .'

I turned around again expecting maybe to see some Porky Pig look-alike in leather-boy drag to emerge suddenly from the shadows, drink in hand, but the disturbed cries for recognition were directed towards the offending object itself, who continued to stagger around in a daze until he manoeuvred his shaky form up to the girl, stared right into her face and burbled, 'Susan', before sidling off in the approximate direction of the bar and almost walking face-first into a nearby plate-glass window.

It took me a good minute of solid staring to visually equate this utterly dissipated apparition with any previous physical incarnation that was ever named Lou Reed. It wasn't easy. For a start, I've never seen a man so utterly paralysed, so completely devoid of life while managing to somehow keep breathing, as Reed had looked that night.

'We were worried when we first saw him like that, too, but what can you do? Louis is such an extremist.' Barbara Falk is the secretary for Dennis Katz, a successful young lawyer who works up on the 37th floor of a skyscraper situated on 59th and Madison. Dennis Katz is also the manager of Lou Reed. 'Dennis and Lou did have a fall-out when Louis appeared with those Nazi crosses in his hair. But . . . like I said, what can you do?'

What, indeed? I mean, what am I even doing having an interview set up with Lou Reed, who, not three nights ago, I'd decided had finally degenerated into little more than a corpse with a heart-beat. I didn't like the new album, considering the reconstruction work on 'Heroin' – and particularly 'Rock'n'Roll' – heresy of sorts, and the few rumours I'd heard floating around ranged from the prominent one that claimed Reed was back into taking speed (popular probably because it helped explain the loss of three or four stone in weight in about as many months) or else that he was obsessed with sadism, had done a recent video with Andy Warhol that has caused him much personal disillusionment and sorrow. And lastly, that he'd written a bunch of new songs, among them one called 'I Wanna Be Black'; another, a mini-opera about a cat and a dog called 'Miss O'Reilly's Dog'.

Anyway, Barbara leads me into a room full of law books and, before too long, I'm joined by Katz and Reed himself.

There can't be anyone cleaner-looking in the whole of show business (never mind the whole of New York) than Dennis Katz. I mean, what's a nice Jewish lawyer like Dennis doing leading in this half-human neo-Nazi? And one of the same faith, already! Well, for a start, Katz is doing all the talking. Reed sits brooding next to him looking disturbingly like a frightened monkey in a studded leather jacket and tight jeans (Katz plays the organ-grinder). Such is the state of the singer's emaciated contours that nothing seems to fit properly. All of which makes him appear even more uncomfortable.

For fifteen minutes Katz talks enthusiastically about how he's now starting to handle Iggy Pop's affairs (which makes him more and more appear like some benevolent missionary for that peculiar genre of ailing, sickly twilight-zone rock geniuses), how Nothing's Happening in New Yuk, how *Rock'n'Roll Animal* is shaping up on the Hit Pick stations, how they had to put *Animal* out speedily because no one quite understood *Berlin*.

'It was intended as a black comedy,' laughs Katz. Ha, ha. I always thought it sounded like the creation of a team of people all suffering from terminal valium hangovers locked away to think up the most grandiosely turgid, depressing piece of brilliance they could muster from among their collective bloated fantasies.

Reed remains silent throughout, except for a couple of attempts at verbal interjections where his voice sounds so parched and dry he literally chokes on his own words. All hopes for some transcendental dialogue have temporarily been shelved. I'm more concerned about seeing Reed actually speak up and give one coherent reply. The first question I finally address to him is a throw-away concerning the reported traumas that went into the making of *Berlin*. The cogs begin to turn and out croaks a subdued, uncertain sound.

'*Berlin* . . . I mean, I had to . . . I had to do *Berlin* . . . If I hadn't done it . . . I'd have gone crazy. And everyone was saying, "Don't do it – you'll get killed." It was insanity coming off after a hit single . . . but . . . but I mean, it was all written. If I hadn't got it out of my head I would have exploded.'

Long pause.

'It was a very painful album to make . . . and we got killed under it. And only me and Bobby [Erzin, the producer] really knew what we had there, what it did to us . . . I . . . I don't wanna go through it again, having to say those words over and over and over again . . .' Reed beats his fist against the table to emphasize the 'overs', looking more glazed and fatigued by the second as he relates the pained saga.

Ah, but c'mon, Lou, shape up and don't get so maudlin about it. Wasn't Dennis over there just telling me it was all one big black comedy? Reed fails to light up to the idea, however, and stolidly insists on pacing his words at an ominously slow rate – almost in reverence to the trials presumably incurred during the recording of the album.

'No, there was no black comedy as far as we were concerned. I knew we were open to that, seeing as it came off, uh, after *Transformer*. I mean, I love *Transformer* . . . It's a fun album, y'know . . . *Transformer* is a fun album and *Berlin* isn't.'

So what about *Rock'n'Roll Animal*, which was recorded live at the Academy of Music with what has since become his old band. All except guitarist Dick Wagner have since split the roost, leaving Reed and manager Katz to pull together yet another back-up band. The sound on the album is all 'pomp and circumstance' heavy-metal thunder, expertly wrought but obviously far too session-musician finicky professional to hope to approximate the magical ineptitude that personified the Velvet Underground sound. Still, you don't argue, at least for the moment, because Reed is more than a little adamant about his feelings concerning the appropriateness of the new versions.

'It's the way those things should be done and hadn't been done' – more fists banged on the table to press the point home – 'correctly. And it finally *was* done correctly! So just like

Berlin had to be gotten out of the way, that had to finally close off and finally finish the fuckin' thing! That's the way I wanted those songs to sound from the very beginning. For better or worse, that's it.

'But, you see, when people think of the Velvet Underground they think of "Heroin". I was always more fascinated by "I'll Be Your Mirror." [*Pause.*] *Rock'n'Roll Animal* is a clarification of my old work . . . I think. I've had my hit single and I want all those kids to know what came before that. Because they don't know and I want them to be aware of exactly what predated "Walk on the Wild Side".'

The slow deliberate tone of his voice sounded not a little disparaging when the aforementioned hit single is brought up. So, d'you still stand by all that Max's back-room 'chic' mentholated blubbering?

'Oh sure – it's cute,' gurgles Reed. '. . . Doo-doo-doo-doo-doo . . .' He sniggers into his Jack Daniels.

This is progress.

OK, Lou, so let's get down to business. How d'ya lose all that fat then? Huh? As if on cue, Reed returns to his zomboid drone and the pauses between commentary become even more elongated and strained. Barbara Falk, ever the helpful soul, offers, 'He just stopped eating,' before Lou speaks up.

'Uh . . . it's like . . . uh, the guy I studied under . . . a poet, Delmore Schwartz. His friends wouldn't let him drive a car because in his own words. . . . uh . . . "Life as he had known it had made him nervous." [*Sniggers.*] . . . And I guess . . . uh.' [*Long pause.*] '. . . It depends on boredom . . . And tension. Getting interested, y'know, in things after you get things settled. Getting involved again . . . Not being bored. Because when I get bored . . . uh, funny things happen.'

So were you bored during the whole *Lou Reed/Transformer* period?

'Well I wasn't exactly exhilarated or thrilled by the whole thing. Boredom isn't the proper word. I knew things weren't right and I was waiting. And while I was waiting . . . uh . . . These other things sort of just happened. Like my marriage. It was kind of a pessimistic act. Nothing else to do at the time. Kept me off the street. "So what's new this week?" "Well, I think I'll get married." And that's when I really started gaining weight. Then one day it dawned on me that it was all like a movie. And the thing about movies is that if you don't like 'em, you can always walk out. And as soon as that became clear, it was all very simple. Now I don't get headaches anymore. And I'm poorer. All the money I make, she gets. They call it alimony.'

So does all this augur a spanking new positivism in the philosophical make-up of Lou Reed?

'Well, I'm not pessimistic. I really like the way things are going and I love the new songs.'

Reed's conversational prowess, however, reaches some kind of burlesque nadir when he actually gets around to trying to describe these new gems of musical/lyrical inspiration.

'Uh . . . well, there's one about . . . [*Long pause.*] Uh, what *are* the new songs? . . . I've got them on tape, y'know, but I keep forgetting them . . . [*Another long pause.*] Oh yeah, there's one called "Kill Your Sons" about parents sending their kids to psychiatrists and giving them shock treatment. The songs seem to all have movement from the general to an example all of a sudden [Uh?] . . . not intimate but specific detail. [Uh?] . . . They all seem to move that way. Constantly.

'There's another called "Babyface" which is about two guys living together and it all comes down to the one saying to the other, "Well, you're not the easiest person to get along with." It's about interpersonal relationships on a one-to-one level. Of the others, "I Want to Be Black" – it's about young middle-class kids who . . . uh, seem to go through this phase of wanting to be . . . like . . . uh, Black Panthers – isn't going to be recorded.'

However, that disappointment is more than compensated for by Reed's description of his forthcoming masterpiece, 'Miss

O'Reilly's Dog' (a song which actually saw the light of day entitled 'Animal Logic' on the *Sally Can't Dance* album).

'Oh yeah . . . It's about this woman who has this dog . . . uh . . . and it gets shot 'cos it barks too much and the neighbours get upset . . . and then this cat . . . uh . . . I forget what happens to the cat but something happens to the cat . . . Anyway the dog and the cat meet. Yeah, the dog's dead, I guess . . . I dunno how he's still alive but he's alive and then, uh . . . some dude sees 'em both and puts a board between 'em.'

And then what happens?

'. . . Uh, I think they both get high . . .'

I see.

'I like these songs a lot. I think they're the best I ever did. Nah, there's no . . . uh, concept, but I notice as I listen to 'em over and over again that interpersonal-relationship theme seems to be running through.'

So there are no obsessive topics to be incessantly dwelt upon this time? Like the last one was suicide, right?

'Yeah, it was . . . *But not mine!* Hers! . . . Someone standing there holding a razor blade up and she looks like she might kill you but instead she starts cutting away at her wrists and there's blood everywhere . . . Yeah, you could get interested in suicide.'

Ol' Lou just drools on, his Peter Lorre bug-eyes set in a lethargic stare. But, like he says, suicide was last year's thrill.

'We got down to the point where we were saying, "Well, you don't cut this way, you cut *that* way"' – symbolically sliding a finger across the lower veins of his left arm – 'But me? Oh no, I wouldn't do anything like that. It's so easy in a way: the actual process . . . [*Long pause.*] I mean, I've seen so many people like that. You either do it or you don't. And I . . . I know where I want to go. I'm in control . . . uh, I know that there's this level and then there's *this* level' – measuring up with his hand – 'and I've seen over *that* level and I'm not even going to go near it. Ever. I'm in control, that's for sure.'

But hey, Lou, then why do you look so godawful? I mean, don't you want to be healthy and clean yourself up a bit? Quit getting the shakes and get a bit of colour in those pallid cheeks?

'Well I'm getting healthier, y'know.' He croaks. 'My drinking is . . . uh, minimal now. I get into that when I'm bored. So much of that shit is behind me. I don't write too much . . . but then I would only write a lot if I had no direction.'

The funeral pace of this discourse takes on an almost poignant tone when the matter of Andy Warhol's failed attempt to videotape Reed recently is brought up.

'Oh Andy . . . It was very sad because he said while we were doing it . . . "You know, it can never happen again." And he was right. Y'see, Andy's situation is kinda harsh. All that sixties energy and now we're in the seventies and there's nothing there. He seems to be waiting but . . . oh, he's so fantastic. People still don't realize how great he is. Oh, he's made the transition, sure, but so have I, y'know. I'm just doing different things. All the rest have been left behind. I didn't even think I had an image. I mean, what image? Now onstage . . . Well all those songs are real and I become that song. But it doesn't affect me outside that particular song.

'There are certain things I just can't do, image or no image. I mean, I did go down to Lexington – I did all the stuff then. But I don't now, and I think it's kinda sad that people are still caught up in that. "Candy Says" . . . "Pale Blue Eyes", those are *my* songs, from my personal experience. And "I'll Be Your Mirror".

'I mean, one night Nico came up to me and said, "Oh Lou, I'll be your mirror," and it bowled me over. I wrote that song for her. Most of the time I just write through other people's experience. Yeah, you could say I'm a voyeur. But I'm not, y'know. I was just talking about what was going on around me. I've always been listening – to this day I still do. Like, I'm not heroin, or I'm not speed, or I'm not liquor, or I'm not up or down. It's like a circle. I write songs, that's all. And I try to make 'em as real as possible. And the way that happens is because they are. They're not necessarily about me, though. That's where everybody gets confused, y'see.'

Finally, Reed is joined by a comparatively vivacious-looking New York girl called Barbara, who appears to be his girlfriend. Dressed in the current thirties-style glad rags she buzzes around him, while he remains seated, his skull creased by a lazy smile. Later in the evening I run into an old friend of his who laughs at my original odds on Reed's chances for that big date with Sharon Tate.

'Oh, he's got his problems, but I bet he'll outlive all of us. He'll probably be around even to read his own obituary.' Why not? He must have read enough of them already . . . Oh yeah and those Nazi crosses? They were actually World War One insignia of some sort. I mean, a nice upper-middle-class Jewish boy like Lou sporting Nazi crosses? His mother should live so long!

Sid Vicious: The Exploding Dim-Wit

January 1978, Sticksville, USA, through whose big old heart a big old bus travels bearing the fabulous Sex Pistols on a tour that will conclude with the group's self-detonation. A deluxe vehicle, its inhabitants comprise the four Pistols, one Malcolm McLaren, some roadies, a Warner Bros. exec and two photographers. Anyway, Sid Vicious is staring out the window – the obligatory beer can in one paw, a sandwich in the other, a blowjob on his mind and dreams of a syringe in his arm – when he turns and those scrawny eyes alight on a wondrous vision. *Motorcycle boots*, to be precise, but not just any old motorcycle boots: these, like, *unbelievably* heavy-duty storm-trooping creations of leather and steel. They were, however, being worn by one of the photographers; some *fuckin' Yank* called *Bob* that McLaren was matey with or something. Sid didn't dislike this bloke, mind. Didn't much like him either. He meant fuck all to Sid really; he was just like, there. But the boots were espied and Sid was smitten. He got well intimate then. Nothing extravagant of course. Just yer basic, 'All right then, mate? Uh, bet you got some fucking good snaps eh?' Then with nary a pause, Vicious asked the fellow to flog him his boots *'cos, like*, he really *fancied 'em*.

Unfortunately, there was a problem here which Sid would have instantly recognized as 'insurmountable' were he, the mighty Sid Vicious, capable of comprehending the concept, never mind understanding the word. Bob wasn't some biker fop: it was just that, so spacious were the boots that a whole camera, simply dismantled, would fit snugly inside the lining. They had become a necessary appendage to his vocation. Sid took this in. It's debatable whether he fully grasped the reasons, but he understood a guy saying 'no'. Still, Bob stemmed the tide of pleading he sensed fast approaching by allowing Sid to wear his boots onstage that night at whatever redneck club the group were scheduled to trash.

Once Sid got his feet in Bob's boots he felt himself undergoing a considerable transformation. The truth be known, lately he hadn't been feeling his old self, but on the stage that night Sid felt his whole stance increased. The fact that he was performing the wrong bass parts for most of the set was inconsequential. Lydon was acting like a stuck-up wanker, a bloody ponced-up pop star who wasn't like, even *involved* in the spirit of the thing; in those boots, those precious boots, Sid felt himself invincible. Still, they weren't his.

Bob again allowed Vicious to wear them the next night that the Pistols performed, and *again*, the fact was made resolutely manifest: Sid and these boots were made for each other. He struggled to find the right solution. Bob wasn't budging – this was clear. The boots were back on Bob's feet so stealing them was not feasible. The answer struck home: in order to get those boots, Sid would have to kill him.

It was approaching 3 a.m. and virtually every passenger on this downbound bus was sprawled in positions appropriate to some condition of sleep. Providential indeed, then, that one of the party should awake just in time to look upon a chilling spectacle. Bob was sound asleep in a vaguely upright position, his backbone curved against the slight dip in the posture-sprung seating. Directly behind his prone form stood Sid Vicious, his right hand brandishing a Bowie knife.

Amassing what strength he could muster, our interloper managed to tackle Vicious from behind, jerking both arms up behind his ('Vicious') head and removing the weapon almost at once. Vicious didn't scream or attempt to unfasten his gangling limbs from the hammerlock. Amazingly, the action itself roused not a soul, not even Bob. The interloper, a longstanding colleague of McLaren, had encountered Sid on various occasions, though never remotely in such circumstances. He was stunned. Vicious was also stunned: the interloper's shocked stare bore down on him. The first person to break the silence was Sid. Shamefaced, he pleaded with an earnestness that undermined any possibility of it being a humorous remark.

'I would have woken him up before I slit his throat,' he kept repeating.

That is my favourite Sid Vicious story, not simply because it packs that good hearty *thwack* of sensationalism, but more because it is a perfect example of the psychological bomb-site upon which John Simon Ritchie invented his own Action Man in the persona of Sid Vicious.

Ritchie was born in May 1958, a suitably turbulent year that witnessed the lascivious rise and fall of Jerry Lee Lewis, infamy's most indomitable living practitioner, the slayings of young Nebraskan Charlie Starkweather, and the celluloid vision of Elvis Presley, a young god, explaining his physical predilections to some corn-fed belle thus: 'That ain't tactics, baby, that's the beast in me.' In a way, the stage was set.

He grew up in and around the outskirts of London – principally the East End – the only child of a single parent, and in those crucial seven years of life – well, one can surmise. Imagine claustrophobic estate blocks, spurious influences and the presence of something inexplicably disturbing, impersonal and sickly scented: some stranger lying comatose against a bean-bag. Children around junkies are given few options in life. Our little prince was given two: he could stare at the wall, or he could throw himself against it. He chose the latter, time and time again.

Most rock stars of the rebellious mould use their parents' values as the source point of their desire for reinvention. John

Simon Ritchie used the world as a whole, but, lacking vision and the potential to apply himself, his alter ego was fashioned more by a colleague, John Lydon. He, Lydon and others were a gang, sneering and puerile, with Lydon the brains and the rest the brawn, and banter. Because virtually all this mob were called John, making it hard to know whose round it was, nicknames were compulsory. Lydon rechristened our lad Sid – a name he loathed but duly lived with.

Sid initially adored Lydon, with his higher intellect and a clear cutting edge to his loathing. When the latter was asked to join the Sex Pistols, Sid and the others became a leering gestapo for Lydon's Top Cat persona. Fuelled on sulphate and acid, they were the big noise now. *They knew the truth* and anyone threatening that autonomy was needful of a lesson in intimidation.

In June 1976, Sid was dispatched to give such a lesson to a journalist at a Pistols gig taking place in the 100 Club. Assisted by another psychopath accomplice, who held a knife some two inches, no more, from this music writer's face, Sid aimed five good scalp-lacerating hits with his rusty bike chain. Only once did he hit his mark, causing much bloodletting but little damage. The blow, however, warranted an ebullient Lydon to grant Sid a new surname: 'Vicious'.

Infamy was now calling the shots: Sid was quoted at length in punk exposés: he abhorred 'sex', 'uniforms', 'hypocritical bastards', 'hippies', 'poseurs', prescribing a good kicking for all and sundry. A century earlier another young hellion had struck fear into the hearts of the law-abiding. Billy the Kid, like Sid (Ritchie or Beverley), boasted two surnames: Bonney or Harrigan. Also, like Sid, he first killed at age fourteen. Bill's victim was a drink-sodden *hombre*, one Belisano Villagran, a gun-fighter of local renown around the tumbleweed-strewn badlands of New Mexico. Sid's victim was a cat: swinging it by its tail repeatedly, he beat the feline's brains to mush against a brick wall. Both also died aged twenty or twenty-one. Billy the Kid, however, had cold-blooded guile and a devastatingly quick left hand to back up his reputation as the fastest gun in the West. Twenty-one victims were notched on his holster ('not counting Mexicans'). Sid Vicious, however, only managed to foul up everything he got involved in. No stamina, no gumption. As one quarter of the Sex Pistols – at their best the musical equivalent of a car wreck – he displayed all the dexterity of a one-legged man at an arse-kicking contest. As a hellion, he was feeble. Whereas the desperado or snake-eyed boy let his weapon do the talking, Vicious would solemnly intone, 'Well, I think that I'm not, like, *really, really* vicious, y'know . . .' He'd pause, lost in half-baked exegesis, 'but I'm pretty wild!'

He was just another dirty fighter. He couldn't throw a punch and lacked the bearing, the stance, of a good scrapper. A good scrapper works from his heels, uses his wits, develops a technique for felling the opponent. Vicious just bottled in, all gangly limbs and mock sneer. He was only dangerous because pain – physical pain – wasn't a concern he seemed remotely aware of. Instead he would wantonly gouge his torso with broken glass, razor blades, knife cuts. He would do this when he was 'bored'. Boredom was intolerable, as the great George Sanders pointed out in his suicide note.

Love, for Sid, was another wretched contrivance, be it 'universal harmony' or the more intimate variant. By the autumn of '76, as an oft-quoted celebrity in the vanguard of punk's disaffected youth, he boasted that he was the most sexless creature in the world. Then, some four months on, he encountered Nancy Spungen and duly revised his opinion.

Vicious first tried heroin not in the company of Spungen but in the company of Heartbreakers Johnny Thunders and Jerry Nolan. The former would wave a syringe in the face of some uninitiated, impressionable shill. 'Are you a boy or a man?' he would tease, turning the issue into a matter of puerile machismo. Vicious, of course, tried it – twice, in fact, while in their company. He threw up a lot and found the experience less than awe-inspiring. However, when Spungen, a maladjusted harridan who'd flown to London in the vain hope of recommencing her fleeting affair with drummer Nolan, found herself in Vicious's company, she sensed the malleable nature of Vicious's hedonistic potential and steered him into the murky precincts of filtered cottons and that same acrid stench he must have recalled offending his senses as a child. For a short while there was a sexual rapport that Vicious had never believed could exist: the archetypal mixed-up restless little boy and maladjusted, self-fixated little girl looking for that golden-armed handshake from a white-knuckled world. Some would call it 'love' – but I prefer to concur with Lou Reed in 'Street Hassle': 'It's called bad luck'.

Infamy is a flint-hearted vocation to live with, requiring lightning reflexes and an abundance of quick-wittedness. Vicious and Spungen had neither. Two months of enchantment curdled overnight into a year of entrapment. Romeo and Juliet they weren't: their relationship was closer to a hopelessly juvenile version of Jack Lemmon and Lee Remick in *Days of Wine and Roses*. On 12 October 1978, ten months after the Pistols' detonation, during which time Vicious had alienated everyone he'd ever known but his soul-mate, the affair came to a predictably gore-spattered conclusion. At 10.50 a.m. a barely coherent English accent phoned the Chelsea Hotel switchboard, asking someone to check room 100 because 'someone is seriously injured'. The Manhattan police arrived to find Vicious stunned, seated on the bed, while in the bathroom the dead body of Nancy Spungen lay under the sink, a trail of blood running from the bed to her final resting-place. When probed, Vicious stated that the fatality had occurred because he was 'a dog, a dirty dog'. A moment later, suddenly acquainted with the enormity of his circumstances, he said, 'You can't arrest me. I'm a rock'n'roll star.'

Ten days later Sid was free on bail. Old acquaintances had sprung to his aid. His mother had flown over; Malcolm McLaren (who, weeks earlier, had refused to take a phone call from his former client) was in town, determined to free 'his boy' even if it meant employing the services of F. Lee Bailey, America's most prestigious defence lawyer. Conspiracy theories were being tossed around: Spungen had been the victim of a drug syndicate hit; a mugger had attacked her while Vicious slept. Optimism reigned, or so it seemed, but Vicious was far from jubilant. His metabolism had been through hell while he was ensconced at Ryker's Island jail. Also his conscience was riddled with a gnawing remorse.

That evening he locked the door to the bathroom and, finding only a Bic razor and a broken lightbulb, he slashed away at every vein in his arms and legs. His mother respected her son's wish to die and sat by him as the blood seeped from his body. By the time McLaren and Joe Stevens, Vicious's un-official minder, arrived, they were confronted with a scene of extraordinary hideousness. Vicious was so far gone he could no longer control his bladder and urine kept spurting over the blood-soaked sheets.

Mrs Beverley immediately rounded on a dazed McLaren, informing him that this was a suicide pact and not to interfere. Sid meanwhile, still conscious, begged his manager to go out and score some downers so as to stop the pain. McLaren walked to the door not knowing what to do. Stevens knelt next to Vicious and with a small cassette recorder in his hand pressed 'record'. The first words are his. 'So, Sid, on that night, what really happened?'

The tape lasted half an hour. Lapses occurred, the voice receded, yet the clarity of recollection was consistent.

They'd been waiting to score, having received a wad of dollar bills – over $1,000 in cash – for an upcoming gig. However, no narcotics could be found. Their dealer, a guy nick-named 'Rockets', gave them Tuinol, a heavy barbiturate which, mixed with alcohol, caused Vicious's withdrawal symptoms to worsen. At one point he left the room and began knocking on all the doors of the Chelsea Hotel, screaming for drugs.

This alerted a suitably imposing black custodian, who, having verbally warned Vicious – only to be called 'a fuckin' nigger' – began striking the puny twerp, in the process breaking his nose. Vicious crawled back to the room to be confronted by Spungen equally enraged. She slapped his face, striking the broken nose and causing the brutish pain to intensify. Vicious, standing by the table on which a 7-inch knife was placed, reciprocated: one clean lunge at the stomach of his beloved. It was hopeless, stupid and typical of their relationship. Minutes later they were embracing, reconciled. Unfortunately, Spungen removed the blade and omitted to cover the wound with a bandage of any sort. She lay down on the bed, while Vicious, similarly negligent in matters of basic hygiene, dashed off to keep an appointment at the methadone clinic. When he returned, his beloved Nancy was deceased. She was not yet twenty-one.

As Vicious finished the halting recitation, McLaren returned not with a handful of downers but with an ambulance. Two weeks in Bellevue Hospital had Vicious patched up. His morale also changed: guilt and remorse were no longer concerns worthy of a wild and crazy desperado like Sid Vicious. Like all hopelessly self-absorbed rock stars he detoured away from moral considerations and believed what he and his fans wanted. He wasn't guilty and the realization that he was once more a big noise – possibly capable of literally getting away with murder – excited him. He had a new girlfriend, who, like Spungen, was a well-known hardcore groupie, and that cocky psychopathic attitude – 'I'm a rock'n'roll star. You can't arrest me' – was suddenly back to the forefront.

It ended in the second week of December 1978. Vicious, back to his initial kamikaze oafishness, had lewdly propositioned the girlfriend of Todd Smith, brother of Patti. Smith had verbally reprimanded him only to have Vicious smash a broken bottle into his face, almost blinding him. Smith pressed charges and Vicious was back in Ryker's Island alongside the 'niggers' who beat him bloody, the 'spicks' who spat at him, the hardcore bad-arse élite who took no truck from some fucked-up limey pop star whose choices and options they never had. In Ryker's Island punks weren't spiky-haired rebels with guitars and wild, crazy attitudes. They were the broken spirits, the losers who could only survive via homosexual liaisons that would offer them protection.

Vicious was released almost two months later, on 2 February. He boasted to Jerry Nolan that he'd got on well with his cohabitants; that these desperadoes could see that he, Vicious, was cut from the same leathery fabric as themselves. In reality he had been treated like scum. Arriving at a celebratory bash, clean and in good spirits, he injected some heroin his mother had bought for him, fearing that he'd try scoring himself, thus jeopardizing his bail *again*. He immediately blacked out, his complexion tinged with the blue signs of overdose – but after a short exercise he came to and continued, in good spirits, to muse about the future.

Yes, he could still fantasize. But then reality would impinge and he'd realize that no matter which defence lawyer was involved, no matter how much he could kid himself he was innocent, it was over. No, Ryker's Island was not going to see him languishing with the other lifers, perverts and losers. While his new girl friend slept, he found another packet of the deadly powder. This time there was no one conscious to wake him from the abyss. He heated the spoon, filtered the cotton and – his life revolving around him – turned to dust. The scum that also rises sank into an unmarked grave.

*

But then, when you break it down, decomposing was their greatest achievement. A mere seven hours after expiring, Nancy Spungen was already *smelling* of death. It takes up to forty-eight hours before the putrefying odour commences in the corpses of the old. At the age of twenty both had wasted themselves beyond belief. Let them rot.

Horn-Rims from Hell: Elvis Costello

First, let it be known that young Elvis Costello is no shrinking violet when it comes to arm-wrestling manfully with the chilly tentacles of controversy. Why, even the National Front have been trying to cast their long unpleasant shadow across his path ever since the release of his début single 'Less than Zero', the song itself being a tacitly fanciful depiction of the landed gentry's fave black-sheep boy of the Isherwood era, Oswald Mosley. Our El croons about Mosley's swastika tattoo before pointing out in a ream of impressive if often fairly hard-to-grasp couplets, the innate British hypocrisy afoot in the double-moral standard twists that forbid your favourite new-wave band, say, from polluting the main media outlets while some gnarled pathetic self-confessed anti-Semite like the senile Mosley can blithely saunter into the BBC studios and run off at the mouth for forty-five riveting minutes over his sordid reminiscences. The marchings, the beatings, the black shirts, the foul sub-Nietzschean rhetoric – the nation 'tut-tutted' at the time but now it's OK 'cos the old fool's past it and virtually everything in this scum-pit that is England gets a benevolent white-washed canonization as time goes by.

It's OK for everyone except for one feisty young computer operator married with one child and living in Whitton near Twickenham whose brain has somehow been left unparalysed by the sickly rays of television and who is moreover downright offended by having this slimy old fascist drooling away in his living-room and who, instead of penning a barbed missive to his local MP, sits down and writes a sly little song full of jaundiced spleen.

We're in a pub just round the corner from Island Records' St Peter's Square building, the man who would be king and I, talking about the subject matter of 'Less than Zero', when his garrulous speed-freak Jerry Lee Lewis wanna-be of a manager Jake Riviera suddenly pipes up with the information that all the Yanks who've heard it think it's about Lee Harvey Oswald. 'Yeah right,' Costello's terse, gruff voice breaks in. 'In fact' – he's quite animated now – 'just for the States, I'm going to write a new set of lyrics to that song about . . . a guy, yeah, this guy's watching the box when he suddenly sees his girlfriend right behind Lee Harvey Oswald just at the moment when Jack Ruby shoots him. And the screen . . . the shot freezes, y'know . . .'

He sits back with a self-satisfied smirk, savouring this perverse little morsel while even Riviera, whose job it is to deal with all the little weirdnesses spurting from his client's lively mind, is temporarily rendered speechless by this information: no mean feat. Costello is temporarily fulfilled though. He looks pleased with himself, pleased enough that maybe he'll actually go ahead and toss just that very plot-line into a song tonight when he takes the train back to Whitton.

That's how these songs of his seem to come to him anyway. They start from simple everyday occurrences the composer finds himself running into on the tube, say, or maybe on his way down to the off licence. And then they blossom into raging chunks of perfectly matched melody and savage eloquence. Like even *I* am in an Elvis Costello song. Costello reckons he saw me one night on a tube bound for Osterley and 'you were obviously pretty "out of it" 'cos you didn't even notice all the other people in the compartment staring at you. I was just amazed that one person could draw that much reaction from others. After I saw you there, I came up with "Waiting for the World to End". You're the guy in the opening verse.'

I touch my forelock at the imparting of this factoid. After all, being in a Costello song is a deal more prestigious than being a name in this little black book he carries around with him, full of the names of folk who have crossed him up, so to speak, who have hindered the unravelling of his true manifest destiny these past years. Maybe they were responsible for not signing him to their label (prior to the Stiff inking this is) or maybe they referred to him as another guitar-strumming Van Morrison sound-alike just like all those other squat, nervy types with short hair and glasses with whom such parallels appear obligatory in today's music press. Whatever the cause, they're all marked men, cows before the slaughter, names and livelihoods about to come under the thunder of the raging spleen of Elvis Costello.

'The only two things that matter to me, the only motivation points for me writing all these songs,' opines Costello with a perverse leer, 'are *revenge* and *guilt*. Those are the only emotions I know about, that I know I can feel. Love? I dunno what it means, really, and it doesn't exist in my songs. Like' – he's into this discourse now – 'when I played earlier in front of all those reps or whatever they're called – all those guys working for Island – did you hear me introducing "Lipservice"? "This song is called 'Lipservice' and that's all you're gonna get from me." That was straight from the heart, that, 'cos last year I actually went to Island with my demo tape and none of them wanted to know. Back then they wouldn't give me the time of day. But *now* . . .'

Now, Elvis Costello is gloating because after years of playing pub rock with country overtones as D.P. Costello, lead singer of a bluegrass group called Flip City, suddenly he's one of the new breed golden boys, already a name to be bandied about, with two excellent singles under his belt and a much raved-over album finally in the shops after a couple of months collecting dust in the warehouse while Stiff and Island rejigged terms of distribution.

''Course nobody wanted to know back *then*,' he continues acidly. 'None of yer rock hacks were around *then*! And neither were *you*! I remember the time you came down to the Marquee when we were supporting Dr Feelgood and you spent all your time in the dressing-room talking to Wilko Johnson. You didn't even bother to check us out. Oh no! And I really resented you for that, y'know. For a time, anyway. You were almost down there on my list.'

Costello always seems to double back to this unhealthy infatuation of his with wreaking vengeance on his self-proclaimed wrong-doers. He absolutely relishes the fact that literally every record company he approached with his demo tape turned him down, and admits that the years of bottling up the vast frustrations of being a nonentity out in the cold looking for a foot in the door have conversely granted him the basic ego drive with which he intends to bring the whole music scene to its feet right now.

But let us return for a moment to the mystique building up around the Costello past. Facts he cares to own up to are these: born in the London area, spent most of his formative years in Liverpool, the only town in the world he still looks upon with any kind of affection, where his father was a professional singer for big bands and his mother worked as a part-time usherette for the Liverpool Philharmonic. He was also raised as a Catholic – 'I had to be either Catholic or Jewish now, didn't I' – and got married when he was in his late teens. He refuses to talk about his wife Mary and one child, a boy named Matthew, or the nature of his relationship with them at all, slyly noting, 'I'm very, very "country music" in my attitude to talking about my marriage.'

Musically speaking, Elvis Costello's career commenced in 1976 when he sent a home-made tape in answer to an advertisement placed by Jake Riviera, who was searching for acts to release through his label, Stiff. Riviera himself takes up the story from here. 'Elvis's tape was actually the very first tape we received at Stiff. It was so weird because I immediately put it on and thought, "God, this is good" – but at the same time I was hesitating because after all it was the first tape and I wanted to get a better perspective. So I phoned up Elvis and said, "Listen, I've listened to your tape, it sounds really good and I'm interested, but could you give me a week in which to check out a bunch of other tapes and I'll get back to you?" Elvis said "Fine" and so I waited a week, received a load of real dross in the mail and immediately got back in touch.' Costello himself has less exalted views on the music he recorded on that tape: 'I just grabbed at the chance and did fifteen songs in that hour, often just making stuff up in my head as I went along.'

Anyway, the interview is going along quite amicably, if a little on the stilted and impersonal side, in the garden of this pub, when all of a sudden a delegation from Island Records corp. descends upon the scene. Costello eyes them all suspiciously as they file past, before resuming the thread of our chat. Then one of the delegation chooses to seat herself at our table. At first she just sits there, causing Costello and me to look at each other uneasily. Then she opens her mouth. I cower back, but Elvis seems in the mood for a bit of retaliation. This, after all, is just the sort of person he loves to hate: a bourgeois glamour victim who thinks she's the cat's pyjamas. Her approximate stereotype has been set up to be ripped apart in numerous Costello songs: she's the classic 'Natasha who looks like Elsie' out of El's brutal 'I Don't Want to Go to Chelsea', a prime exponent of 'Lipstick Vogue' chic.

Anyway, she makes her point. She says she's very interested in Elvis. She wants to know just what 'makes him tick'.

'Oh, I'm thoroughly despicable,' retorts Costello with a disturbing grin on his face.

'But don't you have any friends?' she enquires.

'Absolutely none,' comes the reply.

Elvis goes on to inform her that success means nothing to him, going to America means nothing to him ('I'd rather go back to Liverpool'), that everything – in a nutshell, all conventional desires – means less than zero to her sudden object of fascination.

'Oh, all you people are the same,' she retaliates, her initial disappointment now growing into rabid aggression. 'You're all so boring.'

'Oh, yes, that's it. I'm absolutely despicably boring. You're so totally right.'

Getting nowhere with her enquiries, the girl finally gets up from her seat, feigning extreme boredom with a low farting noise issuing derisively from her lips to register full disgust. As she retreats back to her noisy friends well away from our table, Costello's face has a menacing glow to it. He's now close to being fairly drunk – after one amiable Islander innocently asked him what he was drinking and consequently had to foot the bill for a triple Pernod. He leans over to me in a confidential gesture: 'I was just waiting for her to bring that macho boyfriend of hers over. That would have really been a fuckin' confrontation! I'd have either smashed my glass and gone for him that way or . . .'

The words trail off into a pause so pregnant I thought of alerting a midwife. His eyes stare coldly out from behind the horn-rims and our El quietly digs his hand into one of his four jacket pockets to produce an enormous bent steel nail, something ideal for pinning whole limbs to crosses at a crucifixion. This, he is stating wordlessly, is his chosen weapon of defence. It glistens menacingly against the glasses strewn over our table.

Somehow, this sordid little contretemps has afforded us a neutral terrain, common ground on which to consummate an easier intimacy well away from the usual rigid mode of communication common to such interview encounters. Costello's already well pissed and I've started throwing the booze back just to keep up, so that all of a sudden it's like we're two opinionated old geezers hunched around a spittoon who've known each other all their lives. Costello's nervy abruptness has simmered down to be replaced by the style of a man totally coldly, calculatingly confident. The real Elvis Costello finally seems ready to express himself.

'Yeah, Gram Parsons, he had it all sussed. He didn't stick around. He made his best work and then he died. That's the way I want to do it. I'm never ever going to stick around long enough to churn out a load of mediocre crap like all those guys from the sixties ended up doing. I'd rather kill myself. I mean, Parsons' exit was perfect.'

So you're basically saying you want to snuff it about four years from now, OD'd on morphine on the floor of some cheesy motel in the desert with ice-cubes up your arse and some moron groupie giving you a hand-job?

He considers this for a moment. 'Well, not exactly like *that*, I suppose. I see my exit as being something more like being run over by a bus. But . . . you think I'm joking, right. I'm deadly serious about this. I'm not going to be around to witness my artistic decline.'

That should take a while. You told me you had at least 400 songs under wraps . . .

'Well by 400, I mean songs that aren't finished. A lot of them are just ideas – songs I won't use – but lines and couplets that I'll take and add to new things. So, saying I've got 400 . . . I mean, that number means absolutely nothing, OK. But what you're asking, no I'm not into stock-piling material for "if" and "when" I dry up. I'm not into doing a Robbie Robertson.'

OK, but this Gram Parsons fetish (G.P. is El's very favourite album, by the way), I mean, he was a champion drug abuser and you don't look the type who'd be into that at all.

'Yeah, right. I don't take drugs. I mean, I can't even be in the same room as other people doing cocaine because just being in contact with them, I get three times as wired as them just being there. [*Pause*.] But . . . but I do know what it's like being out of control. I know all about alcohol, for example, because well, let's say I went through my phase of drinking heavily. Really heavily. But, ah you're not going to . . . I mean, that's a bit too obvious isn't it, making a good quote out of me being miserable and unhappy working with these fuckin' computers and being a secret after-hours drinker [*laughs*]. No, I'm not going to fall for that one.'

Costello's not over-anxious to go into details concerning those years of clouded anonymity cloistered among the computers, just as he adamantly fends off queries concerning his wife and child. It's only some weeks later that I'm informed by another source that the exact nature of his job was a computer operator for the firm run by 'beauty consultant' Elizabeth Arden (thus the autobiographical snippet about working for the 'Vanity factory' on, I think, 'I'm Not Angry' for the *Aim* album). He claims that he was viewed as a factory 'freak' – an object of mild affection and ridicule even though he looked as pastily anonymous as he does now (he's worn the same hairstyle, clothes and bifocals for years now, or so he claims).

Also, his job, he reckons, could have been performed by any unskilled peon off the block and he's basically overjoyed at having seen the last of the miserable building since he left that place of employment something like three months ago. (Interestingly enough, Jake Riviera recently attempted to get BBC2 interested in filming a documentary on Costello's progress from the computer factory out into the big, bad world of rock'n'roll. Predictably enough, no one expressed any interest in the idea.)

Immediately prior to his going 'professional', Costello's forays into music-business-land were kept down to hyper-anonymous trips to Highbury's Pathways Studios where the *Aim* album was recorded with Nick Lowe producing (Lowe and Costello had actually first met some years before this, making backstage at Eric's in Liverpool after a Brinsley Schwarz gig). Or there was the occasional trip to the Stiff offices, where Costello would sit almost hiding behind a newspaper, just waiting, biding his time until his secret weapon was unveiled and all the biz would swoop down eagerly to chew on his toe-nail clippings.

Now, of course, he claims he knew all along about the massive shake-up his talents would cause the music business, that all the drool-soaked rave reviews and budding cult acceptance would surge in and wash over his ego like water off a duck's arse. Cults, thinks El – who needs 'em? He'd far rather be scowling out of 10 million TV screens on Thursday night with Jimmy Savile's bazooka cigar and the usual posse of silly disco-dollies milling around. The album itself – well, he read all the reviews, of course. Didn't agree with any of them.

'I mean, that . . . "masochist" accusation I keep getting is only relevant for two or three tracks. On "I'm Not Angry" it's there, plus "Miracle Man" – but it's an interesting point because, as far as I can see, those are the only songs in the rock idiom where a guy is admitting absolute defeat – taking all this sexual abuse, say – without either doing the old James Taylor self-pity bit or coming on all macho with the whole revenge bit . . .'

Hold on a minute. What about . . . well, take John Lennon's 'Jealous Guy'?

'Ah, but with that one, Lennon's saying sorry that I made you cry. That's the key line because he's already got her back. He's triumphed. So all that self-confessed "I'm so weak" stuff is stated from a position of strength. No, I'm talking about being a *complete* loser. That's something totally new to the rock idiom, which by its very nature is immature and totally macho-orientated in its basic attitude. Only in country music can you find a guy singing about that kind of deprivation honestly.'

Finally, if they ever do another *Rock Dreams* book, Elvis Costello will surely be there along with the rest. He'll be the mousy figure, all insect anonymity, seated in a tube train carriage in his insurance clerk suit and misty bifocals mostly hidden by a copy of the *Evening Standard* with Elvis Presley's death announced in grandstand type alongside the latest tales of National Front marches and King's Road Punks–Teds confrontations. Only his hands will be prominent – all shot through with cold-blue veins bulging as they form clenched fists, the knuckles of which scream forth with two blood-red tattoos. The left fist reads 'Revenge'. The right reads 'Guilt'. The main headline will read: 'A WALKING TIME-BOMB – THE MAN WHO WOULD BE KING'. Watch him closely.

'When we met up in that pub opposite Island Records and I got really drunk on Pernod and said all these really exaggerated things which you wrote up so dramatically,' Elvis Costello is reminding me some fifteen years after the event, 'it set me in good store, y'know. It didn't do anybody any harm. That was pretty potent stuff. Y'know, and a lot of it – your imagery mixed in with the iconography of the first two albums – you've got to accept it was consciously very hip. It's just a very hip image. It's like James Dean. But after three or four years it started to become a complete bloody millstone because people without imagination only wanted you to reconfirm that preconception over and over again . . . Nowadays, of course, I don't get so involved in all that side.'

So, did you really believe that line about 'revenge' and 'guilt' being the only emotions that inspired you to write your songs?

'I probably did mean that, yes. I was probably exaggerating more than a little bit. But I was shrewder than most people realize because I knew there was only going to be one chance to get my foot in the door. And if I didn't make a *really* strong impression then I wouldn't buy myself the time and space to do other stuff. Because, as you know, there was a whole other bunch of stuff I could've done even back then. However, I tailored my songs and style very purposefully because I knew which way the wind of prevailing trends was blowing and that it would also steam-roller anyone who happened to be going against it.

'I mean, just look at the guys who backed me up on my first album [a San Francisco country-rock band called Clover]. They were a good musical band and one of them went on to become a huge pop star [Huey Lewis], but they had the gross misfortune to come to London in '76. Forget it! All those qualities were the worst things they could have had going for them *then*. Now I could see that. I wasn't a fool, though I was still pretty naive about a lot of things. But that wasn't one of them. So I made sure I made enough of an impression, claimed enough space and cleared enough ground for a lift-off. Particularly with a very aggressive group and a very, very aggressive manager and the whole thing guaranteed to get people unnerved, if not downright scared of you.

'Like, all the problems over in America with my first record company . . . I'd been with Columbia for ten years, the first two and a half were great. Then things got very ugly . . . for a whole series of reasons, and by the end of it they were just releasing my records and burying them under a stone. Plus I owed them a million dollars. The simple fact is that anyone with any talent at Columbia was never given a chance. People would suddenly become invisible . . . almost non-human . . . if they transgressed certain codes. And I never wished to socialize with any of the heads of the company. I would never have my picture taken with them, in case it turned up as evidence in some FBI mafia investigation [*laughs*]. There's always that possibility with those kind of people.

'Mind you, I'm not particularly proud of some of our scare tactics because it often came down just to bullying people to get out of your way . . . I'm talking about people in the business, not musicians. And some of it comes back to haunt you . . . You learn to live with it. Fuck all that! Those things happen. But when you've done all that, you say, "Well, what am I going to do with all this space?" Then you want to broaden out. You start to want to say tender things as well as aggressive stuff. So you're not stuck with some one-dimensional image.'

To this end Elvis Costello has been attempting to slyly reinvent himself with virtually every album he's ever made. First there were the confusing 'genre' exercises – the cut-price soul of *Get Happy*, the Nashville homage of *Almost Blue*, or an ersatz *Sergeant Pepper* for the eighties in *Imperial Bedroom*. By the mid-eighties he'd started even changing his identity. For 1989's *Spike* he was the Beloved Entertainer; before that, Napoleon Dynamite, the tormented *alter ego* of 1986's *Blood and Chocolate*. To make matters even more complicated, earlier that same year he'd changed his name back to Declan McManus for *King of America*. The 1990s find him all grown up with long hair and beard dismissing contemporary pop in favour of classical music and determinedly romancing the 'forty-something' icons like Neil Young and Van Morrison, both of whom he performed live with, Paul McCartney and Tom Waits, who he's writing songs with, as well as Roy Orbison and Johnny Cash, who he's written songs for.

Meanwhile, his two most recent albums, *Spike* and *Mighty as a Rose*, have been full of wit and detail but lack an awful lot as well – memorable melodies certainly, 'focus' perhaps and the old 'intensity' definitely. But that's probably the price to be paid for the degree of domestic contentment he claims to have achieved with his second wife of six years and some-time creative collaborator, the former Pogues bassist Cait O'Riordan. After all, as Costello freely admitted to me, he's more of an observer than a willing participant in his own lyrics these days. (Still, in 1994 he reunited with the Attractions and recorded an album that can stand with his very best entitled *Brutal Youth*. However much he may get lost in diversification, it's impossible to ever count him out as a relevant talent.)

When I last spoke to him, he was finishing two projects: more writing with Paul McCartney and his first-ever foray into classical music composition and performance with the Brodsky Quartet:

'To even start to express yourself in classical music, you've got to do a hell of a lot of training. Some people might complain about the lack of spontaneity in classical music but that's utter bullshit. That's like saying Beethoven isn't as good as Robert Johnson – just pure fuckin' idiocy. One is really spontaneous and visceral and the other is probably also that way but it's on a whole different level of musical complexity which still doesn't prevent it from being primitive and transcendent. The poetry in the lyrics is arcane but no more so than Hank Williams is now. It still means something real.

'I'd rather go and see Brahms's *Goethe* than check out the new Happy Mondays record. At least, it stands some chance of genuinely touching my soul a little bit. By that I'm not claiming that classical music is better. It all depends on how it's being performed . . . Still, I knew we were in deep, deep shit when Manchester suddenly became the centre of the musical universe. I thought, "Now, pop music's really fucked." Jesus Christ! "I'm really hard and I take drugs . . ." So what! Go fuck off and write some songs then.

'Working with Paul McCartney is a big thrill for me too. It's funny – you take an opinion poll on Paul McCartney and you'll find that almost all music critics dislike him and almost all music fans think he's great. I mean, compared to *who* is Paul McCartney not any good? Compared to the Inspiral fuckin' Carpets? I don't go in for all this "knocking" him. He's who he wants to be. Paul McCartney survived being one of the most famous people ever in the world – and this was back when being famous actually meant something. Nowadays any fuckin' clown can get on international satellite TV and become famous simply by shooting someone or releasing some inane fucking song. Of course, fuckin' Madonna is fuckin' famous – she's on TV every fifteen fuckin' minutes!'

Don't you think you've often been guilty of being too diverse and too wilfully obscure for your listeners?

'Yes, I do feel I've been too wilfully obscure for my audience at times. But then it depends on what you're trying to achieve. If I'm trying to sincerely follow my own feelings about music, then I'm right to do records like *Almost Blue*. If I'm thinking about being ever so famous for a long, long time, then obviously I was completely wrong. I always find myself starting to lose interest in the limited areas of music I operate in. But everything I've done on record – good or bad – I've done with all my heart. And I stand by every record I've done, even records that I don't think nowadays have any virtue. I've made bad records but I've never made a dishonest record, let's put it that way.

'One in particular – *Goodbye Cruel World* – has to be the worst. That was a really fucked-up record. That's the worst one, really, because I had all the arrangements arse-backwards, picked the wrong producers, then asked them to do an impossible job . . . My marriage was breaking up. It all sounds like a fuckin' sob story now but it probably was the worst period of my life. Like one of the songs on that album *The Comedians*, I rewrote it for Roy Orbison partly because he really likes stories in his lyrics but mostly because the original lyrics are so fuckin' enigmatic I've forgotten what they actually meant!'

Does this happen a lot to you with your old songs?

'Yeah, with some of them. The thing is . . . to be blunt about it, the trouble with being an adulterer and a songwriter is that you always write songs in code. You know, when I started I swore to myself I'd always try to avoid writing songs about hotel rooms. But then inevitably many of my most lurid experiences in the past have taken place in hotel rooms so [*laughs*] that's just part of the job. I mean, I'm not glorying in that. And I'm still not at all happy about all the pain it caused my ex-wife . . . But it's a fact and I'm not going to try and hide from it. It's just life. You get over it. And that's why most of my early songs are more obscure than my more contemporary material, where I express myself a lot more openly. See, I'm not chasing loads of women around nowadays . . . I'm pretty calm and stable these days and I think it actually makes me a better writer in a way because . . .'

You've got a lot more time . . .?

'True. [*Laughs.*] And lower phone bills. But also because now I'm synthesizing personal experience with observation. As opposed to just projecting feelings on to someone you barely know or chasing some illusion. Now, I'm more into observing illusions taking their toll on other people. I feel pretty good about life these days. I'm practically forty and I don't want to be like some ageing starlet who's still trying to look young and cute when she's in her bloody forties. Staying young, looking young . . . I don't care about that. No one ever bought one of my records because of my looks . . .'

Yeah, you and Van Morrison both . . .

'Well, I don't feel I look quite as rough and ancient-looking as poor old Van . . . But, um, I know what you mean. Looks have never mattered to either of our careers, that's what you're saying. But I sure added to the problem by subverting a stereotype – which is what I did with the "Elvis" name and the big glasses and putting that to the fore. I could've gone without the glasses, worn contacts and tried to look handsome . . . But actually my early image ended up looking kind of sexy. Who would have thought it? It's idiotic as far as I'm concerned. But it worked. Personally I think it's my big nose. [*Laughs.*] It's not the glasses or the silly walk. Forget the long hair and beard. It's the big nose every time.'

Morrissey, the Majesty of Melancholia and the Light that Never Goes Out in Smiths-dom

Morrissey has a certain way of defining those he most admires: he calls them 'the kind of people you just can't brush aside'. So it was with the Smiths. From the outset they were audacious and totally independent-minded. Hearing their first broadcast on UK radio, Sting offered them a support on a Police tour only to be turned down by Johnny Marr simply 'because we're a hundred times more important than the Police will ever be'. They were incredibly insular, mistrustful of anyone outside Manchester (not that they trusted many Mancunians, come to that), and that insularity, under more and more pressure to go world-wide, certainly sowed many of the seeds of their premature destruction.

Mostly, though, it has to be said they were a real group, the only truly immortal group of the eighties, but their lyrical vision was of course Morrissey's alone. Just as the basic drive was also his, a drive grounded in a seething desire to enact his revenge on a world that had repeatedly mocked and jeered and 'brushed aside' his every former display of self-expression. 'In the Manchester scene he was like the village idiot,' Paul Morley once remarked to a colleague of mine disdainfully. 'In the Joy Division days, when everyone was going around carrying copies of Nietzsche very prominently, you'd see Morrissey at a bus stop somewhere looking hopeless and reading Sven Hassel instead.'

'Fame is a type of revenge. You hate so many people,' the singer would counter. 'It sounds very juvenile now, I suppose, like smashing someone's windows. But then what else can you do? It was like a weapon, something to make them gnash their teeth. Otherwise people will always have the finger on you. Always.'

This is how Morrissey spoke when I first met him in the cold December of 1984, the last month of a year in which England had suddenly catapulted him from his previous state of provincial nonentity-dom to the condition of a virtual deity. Thus, 'the past always tends to seem a little embarrassing, even though at the time it was anything but . . . It's like saying you might be this now but you were once that, you used to do this and you bought this awful record and thought it was wonderful. You see, I can describe the key incidents as far as I was concerned; I recognize them very clearly. The key incident for me was that I never had any friends. And I realized that in order to have friends and impress people, I had to do something extraordinary.'

In order to decode the full dark complexity of the Morrissey enigma, and certainly in order to decipher the nuances of his extraordinary lyrics, one has to do a deal of private research into this most singular of pop lives. Steven Patrick Morrissey was born on 22 May 1959, preceded by a sister Jacqueline, into a working-class family (mother a librarian, his father a hospital porter), then living in the Hulme district of Manchester. Life, according to the singer, was agreeable enough up to the age of seven or eight, when two significant events took place. One was the first spate of discord between his parents that would end in divorce ten years hence. The other was, if anything, even more traumatic to a seven-year-old with an imagination that, where others fixated on Mars bars and Sherbet Dips, seized on the barbaric rituals of those dissolute lost souls drawn to the Manchester fairgrounds of the late sixties in search of love bites and knife wounds, 'under the shield of the Ferris wheel'. ('Rusholme Ruffians' relates just such a child's exposure to the mindless thuggery the grown-up Morrissey so abhors.)

In 1966 Ian Brady, a Glaswegian transplanted to Manchester, and his secretary and mistress, a Mancunian named Myra Hindley, were sent to trial on charges of procuring, torturing (sexually and otherwise, often photographing and taping the atrocities) and ultimately murdering one nine-year-old boy, an eleven-year-old girl and a seventeen-year-old youth. Two other youngsters also went missing at the time. The whole of Manchester was aghast and seven-year-old Steven Morrissey was more than susceptible to the shock-waves.

'I happened to live on the streets where, close by, some of the victims had been picked up. Within the community, news of the crime totally dominated all attempts at conversation for quite a few years. It was like the worst thing that had ever happened, and I was very, very aware of everything that occurred. Aware as a child who could have been a victim. All the details . . . You see, it was all so evil; it was, if you can understand this, ungraspably evil. When something reaches that level it becomes almost . . . almost absurd really. I remember it at times like I was living in a soap opera . . .'

By the age of nine the child had become a distinct problem. His father he rarely if ever refers to, but once let slip that the former considered his only begotten son 'a complete fruitcake' during those years of frenzied brooding. His mother, however, saw an artistic bent in her son's otherwise perplexing inertia. A librarian, she introduced him to the works of Thomas Hardy and Oscar Wilde among many, the latter sparking a particularly fervent infatuation that persists to this day.

And then there was music. He bought his first disc at age six – a year before Hindley and Brady's gambols on the moors commenced. The record featured the virginal entreaties of a very young Marianne Faithfull singing 'Come and Stay with Me'. The mild sexual overtones of the lyric went well with the halcyon blend of folk guitar and baroque pop. Indeed, Ms Faithfull was Morrissey's first love, and in a world where first loves never die it's intriguing that the only two non-originals the Smiths have attempted were her 'Summer Nights' (a thrilling harpsichord-led piece that foreshadows some early Smiths songs) and the 'Sha La La Song'. Quintessential British pop, an influence either due to the radio or elder sister Jacqueline or his own simple rationale: 'I was brought up in a house full of books and records . . . I devoured everything.'

Though he found himself 'disgusted by the savagery of funfairs [he] went to in the sixties', he sought out music that embodied that atmosphere: the treble-and-reverb lamentations of Billy Fury, king of the fairground swing. Similarly, a cute doily of a song, the Tams' 'Be Young, Be Foolish, Be Happy' he always cherished.

'Because of the sentiment. Not that I could ever relate to it. But then maybe that's why I found it so appealing in the first place.' Morrissey's placement at St Mary's Secondary Modern was, from all reports, the grimmest fate conceivable for one of such a haphazard temperament. He carved out a niche of sorts, but not by reciting Oscar Wilde or displaying his growing aptitude for the written word.

'I happened to be very good at certain sports. I was really quite a fine runner, for example. This in turn made me act in a somewhat cocky and outspoken way – simply as a reaction against the philistine nature of my surroundings. This the masters simply couldn't take. It was all right if you just curled up and underachieved your way into a stupor. That was pretty much what was expected really. Because if you're too smart, they hate and resent you and they will break you. When I found out that I wasn't being picked for the things I clearly excelled at, it became a slow but sure way of destroying my resilience. They succeeded in almost killing off all the self-confidence I had.'

Music again offered escape and excitement. Early in 1972, at the age of thirteen, Morrissey witnessed his first live gig: Marc Bolan's T. Rex at Manchester's Bellevue Theatre. 'All the kids at my school were into either Marc Bolan or David Bowie,' he recalls. 'You couldn't like both of them. But it was the New York Dolls who were the real beginning for me. They were so precious . . .

'You see, rock'n'roll, or the traditional, incurable rock and roller, never interested me remotely. He was simply a rather foolish, empty-headed figure who was peddling his brand of self-projection and very arch machismo that I could never relate to. The Dolls on the other hand . . . Well, firstly I always saw them as an absolutely male group. I never saw them as being remotely fey or effeminate. They were characters you simply did not brush aside. Like the mafia of rock'n'roll.'

Upon falling out of St Mary's into the outstretched arms of the dole queue in 1975, Steven Morrissey's life appears to have revolved around the music of the New York Dolls and sixties girl singers, the crucial 'symbolic' importance of James Dean, and the continuing lure of the written word. He claims at fourteen to have been initiated into the doctrines of feminism, citing a book titled *Men's Liberation* as shaping what has since become a key concept in his own lyrical observations. But it was the New York Dolls connection that afforded him a certain notoriety. His small ads in the music press seeking to swap fax and info with fellow Dolls fans caused him to become one of the few ersatz personalities to feature in the punk explosion that hit Manchester, the first stop of the Sex Pistols' infamous Anarchy Tour in 1976.

'With punk I was always "observing". I mean, I seem to recall being a spectator at almost every seminal performance in the movement's evolution, especially in the North. But the aggression was just bully boy tactics. It was, I feel now, a musical movement without music. I mean, how many records were really important? How many can be remembered with fondness? Not many . . . The Ramones' first album I recall as one. Also the Buzzcocks, who, I must be honest, seemed, out of this massive sea of angst-ridden groups, the only ones who possibly had sat down beforehand and worked out what they intended to do.'

By this time it would be fair to assume that Morrissey harboured genuine musical ambitions. His main obstacle, apart from 'a shyness that was criminally vulgar', was his fear that a rock music backdrop would place him 'in circumstances where I would be a very . . . timid performer'. Perhaps, then, he would be temperamentally better suited to music journalism. Turned down no fewer than five times by a certain *NME* section editor, he went on to supply record reviews to *Record Mirror* under the *nom de plume* Sheridan Whitehead. Various punk fanzines were also created by him, and he is remembered by Richard Boon (the Buzzcocks' manager) as being a frequent visitor to the Buzzcocks' office. In 1978, owing possibly to his parents' final bust-up, Boon recalls Morrissey becoming extremely close to the group Ludus, principally the singer, Linder, for whom he seemed to be nursing a growing infatuation.

Linder was deeply affected by the work of certain feminist writers and was prone to carry around such tomes as *Genealogy* and *The Wise Wound*. Morrissey duly moved with Linder and Ludus guitarist Ian into a less than salubrious abode in the red light area of Whalley Range, where they lived for approximately one year. This is the location that inspired songs like the pummelling 'Miserable Lie' from the first album. Similarly, certain sources intimate that 'Wonderful Woman' and 'Jean' refer to this relationship.

After the Walley Range episode Morrissey actually took the audacious step of flying to New York, where he stayed with his 'Aunty Mary'. He recalls seeing Patti Smith, then newly retired from rock, giving a poetry reading in which she 'made farting noises for almost one hour . . . it was both peculiar and singularly depressing'. He soon returned. Around this time he almost got involved with joining a group. However . . .

'There was always an obvious ideological imbalance with whoever else approached me. The one occasion I walked into this group as a potential singer, I said – the very first thing – "Let's do 'Needle in a Haystack' by the Marvelettes." These were four individuals who seemed in tune with this mode of thinking. It wasn't "camp surrealism" or "wackiness". It was pure intellectual devotion that made me want to do a song like that.'

Perhaps it was this ensemble that Howard Devoto swears he witnessed supporting Magazine once in a Manchester club. Devoto doesn't recall much: a guitar, drums and bass line-up, with Morrissey singing while lashing his hair out of his eyes. And so it goes. If it happened at all, it was short-lived.

'The main reason for my not being able to do anything really constructive before Johnny Marr's arrival', Morrissey now concludes, 'is that, with all the desire I had been harbouring for years, if anyone else existed out there who shared the same creative urges, that person was invariably incredibly depressed, totally disorganized and somehow unsalvageably doomed. In other words, a complete slut.'

Richard Boon recalls the last pre-Smiths utterance from Morrissey. This came in 1980 in the form of a demo tape on which was recorded firstly a spoken apology for both the lack of any backing instruments and the low fidelity of Morrissey's singing voice. This was due to the fact that someone was asleep in the next room. Of two songs he definitely remembers hearing one was a version of 'The Hand that Rocks the Cradle' sung to a different melody. The second was a truly ironic choice. Just two years before Marr would come and pull our ailing hero out of some sick sleep and into a partnership that would take them to places they never imagined even existing, the gaunt young Mancunian had chosen to interpret a little-known Bessie Smith number. Its title? 'Wake Up Johnny'.

Johnny Marr had first woken up as John Martin Maher on the last day of October 1963. He modified his surname in his teens in order not to be mistaken for the Buzzcocks' drummer of the same name, but also to avoid police investigation into his reputed involvement with some jewel thieves who heisted a series of T. S. Lowry prints from a museum. He was born in Ardwick Green to a working-class couple of Irish descent, the father employed in the construction trade. His parents are still together and he has a younger brother and sister. Unlike his more erudite lyricist he passed his 11-plus but ended up in a comprehensive school – Withenshaw – where he found himself more interested in experimenting with the soft drugs that a predominantly older crowd of local musicians were introducing him to. He left school with no O-levels, a vendetta between himself and his father since resolved, and a 'friend' he'd been originally asked to keep an eye out for by the school's headmaster when the latter had discovered that 'this posh kiddie with a chip on his shoulder' was courting a potential barbiturate problem.

The latter 'posh kiddie' had been future Smiths bass player Andy Rourke at the age of thirteen. At the ages of fourteen (when various friends and Marr toyed with the idea of working with a girl group) and seventeen (when he and Rourke were again put off by 'how bad everybody was'), attempts had been made to form bands. Joe Moss, owner of Crazy Face, a Manchester boutique where Marr had also worked, and also where the guitarist gained most of his musical education from Moss's extensive record collection, is the figure everyone points to as the one who brought Morrissey and Marr together in the first place. Moss coaxed the guitarist to journey over to where Morrissey lived.

He was nineteen years old, wore his hair in a pompadour and his fingers left chocolate stains on the front window that almost caused him to be ejected on the spot without any further discussion. Morrissey warily let him enter, and in his bedroom, beneath a huge crucifixion poster of James Dean, Marr spoke excitedly about the reality of the two of them possibly forming a songwriting partnership as well as a group. Morrissey listened without saying much and then asked him to choose a record from his sprawling collection. Marr chose 'Paper Boy' by the Marvelettes and it was this decision that first cemented their union. He returned next time with a guitar and after two failed attempts to write a song was shown the lyrics to 'Suffer Little Children', his remarkable meditation on the monstrosity of the Moors Murders. Marr wrote a lush and complicated set of chord changes for the lyric. Morrissey settled finally on utilizing only one quarter of what Marr had written and their partnership was consummated.

But oh, what an odd couple they made. There was Marr with a joint in his mouth and two freshly rolled behind his ears, the exuberant little hedonist full of restless energy and unneurotic enthusiasm for life. And then there was Morrissey, the human daffodil with his down-beat ardour and his fastidious craving to remain celibate and distant from all physical contact. 'I don't have relationships at all,' he told me once. 'It's out of the question . . . Partly because I was always attracted to men or women who were never attracted to me. And I was never attracted to women and men who were attracted to me. I've never met the right person. I'd like to take [one mad plunge]. But not just with anyone; it just doesn't come naturally to me.

'Throughout the Smiths' career, I was entirely crippled [sexually]. I was bound to a wheelchair; I have no doubt of that. When the Smiths performed live . . . I don't remember any of those nights, to be honest with you. Every memory to me is that I was simply a catherine wheel. That was as far as it went. I can remember a few times when I was literally pushed on to the stage. I was pale. I was ill. I needed a meal. I needed a lie-in: all those natural things you need when you're being pawed about.'

'He is very shy, you've got to understand that,' Marr would always emphasize, clearly as enamoured of his partner's creative side as he was deeply puzzled by some of his personal eccentricities. 'We all look out for Morrissey. It's a very brotherly feeling. When we first rehearsed, I'd have done anything for him. And, as a person, Morrissey is really capable of a truly loving relationship. Every day he's so open, so romantic and sensitive to other people's emotions. But', the young guitarist quickly adds, pausing only to take a deep draw from the newly lit joint he's just removed from behind his left ear, 'I must say that when he gets really upset, frankly I think it's just because he needs a good humping.'

Morrissey and Marr broke up messily and rather stupidly in 1987 when their individual paranoias and differing lifestyles mixed in with a lot of fatigue and over-excitable ego conspired to break the spell that had drawn these two disparate individuals to find a common purpose in composing the most haunting and beguiling collection of songs written during the otherwise garish and soul-stunted eighties. Marr, the villain among Smiths fans basically because it was his leaving that broke up the quartet, has since collaborated with numerous groups and musicians, including the Pretenders, Matt Johnson's The The, Kirsty McColl, New Order's Barney Sumner, with whom he created the duo Electronic, the Pet Shop Boys and most recently, Ian McCulloch, formerly of Echo and the Bunnymen. Everything he's been involved in has been solid enough, hard to criticize for its breezy melodic quality or for the delight it displays in experimenting with the latest technology. But not a single note of it has resonated with the same magical quality that informed almost all his Smiths music.

Meanwhile, Morrissey has continued as a solo artist, recording prolifically and picking up musically pretty much where the Smiths left off. His first solo album, *Viva Hate* had its moments, and though the follow-up, *Kill Uncle*, was an out-and-out dud, *Your Arsenal*, the album he recorded with his Camden Town quarry of former rockabilly musicians and with ex-glam rocker Mick Ronson as producer, was every bit as good if not better than *Strangeways Here We Come*, the

Smiths' disappointing final studio album. Still, after six years without contact, both seem to realize that they're bonded by destiny just like Burt Bacharach and Hal David or Lennon and McCartney. So in 1993 they began cautiously socializing again.

'If Johnny phoned and asked to work with me again,' Morrissey had confessed the last time I ever saw him, back in late 1989 when he and Marr were at their most disconnected, 'it's no secret I would be on the next bus over to his house. He wrote great music and the union was perfect. I write all the time but obviously now, post-Smiths, it's only whenever I can get hold of a tune that really starts me humming. But', he added slowly, gravely, his eyes cast downwards and cloudy with sorrow and regret, 'that exuberant music, it's very few and far between, right now.'

The Moon, the Gutter and Shane McGowan

It is June and the Pogues and I are all travelling along in a big green tour bus to another gig. All, that is, except for Shane McGowan, who is teleporting somewhere off the milky seas of Venus as I attempt to interview him in the rear of the tour coach where he sits, alone in all his ruin, not so much removed from the rest of the band as utterly dislocated from the straight world in general. His eyes are mad, conspiratorial beacons and his thoughts are cluttered and half-digested.

'Are you wired for sound?' he keeps asking me, until it isn't even remotely amusing anymore and yet he's still ogling me with that totally meaningful look acid heads give you when they're saying something totally meaningless. 'No, Shane, but you're wired for life!' a roadie indulgently ripostes.

It is an appropriate rejoinder just as the condition it indicates is not altogether unexpected. But it's frustating and a little disheartening to witness because, in between those moments when his brain isn't being swamped out by some oppressive agent of stupefaction, it's clear Shane McGowan has something he wants to tell me. So why do you think you have to torment yourself with all this drinking and drugging you do, I ask him.

He once more laughs his trademark 'Kssshh' laugh, the sound of a portable toilet flushing itself. 'I don't take drugs to torment myself – ksshh-h-h. I've already got life to do that for me!'

But how do you feel when everybody sits you down and lectures you about being too out of it?

'I try my best to hold my temper, that's what I do. S'none of their fuckin' business what I fuckin' do to myself, right?'

Yes, but good God, man, you've got, whether you think this way or not, you've got a God-given talent that, the way you carry on, you're suffocating as much as you're expressing. Don't you think you owe that talent the option of something approaching sobriety if only in order to allow yourself to grasp the nettle of its full potential?

'I've been straight,' he retorts a touch petulantly, 'well, not like recently, kssshhh! But I've done all that.'

And it didn't work?

'Nah, it worked perfectly. 'Cos it proved to me once and for all that I never wanted to be that way ever again. If I could help it . . . I don't believe in the fuckin' work ethic. This "work is what life's all about" shit is just a bunch of bollocks, it's just a fuckin' English bourgeois guilt trip invented by the fuckin' English bourgeoisie to keep people in line, y'know, like a bunch of happy fuckin' slaves. Bourgeois guilt means fuckin' nothin' to me.

'Now, Catholic guilt, I can, like, relate to that. When I was a kid, I was very religiously minded. I'd be down at the confessional talking to God with my rosary . . . [*Ardently*] I was a good Catholic boy. I believed. This is all like before I was put in this fuckin' mental hospital in Dublin. That taught me a thing or two, right? They put me in to try and get me off these Valium this fuckin' doctor had put me on when I was sixteen. The bastard put me on eighty fuckin' milligram a day, right, and after a year they reckoned you have fits if you just stop, which I quickly found out is true. So they put me in there, right, and I'm next door to some poor junkie bastard who's detoxing and screamin' for his fix, right, while on the other side there's some old man who's screaming all night every night 'cos he keeps reliving his mother dying, which happened, like, thirty years before all this. And I didn't know what the fuck was going on or why I was in there, right? I was really, really terrified. Seeing and hearing all that fuckin' horror and misery changed a lot of things for me, right. Taught me a lot. Like the word "mad"! That word doesn't have any fuckin' meaning for me. In this life, some people are just less mad than others. That's all.'

Many people still call Shane McGowan another *beautiful loser*, but he's never been a beauty and neither, all desperate appearances to the contrary, is he a loser. Rather, he's a loser who chose to lose and came up winning more than he ever dared dream. The severity of that contradiction haunts him, but then McGowan's whole life is shot through with raging contradictions. He is extremely shy yet makes his living standing stupified and being stared at by thousands at a time. He is extremely bright and perceptive but seems to do everything in his power to bury these characteristics behind as much grimy sensory deprivation as he can muster. Stupefaction seems his only defence and intoxication his muse, yet his best songs betray a depth, a longing and a clarity that mock those tawdry implications.

He is obviously ensnared in the grand romance of his Celtic heritage, but his manner and bearings are all those of the London wide-boy punk. Certainly, as traditions go, he has a rare talent for mixing the Byronic with the moronic.

Still he's always been true to his vision. His notoriety as one of 1977's seminal punk faces is all a matter of public record now. The first time I saw him that year he looked like he'd already been a member of the 'count me out' generation probably from since before he could count. A few months later I remember we had a barney that stopped just short of blows; this was just after my immortal spat with Sid Vicious, mind, and I was fair prey to every 'aspiring young psychopath' in club-land who wanted a quick mention in the weekly music comics. He wasn't physically threatening (nor was he – or is he – genuinely psychopathic, certain appearances to the contrary), but he was on so much speed he was shaking and his eyes had an unnervingly demented quality to them. At that moment I needed him berating me like I needed cancer. We enjoyed a very singular relationship after that. For what must have been eight years I'd see him once a month in some crowded sweaty room, always half-cut (but then so was I usually) and we'd just scowl at each other wordlessly from our different foetid corners. As the years elapsed his appearance grew increasingly bedraggled and his mouth lost most of its teeth, but his compulsive appetites seemed only to harden – as apparently did his constitution, to that of a horse. It was obvious too that the persona he adopted took a lot of its cues from his hero Robert De Niro's great lost boys, characters like Johnny Boy and the patron saint of the whole seventies psycho-chic experience, Travis Bickle. A friend who provided sanctuary for Shane after he'd been run over by a taxi cab in Westbourne Grove told me that he used to recite De Niro's dialogue from *Once Upon a Time in America* every night in his sleep. From the first days of the Pogues' formation, six years ago, people have been giving him no more than six months to live, just as his consistently besotted condition on and off stage blinkered many to view the group as nothing more than one long mangled advertisement for alcoholic oblivion. On a bad night they had a point, but on a good night, when everything connected, stupefaction would be alchemized into blinding fury and the Pogues would rage with riveting abandon, irrepressible and justifiably unstoppable.

'It's all in the bollocks where Irish music and rock music meet each other. The centre of gravity – the bollocks. Rage, anger, desire and all that shit.' That's how he summed up the Pogues' mangled essence only last year. He'd used much the same analogy when I first interviewed him in 1986. I still remember two things about that evening. Firstly how, once he'd rid himself of his initial doubts, he spontaneously transformed his whole stance from the habitual dull-eyed, slack-jawed Shane McGowan stupor into a state of dauntingly focused and learned articulacy. The second image was quite different, however more appropriately 'hellish'. At four in the morning we'd trooped out to King's Cross, where McGowan, dressed only in a T-shirt, jeans and ragged bedroom slippers (and this was mid-January, mark you, brutally cold), purchased a bun wedged only with grease and copious onion rings then handed out the rest of his wealth in bank notes and loose silver to three beleaguered-looking tramps clumped haphazardly around the makeshift hut that sold refreshments and cigarettes to the area's destitutes and insomniacs. As he was dispensing his booty, a solitary one pence coin dropped from his pocket and rolled into the gutter. Instantaneously he followed its descent, throwing himself down on to the cold, dank concrete sewer and crawling on all fours, his eyes stricken with the mad wallowing frenzy of those whose lives are one long exercise in seeing just how far and how *low* they can keep going.

Now take a picture of this. Shane McGowan has a vision he wants to share with me. 'Young white psychopaths, young black psychopaths, young Paki psychopaths, young gay psychopaths – all fuckin' races and creeds together on Ecstasy right, dancin' in a line like the fuckin' conga, really connectin' . . . This great fuckin' swamp of humanity . . . Kssshhh!'

Twelve years after McGowan's summer of punk he was back in a 'rest home' again, though some refer to it as a health farm, summoned there at either the group or his family's instigation (or both), only to resurface in London in time to hurl himself headlong and screaming into the sensory wilderness of acid house. 'It was fuckin' great, acid house. Well, the music's bollocks in a way – but no, some of it's good. No, really! You got to be on Ecstasy or acid to listen to it, of course, ksshhh! But that's no fuckin' different from punk and all the speed you had to take to listen to that, right.'

It was to prove a nightmare bender for everyone else, however. 'Shane is extremely shy and self-conscious, extremely bright, extremely intense and obsessive,' an acquaintance once remarked. 'The ugly things about life that everyone else hold at arm's length he kind of feels he has to madly embrace. As a result his defences are much lower than other people's and it's always made his whole personality a little bit fractured. And acid has only probably helped magnify those fractures.'

The Pogues would go further than that. 'Yer man McGowan on acid . . . eight or nine tabs at a time, every day . . . One big fockin' nightmare,' remarked manager Frank Murray. 'It was terrible him out his head on acid in the studio. He was bein' impossible, gettin' into a couple of big bust-ups with Steve [Lillywhite]. Tryin' to get him to finish the fockin' lyrics to a new song, y'know, was bad enough. Then he couldn't sing properly some days.' As a result, sessions overran by an extra month (at 1,000 pounds a day) in order that McGowan's vocals be 'suitably' recorded. And he lobbied in vain to get the Pogues to record a twenty-minute acid house track he'd written entitled 'You've Got to Connect Yourself'.

'We had to tell him right there,' claims Murray, 'Shane, man, keep that fockin' acid house for yer solo album.'

Murray, certain idle gossips have indicated, has perhaps done McGowan's compulsive nature no favours by committing him and the rest of the Pogues to such an arduous work regime these past few years. These criticisms, however, simply don't take the facts into account, as McGowan's self-destructive tendencies only magnify when he has no regimented workload to half-way stabilize him. Trying to manage such a wayward individual, though particularly over the last year, has often brought Murray close to the end of his tether. And right now no one in the organization seems able to gauge what's really going on in the back of Shane McGowan's mind, whether his bent for stubborn petulance and general 'out-there'-ness is an indication of some frivolous 'altered state' or the more deep-seated manifestation of a craving to hasten his own imminent retirement from the front line of Pogue-dom.

For their part, other members make no bones about publicly expressing their discontent over McGowan's condition. 'Enough people have tried to get through to him,' bassist Darryl Hunt told me. 'Nick Cave tried recently, he was being gentle about it but the message was clear. And Ali Campbell just last week on the coach' – the Pogues have been supporting UB40 at various European stadium gigs – 'really lit into him. "You're pathetic, you know that! Why are you always such a miserable cunt? You never talk to anyone! You never fuckin' socialize. You just sit in the back of the bus quietly fuckin' yourself up!" Sometimes it registers and sometimes it doesn't.'

Six weeks before had been a red-letter day for the Pogues, a day when the world's most ostensibly dissolute band had to read the riot act to one of their own. McGowan, tripped on an alarmingly pronounced dosage of acid, had been impossible to communicate with, from the sound check, which he'd performed with his coat over his head, to the gig itself, where in front of ten thousand he'd stumbled about, continually interrupting his vocal performances to relocate his portable off licence or converse with other galaxies.

'Altered states . . . Yeah! Kssshh,' he remarks, grinning manically, his mouth a veritable dental graveyard. 'See, I'm a hedonist, right.'

This is scarcely a major revelation. I ask him if intoxication really is his only muse ('I've got to be out of my head in order to write,' he'd told a journalist only three months before) and he immediately rejects the word 'muse': ' 'Cos, like, it infers that the songs I write sort of come through me. And that's bollocks, mostly. Songwriting's a craft, that's all. Like, a lot of people analyse my lyrics but they miss the fuckin' point. I always knew my lyrics were better than anyone else's anyway. I just edit more than other people, that's my fuckin' secret. Constant fuckin' re-editing. Also I never sleep and that helps too. You've got more time that way, right.'

So are you really just another of those 'life is shit and then you die' type of guys?

'Nah, I hate that. Life is great. This is a beautiful world, y'know. It's all here. This is where you get to experience heaven and hell . . . Heaven? Heaven is Thailand, OK. Kssshhh . . . A blinding civilization full of strong, gentle, good-hearted people with suss, right. A noble race of people, an easy-going race of people a lot like the Irish before the fuckin' British soldiers occupied their country. The fuckin' Yanks never went near 'em, right. Thailand's an undefeated country, right. And, like, everyone smokes opium, right, but it's cool. It's all part of the scheme of things.

'Where do these drugs come from? From plants right, growing out of the fuckin' ground. If God didn't mean us to take drugs he wouldn't have created them in the first place. I don't go for all this bollocks about "sin". Evil is torturin' other people, not yourself, right. I believe in reincarnation. And the laws of karma. You do wrong and it comes back to haunt you in your next life. Then after you've come back over and over again your spirit is finally put to rest and shunted out into the fuckin' void. And that really is heaven.'

And where is hell?

'Hell', he shoots back, indicating his immediate surroundings, 'is all this.'

Though he admits to being 'very, very unhappy' at the moment, press him on whether he really wants to retire from the Pogues or not and he seems uncertain, if not a little shame-faced. He talks about 'commitments I can't turn my back on. There are, like, fifteen blokes depending on me in this organi-zation and whether I personally get on with most of them or not is like beside the point. We're still comrades.'

'So where's Mr Magoo then?' It is seven and the Pogues are in the lobby waiting for Shane to join them for the gig tonight.

'He's in his room rubbing wintergreen into his girlfriend,' retorts James Fearnley.

'He's looking for his third eye,' pipes in Jem Finer.

'No, he's polishing his third eye, looking for his fourth eye.'

You can't blame them for their barbs too much because in 1989 the image of the Pogues as a bunch of drunken yahoos is, barring McGowan and his bosom buddy Spider Stacey (oddly subdued this day), really a thing of the past. Everyone's past thirty now, some nearer forty, and consequently they've become more professional, less abuse-conscious, more into pacing themselves. What started out as just a good crack has developed into a lucrative vocation. They tour the world in comfort, play to appreciative, often adoring masses and then have heroes like Lou Reed and Tom Waits wanting to come up and shake their hands after the show. Is it any wonder they find it so frustrating to work with a frontman who spends half his life in conditions that constantly threaten to jeopardize their very future?

Later, on the coach, Philip Chevron remarks that 'being around one person who obviously overdoes it can make everyone else sort of question their own vices ... Shane is obviously irreplaceable to the Pogues, but then so is everyone else in this band. I still believe that if anyone needs to take an extended break from the group we can accommodate that ... People seem to think that if Shane wasn't involved in the Pogues he'd be more stable or something. But that's really a fantasy. He's never lived a normal life and he probably never will. It's too late for him to start now.'

The gig is neither splendid nor is it particularly disastrous, but that isn't the point. The band is seethingly professional (no small thanks to their rhythm section) but the mythic 'bollocks' factor seems absent tonight. Shane for his part manages to hang in with the rest while seeming to be forever out of step, like a sleepwalker almost. He doesn't seem quite connected and only comes alive when he purposefully falls on to the stage twice in the middle of dancing a mutated Irish gig. Without him there, though, the conclusion is obvious: the Pogues would still be hugely entertaining but they would also be quite 'irrelevant'.

Whatever happens next is anyone's guess. 'There's a limit to everything,' he stated ominously last year before describing the Pogues experience as 'educational . . . The education of a young suicide.' Still, there's another way of looking at this life, I suppose. For, like Frank Sinatra, Shane McGowan has done it his way and what he has already achieved is to provide an authentic and stirring body of work for all the poor outcasts too sensitive or maladjusted to compete with all the grasping bullshit of the eighties to harken to. Just for the bare facts of what he and his success represents in Great Britain he will probably be remembered as the very stuff of Margaret Thatcher's worst nightmares.

But he is doomed. 'I don't see it as any fuckin' tragedy, my life. Everyone thought I'd be a failure and a liability.' And he can still be spotted on the same dark London streets at night dispensing great bundles of 'dosh' to the tramps and destitutes who litter his path. 'It's not, like, a ritual though,' he reasons. 'I do it so they'll leave me alone . . . But also because I'm very, very aware, right, that there but for the grace of God go I. I'm just lucky. 'Cos I'm no different from them. I just get to behave like they do in front of 24,000 people, that's all.'

The Daze of Guns'N'Roses

'Let me tell you about when Guns'N'Roses really first . . . like, the moment of revelation, the moment which began this whole . . . *movement*. It was when our car broke down a hundred miles into the fuckin' desert when we were drivin' to our first ever gig. Duff, when he joined – like we said, "Hey, wanna jam?" He said, "Yeah!" – he got us these gigs in Seattle to play. Duff said, "Yo! Seattle, it's right on top of America." We said, "Hey, cool," y'know. "Let's fuckin' go." It was a complete disaster.

'So we're stranded in the fuckin' desert, right. Ain't no way we're going back to Hollywood. I mean, these are 300 bucks a night gigs we're talkin' about here . . .

'So we hitchhiked. After two fuckin' days in the desert a guy in a semi picked us up. Finally we made it to Seattle. We played. There were ten, maybe twenty people there. We didn't get paid. Finally we had to steal another car to drive back to LA again.

'And from the day we got back to Hollywood, it's been, like, whatever goes down, y'know, we're still united in this conflict against . . . everything, really. Guns'N'Roses' motto from like that day on has been "Fuck everybody," y'know. "Fuck everybody before they fuck with you."

'"*Fuck the whole fuckin' world*," y'know. Just let's keep movin'.'

And so it is that we are moving, Izzy Stradlin and I, in a long black limousine no less, hither and yon through the empty August streets of Paris, searching – always in vain – first for a guitar shop, then a pizza house, until finally we're just in transit, completely rudderless, no particular place to go. Just moving. On one lazy infamous street, a single desultory prostitute stands, old and defiant. 'Is this the . . . uh red-letter district,' he asks me uninterestedly in his slightly paranoid half-whisper of a voice. A lantern-jawed Midwestern farm boy with haunted eyes and a monumental Keith Richards fixation ('the guy is just so far out! I imagine he must be, y'know, just really, really *numb*, y'know what I'm sayin'?'), Stradlin's supposed to be on holiday, but today (Wednesday) is this interview and tomorrow's Germany, where he's going specifically to 'have all this new scientific shit pumped into my gums so my teeth won't keep fallin' out'. In between involves going through Customs and this imminent reality is clearly not sitting well with him at all. Though maybe it's just a pathological reaction dating back to a year ago, when on a flight to Japan with the other Gunners and ordered by his manager to get rid of all drugs about his person before landing, Izzy had done accordingly, sending himself straight into a coma lasting thirty-six hours that almost necessitated cancelling the gigs they'd come to play.

But there is worse than Customs awaiting Stradlin the day after (Friday), when he must return to America ('which is just about to explode, man! The pressure there is too intense!'), specifically to LA, where, 'if I'm there over a month, you'll have to pretty much dig me out.' There he is set to regroup with Guns'N'Roses ('the only guys I can really relate to on a day-to-day basis. You could say we live in our own little world. We see things in our particular way and that's it'): with Axl Rose ('he's completely crazy . . . Without the other four of us around, I wouldn't even *want* to imagine what the fuck would go on in his head. Or his life'); guitarist Slash ('Slash was born in Stock . . . Uh, Stoke-on-Trent, when he was just a little kid, you know what I'm sayin'?'); bassist Duff ('he plays sort of like a rhythm bass sort of thing, y'know'); and drummer Steven

Adler, hereafter referred to as 'fuckin' Stevie' – in order to once more attempt the seemingly impossible dream of completing their next album without anyone dying – or 'having their lives turned into absolute shit' – in the process. Scott Fitzgerald made that famous quote about there being no second act in American lives, and Guns'N'Roses, America's premier outlaw attraction of the eighties, currently the world's biggest selling rock'n'roll band, are having a hard time disproving it long enough to achieve even the making of a second album. (Their second actual release, 'Guns'N'Roses Lies', is always referred to as an 'extended EP'.)

With G'N'R mania at its nerviest peak in America, you could be forgiven for thinking the whole country is just waiting for one of these guys to die. I ask Stradlin what it's like to open *People* and *National Enquirer* every week and be told over and over again that you've got between three and six months to live.

'It's sick. Freaks me out. Like the last thing . . . Just before I left the States to come here . . . I saw this thing in *National Enquirer* and . . . It's fuckin' Stevie, man. Apparently he went to Nevada, got fucked up, met some girl and, like, ended up marryin' her or somethin'. And the headline, y'know . . . It read something like "G'N'R DRUMMER MARRIES GIRL: SAYS I CAN STILL FUCK AROUND". *In*-credible!

'Talkin' of *sick*,' he seemingly free-associates. 'Y'know Mötley Crüe?' 'Sick fuckin' guys, man! Real sick fucks, those guys! In '87 we were supposed to come . . . here . . . to Europe, man . . . with fuckin' Mötley Crüe, and they burnt out on us and had to go into detox. You wouldn't have believed these guys. Like they're doin' an ounce of cocaine each a fuckin' day. These guys are walkin' into fuckin' walls, man. And they're doing this shit . . . Y'know, havin' this chick tied to the bed and stuff. And they tried to get us into that shit too, just to fuck us up, right. Which is what happened.' And here he straightens up. 'I mean, can you believe . . . These guys gave fuckin' Stevie fuckin' *Ajax* to snort all fuckin' night. *Fucked him up*. You don't pull that kinda shit on another musician!

'Then after Mötley Crüe burnt out on us, we got a call sayin' Alice Cooper had like two weeks of support dates in the Midwest. We said, "Alice Cooper . . . Fuckin' A!" Hey, I grew up listening to, y'know "Sick Things", "I Love the Dead". It was a lot better than fuckin' reality. So we did 'em. Alice was cool. He's still . . . y'know . . . "Alice". Anyway, after like a week Alice's old man died or somethin', a gig was cancelled and we got, like, really slaughtered in a Holiday Inn like somewhere in West Michigan. And it's snowing, right, fuckin' Stevie's fucked up, he goes and punches out a fuckin' electric light bulb in the fuckin' street, man. His hand's fuckin' swellin' up like an egg and he's on the bus cryin' and shit. We're goin', "Shut the fuck up!"

'And like now, we're doin' this new album and one of the biggest fuckin' hang-ups . . . uh it's just so hard to get everybody in the same direction, y'know. For example, you can be into two bars of a song and you stop and Stevie just goes off, man, for no fuckin' reason, playin' this fuckin' drum solo bad-ada-da jazz fuckin' shit, right. And you're like sittin' there right screaming at the guy, "Shut the fuck up!" This shit tends to use up an awful fuckin' lot of our time.

'But see,' he adds ruefully, 'whenever we've played with other drummers . . . I mean, these guys can be meter-perfect but it just has never worked. Stevie's timing is all "up and down", "up and down". It speeds up. Then it slows down. It's fucked up but it works. And like that's the thing about Guns'N'Roses. The more fucked up things are the more they seem to work for us.'

Strictly on a *cartoon* level, Guns'N'Roses are probably the most singularly entertaining and titillating group in the whole of late-eighties rock pop culture right now. After all, they're the youngest, the thinnest, the rowdiest, the most calamity-prone, etc., etc. Plus there are a number of Spinal Tap comparisons (the ongoing drummer problem, the fact that the G'N'R manager, New Zealander Alan Niven, apparently bears an uncanny resemblance to the Tap's long-suffering celluloid counterpart). But to just brush this group off as another tasteless fad – like hula-hoops or something – is to miss the point entirely. Many have argued that Guns'N'Roses have single-handedly brought rock'n'roll back to life, that they are to the eighties what the Sex Pistols were to the seventies – a short sharp shock to the youth culture, bristling with authentic rage and outlaw irreverence.

Their music when you confront it is rock stripped down to its absolute pig-iron fundamentals. That is to say, there is no real imagination at work here, no wit, no joy, no irony, certainly no originality whatsoever. Their sound is all relentlessness and paranoia, all 'they're out to get me – I'm fuckin' innocent', all 'the world is fucked up and so are we'. Basically, their music is primeval ('It's just such a twisted and demented effort for all of us,' Stradlin claims). It confronts you, it gets right up into your face with its one barbaric message: 'Love us or let us run wild. We're Guns'N'Roses. What are you going to do about it?' Of course, in America the hype says that they're the new Rolling Stones and it's a hype that the Stones themselves have bowed to, finally after months of public speculation inviting the Gunners to share the bill with them for two mid-October Los Angeles shows – a sort of late-eighties rock'n'roll Pat Garrett meets Billy the Kid affair, if you like.

And even though the G'N'R rhetoric has more in common with the Hells Angels of 1969's Altamont than the gloriously disengaged insincerity of Mick Jagger, there are obvious similarities between the two in that G'N'R currently pose the question that Nik Cohn asked about the Stones twenty years ago: 'What's so good about bad?' For as one-dimensional and cartoon-like as they can sometimes appear, Guns'N'Roses' popularity is maintained by dint of a genuinely raw charisma that one can't help but view as also being genuinely 'diabolical' as an influence on young people. 'The kids understand us,' they say, but what is there to understand here? That 'you can say we're not exactly life for life's sake kind of guys'? That already fans have been killed at their concerts, specifically at last year's Donington festival? That, in the nineties, cutting edge rock'n'roll will be all about death and dissipation, dumb racism and even dumber isolationism?

Thus it was that I went along to this interview not so much to come to terms with Guns'N'Roses as to *further define* terms with them:

Let's get personal here. How are the other members of Guns'N'Roses right now?

'Well, uh, Axl is probably the most, uh, physically ... together of us right now. Slash? I hear he's doin' better, y'know. Haven't seen him in three to four weeks but I hear he's doin' better than in a long time. He seems to realize now that with this new album to be made there's like a ... uh, time period he has to be sustainin' right. Which he couldn't do before because of the way he's livin' his life.'

Hasn't your drummer Stevie been in and out of detox clinics in the last year like a proverbial yo-yo?

'Uh ... uh ... Who ... Stevie? Uh ... When somebody in the band just gets too fucked up, sometimes the manager will just ... No. No, I mean, yeah, Stevie has probably been on several of those missions, yeah.'

Isn't there a time limit involved in all of this ...?

'Uh, it depends. [*Pause.*] Definitely, I'd say. Like, when we're touring it's like we have to be on ten all the time anyway, right. So you can indulge a hundred times more, right. Because a lot of that physical and mental abuse ... You can take it, it just drops off you like fuckin' dust and you can walk away. 'Cos you're movin' all the time, right. But if you're sittin' around in Hollywood with your adrenalin charge shut off, then ... bad shit can happen. If you're the sort of person who takes drugs, man, that's when it gets to you.'

Are *you* currently addicted to drugs?

'Uh . . . addiction . . . That's a very heavy word . . . That depends. [*Another pause.*] Do you mean physically or mentally?'

Are you *physically* addicted to *hard drugs* I mean, that's what everybody infers about you guys. The big national rumour is that you're all junkies . . .

'Listen, I can't even . . . I don't . . . I'm OK, y'know. Everyone in the group's OK. I mean, everyone's talkin' about this shit all the time. I mean, *I* never said nothin' about "drugs". Everyone has to know their own limits. That's all I wanna say.'

Well, the other thing I wanted to ask you – irrespective of whether you are addicts or not – being the most famous and visible examples of that kind of lifestyle, don't the police or the CIA or FBI or whoever keep constant tabs on your activities?

'There's a *lot* of that bullshit, yeah! Put it this way, when I'm on the telephone anywhere in the USA I'm always very careful what I say. Always. It's all so new, this shit, that only *now* am I starting to understand it. Strange people come to your door . . . Even in hotels they just walk into your hotel room and try to sell you stuff, y'know what I'm sayin'. I have to be very careful.

'And LA is the pits, man! I'm fuckin' . . . I'm supposed to go back on Friday to do the album and already it's worryin' me 'cos the police have our names and numbers there, y'know. And I've been arrested once already. It's just a nightmare. I don't go out anymore. All my friends are the same way. But that's LA for you. I go out for a drive, I get pulled over. First thing, the cop pulls a gun in my face. I'm sittin' there . . . "Officer, what did I do?"'

So what sort of perspective does being the premier outlaw band of America give you about the current state of your country?

'America is about to really just blow up in some kind of drug war. There's just so much of it around. Right now in West Hollywood it's a complete Gestapo situation. If you're walking down the street they'll jump you, beat you up, plant shit on you and haul your ass off to jail. Then you're in court and it's your word against theirs. I mean, who are they going to believe?

'When I go back, I'm just going to stay cool and not hang out in the city. I've seen too much shit go down. I know too many people associated with Guns'N'Roses whose lives have turned into absolute shit because of this drugs media angle. I mean, that's why I'm over here.'

A number of other rock acts have commented on the 'undignified' way you're handling success . . .

'Fuck them! What do they know? There's all these burnt-out old fucked-up rock stars we get to meet in clubs and bars in Los Angeles, y'know. They want to talk to us but they've mostly all got this attitude . . . like they're a bit "interested", a whole lotta "jealous" and a little bit "fuck you", y'know. Fuck man, it's not success that's hard to deal with, it's . . . uh, the other thing. But we've got it licked. We'll just make this record and then just keep on movin', y'know.'

But let's talk more about success, about your success.

'Well it's frightening, that's what it is. I mean, a week ago I flew with Axl from New York to Lafayette, Indiana, with one lay-over flight and by the time we hit Lafayette there were people just milling around the fuckin' airport. Mainly for him. Axl really brings out the fuckin' crazies, man. They relate to him particularly in this very weird, intense way. But that's the same with all of us, y'know. It's like a sickness. 'Cos they don't want to shake your hand or get your autograph. They want to scream in your face or mess with your head, sneak around your house, sneak into your hotel room and fuck with your head. It puts you right on edge, man, all the fuckin' time. Because a lot of these kids carry guns, right. And you never know what the fuck they're up to.

'And that's not half the shit. I've been ripped off . . . nine months ago I moved into the Valley; in one week I was robbed, y'know, of everything. Four months later I had to crawl out of LA and cool out in the Midwest. I find a place there and four days later it's been stripped clean. You figure you have to get rifles. Just to deal with these people. You don't want to shoot anyone but hey, if that's how it goes down . . .'

I'm sorry, are you saying your fans actually pull guns on you?

'It's happened, man. I'm walking into my house, there's five guys parked in my yard, just waiting for me, right. One gets out – "We wanna autograph!" I tell them to get the fuck out of my yard. But they don't see it that way.

'I've had my windows shot out. Many times. You think, "Why the fuck would anyone wanna shoot my fuckin' windows out?"

'I mean, there's currently a wave of fuckin' murders in Los Angeles involving "personalities" . . . Some actors just got blasted point blank in a place on Fairfax on the same fuckin' block we used to live in. It's bullshit and I don't like to think about it but sometimes it gets to you, y'know.'

You keep talking about 'explosive pressures' in your country. You talked just back there about an 'imminent drug war' . . .

'Listen, America right now is one big fuckin' drug, OK. Like, cocaine is . . . It's like this cigarette [reaches for a Marlboro]. And the press can talk about it, say, "Don't do it. Just say no . . .", it don't make a fuckin' bit of difference. Because, hey, South America and Mexico – where the stuff originates from – are right below the Southern USA – You got Florida, Texas and the Tijuana border over to LA . . . It's a sick joke. A bad fucked-up sick joke. They should just legalize it. Instead they're just crowding out the prisons.

'I mean, I know this for a fact, right? The prisons are so over-crowded – and it's a 70–80 per cent drug offences ratio – that the powers that be are currently doing up all these defunct old army bases all along the Mexican border for the express purpose of taking the overspill from the jails and doing experiments on them. Like the Germans did during the fuckin' war. You can bet neither me nor the rest of Guns'N'Roses are going to be around for any of these experiments.'

There's so much paranoia and belligerence in your music . . . Isn't all this violence you give off very contagious?

'Yeah! We seem to stir up real violent emotions in people! I've noticed that. But, see, violence happens only when we're being fucked with. I mean, like you're tryin' to make a living playing your music. And you've got these assholes who work in these clubs – they're just fuckin' animals, these people – who just want to push you around. Treat you like you're just another fuckin' band. Shove you in the ass. And we were only doing our own thing. Then things would happen, y'know. Some fucker would get onstage – some drunk would fuck with you – and that was . . . that was it. We'd just dust 'em, just kick them down. Kick their asses to the back of the stage, back into the fuckin' crowd. Why? I don't know why. 'Cos they're fuckin' with you, I guess.

'So that's part of the violence. The other is this bullshit whenever we've been a support act . . . like, you open a show, you get your standard thirty, forty minutes, right, which we always tried to play over. So the headline act would pull the fuckin' plug. Fights used to start a lot 'cos of that.

'We know what it's like to be fucked around. Even still today we get fucked around. I mean, and who knows, man? Maybe the Stones are lettin' us play these two gigs with them just 'cos they can fuck with us? Maybe the Rolling Stones want to fuck with us, y'know what I'm sayin'. That would be . . . a trip.'

How do you respond to guys like Jim Kerr of Simple Minds and U2's Bono who say they're playing rock'n'roll to save the world and that Guns'N'Roses just want to pollute and destroy the world with their music?

'We don't want to destroy fuck. We're just writin' and singin' about what we see. Maybe those jerks see somethin' different. I don't give two shits about them and their world anyway.'

But your world lyrically is seen through the eyes of your singer, Axl Rose, and he's completely mad . . .

'Yeah, he is! He's *very* crazy, y'know. Like, sometimes he can be very rational and other times he's just deep left-field. It's always up and down, up and down with Axl. He just has a very hard time relating to other people.

'Sometimes he just goes off the deep end and if anyone can make sense to him in those states, I think it's me. Because we still relate as friends coming from "bumfuck" Indiana. The rest doesn't mean much. I can kinda talk him down when he freaks out and locks himself in his room and we've got to play a gig or record.'

How do you relate to some of his lyrics – like the immigrants and faggots slur in 'One in a million'?

'I have a big problem with that lyric. I've talked to Axl many times about his lyrics. "You don't need to say that, Axl. You're a fuckin' immigrant yourself. Everyone's a fuckin' immigrant in America. Don't you see you're putting down the whole of fuckin' America? And if they're faggots, well so what?" Axl . . . is very . . . confused.

'But I was pissed off. I was very against that shit going on our record. "Why'd you have to say that, Axl. It's hard enough just gettin' by." [*Pauses.*] But at the same time, y'know, this is just fuckin' rock'n'roll music. When it's fucked up, it's more interesting. Whoever said this was *responsible* music, y'know? We're not fuckin' role models. At all.'

But 'One in a Million' is just flat-out racist. That line about niggers trying to sell you gold chains. I mean, I think Public Enemy and NWA are racist but . . .

'Have you heard Niggers With Attitude? They write about exactly the same area that we wrote "Welcome to the Jungle" and "One in a Million" about, the same fuckin' area we're going to be playin' with the Stones in a couple of months. You wouldn't believe this fuckin' stretch, man. Talk about racial differences! You park your car there, they'll sell you the parking space, then they'll strip it of tyres! A guy livin' there goes out for the evenin', he comes back, someone's sold his house *and* his yard behind his fuckin' back! . . .

'There's just so much fuckin' friction there between black and white. This "we've got to live together" shit . . . it just isn't real, y'know. It's not realistic. I can't save the world, man. 'Cos what's going on out there is just a fuckin' jungle. We just observe it.

'But Niggers With Attitude – man, they are *baaad*! They dig us too. They wanted either to do a cover or do a sample of "Welcome to the Jungle". They rang up the office. I don't know if Axl was too . . . receptive to the idea.'

Tell me about Donington.

'That was . . . very strange. I mean, I saw it all go down. I stopped the gig three times. Kids were lookin' at me, givin' me this real intense look, like "something really, really bad is going down". You could read it all in their faces. I tried to stop the band . . . like three times . . . but they just kept playing, y'know on and on. Then I turned around and I could see the bodies being pulled out.'

Didn't you think by then that there really was a genuine hex on Guns'N'Roses?

'I just realized that Guns'N'Roses had become way, way bigger than anything you could possibly hope to control as a musician. I mean, when you play clubs you're pretty much in control. But the energy forces in these stadiums and arenas are beyond anything . . . It's frightening, y'know.

'And the fuckin' money that's involved . . . like with us, then with this Stones tour . . . I mean, what are the promoters goin' to offer us next? Are they goin' to buy off whole cities so we can play there? Is that next? Y'know, "Come to our city and take all these drugs." Listen, the last time the Stones played the

Coliseum, eight years ago, it was insane! I didn't have a ticket but I was outside hangin' out. There were, like, 50,000 inside and 20,000 outside, selling drugs, selling fake passes and every-thin', man. Undercover policemen. When the Stones went on . . . y'know, "Under My Thumb", the fuckin' trees were movin'. I'll never forget that. Then a riot broke out at the back of the Coliseum. Me and this little kid were in a fuckin' tree peering around these pillars. Then I see these pigs on horses with the shields and all the riot shit on, just mowing these people down, man, crackin' black skulls, hispanic skulls, you name it. Then a whole bunch came crackin' and beatin' us out of the trees.

'And to think now, in 1989 with what's going on in America and particularly the West Coast – and where the Coliseum is is one of the worst racial areas you can go to – that *we're* going to do these two gigs with *those guys there*! It's going to be very interesting.'

You mean, 'interesting' like Altamont?

'Maybe. If that's how it goes down. It's going to be . . . a trip.'

The Mancunian Candidates:
Happy Mondays and Stone Roses

'Last night 'is bed caught fire 'cos o' smokin that. There were flames comin' up from 'is pillow. 'E didn't know owt about it tho'. 'E were fookin' comatose.'

The Happy Mondays' infamous dancer Bez, whose bed it was, holds aloft a pellet-sized lump of hashish the colour of a particularly malnourished bowel motion towards the gaze of the Stone Roses drummer, then flashes him a good conspiratorial 'mad' look before stating without any intended irony whatsoever, 'Aye, when your bed's on fire you know you're dealin' with top fookin' draw!'

Across the room the Mondays singer Shaun Ryder is being asked by a journalist just exactly what he and the rest of the band want out of 'the drug experience'. Ryder squints his weasel eyes, the eyes of the terminally 'sarky' Northerner, and gives the question due thought.

'Uh . . . well . . . uh . . . illumination, pal. Yeah! Illumination, definitely. Well, illumination, like, half the time anyway. 'Cos t'other half we just like to get fookin' roarin' shit-faced y'know wharramsayin'.'

Welcome to the New Power Generation. A hundred years ago most of this mob would have ended up on a press-gang. Today, one month shy of 1990, they're the two great dark British hopes of pop for a whole new decade. Talk about the decline of civilization. 'The nineties actually began during the six weeks that *Ride on Time* by Black Box was Number One in England,' states Factory supremo, Happy Mondays' pet Goebbels, Tony

Wilson. 'Happy Mondays and Stone Roses entering the charts together the same week and getting their first *Top of the Pops* together as a result . . . That makes this decade now well and truly declared "*open*". This makes it *official*.'

To boost these young Mancs' jubilant moods further, a big black beatbox stands proudly at one corner of their communal dressing-room blaring out alternate selections. The Stone Roses boys instigate a session of the Beatles from one speaker played against some acid house whooping and looping out of the other. Every now and then the Happy Mondays change the music by Shaun Ryder simply turning off the Beatles and leaving the tape of atonal honks and scrambled rhythms to ricochet through the room. One can't help but see something symbolic in all this.

'They're the only other group we can just sit down and have a drink with, like,' says Stone Roses singer Ian Brown, indicating Ryder and his cronies. 'The Mondays and Stone Roses have the same influences, really, 'cos we've been to the same clubs. Blues nights, reggae nights, house nights, a bit of Parliament, a bit of Funkadelic . . . We're all takin' it from the same record collections, just doin' it up different.'

'Y'll find no rivalry here, pal,' mutters Shaun Ryder, before pausing to think. 'Well, the only rivalry 'tween oos and the Roses, like, is over clothes, really. There's always been a bit of a race on to see who's got the best flashiest clothes, right, and what part of the world these clothes come from. 'Cos we're both flash cunts, y'knowwharramean!

'They're dead brilliant, Stone Roses. They're more tuneful than us but we're a top band too so it works great together, I reckon. I mean, I can call 'em mates. Ian! Fookin' Mani! Friends, y'knowwharramean. And particularly fookin' Cressa, man! Whooray, we taught 'em everythin' 'e fookin' knows.'

Talk turns to the subject of another shared experience, producer Martin Hannett, the troubled Phil Spector of the North. 'We went in with him in 1985 and he produced the first version of "I Wanna Be Adored",' Brown is telling Ryder, 'and a bunch of other stuff. Riffs that weren't songs. It was a disaster. 'Ee were only half-there.'

Shaun Ryder counters: "E's a fookin' mate to the Mondays, Martin. He's great when 'e's with us, man. Mind, 'e likes workin' with us 'cos we give 'im a lot of E durin' sessions, right! E sorts 'im right out! During the *Hallelujah* sessions we were givin' him two a day and this were when they were twenty-five quid a go, right. But it were worth it 'cos he kept saying, "I can't feel anything but I'm in a fookin' great frame of mind." Plus it stops 'im gettin' too bladdered.'

Most members of both groups are paying little attention to the music and the conversation, preferring to huddle over the week's music papers, notably those pages that tend to feature themselves (which, this week, is a lot). Each review they doggedly peruse seems to have signed off with some excitable reference to the Mondays–Roses progress being akin to 'the North rising again', but the only rise Shaun Ryder is concerned about at the minute is situated somewhere inside the over-generously well-ventilated crotch of his black Oxford bags. He sidles up to the statuesque make-up girl brought in specifically to make him and his band look 'presentable' to a peak-viewing audience and mutters apropos of nothing in particular, 'So do you reckon mee willie'll look big enough to the world hangin' there in these fookin' strides, then, luv?' He starts rubbing his genitals vigorously.

The Stone Roses would like to take this opportunity to clear something up. At least their manager would. We're all in the bar now and Tony Wilson is busy pulling all the stops out in yet another of his over-generous Mouth Almighty routines when he turns a bit patronizing on the Stone Roses and accuses them, in front of this writer, of unprofessionalism at a certain gig due to excessive drug use. The easy camaraderie freezes for an instant as the Roses manager reaches out his hand and places it softly but firmly over Wilson's mouth. Then he whispers something in his ear that causes Wilson to stiffen momentarily. Then he turns to me: 'You should know the Stone Roses don't take drugs.'

What he's trying to say is that the Stone Roses don't take drugs in remotely the same way Happy Mondays take drugs. But then no one takes drugs like Happy Mondays. The Mondays' recent trip to the States was highlighted by (a) the lads introducing themselves generously to PCP ('Top fookin' gear, man! If it's good enough for James Brown, it's good enough for oos') and (b) yet another drug bust, this time on their second day in New York, where several of them were busted smoking 'something inflammable' with 'a bunch of black geezers in some park, like'. The reviews they received were mixed and troubled. Americans evidently found it hard dealing with the concept of real Northern hooligans on ecstasy. But that didn't stop Tony Wilson from egging on Factory's press officer to wangle Happy Mondays' every drugs transgression into the tabloid press.

All of which leads to one inevitable question: 'Do I have any problem with any of Happy Mondays dying on me?' He looks at me while both the Mondays and Stone Roses contingent look on a little aghast. 'I have absolutely no problem whatso-ever with any of these guys dying on me! Listen, Ian Curtis dying on *me* was the greatest thing that's happened to my life. Death sells!'

Doesn't that make you just a voyeur?

'I've got news for you, pal. I am a voyeur!'

'Tony's just a businessman, really,' Shaun Ryder opines shortly after Wilson's outburst. 'Someone like him . . . I mean, he likes us . . . at least, I think he does . . . But he's got to use the drugs angle to sell us, y'knowwharramsayin'. I mean, what the fook could Gaz, Bez or me be like without someone like Tony exploiting us? We wouldn't 'ave jobs 'cos we can't do fookin' jobs. That's just a fookin' fact, right!

'I mean, 'e's exploitin' us, right, but we're exploiting the situation he's given us 'cos like two years ago we 'ad to 'ave drugs on our person 'cos we were sellin' 'em, right. So if you got caught then it were a bigger problem. 'Cos it were bigger amounts we were carryin'. But, like, *now* we always carry the name of a good solicitor around with us. I've got this card, right, and I just show it 'em, the filth, when they come pryin'.

'Whereas before when they'd search me they'd always find, like, forty-seven plastic bags and *no* solicitor's card . . . Fookin' hassles, y'knowwharramean!

'We've chosen to live like this and that's it. We're just playing a game, the same game we've been playing for a long time. That's the one trouble with being on *Top of the Pops* though. Someone in the force might get clever. The police are thick. They're dirt thick. We all know that. Bez's dad's a nasty fuckin' high-rankin' CID officer. A real nasty bastard. One of those fookin' working-class cunts as likes to dish it out. Now this bastard hasn't seen Bez for five or six years. He doesn't know anything about him or Happy Mondays. Until 'e sees us on *Top of the Pops* . . .

'We just see Happy Mondays as this licence to do what we want *right now* as much as possible. The police and that can't do worse to us than what they've already done, like. And if I do get banged up, it's not like it's somethin' that's never happened before. Jail's nothing new to me, man. Bird, like, it's all down to how you use your time really. I mean, you can read a few books. Or study a foreign language. It's a bit of a lark really.

'The Mondays, we've been friends for over ten year, pal. There's no one else we'd rather be with for doin' the things we wanna do. When you've been friends that long . . . well, for a start you can take the piss out of each other somethin' rotten and get away with it. Gaz can call me some right snide things an' I won't fookin' crack 'im one.

'But, like, our keyboard player's off 'is fookin' trolley! Daft as a fookin' brush! 'E's a top lad, our Paul, but 'e don't half talk some fookin' toss sometimes. Y'ave to tell 'im, "Shoot the fook oop." If 'e were 'ere right now 'e'd be over 'ere talkin' daft! And you'd probably hate 'im 'cos 'e's a bit of a bastard too. You just 'ave to say, "Shurrup, our Paul, and listen to wha' yer sayin', ya great fookin' knobhead." But he's daft. That's just 'is way.

'People keep askin' us about Manchester . . . We never ever really stayed in Manchester. We get around, pal. London . . . Paris . . . Bez was found livin' in the fookin' Sahara Desert in a fookin' cave, man. It's the fookin' truth, that. Manchester's just where we're from.

'Well, our sound's all sorts really. Funkadelic, "One nation under a groove", being eaten by a giant sandwich . . . that were fookin' tops, that . . . Northern soul . . . punk rock . . . Jimi Hendrix . . . fookin' Captain Beefheart. And a lot o' drugs on top o' that. It was thru' Bez with E . . . just, "Get 'em down yer throat, son! More! More! Go on! Throw 'em down yer neck!" . . . That's how we really got to see how E can get you, like, right out there. You've just got to pelt it down yer.

'I don't want to get serious with music. Our music is about not even thinkin' about havin' a future. It's all going now. Right now, we're it. When it stops, it stops. We're just doin' what we're doin'.

'Me old bloke, 'e works for us, right. 'E's basically one of those workin'-class geezers who never 'ad a fookin' clue, always gettin' banged up or fucked over. Me mam was a nurse . . . she's like a three-year-old really . . . good woman an' all . . . but she's a worrier . . . too nervous . . . Well, y'can't blame 'er what with the phone goin' all the time and the police tellin' 'er I've been booked, y'know . . . But me old bloke always like instilled in me this belief that we may not be big 'ard blokes but there's not a situation we can't handle. And that's how we live our lives for better or worse.

'I mean, I'm in this for the fookin' money, man. I was more interested in money than learning at school. Money, wearing the flashest clothes and fookin' around! Naught's changed, really. We all wanna make a fookin' pile. But at the same time I think we've got, like, principles . . . a fookin' sense of loyalty. You can't buy our loyalty. We'd never leave Tony and Factory, like. [*Pauses.*] Well, not unless someone offered us seven million or summat dead tasty like that!'

'Positive thinking, that's all we've ever really believed in. You've got to make things happen for you . . . Positivity comes from inside. We can see right from wrong. Why be glum? Why celebrate sitting around being lonely in bedsits. You should encourage people to go out and talk to each other. Communication makes things go round.'

Stone Roses make statements like that with a straight face. In the company of the Happy Mondays and their walking *Viz* cartoon workshop of personal magnetism they seem a bit vacant. But here in isolation in some other room in a nearby hotel their vague statements come across buoyed by a certain quiet authority. The main thing about the Stone Roses is that, unlike Happy Mondays, they're going to be really huge, foreseeably as-big-as-U2 huge.

'It started in February really with "Made of Stone" coming out. We played the Hacienda then and sold it out. It was just the atmosphere. People were just willing us to go on.'

Then came the album on Silvertone and everything seemed to explode. Mick Jagger purportedly asked them to support certain dates for the Stones (some people at Silvertone now question this) on their American tour last year: 'But we said no 'cos everyone else'd say yes. We're against hypocrisy, lies, bigotry, show business, insincerity, phonies and fakers . . . There's millions of 'em and they're all pricks. People like Jagger and Bowie . . . They're so insincere now they're just patronizing.'

Then came Europe and Japan, where 'everything was boss. It was all getting chased around train stations. And havin' our hair pulled. It was mad. Unreal. It was like being in *Help*.

'Being bigger than U2? Well, they're empty anyway – what does all that emptiness say to all those people? But, yeah, I think we can deliver on that. We've always felt we could be the top group in the world. It's only now that others are saying the same thing. We can handle it.'

'From now it's just gonna be the five of us sealed off into our own little world,' states singer Ian Brown, whose face bears the sculptured cuteness of a perfect pop idol. 'It's inevitable really, isn't it. But the bonds are strong enough. I've known John since I was four now, twenty years ago. Mani for ten years . . . Reni for ten years. It's too strong. Nothing can stop it. We were on the dole for five years. Now we're earning so we've got to stay and take it all.

'We wanna keep moving. The world's too small. It doesn't end at Manchester. I don't see us as part of a Manchester scene as such. I want to get out as fast as I can. I know every fookin' street. I've seen it all. Still, it's home. And there's always been that scene. Before, it was the Boardwalk and all the bands that played there and knew each other. And we were always not included. And neither were the Mondays. They were off in Salford somewhere. Now we're the scene but in fact we were always outside the so-called "Manchester scene".

'Tony Wilson, 'e's all right, I suppose. He put the Pistols on, didn't 'e. Built t'Hacienda. But he shouldn't go around like he's the spokesman for Manchester 'cos he's too out of touch. And Jonathan Ross is a tosser. We're saying we're going to do his show now' – Ross had been disparaging about Stone Roses on his show two days before – 'then at the last minute we'll pull out. Don't wanna be treated like a fuckin' monkey.'

John Squire, the group's guitarist, declares, 'The next album will be more positive, tidier, looser, better. The idea with the first album was to make each song extremely different from the last but we didn't get it. So that's the aim with the second. We don't want to sound like a band.'

'It's not about bands with us,' adds Brown. 'It's always been about records. No one's ever made much over three or four good records. And that's our big aim. To make some of the best records anyone's ever gonna make and still come out of it all with our self-respect.'

'Our vision of the nineties?' asks Squire.

'Time to see who's who, isn't it,' affirms Brown.

Well it was time to see who was who in the eighties but nothing happened.

Brown looks at me and suddenly he hasn't got a real answer.

'Yeah, I suppose you're right,' he offers.

'You can't say it hasn't done some good, Ecstasy.' Ian Brown is still talking and somehow the conversation doubles back to the topic of this strange designer drug and how it appears to hold the key to unlocking the essence of both the Mondays' demonic howl from the hooligan North and the Stone Roses' tricky megapop. 'Ecstasy has loosened people up who maybe weren't really in touch with their own spirit. But I was in touch with me own spirit before so I don't believe it's changed me. But I can see it's changed a lot of other people. Only last year people were taking it to extremes, using it to dance themselves into a trance with. I mean, fook that. You've got to stay conscious, stay awake. Or else you're just like some old 'ippie . . . Am I right?'

'E were great two years ago, y'know.' Shaun Ryder is pausing for his last reflection of the afternoon. 'It made every-thing peaceful. But now the violence is comin' back in the Manchester clubs. There's too much free-basin' goin' on, that's what I think. It's takin' over in Manchester . . . like everyone in Mani 'ad a binge on E, right, only the people who had a binge on E from the start are now 'aving a freebase binge on cocaine. All the lads we know in London . . . it's the same.

'Y'know, two years ago, I'd've said legalize E. Yeah. No problem. But now . . . I don't know, like. 'Cos E . . . it can make ya nice and mellow but it's also capable of doin' proper naughty things to you as well. Proper, *bad* naughty things to you. E can get you into big fookin' bother!

'Mind, drink's worse. But E and drink together's worse than that. Fuck, if we legalized E, man, we'd probably have a race of fuckin' mutants on our 'ands!'

'So ah says to 'im, "Just 'cos you got 'airs round yer lips, our kid, there's no need to talk like a coont . . ."'

Finally, most of the Stone Roses and Mondays have exiled themselves off to the make-up room, when a haughty Home Counties-type BBC employee strides into the communal dressing-room and demands of those present, specifically the groups' two drummers and myself, if we'd start dismantling the sacred black beat box toot sweet. 'It's not just that noise' – she gestures at some mind-warping rendition of 'Ballad of John and Yoko' currently being sampled and cross-taped into hyper-space – 'it's . . . all this.' Her hands wave neurotically at the gargantuan power cord running out into the reception hall that the groups' roadies rigged up for the occasion.

It's a moment to savour, this: Ms Jodhpurs *vs* mangy Gaz, the beetroot-faced Happy Mondays drummer, not so much a human being more an apprentice troglodyte. For if there is a moment for the North to 'symbolically' rise into the nineties and tell the South to stop sitting on its face, then surely why not let it be this one? But it doesn't really register with Old Gaz who just turns a bit sheepish before sloping out to do the required dismantling. Welcome to the no-power generation.

The Four Ages of a Man Named Pop: Pictures of Iggy

The first time I ever met Iggy Pop, it was in early February 1972. The sixties were not long over and he was celebrating the fact by sporting a pair of 400 dollar silver leather pants and a tacky pregnant woman's smock with a big ugly flower embroidered on the front. He had long flaxen hair past his shoulder and big penetrating Bambi eyes staring out like approaching headlights on a long black highway. When he finally spoke, this deep, rather suave-sounding 'he-man' voice emerged, edged with a manic chuckle that would send it momentarily spiralling up into an altogether higher octave range. Though he carried himself in a robust sort of way, he was pretty frail and feminine-looking, and at 5 foot 7 inches he wasn't exactly tall either. But then, to me, it seemed like he was towering above the rest of the world.

Which was true, at least in the sense that here he was, still a young man in his early twenties, and already he'd changed the whole shape and artistic vision of rock'n'roll music not once but twice. There was one slight problem however: hardly anyone had noticed his accomplishments. In fact, it wasn't so much that they hadn't noticed, more that they'd been actively repelled by the music they'd heard coming from the Stooges, Iggy's chaotic anti-social rock band from the suburbs of the Motor City there in that stretch of America known as the Midwest.

In the late sixties, the attitude among most working rock bands became increasingly fixated around long, improvisational jamming segments with appropriate displays of technical expertise, but the Stooges weren't interested in 'straining and soaring against the entire dark ages of music', as some insufferable bore once described just such an example of that approach – the British power trio Cream on British television. On the contrary, they were hell-bent on taking a time capsule right back to the darkest ages of music they could hope to sink into, back to that dim time when the world was one big, pulsating swamp which shook with the terrible thunderous rhythms of nature's raw elemental power. To this end, they beat out this muddy, brutal, ecstatic music that grabbed anyone in its path roughly by the scruff of the neck and hurled them headlong into the very wilderness of the senses that lies stretched out just beyond man's deepest primordial fears. For some, like myself, being exposed to music this raw and alive had a profoundly liberating effect. But most people in the late sixties and early seventies who came into direct contact with it found the experience unsettling and often bordering on the frankly repugnant.

Not that the Stooges themselves ever gave a tinker's cuss what anyone else might have thought about them and their music. They had this gang mentality that was the usual 'four losers against the world' riff except they took that riff and blasted it through the loudest PA system they could construct, until all the nervy punk bravado wriggling around in their gut was pushed right up in the audience's collective face and you either became duly smitten by what you experienced or else you pretty much wilted under the sheer horrendousness of it all. Being a proper gang, of course, involved the added responsibility of creating your own 'cool' vocabulary. 'Boge' was one such word – short for 'bogus' – that the Stooges had invented to describe, well, everyone else in the world apart from themselves, quite frankly. Another key phrase for them was 'the O-mind', or just 'O-mind'. It referred to those times when the individuals in the group spread out around the communal 'bong' and got even more righteously stoned than was normally the case. At this stage, all conversation would cease, eyes would fall shut, heads would tilt back and minds would feel like they were opening up, like there was a big 'O' shape where their brains had formerly been, this hole looking down through to the subconscious and then back through to the dawn of time itself, back to when dinosaurs still roamed the land, when strange birds of prey hung in the skies and where large prehistoric amplifiers vibrated with the horrendous howling of strange tribal madness. This was the Stooges' fundamental vision, anyway, and the reason why they created this monstrous tribal music with Iggy's free-expression vocal gymnastics giving it a most singular context and charisma. They were so raw to begin with that the ability to actually write a song with riff, verses and a chorus only came to them a couple of nights before they went into the studio with John Cale to record their first album for Elektra records. The eponymously titled result got immediately slammed by a *Rolling Stone* critic for being a one-group definition of musical juvenile delinquency and sold abysmally, but seven years after its release in the summer of 1969 a whole new lost generation looted the sound, content and attitude of those pithy pissed-off little songs wholesale to help create some splenetic musical outbursts of their own over in England that got tagged together as something called 'punk rock'.

Then came *Funhouse* a year later, which found the Stooges working on a darker musical terrain altogether, mixing pioneering metal riffs and free-form jazz saxophone honks with tribal grooves and a lot of hard funk as well. Iggy was in his element with this kind of heathen backdrop, because he could stretch out and do his James Brown-inspired King of the Jungle routine with all the ear-shredding screams and deep animal grunts. It was real 'heart of darkness' music in the classic Kurtzian sense and a lot further down the river of no return, sonically speaking, than their début. One of the key reasons for this downward shift was the fact that the Stooges themselves had shifted away from the old regime of pot and psychedelics towards harder, more deadly chemicals. It's useful to recognize that, when the Stooges started performing, Iggy always felt compelled to drop two acid-tabs before each gig, about ten minutes before he'd actually hit the stage. The tabs would quickly start kicking in and he'd feel the first lysergic flashes as soon as he saw the audience's hungry eyes. For the next forty minutes he'd feel the music his band was playing surge through him with such absolute intensity it would involuntarily throw him into the extraordinary contortions and acts of wanton self-destructiveness that would most inform his future legend. (That's also why Stooges gigs were so notoriously short: after forty minutes he'd start hallucinating so intensely he'd usually become completely incapacitated.)

But then everything in this daring young man's egg-shell psyche started getting a little overheated because of all the sensory upheaval going on, until one night in early 1970 when a Stooges roadie introduced him to heroin. The effect was so calming, like suddenly finding yourself lying under the stars in a perfect little island all of your own creation, where gentle sea-breezes caress the skin and a sweet seductive music comes wafting through the air, like the sound of Javanese bells ringing in strange beguiling tonalities with the voice of a woman singing wordlessly against its rhythm. Anyway, in no time at all the guy was a full-tilt junkie, as were most of the rest of the band. This in turn prompted a number of very ugly episodes, and after most of the Stooges' equipment got pawned for junk and Iggy had overdosed several times, the group dissolved, leaving most of its individual members no other option than to sign on at a local methadone clinic in Michigan.

When I first met Iggy he'd been straight for some months, as had his partner, James Williamson, a young guitarist with cold, angry eyes and a severely acne-ravaged complexion who'd been in one of the Stooges' final line-ups. After cleaning up in Ann Arbor, Iggy had travelled to New York late in 1971 to consider his next move, when he met the London-born singer/songwriter David Bowie, who alerted his new manager, Tony Defries, to sign up the performer. Defries had duly secured him a deal with Columbia records and had flown him to London – with Williamson alongside – supposedly in order to monitor his career at closer range. So there they were, these two black-hearted ominous-looking individuals from the Motor City living together in a little house in tame, salubrious Maida Vale, looking for some like-minded limeys to fill in on bass and drums so they could record the Stooges' third musical chapter. I remember asking them how they envisaged this third musical statement might end up sounding. Iggy pondered the question for a moment while dangling a wine glass he was sipping from rather daintily from his left hand. Then he drove the glass down hard on to a little table directly in front of him, noisily shattering its base. 'Something like that,' he then replied evenly.

Of course, everyone they tried to play with was lacking in some requirement or another, so after a couple of months Iggy imported his old Stooges buddies Ron and Scott Asheton over to round out the sound. These two had been raised in Iggy's own little Michigan suburb, Ann Arbor, mostly by their mother Anne after their father, a Marine Corps pilot, had died while both were still in their early teens. So they weren't too strong on discipline, having been left to pretty much run wild since puberty. That said, Ron was by far the more responsible of the two: in fact, he was the real straight-arrow of the Stooges where drugs were concerned. His brother . . . well, let's start by saying that Scottie Asheton was the youngest, sweetest and most hopeless member of the Stooges. If Terry Malloy, the valiant simpleton Marlon Brando portrayed in *On the Waterfront* had been plucked from his place in the dockland conflicts of the fifties and restationed one whole decade later in the suburbs of Michigan, where he would come to find his destiny in bashing out primitive rhythms on a set of drums he would later end up pawning to further feed his love of substance abuse, well, that was pretty much Scott Asheton for you. He even had a bit of that Brando-esque 'noble savage' look about his features, which peered out, adopting looks of casual menace from behind two lank curtains of greasy black hair; but mostly he resembled a hard-core biker type pondering his next act of imminent barbarism. Scott's talent for creating mayhem was also something to be considered. His *pièce de résistance* in this area had to be the time in 1971 when he drove the Stooges' bus – with all their equipment inside – under a 12 foot high bridge without considering the fact that the vehicle he was piloting measured over 16 feet in height. Talk about raising the roof. The resulting crash sent all the occupants and their cargo spilling out on to the highway, breaking all the instruments, injuring several people and basically putting paid to the Stooges' immediate future.

For a while there Iggy hadn't particularly wanted to see Scott again, but at the same time he knew that, without his bone-headed percussive attack and the presence of his spoiled brother, the Stooges just wouldn't be, well, the Stooges. So they were back in but neither was at all pleased about having to play second banana to guitarist Williamson's abrasive arrogance. Iggy called James Williamson his 'secret weapon' and that's exactly what he was, at least in a musical sense. He played his guitar so intensely hard both his hands were a constant blur. In fact, at his best, he played guitar just as fast and as loose as the way he lived his life. Which was always very fast and loose indeed. The Stooges were quite obsessive in their quest to constantly project an overtly delinquent persona, but Williamson was the only bonafide delinquent of the four, to the point where he'd actually got locked up in reform school for stealing cars and speed-taking in his early teens. After his release he'd gone on to establish himself as one of Detroit's most powerful young guitarists and one of its most notorious junkies. Even Scott, who didn't give a fuck about anything or anyone, was frightened of him because James was the best fighter too.

Iggy had him right by his side, because he wanted a Keith Richards-kinda guy carrying half the creative weight in the Stooges, playing guitar riffs that hit the listener like kidney-punches. But he also deeply admired the way James could project this image of withering malevolence. Evil was much on his mind at the time. He'd walk around the streets of London in his leopard-skin jacket and Beatles boots and all he could feel was hatred in his heart for this whole slow-witted conniving world he'd been born into. All this 'cute' shit – this glam-rock – was selling up a storm over in limey-land and all it was was a bunch of wimp pop written by more cynical hack cock-suckers and sung by talentless dorks wearing too much make-up who were too dumb and lame to even be mistaken for real faggots. Over in America they were lapping up this homogenized crap by the Eagles and all these other clowns singing about feeling like Jesse James and James Dean and pretending they're modern-day rock'n'roll outlaws when, in reality, they were just another bunch of denim-draped self-obsessed faux hayseed hippie morons. Meanwhile, the Stooges were in exile in this piss-ant isle, unloved and living in the shadow of David fuckin' Bowie, whose manager they shared suddenly seemed to consider them less like one of his clients, more like some vague afterthought. There was such poison in his heart, so much rage and such a deep loathing of mankind in general, that it just flooded into the creative marrow of the Stooges' greatest creation – the body of songs that got released on an album entitled *Raw Power*.

There was an extract of howling spleen entitled 'Your Pretty Face is Going to Hell', about a girl he'd known called Joanna who he'd become infatuated with even though she'd treated him scornfully. Still, now she was losing her looks, so screw you, sister! But mostly it was one man's rumination on his own loveless exiled condition. The track straight after that had him crooning to some imaginary pretty baby about danger, disease and nothingness. The final number was entitled simply 'Death Trip'. By the same token the sound they created was obscenely alive, real raging two-fisted hell-fire sonic abandon. If Iggy, Williamson and, later, David Bowie hadn't made such a mess of the mix, it would have been the best and blackest rock'n'roll album ever made, if only for the title track, Iggy's definitive O-mind salute to the great swamp from whence all elemental energies stem.

They were so good and yet destiny was once again not following through with the right breaks. They spent almost the whole of 1972 in London, yet apart from recording *Raw Power* they only got to play one show there, at a cinema in King's Cross. It was a breathtaking performance but anyone there could have told you that the kind of provocative, confrontational sensory assault the group specialized in would never be accepted by the timid Brits, who were still into the glazed-eyes-and-flared-trousered semi-stupor of the late-hippie era that would only be rendered obsolete four years later when punk happened. (Talking of which, one John Lydon was also lurking in the audience that night and evidently took home some pointers from the spectacle for future reference.)

Anyway, the Stooges relocated to Los Angeles by the beginning of 1973 in readiness for *Raw Power*'s release in the early spring of that year. They got set up in a big house right on top of the Hollywood Hills, right there in the heart of the city that loves to corrupt. The Stooges loved to be corrupted, so you can probably imagine what happened next. It began with hard drugs and quickly moved to under-age girls. Hollywood was suddenly crawling with these packs of fourteen-year-old girls stoned on their mothers' tranquillizers and waving their fathers' credit cards all over the place in hot pursuit of sexy, emaciated-looking rock dudes to have sex with. The teenage lust factor was considerable of course, and it was partly their way of rebelliously extending the permissive standards of the sixties. But it was also a hell of a lot to do with wreaking revenge on their inconsiderate (and usually divorced) parents. Most of these girls were only seen on the weekends when they weren't constrained by school schedules, but there was a hard-core bunch who didn't feel compelled to attend school at all. They'd always get the manager of whatever rock group they were having sex with to write them an absentee note and hang out along the Sunset Strip seven days a week. These were the girls that the Stooges became particularly close with.

The centre-point for all this Barbie-meets-Satyricon lust action was Rodney Bingenheimer's English Discotheque, hosted by an anaemic-looking anglophile disc-jockey: a kind of *Beyond the Valley of the Dolls* scenario come to life in a cramped little room surrounded by mirrors and full of satin-swathed heavenly bodies forever being serenaded by the tacky glam-rock bombast of Suzy Quatro, Sweet and Gary Glitter. I saw Iggy there many a time, stoned out of his gourd, lost to the world and to himself as well, staring at his face and form in those mirrored walls. He'd stand there for hours, it seemed, sometimes moving slightly in a style that could be said to have boldly predated the whole 'vogueing' trend of the late-eighties, but always staring at his reflection like Narcissus drugged out in teenage-disco-hell. Was he looking deep inside himself, trying to locate some semblance of his soul and natural vitality that would tell him to shape up, or was he becoming more and more mesmerized by the motions of his down-bound mystique? I sensed the latter.

Then the really ugly stuff started, because Defries tried to fire Williamson for being a disruptive influence, which duly prompted the Stooges to walk out on Defries. They soon lost that big house in the Hollywood Hills as well as the equipment and those fancy stage costumes that made them look like the Sex Hooligans from Outer Space. Yet still they persevered, getting themselves booked into a host of sleazy clubs across America on a never-ending tour starting in mid-'73. No one remembers those times with much joy. Ron Asheton lays the blame for the Stooges' final ill-starred passage squarely on Iggy's shoulders: 'The guy had a lot of problems. I mean, on that last tour he was just so self-obsessed . . . so into this "I feel pain" thing all the time.'

Even the rowdy Williamson concurs, citing a particularly disastrous show in Philadelphia as just one example of the singer's ongoing decline: 'The gig was one of the key ones for the band. Columbia was there to record us in an attempt to get some product out of the Stooges. By this time, Iggy had completely lost it. He was just completely out of control, beyond anything remotely related to sanity. Anyway, he took these two lines of THC just before the gig. He'd never taken it before and had no real concept of how powerful the stuff is. I can still recall the promoter's reaction when he arrived. He was one of the biggest in the States too. We turned up about an hour late – and when he saw us he took out his gold watch and threw it against the wall in a mixture of blind rage and complete despair.

'By this time Iggy literally couldn't stand up and couldn't put two words together straight. So the band just had to go on and start playing while three roadies got a hold of Pop, two for his arms and one for his legs, and threw him on to the stage. Somehow he fell into the audience and someone stuck a peanut butter and jelly sandwich on his chest which made it look like he'd been stabbed. So they closed the show down after only three numbers!'

It was on this tour, too, that Scott Asheton gradually began losing his mind. He started developing the interesting theory that man becomes automatically closer to God when he decides to wear the same set of clothes twenty-four hours a day, every day. Then he started developing a strange relationship with his towel, the towel he always used onstage to douse the sweat from his body while playing. Sometimes he'd wear it over his head throughout the entire gig. He later told the rest of the

Stooges that hiding under it helped him ward off the negative forces forever preying on the band, but it probably had more to do with getting hit in the face with eggs and rotten fruit thrown by angry audiences night after night. Still, when Iggy took Scott, or 'Rock' as he now called himself – it was short for 'Rock Action' – out on a double-date with two extremely attractive and sophisticated young women in a high-class restaurant and watched speechless as the drummer commenced to pull out his old towel and drop it over his head before he'd even ordered the first course, he knew it was over for the Stooges. He also knew he was probably in even worse shape than poor old 'Rock'.

'But what could I do?' Iggy would plead only a matter of months after the group had disbanded and Scott Asheton was back pumping gas and living with his mother in Michigan. 'Look what I was up against, man. I had Defries breathing down my back, no manager, no direction plus a band that could never begin to fulfil its potential. I was past desperation point. I just wanted to die all the time. Like, that incident at Max's Kansas City. Everyone thought I'd fallen on some broken glass by accident. But . . . I just couldn't stand myself anymore, so I went behind the amps with this piece of broken glass, having decided to cut my jugular vein. I just didn't have the guts, though . . . I was aiming for the vein, but I just couldn't make it. I cut up my chest instead.

'After the tour I just wanted to forget everything that had gone before. I didn't care. I was sick . . . out of my mind. I couldn't sleep. My back had been put out of joint after I'd fallen backwards nine feet off a stage and I was in constant pain. I had to get myself into a stupor just in order to handle it.'

By the early spring of 1975, Iggy and James were sharing a small apartment in a building on the Sunset Strip that otherwise seemed to be inhabited almost exclusively by prostitutes and drug dealers. Iggy was in such bad odour with the rest of LA that most of the dealers refused to let him into their apartments. He'd made such a mess of his life during the two years he'd been based in Los Angeles that everyone had him written off as nothing more than a washed-up loser. The word was out on him in all the clubs anyway, and it wasn't just confined to the Sunset Strip and Santa Monica Boulevard. Open a music paper around that period and you'd often find some 'former acquaintance' running the Pop down in print. Lou Reed, who'd always treated Iggy with a kind of haughty disdain anyway, basically because he was jealous of his superior abilities as a live performer, had the gall to denigrate him during a drinking contest with Lester Bangs: 'Iggy is stupid. Very sweet, but very stupid. If he'd listened to David [Bowie] or me, if he'd asked questions every once in a while . . . He's just making a fool of himself, and it's just going to get worse and worse. He's not even a good imitation of a bad Jim Morrison and he was never any good anyway.'

Then, the same month that Reed's quote started circulating, an interview with Ian Hunter, the cross-eyed old rocker who'd recently left Mott the Hoople, appeared, airing the following views: 'I think Iggy's the most overrated star ever. Iggy has all the attributes of stardom, except that he doesn't deliver on any level. He's the all-time "should-have-but-didn't" and it's because he's just not quite good enough.'

How could a young man stand such taunts without becoming all twisted up with self-hate and low self-esteem? 1975 was a hellish year for rock'n'roll anyway. Appalling groups with names like Supertramp and Gentle Giant were selling millions of records with their hideously insipid 'hey nonny no' concept crap. The Bee Gees were on the come-back trail. Peter Frampton was about to come alive. Whenever Iggy tried to summon up the old spirit, he was left grasping for ghosts. How many dead Stooges were there now? There was Dave Alexander, their first bassist, who'd drunk himself to death while still in his twenties. There were guitarists Zeke Zettner and Billy Cheatham dead from 'smack'. Who'd be next? Well, James was going straight and losing his feel for music since his hand had been badly broken by Alice Cooper's bodyguard, and Ron had always been straight anyway. So now it was between him and Scott. 'I know it's me who'll be the next, though,' he'd mutter with a kind of eerie confidence on any number of occasions. A large part of him wanted to die, too, wanted to die so badly that it would compel him to empty whole bottles of tranquillizers down his neck one after the other. The day I left LA I went over to say goodbye and found him in a car-park wearing a woman's dress and lying flat on his back, having just consumed thirty quaaludes. A month later, he regained consciousness from another binge in an abandoned building next to a partially clad teenage girl just in time to vomit up something that was such a lurid green colour he knew he'd reached the final rung of the ladder. So he voluntarily admitted himself to a Los Angeles mental institution where, amid a colony of deranged middle-aged women recently abandoned by their husbands, he was given his own room and a record player as well. In time, he recovered, and, after playing James Brown's *Sex Machine* album incessantly, his old wild healthy spirit started to rise up again. Then David Bowie started making social calls and a whole new chapter of his life commenced.

It is now the late spring of 1979 and everywhere there are blue skies, crisp sunny days, the merry sounds of people stepping into the light. Yet only darkness and loathing spring forth from the heart and mouth of Iggy Pop.

'I am totally into corruption,' he is telling me. Or, to be more precise, he is assaulting me with this information while crouched on his bed wearing only a pair of vinyl trousers and a little too much eye make-up for my liking. An Oriental girl sits in one chair positioned near the bed. Her face never changes its expression. On an adjacent table lies a cassette recorder, a notebook (his), a mirror, a razor blade and a packet containing cocaine.

'You wanna know about corruption?' he leers at me. 'Okay, well let's say I want to corrupt you. Corruption would be you working for me for reasons that you'd think you were going to get something out of it. But I know you wouldn't, so screw you! It's like W. C. Fields says: "You can't cheat an honest man." Right, he got it! So there you go, that's corruption. You find a dishonest person and you use them. You use their corruption!

'When I got signed to RCA back in '75 . . . every goddam executive in the place, I had 'em researched. I found out their weakness – everything. I played them like a harp 'cos I don't miss a trick, baby. I had a whole plane-load of 'em flown over – at my expense – to preview *The Idiot* at Winston Churchill's old club. And even though I knew damn well *The Idiot* wasn't going to be a million-seller I still wanted the word put out on this Iggy Pop fellow right from the top.

'Also, I wanted it made known – in the most stringent terms possible – that it would be very foolhardy to mess with Iggy Pop. Because – it might take a month, it might take a year – but, buddy, you do the wrong thing by him and you're gonna regret it very, very sorely. See, I started reading in the papers about me being the "Godfather of Punk" and figured, well, if I'm going to be the Godfather, then I'm going to be a real Godfather, Mafia-style. Taking no shit from anybody and screwing anyone who tried to screw me.

'This particular attitude I have . . . it all stems from Nico actually,' he continues. 'She was the one who took me when I was a skinny, little naive brat and taught me how to eat pussy and all about the best German wines and French champagnes. Anyway, one day she said to me' – adopted doomy German tone – '"Jimmy, you have zis one big problem" – I was just a little lad for chrissakes, but I was still game – "You are not full of *zee poison*! Zis is not correct. Zis is not right. How can you perform when you are not full of the poison? Me, I will help you just enough to fill you with zee poison but otherwise you have nothing! We do not want to see a person on the stage, no, no, no. We want to see a performance, and zee poison is the essence of the performer."

'And she'd do things . . . Like, I'd go away for a few days and come back looking healthy. And she'd scream, "Jimmy, what are you doing to yourself? You are ugly. Don't you know you are only good skinny. Skinny as a rail." And Danny Fields [Stooges publicist] was always fussing about my hair in his usual faggy way, and it had reached a point where my hair had become so long and curly it pretty much totally hid my face.

'Anyway, Danny said something about me having my bangs cut. Nico just freaked completely and screamed, "But, Danny, Jimmy's face is not meant to be seen!" [*Laughs.*] And she immediately grabbed this wine glass and smashed it against the table, which made everybody run away. Except me 'cos I knew her little games and wasn't afraid anyway. And she turned to me and said, "Good, Jimmy, now we are rid of them." And she proceeded to carve a most incredible sketch of me – somewhat in the style of Cocteau – with maybe two cubic inches of my face showing. And she summoned everybody back and pointed to this sketch and said, "Now this is Jimmy's face. And if you could see it, it would be a drag!" And I thought, "Right on, Nico" [*laughter*].

'I saw her later though, after things were starting to get bad for her. It was in Paris and . . . oh forget the state she was in . . . she just wanted desperately to get in touch with me. Maybe with Bowie more, but, hell, I'd suffice. And she had me followed. Had radio monitors scanning my every move. Taxi drivers were bribed – just everything.

'Anyway, when she found me I just rejected her immediately. I just said, "You're not good enough for me to expend time and energy on anymore." And the first thing she said' – his eyes snake into a hell-hath-no-fury-like-a-woman-spurned glare – 'was "Jimmy you are strong!". And she got that look that Deutsche get when they're about to bite into a pig.

'She got that vampirism in her eyes. But she wasn't going to be defeated outright, or so she thought. Because her next number was to slyly offer me a snort of heroin. She laid out a line, figuring that heroin would get me into her little web. But, just as the enticing line came close to my nostril, I blew it off the mirror all over the floor, got up and said, "So long baby! Nyah, nyah – fooled you!" And that's the last I've seen of Nico since.

'I tell you, all the bitches – all these women – want me now because they can sense that strength in me. And they want it sooo bad. But they're not gonna get me. Uh-huh. Only on my terms. And my terms are simply phoning 'em up, telling them to be at such and such a place at such and such a time, in good physical condition, to be fucked. And then leave, goddammit.

'Because? Because?? Because I've got more important things to do with my life, and I cannot, and *will not* have my time wasted. It is not just a case of my work suffering. It is more a case of me wanting to go my own way. I want to go all the way. I can't think of one goddamned reason why I shouldn't achieve just that and go all the way to number one. All I have to do is corrupt others instead of them corrupting me.

'See, I'm so damn happy. I'm rich. I'm a big rich man. Rich beyond my wildest dreams. Rich in life, goddammit! I have a job, I have my self-esteem, I have discipline. And I'm becoming a very good entrepreneur. I've just made an album financed on good will and responsibility, on *Iggy Pop*'s name. *Iggy Pop*, who three years ago was a name synonymous with shit! *Iggy Pop*, the guy who'd be tied up in a bag and thrown out of the window at a Deep Purple party two floors up in some hotel! *Iggy Pop*, whose girfriend would run off with Robert Plant! *Iggy Pop*, the guy Ian Hunter said would never make it because he never had any talent!! Well, where is Ian Hunter now? Nowhere is where Ian Hunter is now. And the only chance he could ever have of making anything of his tawdry life would be to listen to one of my albums.

'See, I play hard' – he is shaking now – 'and Christ almighty, I love my revenge.'

Iggy Pop pauses, for the first time in at least fifteen minutes. I have just accused him of sounding fascistic and he's pondering the accusation. (Actually he's forgotten a lot of what he's just said and I have to remind him. But we'll let that pass.)

'Well, I can only see any notes of fascism in my attitude coming from the fact that it would only be in the sense that I know that what I'm dealing with is in essence a military industrial complex, albeit on a small scale, which is what rock'n'roll is right now.

'As for sexism' – here he lights up like a blow-torch – 'well, I *hate* women! I mean, why do I even have to have a reason for that? It's like, why are people repelled by insects? I use 'em because they are *lying, dirty, treacherous* and their ambitions all too often involve *using* me! And however close they come, I'll always pull the rug from under them. That's where my music is made.'

Maybe you just haven't met that special girl, I offer helpfully.

'Oh come on, I've been around. I've met all the women, and I'll tell you one thing, I'm more woman than any of 'em. I'm a real woman, because I have love, dependability, I'm good, kind, gentle, and I've the power to give real love. Why else would you think that such a strong man as David Bowie would be close to me? He's a real man, and I'm a real woman. Just like Catherine Deneuve.'

Only when he says the last sentence does he allow his mouth to slacken into a smile.

'What produces a dork? Usually a kind and loving household. Plus the fact he's usually a decent, bright guy with a distinct lack of aggression.'

It is seven days later and Iggy Pop and I are once again alone together. The Oriental girl is gone, as – providentially – is all that cocaine. 'I'm the man Friedrich Nietzsche could only dream of being,' he boasted to me a week ago. 'A leader who doesn't want to be led.' But this figure in front of me really doesn't look anything like a super-being. Truth to tell, he barely looks like Iggy Pop, leastways not Iggy Pop the love god, death-tripper and all-purpose fallen angel who was so omnipresent the last time our ships passed in the night. No, the person facing me with the big ready grin, the frankly geekish thick-lensed glasses, and dressed disconcertingly like a pro-golfer in his early forties is Jim Osterberg. In short, gentleman Jim, Iggy Pop's *alter ego*, a tender warm-hearted individual with an abnormally high IQ and a firm grasp on the fine art of conversation. There is a new Iggy album called *New Values* to be released and Jim is talking about how he wants this record to finally express 'right up front my real personal James Osterberg feelings. My emotions, all the hideous things I've been through, and the things that have affected me that I should never have let affect me in the first place. I've been through it all, I've been a puppet, the asshole, the dupe, the junkie, and I've come through it all and proved that I'm the equal of anybody you'd care to mention.'

He even divulges the ingredients that first allowed him to summon the best from within. It was 'two grams of biker speed, five tabs of LSD and as much grass as could be inhaled before the gig,' he laughs easily. 'I found this concoction effective enough to completely lose my senses. And then, before a gig, we'd gather like a football team and hype ourselves up to a point where we'd be screaming at each other, "OK, you guys, whadda we gonna do? *Kill! Kill! Kill!*" Then we'd take the stage.'

But what he keeps returning to again and again are the form-ative years. The years spent in exile. The years that made him hate himself so much that he just had to go out and reinvent himself as a human blow-torch. The years of his adolescence he spent as a dork.

'I was transformed into a dork in high school, when I first became exposed to the incredible cruelty that children have at their disposal. Nobody can be more cruel than a child. And there's nobody more equipped or inclined towards cruelty than upper-middle-class children whose folks have lots of spare money and big cars and glib speech. I was burdened by the fact that whenever I tried to express myself I would be laughed at. I was considered weird – this weird kid. I was also very very shy, very unhip, very unglib, and never wore the right clothes. I also had very weird looks, because my father, being a military man, forced a military haircut on me.

'But those days were numbered as soon as I learnt how to become excessively aggressive towards others. I learnt a unique and indispensable skill, which is to make rock'n'roll. I stopped my parents dressing me and started becoming a *conniving cold-hearted son of a bitch*, which I've always been since the beginning of the Stooges' – and suddenly his face, which now looks like a weird cross between Alfred E. Neumann and Klaus Kinski, gets ripped apart by one of those diabolical cartoon smiles of his that announce: 'He-e-ere's Iggy!' – 'right up until the here and now!'

Time flies and suddenly it's late October 1986 and Iggy Pop, just one year shy of the big 4–0, is apologizing for being so tired. 'I'm sorry I'm not, y'know, "Hey, zap, pow I'm the Mighty Pop, rah-rah-rah – and hellzapoppin' have I got a scoop for you!"' He jumps on the table facing me, aping the hyperactive histrionics of his past, before settling back down on the sofa again. 'See, I just can't be bothered to do that right now. But then I don't feel particularly ashamed.

'See, a lot of things have changed for me in the past three years. I want to project myself slightly differently as a result. I stopped the drugging and drunking, found a female companion I felt could support me in a way that would keep me from running wild, and slowly started to reappraise the situation . . . For over a year I couldn't write a song. I was just blank. I'd never been this vulnerable before. It was so new that I couldn't get a focus on it for ages.

'Another thing – I finally got together and started building a relationship up with my son Eric. He's . . . well, he's sixteen now and lives in Philadelphia where he's got his own apartment. He's studying accountancy basically in order to find a way to make large sums of money. That's his thing currently. We get along well now, though there were big problems in the past. He was displaying some very disturbing traits which I feel were his mother's influence . . . Her lifestyle kind of messed up his thinking for a time.

'See, now, I can afford to support him financially in his efforts at self-improvement. I wanted most of all for him to have a person in his life, a paternal friend he could communicate with. When he moved to Philly I started corresponding with him and I've finally established a successful rapport. I just wanted to establish a *healthy* relationship with him. Him being the son of, y'know, "the fucked-up godfather of nihilistic horseshit, the monstrous Iggy Pop" was a big factor in my determination to live a responsible, organized lifestyle. I didn't want him to remember me like, "Papa was a rolling stone."

'I want people who come and see me now to witness a performance that will give them an emotionally cathartic charge. I want them to leave a gig of mine feeling they've witnessed a great, very controlled performance while somehow understanding their lives have been, dare I say, enriched by being exposed to a musical experience that deals with real issues. Issues like personal self-respect. Issues like being true to your heart without feeling you have to drink and drug yourself into a state of mindless abandon. *That's* the final challenge for Iggy Pop now!

'I've become so utterly sick of the whole "rippling torso, leather and chains, animalistic narcoleptic scum-sucking hedonism" tag that my reputation got more and more submerged under, particularly during the two or three years prior to my retreat in '83. I need to prove to myself that I can achieve this transition from "God's garbage man" to someone who can offer the public more than a warped celebration of sex, drugs and dissipation.'

He pauses. 'Does that make sense to you?'

These were different days for Iggy Pop to be sure. The last time we'd seriously spoken – back in 1981 – he'd cut a bit of a tragic figure, worn to a frazzle from incessant touring that had left him strung out on alcohol, cocaine and pills all over again. 'I'd always secretly believed my creative juices were reliant on artificial stimulants,' he would later admit. 'I was scared to be completely straight because I felt I'd dry up and have nothing to say.'

Similarly, his notorious attitudes *re* the fairer sex and his incessant 'womanizing' he now sees as being motivated 'by a basic need to be wanted. That's what it came down to. My sense of self-worth needed the boost, I guess.' By 1981 he would confide that his reputation as a philanderer was leaving deep emotional and psychological scars. He was also psychologically run-down. A three-album deal with Arista had ended disastrously with the final album, *Party*, a brain-addled celebration of 'the rock'n'roll band as gang' concept, instigated by a man who at the same time as he made the record was openly admitting to friends, 'I'll always be a solo act.' By this time the eighties had arrived and, everywhere one looked, inebriated abandon was taking a backseat to 'career strategies'. Even Iggy Pop knew the score, however much he'd attempt to pretend otherwise.

Iggy Pop and the careerist instinct have never been exactly *sympatico*. *Raw Power*, the opiated early seventies and hindsight illustrate that he wasn't striking some hip pose at any time. In the throes of 1977, Bowie boom-time, he fronted one of the latter's spiffy tunes on 'Lust for Life' by sardonically declaring his own approaching success. Even on *Party* – amid all the rah-rah-rah rockism – there was 'Eggs on a Plate', a song in which Arista boss Clive Davis was unlovingly depicted pointing to the big house on the hill that could be Iggy's if only he'd just sell out and became a human cartoon-strip. All the way down the line, whether on his feet or on his knees, Iggy Pop would always end up giving the finger to all the itch-scratching status-seeking top dogs and their mansions because he instinctively knew that all their rooms at the top were only four more walls and one sheer drop.

'I'm now interested in dealing one-to-one with subjects I was too frightened to deal with before, when it got to the point where I was like the Don Quixote of rock, railing at windmills, pissing and moaning all the time. Writing "Cry for Love" . . . just expressing that openness frightened me. The notion of expressing vulnerability was something I couldn't deal with before. It was too close to home maybe. I didn't want to admit I was in need of basic affection. I mean, when I decided to quit drugs and liquor . . . I was in a hospital/detox centre for the ninetieth time cleaning out all the poisons in my system before marching off to impale myself yet again as the Mighty Pop and . . . I'd been writing my book *I Need More*. I knew that book marked "the end". I couldn't go on playing music with idiots who played their hairdryers more than their instruments to audiences who were only interested in the size of my dick. It was the end. Either I was going to kill myself and this time I wasn't fooling around. Or else . . . something had to drastically change in my life. And I mean *drastically*. Then David [Bowie] played me his "China Girl" and that allowed me to breathe a little better, take more time.'

Bowie's 1983 recording of Iggy's 'China Girl' – although 750,000 dollars of publishing proceeds went immediately to the IRS – still provided the song's lyricist with enough ready cash to retire and reassess his career situation. Similarly, Bowie's recording of five Iggy lyrics on *Tonight* helped deter US tax authorities from making the Mighty Pop's life a living poverty-stricken hell for many years to come.

Bowie next stepped in to produce Iggy's 'come-back' album, *Blah Blah Blah*, released at the end of 1986, and though the former was criticized for devoting too little time to the project, the record still managed to provide the singer with his first and only mainstream hit single, 'Wild One'. In 1988 he took matters into his own hands, composing with the ex-Pistols Steve Jones (who'd written with him on the previous album) and moving into a more metal-orientated hard rock groove for *Instinct*. Two years later he signed to Virgin records and released *Brick by Brick*, a credible blending of the old raw raging glory with more 'sensitive' acoustic meditations. In due course it was followed by *American Caesar* – his most recent recording – an assault on a country that's become like some great dazed corporate behemoth stumbling around in its own tracks and sure to fall. ('That record is basically me saying, "Hey, big guy, you're not so big anymore! In fact, you're not big at all!"' he will gleefully explain.)

The last time we met was in the late autumn of 1993 and he looked just magnificent, with his hair all long and shining like it was when I'd first met him over twenty years before. He still throws himself into the crowds he attracts, still pirouettes and puckers up his face before flailing the air with his limbs. And he still delivers a hard cathartic dose of authentic rock'n'roll at its most raw and alive every time he bounces on to a stage. Partly in response to all this vitality, he gets the most desirable women in the world turning up to check his moves. This can sometimes prove to be problematic:

'The young girls who turn up to my shows in LA, for example . . . They all think they're living in a rock video all the time. Those girls torment me when I perform! They act like little kittens [*coos*], "Maybe you'd like to fuck me!" And I know I'm not going to fuck them, so I'm going crazy! This shit drives me nuts.'

There are still more frustrations to contend with; for example, his on-going recording career: 'Every time I make a record for a major label it's such a kicking, screaming battle to get it out the way I want it. And every time I do get one released I honestly think it's going to be my last.' But apart from that, well, business is brusque for the Mighty Pop and life seems more than sweet. Creatively speaking, he is still a contender on every level. He and his wife Suchi share a strong, abiding love for one another, a degree of financial security, a beautiful house in Mexico, a place in New York, as well as a cat they shower much affection on.

And there's always Eric – now in his twenties, who more recently decided to throw off accountancy in order to follow through in his father's footsteps and become a lead vocalist kind of guy. ('His pitching's a little bit suspect' is Iggy's considered verdict on his son's abilities, 'but all the girls want to fuck him and that's 80 per cent of the deal taken care of right there.')

'I think I'm just lucky I didn't get paid enough to drown in the syrup of success,' he was quoted as saying only recently. That's one way of looking at it. As for all those ugly memories from the past: 'My friend Tony says, "Jimmy, you're a pioneer, the pioneers get all the arrows." He kind of has a point of course [*smiles*]. But then there's an altogether different way of looking at what I'm supposed to have gone through. I mean, there's this whole glory trip in rock'n'roll: "I'm the one who never sold out!" Yet in New York and in the Third World countries I sometimes visit I see real people living real lives involving real struggles and real hardship. Let's face it, the only reason rock'n'roll guys are viewed as heroes in the first place is that they usually come from a country that hasn't recently been defeated in any war, where the economy is bountiful and where generally you find that their parents have given them virtually everything on a plate. Just so they can go out and play pop stars. I was thinking about all this recently until I suddenly realized, "Jesus Christ, this describes me as well!" It's pretty ironic, really, when you realize that my dad was out there fighting a war at exactly the same age I was when I first started experimenting with smoking pot.

'It's ridiculous, really. I mean, just the other day, I heard myself saying – actually it was more like boasting – to my wife, "You know, honey, times were hard. I remember actually walking through the snow to start the Stooges."

'I mean,' – and here he can't stop bursting out laughing and sending his voice shooting up another giddy octave – 'big fuckin' deal, y'know!'

Lightening Up with the Prince of Darkness: Miles Davis Approaches Sixty

It was a priceless photograph. Not a classic because of the technique involved, or the lighting, but just because the cameraman had been lucky enough to be there, backstage at Carnegie Hall, and was able to capture a vision of magical confrontation in jazz history. He got to shoot together, face to face, an ageing, ornery Miles Davis and a young, earnest Wynton Marsalis.

The new star trumpeter Marsalis was the one in the business suit while Miles, for this particular shot, looked disconcerting, like some hack SF movie-maker's vision of a species of ebony mutant lizard. 'Macabre' might be an apt description of Miles's strained put-on of a half-smile over the usual backdrop of cat black. It's an effect he's the undisputed master of, even now, with his receding hairline and shoulder-length curls.

In his mid-twenties and clearly a novice next to Miles's propensity for achieving the look of perfect disdain, one still has to admire Marsalis for having the brass balls to get involved in a heart-stopping eyeball-to-eyeball encounter like this. Both are seated, their shoulders hunched, squaring off like boxers trading looks instead of punches, seemingly lost in a contest over who can outglare the other. Marsalis's stance is tense. It's as if he's facing off the once-great Miles Davis who, as far as he, Marsalis, is concerned, has opted to become a buffoon: a role his flinty visage may refute but one which his garish pop star clothing (not to mention the music he's been playing for some time now) cannot deny.

Davis, however, looks barely phased by Marsalis's scrutinizing eyes. His expression, furrowed but adamant, seems to be sizing up this gifted young big-mouth, whose work so clearly apes his earlier idioms, adding considerable polish and an undeniably brilliant technique, but not taking these reference points anywhere further. In short, Miles seems to be drinking him in and spitting him out.

Marsalis came away from the encounter with his suspicions confirmed, or so he later claimed. He and Miles had spoken and, according to the former, Miles was more than ready to acknowledge the younger man's challenge.

'Miles just stated outright that what he does now is a joke,' claimed the 23-year-old prodigy.

'Hell, you know, I believe music – just about everything – *sounds* better these days. Even a car crash sounds better!'

Everything, that is, except the voice of Miles Davis, a charred husk of sound, hoarse and cancerous. He is talking about whether today's computerized recording studio techniques have benefited or damaged the musical process as he, a forty-year veteran of performing and recording, conceives it.

'It's never been better! Damn right! Are there drawbacks? *None whatsoever!* Hell, some damn *critic*' – the word is spat out – 'might disagree but, you see, he don't know! All this shit about me bein' better in the old days . . . Music bein' better. That's reactionary thinking from pitiful motherfuckers who weren't even there. The old days . . . shit! In the old days, when it was alive and happening, jazz was made by this breed of musicians; I'm talking here about creative guys but they were also weird, idiosyncratic cats! Strictly night people, y'see? Somethin' about that night time made it real conducive to playin' blues . . . You know, "Blues After Midnight?"' He gives a parched chuckle. 'Oh yes! Attitude shit.

'Now these cats,' the bone-scraping croak continues, 'they always had their problems. I mean, I'd book a session, let 'em know where and when . . . Hell, half the cats wouldn't be there! I don't *need* that kind of mess! Runnin' around these fuckin' dives lookin' for the drummer, say, 'cos he's probably off somewhere scorin' dope. Bass player's a goddamned lush, always goin' too far at the bar. Trying to get him sober enough to stand up. Meanwhile, the sax player, he's pawned his goddamned horn! *That's* the old days, far as I can recall! Nobody needs that shit. It's demoralizing. Critics say, "Oh, Miles and Bird . . . the golden days!" What's *golden* about a cat all strung out on dope playin' a goddamned instrument with half the keys mashed up? Hell, you tell me 'cos I'm damned if I know!

'But, see, nowadays, you walk in the studio, there's these machines that'll do it all for you. Drum machines – hell, you just programme the motherfucker, press a button, you got that "bim, bam, boom" twenty-four hours a day if you want it. You want it to stop? Press another button. Synthesizers too. I love 'em! I mean, say you want something with a little Brazilian sound, a samba-type groove, then add in a little English-type music, plus a little bit of that Parisian sound – you can mix 'em all together. Get a whole new hybrid. Break down those frontiers! I love the textures you can get from those things. You don't have to be coppin' for no drum machine either. Don't have to wait till midnight to get the stuff down. *That's* how I like to work now. That's how it should be.'

The above is stated absolutely deadpan, with no room for any kind of rebuttal. Nor is one forthcoming because this is after all *Miles Davis*. The *legendary* Miles Davis. The *indefatigable* Miles Davis. The *wickedest, canniest, deepest, slickest, baddest* musician this century will ever see. Miles Motherfucking Davis, three months from his sixtieth birthday, forty-seven of those years spent as a card-carrying professional musician. Miles has decided to open up a little. That's why he's talking down, and I am listening up.

Maybe it's that voice, emanating from a veritable graveyard of a larynx, a voice variously described as 'demonic' and 'chilling', that's keeping me in my place. And those descriptions were made seventeen years ago, before thirty more nodes were surgically removed from Davis's throat, so that now the sound is quite other-worldly: at its most vitriolic, he spits out his syllables like a coiled snake dispensing some deadly poison.

Still, in the 'old days' he disdainfully refers to, Davis was a man of few words. In the fifties, having tossed aside the Juilliard School of Music's academic straitjacket to become sorceror's apprentice at Charlie Parker's mercurial creation of bebop, finally usurping his master's role as kingpin of jazz attitude (four years of heroin addiction having further distanced his bourgeois origins), Miles invented a whole new concept of 'cool'.

Ross Russell's *Bird Lives* captures the Miles persona of that era better than any other account:

> Aloof and disengaged, Miles turned his back on the
> audience, walked off the bandstand to sit alone,
> indolently smoking a cigarette and staring with stony
> contempt at the customers. Outwardly, he seemed
> unemotional, unconcerned and indifferent. Inwardly, he
> seethed with hostility. One of his favourite ploys was to
> shake hands with an old colleague, applying an
> excruciating jiujitsu grip, and, as the other writhed in his
> grasp, hiss 'I never liked you!' Or comment in a snaky
> voice, 'Man, you're getting old.'

When Davis was approached by fans simply wishing to express their love of his music, he would stonily respond, 'So what?' *Then* he could afford to behave with such imperious disdain. The Miles Davis enigma has been shaped in the balance between knowing when to react and when to stay silent. In the twilight sixties, Davis, notorious for not giving interviews, suddenly granted youth-oriented periodicals considerable access, spending inordinate time discussing his new attitudes, his reasoning, allowing young scribes lavish insights into the thought process of jazz's most controversial figure.

Then, just as the seventies began, his guard once more shot up. Having been lauded as 'the Picasso of invisible art' (a term coined by Duke Ellington), he was dubbed 'the Howard Hughes of jazz'. By the mid-seventies his enigma level was unsurpassed. This stemmed more from his bizarre nocturnal forays, however, than the quality of his music, which at that time sounded morose, directionless, perplexingly impotent. Between 1975 and 1980 he refused to enter a recording studio, maintaining an ominous silence as rumours of illness and drug dependency persisted.

Yet Miles has never been short of *direction*. Trace his progress: early years as Parker's oft-humiliated protégé/errand-boy; the recording of *Birth of the Cool* in 1949; the four years as a heroin addict and pimp; the formidable comeback in late '54 through '57 and the seminal modal excursions with John Coltrane (best exemplified by *Kind of Blue*); then, the equally historic Gil Evans collaborations (*Sketches of Spain* and *Porgy and Bess*) of the early sixties. In 1968 Davis opted to work with electric backing creating more seminal music; *In a Silent Way* witnessed Davis's tonal transformation from the elegant blue melancholia of before to the fire-red extrapolations that reflected a mood of vehement black militancy then gripping America.

Commencing with the electric church tonalities and brooding spiritual interludes that made 1969's *In a Silent Way* one of the last albums to break new ground while still affording Miles the total reverence of his hard-line critics, he became immersed, more and more disdainfully rejecting Western concepts of structure, harmony and texture in favour of other idioms. The hypnotic drone imperative to Indian music was fused with an ever-increasing fascination with interplay around the repetition that has always been at the heart of Afro-American music.

At first, Davis worked at a furious rate, clearly elated by the sense of 'command' and 'possession' that the music summoned forth. *Bitches' Brew*, his new recording, became the seminal work around which that dubious collation, jazz rock, was finally established, not to mention reaping sales that transcended the quantities sold by all other 'jazz' records. Gigs were obsessively taped, Miles often performing to predominantly white, young rock audiences as a support act to the likes of Steve Miller, Neil Young and the Grateful Dead. Although there were many formidable moments of supreme ferocity and excitement (the most sustained example being Davis's soundtrack to the movie *Jack Johnson*), the odyssey from 1970 through to 1975 was one that clearly showed signs of taking a down-bound curve both aesthetically *and* commercially. Miles's 'African Bag' – with track titles culled from the names of African guerrilla movements – had begun to exclude other existing textures and juxtapositions. One was suddenly presented with the albums such as *On the Corner*, with its upmarket cocaine dynamic and up-front 'street black culture' attitude. Two live albums from a Japanese tour, conducted some four months before his retirement, show just how lamentable Miles's focus on his music had in fact become.

Davis's retirement at this point has been explained by many factors. He had suffered from bursitis in his wrists and shoulders, a hip joint seemed to be disintegrating, insomnia was wasting him as much as the plethora of pain-killing drugs – codeine and morphine-based medication – which were helping to inflame several stomach ulcers. Probably worst of all, his muse wasn't functioning (his greatest periods of creativity have tended to always correspond to his having attained a condition of excellent physical fitness) and the sound emanating from his horn, bereft of its former spitfire alacrity, sounded incredibly weary and mournful, almost bordering on an aural evocation of cancer of the soul.

For Miles Davis the years between 1975 and 1980 were ones shrouded in mystery, intense rumour and speculation. Davis's numerous ailments – arthritis, bursitis, stomach ulcers, throat polyps, pneumonia, infections, repeated operations on the disintegrated hip – weren't helped by their victim's own attempts to stave off the pain and boredom by means of ingesting formidable supplies of alcohol, barbiturates and cocaine. Injecting various chemicals into his leg with a dirty needle, he suddenly found one day that he was unable to walk and was told he had to face up to the possibility of having his leg amputated. There was another operation and it was mercifully saved, but Davis continues to skin his teeth at fate.

'I was just having myself a good time,' recalled Miles to writer David Breskin two years ago.

Miles's eighties recordings have been greeted to date with a bemusement that he himself has done little to dispel. In 1983, having recorded and released three albums since his return to the studio in 1980 – *Man with the Horn*, the live *We Want Miles* and a Gil Evans collaboration, *Star People* – he brushed them all off, baldly stating, 'I don't like to record at all, live or in the studio, I just do it to make money.'

Ironically, it was 1985's *You're under Arrest* that caused him to change his tune. It was to be Miles performing contemporary AOR numbers: pop songs he'd heard on the radio in his Maserati, taped and arranged with his trumpet as the lead instrument. Having noticed how well received his poignant live version of Cyndi Lauper's 'Time after Time' had been with audiences, he went on to record, according to guitarist John Scofield, some forty songs, including several Toto compositions, Tina Turner's 'What's Love Got to Do with It', Dionne Warwick's 'Déjà Vu', even Lionel Richie songs and Kenny Loggins's 'This Is It'.

Ultimately, Davis included only the Lauper tune, the Toto-penned Michael Jackson opus 'Human Nature' and

D-Train's 'Something on Your Mind', opting instead to toss in some original material composed by group members and arranged by himself. This gave the finished product a schizophrenic quality symptomatic of artistic tunnel vision, but Miles didn't care. He claimed *You're under Arrest* to be his all-time favourite recording. 'The best album I've ever made!'

That album's executive producer, Dr George Butler, is not one of Miles Davis's favourite people. Since the abdication of Teo Macero, Miles's producer since 1959's historic *Porgy and Bess*, Butler became the key figure in playing midwife to the final recordings Davis did for Columbia/CBS. He considers Miles somewhat unpredictable:

'I think that sometimes his whims can get a little out of control. They're in his head, these little gems, so to speak, but the problems arise when it comes to translating them into a reality. He tends to need someone to pull them all together. Even when I worked with him, I often didn't know how it would work out as a complete project. I was usually always pleased with the results. He's still very clever. One of the very, very few.'

Dr Butler is of course a diplomat. He refers to Miles Davis as 'unpredictable' in the same way an adversary might refer to his opponent as a hell of a guy. Miles, never renowed for being pragmatic about discussing those he dislikes, doesn't lay the blame for his problems with Columbia, the label he has been with for thirty years, solely at Butler's door, but he does get rather testy whenever the name is brought up:

'He [Butler] came up to me, this is a year and a half ago, and said, "Miles, you should really put that version you do of 'Time after Time' out. It could really take off, be a smash." I said, "George, I told you that six motherfuckin' months ago!" But he hadn't heard me then, he wasn't listenin'! He just don't know! See, I can't stand a black man who wants to be bourgeois! That's a pitiful condition to be in.

'Another time' – Miles is getting warmed up, that demonic croak lubricated by cantankerous phlegm – 'that George, he phones my house. My daughter takes the call. She comes to me later, tells me he rang, right? I ask her what he wanted. She says, "George wants you to phone and say happy birthday to Wynton!"' His voice registers a sound of exasperated contempt. 'Happy birthday to Wynton! Shit on *that*! Who does he think I am? See, George, he reckoned it would make a nice gesture! He don't understand me, never did!'

Wynton Marsalis, whose virtuoso prowess as a trumpet-player is coupled with his controversial and reactionary views on staying true to the fifties spirit of jazz, has provided the media with their most recent opponent to Miles Davis. Dr George Butler signed Marsalis to Columbia, and when the latter, at the precocious age of nineteen, successfully fronted Miles's classic sixties quintet – Herbie Hancock, Wayne Shorter, Ron Carter and Tony Williams – when Davis himself refused at the last minute to take part in a one-off reunion gig, a confrontation was inevitable.

'Wynton . . . well, he's a good player,' mutters Miles reasonably. 'No two ways around that. But see, I don't want to get caught up in some jive feud thing here. That may be *his* style but it's not mine! He's good but his whole style of presentation, his look, his manner – it's dumb! *Plus* he could do with a few lessons in couth! What's he doin', messin' with the past? A player of his calibre should just wise up and realize it's over. The past is dead. *Jazz is dead*! The whole context has changed and people gotta . . . Why get caught up in that "old" shit? Music shouldn't be this stuff you play to kid your audience into thinkin' that's the way it was. Don't no one start telling me the way it was. Hell, I was there! *They* weren't!

'Some people, whatever is happening *now*, either they can't handle it or they don't want to know. They'll be messed up on that bogus nostalgia thing. Nostalgia, shit! That's a pitiful concept. Because it's dead, it's safe – that's what that shit is about! Hell, no one wanted to hear us when we were playin' jazz. Those days with Bird, Diz, 'Trane – some were good, some were miserable. But, see, people don't understand why I get so touchy sometimes. I just don't want to talk about that stuff. People didn't like that stuff then. Hell, why you think we were playin' clubs? No one wanted us on prime-time TV. The music wasn't getting across, you dig! Jazz is dead. Goddammit. That's it. Finito! It's over and there is no point aping the shit.'

Miles isn't angry, just adamant. His rationale is often wrought from a logic that is genuinely ingenious. At other times his philosophy is shaped from one simple point of view: he is Miles Davis and you're not. Musing over the previous outburst, he settles back to consider the fact that, *finally*, black music has overtaken the white folks' watered-down approximation of same in the market-place.

'Hell, y'know, Lionel, Quincy, Michael, Prince and me together . . . Now wouldn't that make for one hell of a movie?'

This is where Miles Davis chooses to pitch his tent in 1986. After thirty years as a Columbia recording artist, he is releasing his first Warner Bros. album. Initially entitled *The Perfect Way*, after the Scritti Politti number on side two, it has since been renamed *Tutu* after one of five Marcus Miller originals that predominate among the product's contents. Speaking to Warners' A&R kingpin, Tommy LiPuma, late last year, little was forthcoming with regard to how much cash the label had spent on procuring Miles. 'It's standard practice not to divulge such matters,' said LiPuma, another good-natured pragmatist. It was, of course, 'a great honour to have Miles Davis on the roster. He seemed to like our way of thinking. He felt that his association with Columbia had gone as far as it could. He was looking for a change.' Not that LiPuma and Warners had any grand schemes for Miles. 'Let's just say that, when you come to work with a musician of Miles's pedigree, it's not fitting to try and tell him what to do.'

This, of course, was early in the relationship, before LiPuma would become executive producer of the first WB release, at that point tentatively pencilled in for a late spring 1986 release. LiPuma had definite ideas about suitable collaborators: Thomas Dolby, for one, was high on the agenda; and Lyle Mays, the young keyboard player best known for his collaborations with guitarist Pat Metheny. It was then that Prince's name came up. LiPuma reacted immediately. 'I felt that Prince might not be too conversant with certain idioms pertaining to Miles's playing. But his work on the *Family* album displayed a keen awareness of the dynamics inherent in be-bop so, yes, indeed, Prince was ideal.' Miles refers to Prince excitedly as 'that funky little dude'. By the time of the release of *Around the World in a Day* in 1985, the ageing trumpet legend had become totally smitten with pop music's most audaciously resourceful stylist:

'Prince wrote me a letter and along with the letter he enclosed a tape of instrumental tracks he'd recorded by himself in his studio. And in this letter he wrote, "Miles, even though we have never met, I can tell just from listening to your music that you and I are so exactly alike that I know whatever you play would be what I'd do. So if this tape is of any use to you, please go ahead and play whatever you feel over it. Because I trust what you hear and play." I mean, now here's a dude . . . Hell, he's got it *all*! Multi-musician with a damned vengeance! As a drummer he can hold it down, you know what I'm sayin'? There's not many cats can nail it tight what with current technology makin' most drummers damn near obsolete. As a guitar player . . . he puts *out*! Plus, he's a goddamn great piano player. Matter of fact, he's about as good as they get, and I've worked with the best, I should know!'

Did anyone say Wynton Marsalis? Prince is who Miles Davis checks out now. The way he works in the studio – 'sheer genius,' reckons Miles. Hell, it didn't even drag Miles's bag one bit when the boy genius suddenly called through for some typically enigmatic reason requesting Miles *not* to release the tracks he'd sent him. 'I don't know exactly why he decided not to let 'em come out but I respect the boy.

'Do you know who Prince kinda reminds me of, particularly as a piano player? Duke! Yeah, he's the Duke Ellington of the eighties to my way of thinking. Only, back in them old days you couldn't get a man like Duke on prime-time. No, white audiences didn't want to see that elegance, that attitude, 'cos it was too intimidatin'.'

This leads Miles straight into another of his harangues:

'See, this is the thing you got to take into consideration here. Time and again, the black man has fucked up. He starts out with his shit together, then he gets damn side-tracked by white folks, y'know, whisperin' in his ear, "Hey, son, you should do this. Clean it up. Tone it down. Get smart. Get jive. Get yourself a goddamn monkey-suit or somethin'." The white man, see, he's always out to mess with our thing, packaging it, strapping some jive label on it. And the black man, he's fallen for it mostly every damn time. Why? 'Cos he's greedy, that's why! Hell, it's shameful what I'm sayin' here but it's the truth. White man starts talkin', the black man, he listens up, starts seeing dollar signs flashin' and the next thing you know he's selling himself out everywhere. See, *attitude* – that's what the black man's got. Attitude! The white man wants it so bad, he can't help but be jealous. So, over and over, the black man's music gets fucked with. But he don't see it happening 'cos greed is motivatin' him more than his better instincts.'

That deadly voice, shorn of any pitch beyond a gravel-toned whisper, rarely registers an emotional counterpoint to these tenacious accusations. He does sound particularly melancholy, however, when I query him about the absence of Darryl Jones, the young bass-player featured in last year's ensemble. Davis, during 1985's European gig, had tended to behave somewhat mischievously towards his fellow musicians. At London's

Festival Hall he kept resetting keyboard player Robert Irving III's synth patterns to no appreciable avail, while in Paris he brought on John McLaughlin in what could only be interpreted as a bid to upstage guitarist John Scofield. Only Jones was left unscathed by such questionable antics. At Montreux, Miles had even sidled up to the bassist and, his arm around his shoulder, gently coaxed him to the lip of the stage for an ovation. This occurred, mark you, just before young Darryl passed an audition to work with Sting on his *Dream of Blue Turtles* record and tour.

'Darryl? I had to let him go. Same shit as I've been relatin' to you. That boy . . . I liked him too. He could play so good and, hell, I felt kind of paternalistic toward him in a way. But then Sting comes along, offers him more money, high-class accommodation and all that stuff. And Darryl, he got so damn confused, I just said to him, real diplomatic and cordial like, "Man, what do *you* really want?" You know what he said to me? Darryl said, "Miles, I wanna do *cross-over*." God, I almost threw up! Here's a boy with real potential and yet here he is falling for that white man's corporate bullshit. Cross-over my black ass! Don't *mean* nothing! . . . Anyway, the boy has made his choice.'

Curiously, Miles then goes straight on to praise Sting's music.

'See, I like Sting! Yes, indeed! He's good and I like his songs – some of 'em – and his voice. He ain't like Mick Jagger rippin' off Wynonie Harris, shakin' his goddamn skinny white ass and pretendin' to sing the blues. You can take that shit, toss it in the river, watch it sink. Fuck that shit!

'Sade – her too, y'know. I think she's interestin' right now 'cos, see, if she works on her attitude she could shape up to be something good. Like, when she comes on the radio, I keep hearing intimations of Lena Horne comin' through. Now, she ain't that good – yet. But, like Lena singin' "Stormy Weather" – hell, it's something and God knows I love her but, damn, that "my man is gone" shit . . . Women ain't like that *now*! Like, Billie [Holiday] singin' about "her man" and how she ain't worth shit without him. That was real but that was *then*. It would be a lie to do that shit now though, 'cos women have changed. They don't need no pimp! They don't stand for that shit and that's how it should be. I know 'cos I used to be one myself! Had me seven women when I was strung out back in them old days [*mordant chuckle*]. And I'll be damned if I can remember their names . . .

'I don't like to think back to that. Women nowadays are into control. Like that song by Michael's sister, Janet [Jackson]. That's what's happenin'! Anyone who wants to go back to the past, they're too scared to live in the present.'

Miles Davis at sixty years of age is one funny motherfucker. Almost garrulous, when once he was prone to the absolute minimum of verbal expression, the hostility that seethed within him seems now to have dissipated, leaving only the ghost he chooses to inhabit when his pride is threatened.

What remains is indeed complex, hard to pin down. His rhetoric is loaded with odd contradictions yet he remains consistent in more crucial areas than many of his most zealous followers seem able to fully comprehend. He has been criticized for playing at being a pop star but, first, he's not playing and, second, he's always been a pop star: a larger-than-life luminary whose name is recognized by multitudes of people to whom the medium of jazz expression is as alien as the ancient Greek alphabet.

Those millions may know of him because of his notorious past: getting busted for narcotics and a heavy-duty arsenal of weaponry in '52; getting savagely beaten by white cops outside Birdland; having New York mobsters in late '69 riddle his red Ferrari with bullets – the fact that Miles later would boast that both his adversaries (cops and mobsters) had been 'dealt with'. Even the plethora of decidedly chilling rumours regarding his imprisonment of women for days on end during the dark endless nights of the seventies. Maybe they know him because of his single-handed elevation of the fifties black hipster to a realm of treacherous grace which, through his sartorial elegance, his fat, bright sports cars, his beautiful statuesque ebony-skinned women-friends, his feisty hyperactive persona, spelt out to all and sundry, *I'm not as good as you are. I am better.*

And even if they may have only glimpsed one of the five separate periods of extraordinary creativity his muse has been responsible for setting into motion, they recognize that Miles Davis is *great* in a way that defies placing him in an immediate peer group.

Now, after six years of shaping himself up for that sixth shot at further greatness, Miles feels that he is ready. His divorce from Columbia is indeed a brave move, mainly because in so doing he has granted the label the right to release any number of extracts from what John Scofield claims to be some 300 hours of unreleased material; music, moreover, made by a younger, considerably more tenacious personality, whose artistic temperament – the depthless blue pools of longing that lurk alongside the blood-red splashes of tension – has set aesthetic standards his Warner Bros. product is going to be hard pressed to keep pace with. Teo Macero hinted at the extent of an extraordinary mother-lode lurking in the vaults when he referred to late-sixties sessions alone:

'Everything that was done in the studio was recorded. Miles is probably the only artist in the world where everything is intact. I just edited out what I wanted, then the original went back into the vaults, untouched. Whoever doesn't like what I picked twenty years ago, they can go back and re-do it.'

The very idea of a man as prodigiously talented as our subject having to do battle with his own past triumphs at the age of sixty seems one that would cause even the most self-assured egocentric sleepless nights. Miles, however, *seemed* totally unnonplussed by the concept:

'Did I relinquish the rights to my unreleased stuff on CBS? Well, yeah, but it don't scare me, hell no! 'Cos even if they want to release 'em they wouldn't know where to find 'em. Teo, I don't reckon he knows either. And what if they did? Hell, they put the shit out, it won't sell. There's enough old shit of mine bein' issued as it is. I never seen any of it toppin' no charts. No one wants to buy it. Why should they?'

Again, that overwhelming adamancy, that patented *I'm Miles Davis and you're not* vehemence. His past, those gone-dead decades he refuses to contemplate affectionately, filter through, but he looks back only in disgruntled sideways glances. Those damn critics, the same plebeians who used to bug him when he was *Downboat*'s pet king-pin – they're the ones who fucked with his music:

'It's like Duke [Ellington], he said it first and he said it best: "If it sounds good, it is good." But them damn critics, they always had to complicate matters. Pigeonholing my music, they turned off my potential audience. First they said, "Ah, well, this is Cool," or "This is space music." Voodoo? Teo, he came up with that label for *Bitches Brew*. There wasn't no damn voodoo going on, it just sounded good to Teo and, hell, I wasn't in no mood to argue with him. There's more "bottom" to that stuff. More rhythms.

'*Now* they say *Bitches Brew* is a goddamned masterpiece but, hell, those critics hated it. Jazz-rock, my ass! They couldn't see that I was hip to the way black folks were hearing *their* music. I wanted to play for *my* people. I was listenin' to James Brown 'cos James was the Man – still is – where rhythm is concerned. That's what all the stuff I put out from *Bitches* on out was based on.'

Like the Janet Jackson record he admires so much, Miles Davis has always understood the need for control: to possess a firm grip on his life and his artistic destiny. The son of a bourgeois black family, he has succeeded in transcending the values of his upbringing, thwarting a debilitating drug habit, leading numerous formidable ensembles, controlling the music to suit his mercurial personality while, as Herbie Hancock once observed, keeping his musicians intimately involved. He has succeeded, above all, in both understanding and manipulating the key forces at work controlling a vicious business: the power of money, the power of image and taking hold of the power of mystique as a means to an end. As an artist, his role as catalyst is one that has involved an incredible facility for controlling often ridiculously opposed forces, harnessing a tenacious, fiery temperament to front music that has been mostly defined as 'the sound of sadness and resignation'. Similarly he has controlled his music's progression while rarely, if ever, turning his back on 'tradition', always aiming for the 'sophistication of simplicity'.

This year has seen a number of interesting developments. Duke Ellington, Miles Davis's beloved predecessor, twelve years after dying of pneumonia in a New York hospital, has had his profile embossed on a postage stamp. Bill Cosby, the black American comedian who was best man at Miles's wedding to actress Cicely Tyson five years ago, boasts the most popular prime-time TV sit-com in the US. And Quincy Jones, Miles's old running buddy, with his Grammy nomination for *The Color Purple*, the movie he co-produced, has been putting Michael Jackson through his paces in the recording studio for another billion-dollar disc. Miles is ready to ascend from the comfy confines of prestigeville. America's TV heartland has already witnessed this curious image of a man, a skinny figure with gleaming skin and what remains of his hair curling all over his shoulders: his hands grip (what else?) a trumpet, his lithe form is slouched against a small Japanese scooter, his eyes stare out at the viewer with imperious disdain. Then the voice, emanating from that shredded, node-less killing-floor of a larynx, mutters, 'I ain't here to talk about this thing, I'm here to ride it.' Miles Davis, renowned for his taste in the slickest, fastest sports cars, has followed Lou Reed, Grace Jones and Adam Ant into advertising Honda scooters. The money helps but it's exposure he wants. And is getting, if the role of a pimp in a recent *Miami Vice* episode is any indication.

Amazingly, at sixty Davis looks better than he has in over fifteen years. At a diminutive 5 feet 4 inches, he none the less looks formidably exotic, in fact nothing short of stunning. In 1981 he looked awful – overweight and obviously very, very ill. Today he looks like a male Grace Jones – rail-thin, his attitude in his heels, his eyes torching with a gleam that can turn from depthless calm to deadly volatility.

'Yeah, I'm lookin' good, ain't I! I swim every day when I'm touring, have acupuncture, stick to these special herbal diets. Don't fool around anymore. Dope is *out*! Used to get through maybe a third of an ounce of cocaine a day, stay up forty-eight hours, smoke six packs of cigarettes in that time, drink spirits, take sleeping-pills. I was killin' myself. I was a hog and that's . . . See what I mean by black people bein' greedy?' He credits his wife, Cicely Tyson, for saving him from death when his body was racked with painful ailments. His currently gleaming skin and trim physique he attributes to a more unusual source:

'I went to the place called La Prairie. This fella I know took me there. They give you these shots: I got eleven of 'em so far! They consist of, well, basically, it's unborn sheep glands! Yeah, that's right. Goddamn *sheep*! These shots, they make your eyesight sharper, make your skin softer too. Make your sex organs much – [*he issues a low grunting sound*]. It's funny though!' he continues, clearly drawn to the subject. 'I didn't feel that eleventh shot! The other ten – I felt them, no damn problem! But that last one . . . man, maybe those sons of bitches ripped me off! Y'know what I'm saying . . . And this shit costs a hell of a lot for it to be pumped into you. OK! Anyway. [*He pauses.*] Y'know this stuff – when it's in your bloodstream, it's like you're high on cocaine or somethin'. But it's natural! I'll tell you the feeling this stuff gives you. Say, you're sitting in your living-room and suddenly you start feeling kind of hungry. Well, with this sheep-shit pumpin' through your veins, you don't ask nobody to go and fix you something to eat! Hell, no, you get off your ass, go in the kitchen and go fix it yourself!'

Miles is clearly getting quite lively in his old age. With *Tutu* already long completed and down at the pressing-plant, Miles casually states that its successor has already been recorded:

'It sounds hot. Y'know, this new stuff I'm comin' out with is better than anythin' I've recorded in the past. Hell, I don't *think* so I *know* so! I want this shit to get out to the people. That's why I left Columbia, see. I kept tellin' em, "If you dumb motherfuckers keep puttin' labels like "Contemporary Jazz" on my damn records, you might as well stick them up next to beans and molasses." Might as well throw 'em in the river. I had to leave. It was degrading. Now *they* say, "Jazz is comin' back; there's a revival." They don't know! Same people that think that, they'll say, "Bird died for his art. He had a good ole' time doing it!" He died on his knees, man! Broke and broken! He wasn't in control of nothin'! People love that bullshit though. See, death – it's safe. All those fuckers too scared to feel anything: they get into that "mystique" bullshit.

'If I was dead now, they'd love me whatever shit came out with my name on it. Hell, if I was a recluse doin' nothin', it would be the same. Fuck 'em. I don't like to relax, lay back on my old stuff. Show me a motherfucker who's relaxed and I'll show you a motherfucker that's afraid of success.'

I ask him about his renowned quote: 'I've got to change. It's like a curse.' Is it still a curse?

'Funnily enough, someone else asked me that question. That quote, maybe I said it once but now I believe, hell, I *know*, it's a blessing. My music is better than ever. To my ears, I check out the contemporary heavyweights. I'd like to work with

Quincy. He understands, Prince, *he* understands. In fact, Prince said to me, "You don't ask God for what you want, you thank him for what you've got already." Now I'm not a particularly religious person but, hell, I can empathize.'

Max Roach, the great jazz drummer, stated, weeks before the first clumsy return to the stage in 1981, 'Miles is a champion. Champs always come back.' With Muhammad Ali brain-damaged, James Brown an egomaniac bordering on lunacy, and most other 'champs' burned out, the vision of Miles Davis at sixty, still fit and functioning with formidable élan, is one worth cherishing.

'Don't you ever count me out!' he muttered as we concluded our talk. I don't intend to. Neither should you. After all, he's Miles Davis and you're not.

*

Five years after this was written, Miles Davis died from complications arising from pneumonia at his home in Los Angeles. He had been musically active up until the very last days of his life.

'God's Got His Plans and I've Got Mine': The Last Testament of Roy Orbison

It was an unusually wet and gloomy Monday afternoon in the early December of 1988 when I set out to interview Roy Orbison. Maybe it was some kind of premonition, for only nine days after our encounter he died from a heart attack 'cradled in the arms of his mother' at his home in Nashville. That image would end up providing the media with a final tragic closing-shot for their emotive vision of Roy Orbison's life as one long, remorseless tale of woe.

Just as I'd anticipated, he was a most singular-looking individual. Disturbingly thin – a condition much amplified by skintight polo neck and black slacks tapering off with aggressively pointed Beatle boots – his physique – he was also much shorter than photographs might otherwise indicate – actually reminded me of Mr Magoo, the cartoon blind man. And yet he also seemed quite ageless, his movements, gestures and reflexes betraying the agility of an albeit malnourished youth. And that face was just bizarre with his guinea-pig eyes beaming out like beatific orbs through truly weird multi-mirrored and tinted wine-red spectacles. The final touch was the pigtail of jet black hair. Actually I thought he looked perfect.

He looked perfect because in my imagination the Roy Orbison I've listened to for most of my life always looked weird and alien and dark and totally aloof from life's dull equations. I imagined him more like this human beacon beaming down these shards of perfect romantic torment that have cast light into more dark moods than I care to remember.

This is the essence of the great cathartic experience that is Roy Orbison, the essence that Bruce Springsteen picked up on in the celebrated speech he gave when inducting Orbison into the Rock'n'Roll Hall of Fame back in 1986. To wit: 'He had the ability, like all the great rock'n'rollers, to sound like he'd dropped in from another planet and yet get the stuff which was right to the heart of what you were living today. That was how he opened up your vision.'

When he spoke, the myth and the man naturally started to separate, but never in an uncomfortable way. Orbison, throughout the interview, referred to himself as 'totally centred', and frankly it was hard to disagree with him. A shy, remarkably wistful man, he embarked on each answer with a soft, almost bashful Southern burr to his voice. He was unswervingly gracious and polite, especially when discussing topics he must have had to chew over a million times before in such circumstances. His manner was clearly one of elation. As he was the first to admit, it seemed he could do no wrong. The tidal wave of regeneration that took its most crucial momentum from David Lynch's perversely surreal interpretation of 'In Dreams' as the glowing centrepiece of his film *Blue Velvet* had surged into overdrive with the Travelling Wilburys project: a curious assemblage of the great (Orbison and waffy old Bob Dylan) and the not so great (George Harrison, Tom Petty and Jeff Lynne) being wacky and whimsical together in a recording studio. The resulting album has sold well – 'Number nine with a bullet,' he'd positively beamed – and with the radio newly reacquainted with that extraordinary voice the timing could not have been better for the release of Orbison's first album of new songs in years.

However, fate stepped in and now all we have of him is that glorious body of music and the memory of a life marked with great tragedy but much greater good grace and resilience.

'My earliest memories? Well, I was born in Vernon, Texas. Actually, I've since learned that I was born right on the

Chisholm Trail, which is where they drove the cattle from Texas through to Kansas. That trail was the main street in Vernon. It was ranch country really, not very big in size. My dad was an auto mechanic, but we soon moved to Fort Worth, where he worked in defence building B-24s. Then he moved to West Texas, where he worked in oil. Started as a roustabout working up to drilling superintendent. Mom and Dad bought me a guitar for my sixth birthday. We were living in Fort Worth then, just above a drugstore – and my uncle Kenneth and James Littlejohn and a bunch of cousins would come by on their way to the European Theatre – or the Pacific, that was the other one – to sing and play the guitar. And because I'd learned to play, they'd let me stay up and do the singing. And what I recall of it was that their zest and gusto for life was what made those times so supercharged. So that if they were drinking they'd drink a lot, and when they were playing they'd play with all their heart and soul. So I never really knew any other way. And still, today, that's how I do it – with everything I have. That spirit and intensity, the easy camaraderie of musicians, that lifestyle is ingrained in me. By the time I was seven I was finished, y'know, for anything else.'

One thing I've always wanted to know: where did you steal that growl from?

'You mean on "Pretty Woman"? [*Laughs.*] I stole it from a Bob Hope movie I'd seen as a kid. I think it might have been *Son of Paleface*. He looked into the mirror and went, "Grrrr". So I'll give Bob Hope credit for that one! [*Laughs*].'

You've been singled out as the only early rock pioneer vocalist who can still sing his songs in their original key and whose voice has become stronger and purer with age.

'Actually, that's true. It comes from my father. I think his voice has much the same young quality and it never deepened from the age of thirty to fifty. It's a blessing, I guess. My octave range isn't extremely wide, but what I do have, everything is very solid and useful. It's the way my voice kinda portrays what

I'm saying in the lyrics so nicely – that's the real gift. It makes the song more binding. When I'm singing there's never any conscious memorizing process going on with the lyrics. When I sing, I don't think, 'What does this mean?' It's somehow already a part of me and the voice just takes over.

'So I was singing and playing from a really young age. Sang on the radio when I was eight, I recall. The first singer I heard on the radio that really blew me away was Lefty Frizzell. He had this technique which involved sliding the syllables together that just about used to slay me. He left a definite impression. Later, it was certain blues and rhythm & blues singers that had the same effect for me. Hank Williams? I liked him well enough but didn't reckon him as the genius I now perceive him to be – the guiding light of us all in a way. Actually, I found his stuff too tin pan alley-ish for my tastes back then.

'I really don't know where individual influences come from. There was a lot of diversification going on. Like at fifteen I tried to be a lead guitar player playing intricate melody lines and such. I didn't get very far, so by sixteen I'd set my mind to playing just rhythm guitar to accompany my voice. So I was a singer until Jerry Lee Lewis recorded "Down the Line", the first song I ever wrote. The same time that got released, the Everly Brothers recorded "Claudette", the second song I'd written. So it kinda occurred to me that, y'know, maybe I have a talent for this.'

The emotional tenor of your work has always seemed to me a very heightened expression of a very adolescent state of mind. Do you agree?

'Oh, yes, absolutely. Absolutely. It's a condition I related to deeply. For me, adolescence was such a glorious time. The intensity of your emotions at that period in your development is something awe-inspiring, no matter how painful it might sometimes seem. I believe that none of us really grows out of that. At least I haven't, or I just wouldn't be doing what I'm doing. Personally, even though I've since experienced a lot of personal growth, spiritual growth, working on relationships and things, I still feel there's that connection. Even though the love I sang of then is probably not the love I know today. See, it's only in the last twenty years of being married that I can understand what poets talk about when they say how love grows and becomes something you never dreamed it could be. But God has a way of giving you the lyric and the melody, and if it stands up over the years, then adolescence – that innocence – helps to keep its intentions pure. That innocence is the big ingredient that keeps my songs alive, that makes them stand tall.

'Yeah, actually, I do find this obsession with "the Sun Sound" to be overrated. See, all it really was was the influence of the two-track over the one-track recording set-up, using the second track for echo – slap-back is what they called it back then. Plus, all of us – Jerry Lee, Elvis, John and myself – had to have big voices just to get heard in that room over the instruments because there was no separation.

'Sam Phillips – he's sure a big topic, boy! [*Laughs.*] See, I think what he got to achieve came by luck rather than inspiration. Sam was a very short-sighted man in many respects. In the studio he'd just bring out these old, thick 45 records of, like, Arthur Crudup singing "Mystery Train" and then tell me, "Sing like that." The only other thing he'd say was, "Do it again." He wasn't one for advising his artists, was Sam. But he was blinded by the early lack of success his records had enjoyed. Like, Elvis only sold a few thousand on Sun.

'I saw Elvis before I heard him on record. See, Elvis and John were coming from a country tradition to begin with – they were live performers on the country circuit. Country singers, after the war, went out and toured live. Pop singers – the Frankie Laines and the Johnny Rays – they didn't tour, they made records. There was this distinction and Sam couldn't see that what he'd got going on in his studio had the capacity to break that barrier and just explode. I once asked him why – we were next door to the Sun Studio sitting in a café, as I recall – why he'd sold Elvis to RCA. He just smiled one of his crazy smiles and said, "For Carl Perkins and $40,000." He was clearly well pleased with the deal. But at the same time I owe Sam so much. It's just that the money was so poor – he didn't even pay union rates – and he had no publishing house outlet, so all of us just had to leave. The last time I really spoke to Sam was just after my first big successes for Monument. I went back to the studio to pay my respects. Sam just looked at me, smiled and said, "You'll be back." His brother Judd was in the same room. He just looked at me, rolled his eyes and said, "The hell he will."

'I first saw Elvis live in '54. It was at the Big D Jamboree in Dallas, and first thing, he came out and spat on the stage. In fact, he spat out a piece of gum, but that was right away shocking. And he was this . . . this punk kid, a real weird-looking dude. Just a real raw cat, singing like a bird. I can't over-emphasize how shocking he looked and seemed to me that night. He had Floyd Cramer playing piano along with Scotty Moore and Bill Black too. Did "Maybelline", then the kids started shouting. There was pandemonium in the audience 'cos the girls took a shine to him and the guys were getting a little jealous. Plus he told some real bad, crude jokes – y'know, this dumb off-colour humour – which weren't funny and his diction was real coarse like a truck driver's.

'His energy was incredible, his instinct was just amazing, but . . . Actually it affected me exactly the same way as when I first saw that David Lynch film [*Blue Velvet*]. I didn't know what to make of it. There was just no reference point in the culture to compare it with.

'In the "Ooby Dooby" days I was anything but timid in my performances. I was very much an extrovert, sensation-seeking fella. I moved around more than Elvis or anyone. But then it was over for me very quickly. I just felt that for my style it was a bit shallow. Plus the stationary image was done out of necessity because the microphone was there, most of my songs don't have instrumental breaks, and I was most comfortable just being there where I could be most effective.

'At Monument . . . I have to give Fred Foster his due. He didn't necessarily know much about music, but he was the perfect patron for a young artist because his attitude was "Here's the canvas, here are the paints – get on with it." And even though he was credited producer, it was mostly him letting me produce my own sessions.

'I always felt that each instrument and vocal inflection had to be special. And I'd work out vocal counter-melodies. In fact, I'd spend almost as much time on those as I'd spend on the song itself. For the instrumental accompaniment I'd get with the arranger who scored the charts and sing the lines I wanted. Looking back on it now, I feel I was blessed much like the masters, I guess – the guys who wrote the concertos. I'd just have it all in my head.

'People say how dark and melancholy my songs appear, but that's a misnomer, I feel. "Only the Lonely" isn't a sad song, it's just a lonely song. Each song highlights one feeling, and whatever that feeling, I think I've succeeded in showing the positive elements along with its gloomy side. Like "Crying": I didn't mean that song to be taken as neurotic, I wanted to show that the act of crying, for a man – and that record came out in a real macho era when any sign of sensitivity was really frowned on – was a good thing and not some weak . . . defect, almost.

'"Runnin' Scared" I got from a newspaper headline on a flight to New York. I could relate to the concept because every relationship I'd ever been in, the girl already had one going when we first met. Even as far back as kindergarten. "In Dreams" – now that song was given to me one night when I was literally falling asleep. I'd written a couple of songs in my dreams and I'd thought they were someone else's. So I'm half asleep and my thoughts were still racing when that whole introduction just came to me. I thought, "Boy, that's good. I need to finish that. Too bad these things don't happen in my dreams." I woke up the next morning, twenty minutes later I had the whole song written.'

There's an element about 'the context of pop' that is incredibly fickle. For everyone who's succeeded in attaining longevity there have been periods of great acclaim tempered by periods when they've seemed incomprehensibly old-hat, almost obsolete for a time. Then it snaps back and they become utterly contemporary again . . .

'Exactly, but that comes with the territory. It's an outside influence that's not even affected necessarily by stuff like marketing techniques. It's something, some energy that comes in and says, "This is too plain, this is too accepted, too ordinary for now." Then it kind of settles back down. But I've felt the sting of that. As the sixties turned into the seventies I didn't hear a whole lot I could relate to so I kind of stood there like a tree where the winds blow and the seasons change and you're still there and you bloom again. With time. Right now, I feel very, very viable. I genuinely feel that I can put this new album next to anything I've done in the past and it won't seem diminished by the achievements I'm chiefly regarded for. See, being contemporary – you don't chase it. Certainly, if I chased after what I thought might be contemporary, I'd be completely lost and coming up behind. In my case, I've always felt there were no limitations. I remember when I was at school, two or three years before it really began. I was totally anonymous – I mean, I was virtually unknown even at my home. Then, after thirty months, I had a number one record round the world. I didn't see any limitations then. And still to be viable while being viewed as one of the pioneers of rock is in validation of that.

'I was standing at the side of the wide stage at the Rock'n'Roll Hall of Fame ceremony, and I thought Bruce Springsteen was just going to say, "Ladies and gentlemen, da-da . . ." y'know. Anyway, he went into this . . . soliloquy almost, about me and how my music had really touched him and I'm just *wilting* as he's doing it in front of everybody. I mean, I was really touched, really deeply moved. I felt I had been truly *recognized*, y'know, justified. "Validated" may be the word. At least in that room, for one night . . . You can't instigate these things. God just has his plans and I have mine.

'Like, it was 1978 or something and I was together with Linda Ronstadt and Emmylou Harris and this tall young guy, real sweet, came up to me and said, just straight out, "I got into showbusiness because of you." He told me he'd seen me play once in Winnipeg way back when and he just said, "You really moved me. Your performance that night made me decide to really go for becoming a professional musician." And I only found out later – he was Neil Young.'

You said you were initially shocked by David Lynch's interpretation of 'In Dreams'?

'Oh God! I was aghast, truly shocked! I remember sneaking into a little cinema in Malibu, where I live, to see it. Some people behind me evidently recognized me because they started laughing when the "In Dreams" sequence came on. But I was shocked, almost mortified, because they were talking about "the candy-coloured clown" in relation to doing a dope deal. Then Dean Stockwell did that weird miming thing with that lamp. Then they were beating up that young kid. I thought, "What in the world?" But later, when I was touring, we got the video out and I really got to appreciate not only what David gave to the song and what the song in turn gave to the film, but how innovative the movie was, how it really achieved this other-worldly quality that added a whole new dimension to "In Dreams". I find it hard to verbalize why, but *Blue Velvet* really succeeded in making my music contemporary again.'

Do you feel this image that hangs over you like a shroud – the singer who lost both his first wife and later two children to accidents of fate, the solitary man enmeshed within a life of great tragedy – is a myth?

'Well, yes, I do. See, those tragedies are things that happen to you. When I realized – and it took a while – that those kinds of things happen to everyone, I didn't feel so isolated in my sorrow or as put upon as I did initially. But see, Barbara and I will be married twenty years this March, so it's also a long time ago.'

But you haven't seemed embittered by those tragedies. Unlike, say, Chuck Berry, whose experiences – albeit different from yours – have made him a very bitter man.

'But that would be terrible. You have to be forgiving and you have to also acknowledge the love that people give to you. You have to remember the people who called up or took the time to come by and say, "Look. I'm with you." But most of all, you have to recognize that it's not a personal attack being made on you. It's not your fault or any kind of weird process. And I don't want to be intellectual about it, but you've got to somehow let the sorrows of the past go and become just another part of your experience. Looking back, I truly feel that I have spent most of my life in a state of genuine contentment. I've always felt myself to be self-sustaining from as far back as I can remember. A part of, but apart. I still feel that way. And once I got over the anguish of those times, a natural balance started to exert itself within me and that came from acknowledging how exciting the times I've lived through have been and how I've been a party to so many wonderful experiences . . . Now, having established a working relationship between myself and Jesus Christ, I feel I am truly centred and truly focused. There are churches I go to when I can get to them. Not the church I was brought up to believe in, the Church of Christ in Texas, when I was a young boy. I drifted away from that because they didn't believe in dancing, but I was playing for dances. So there was a conflict – the Church or me. I'm only telling you that to get this in perspective because I still consider the Church to be Jesus Christ and that is my source of strength and balance. We're all on a spiritual path, one way or another. It's like I said, God has his plans, and I've got mine.'

Neil Young and the Haphazard Highway That Leads to Unconditional Love

About thirty miles back the roads had been sprouting forth like healthy veins just like he'd once described in an old song of his. Then everything tapered off, and now it was one long winding stretch of black tar bounded on both sides by rugged elms and tall, proud oak trees with patches of violets growing wild at the base. He didn't know where on earth he was, if the truth be known, but he didn't care. It was somewhere in the high country anyway, because he'd seen a deer sprinting through the slashes of light between the trees while they were driving, and had just told the guy at the wheel of his tour bus to pull over, let him off, and wait up for him a couple of miles further along the road. At first, he'd stepped out to get better acquainted with the lie of the land, and let his senses feast on nature's bountiful gifts awhile. There were the sounds of wild geese flying westward right above him, while not far away the babbling sound of a small stream was starting to fall within his ear-shot.

But as he walked with that intense purposeful stride of his, back slightly stooped, his wise old owl's face mostly hidden by a remarkably cheap-looking pair of sunglasses, he was no longer hearing that stuff. Instead, he was tuned into the sound of galloping horses pounding along inside his brain like in an old John Ford movie when the fort's about to burn down and the cavalry's thundering hooves are starting to dust up the horizon. Over that, he could also make out a loud raucous guitar twanging out a riff that sounded like it was churning between the chords of G and E minor. There were no lyrics yet, just the image of these unstoppable horses with steam rising off them, ploughing through a dense mist, ridden by gaunt-faced slit-eyed individuals whose features seemed utterly devoid of humanity. Where were they going and where had they just come from? That he still had to figure out.

There was a rustling sound from behind a fallen stump of timber just to his left that startled him. In the distance, he thought he could hear a church bell ringing. Then the rhythm started up again in his head with that guitar riff that kept reminding him of the *Rawhide* theme as sung by Frankie Laine and his voice of true pioneer grit lighting up the prairie fires and the TV dinners of his youth. And as he heard the voice reverberating through his mind, he cast his mind back to those early mornings back in Omemee, the place he was first brought up in and the place he wrote 'Helpless' about. He'd be walking down a railroad track at age six or seven past a hobo's shack, strutting along with a little transistor radio jammed to his ear and Frankie Laine's rich, unflinching voice intoning mellifluously about the wayward wind despatching lost and broken souls to dwell, heads bowed, in just such lowly make-shift accommodations forever to be haunted by the sound of ghostly train whistles.

The road came to a head and then there was a slight bend. Once Young was around it, he could see the bus parked not too far ahead. Those horses and their riders were still waiting to gallop into some kind of story-line but that would all be taken care of just as soon as he got hold of a guitar. It's like there's a mighty reservoir of songs that no one's ever heard up there in heaven and there's a tap in Neil Young's brain that's somehow attached to it. All he has to do is ease his mind into the right gear and something will always come trickling down.

'Writer's block? I would never recognize it. I don't know what it is,' Neil Young will tell me ardently in Paris only a matter of days and several time-zones from that afore-depicted pastoral trek. 'See, I'm not trying to write. It just comes out when it comes out. So there is no block! Like, I'm not sitting down, going [*frantically*], "Oh my God, I've got to write a song! I really, really have to . . . Oh my God!" Hey, if I don't write a song, I don't record a song. Hell, it just gives me more time to do other things.'

For over thirty years it's been like that: Neil Young rolling down the road with a song coming alive in his head, a dreaming man endlessly driven to kick-start the creative moment as quickly as possible and then to share his fantasies with a world going at a mere fraction of his natural speed. Try and isolate the one common denominator threading together Young's stout body of work and you have this image of characters constantly on the move, be they ancient Aztec warriors, motorcycle-riding waitress-divorcees or, most often, guys who are a little paranoid and a little troubled, noble-men-of-destiny types who smoke too much pot and analyse their own feelings too relentlessly, who are always looking out for a genuine soulmate but who are also aware they are way too self-obsessed to give enough of themselves to make any relationship truly work, so there is always this contradiction tugging at their souls like a sort of sadness, giving their outpourings a strange cathartic twinge. Guys, in other words, almost exactly like Neil Young was throughout the sixties and for most of the seventies.

'I've often been singled out for extreme things to happen to in my life,' he'd calmly observed late in the eighties after nature had played a particularly hideous trick on his family. But it has always been that way for Young, the younger of two sons born to Scott (a well-known Canadian journalist) and Edna ('Rassie') Young in the early morning of 12 November 1945 in the city of Toronto, Canada. Early photographs portray him as a chubby little infant with hair standing up like a porcupine's quills and a grin big enough to split his face like a coconut, an early image of himself he'd later recall in song. His joy was not unconfined, however, for at the age of only five he'd become stricken with polio and almost died. Only a few years later, just as he was about to enter his teens, his parents would separate and the whole family split down the middle. 'Sure, it was pretty traumatic,' he would later recall to me. 'But not *that* traumatic! I knew my dad still loved me and my mom was still there. Actually, it was kind of exciting, now I think about it. It was a change. We'd had ten or twelve years of living together, then my mom went off to live in Winnipeg.

'Looking back on my childhood now, there's a sort of glow to my reminiscences. It's like my memory has blocked out most of the bad stuff. I just remember all those glorious sunny days and good times. You need to have good memories from your past. You never know when you're going to have to depend on those memories just to see you through a bad patch in your adult life. See, my family were like nomads. We travelled all over the place and I ended up going to eleven or twelve different schools as a result. That's partly why my education left a lot to be desired. I mean, I dropped out at eleventh grade [*laughs*]. Success and failure at the same time – that's the feeling I remember the day I left school for the last time.

'Originally I wanted to become a farmer. I was planning on going to agricultural college and getting my own farm. I was going to raise chickens at the beginning. Then eventually branch out into a full farm. I started seriously working on this project when I was about ten years of age. I even got the chickens and set up a coop for them. But then something unexpected happened. I heard Elvis Presley for the first time. And then, along with Elvis, I heard Chuck Berry, Ronnie Self, the Chantels and this whole other galaxy of strange bewitching music which you could pick up on radio from transmitters down in the Southern states of America. Also, it was getting played on a Toronto radio station known as CHUM.

'I started playing musical instruments when I was fourteen. I mastered the ukulele, the banjo – y'know, four-stringed instruments of various kinds. The first thing I learned is that three chords are the basis to a lot of songs . . . It's a blues-based idea. You start on G, go to C and resolve it all with a D chord. So I learnt how to work those three chords and then got into the thing of working in different keys. I basically just taught myself, figuring out as I went along.'

By the age of sixteen Young had lost all his childhood puppy-fat and measured a long, raw-boned 6 feet 3 inches in height. He had his mother's piercing eyes and his father's same shock of abundant black hair. He carried himself with a certain ironic detachment, and it's tempting to portray him day-dreaming through the windy streets of Winnipeg all scrunched up in his tiny denim jacket and dilapidated jeans as some prototype early 'slacker'. But Young was no diffident hippie slouch. On the contrary, it was like he was on fire where his music was concerned. He'd already become obsessive about following in the footsteps of perhaps his greatest idol, the melancholy but indefatigable Roy Orbison:

'This all happened in '62. I saw him in Winnipeg, saw him all over the place that year. Got to talk with him once outside a gig. He was coming out of his motor-home with his backing band, the Candymen. That had a profound effect on my life. Period. I always loved Roy. I looked up to the way he was, admired the way he handled himself. His aloofness influenced me profoundly . . . His music was always more important than the media. It wasn't a fashion statement. It wasn't about being in the right place at the right time making the right moves. That didn't matter to Roy. Just like it doesn't matter to me.'

His mother had helped him buy an orange Gretsch guitar and he stalked the streets of Winnipeg brandishing it proudly in a fine white case. At fifteen he began playing guitar with the Esquires, a semi-pro teen band who had got as far as printing up their own business card, which read 'The Esquires. Instrumental and vocal styling. Fine Music & Entertainment', but no further. Then came another brief spell in an outfit known as Stardust, but by the end of 1962 he had his own band going for him – a bunch of interconnected school buddies who called themselves the Squires:

'We were doing our own stuff – mostly instrumentals in the style of an English band called Hank B. Marvin and the Shadows. The big early influences? For me, OK, there was Hank B. Marvin obviously . . . Lonnie Mack – "The Wham of the Memphis Man" – the lead guitarist in the Fireballs . . . his name escapes me but he was just great [George Tomsco] . . . Link Wray . . . "Rumble" . . . Oh, man, Link Wray's right there on top of the list . . . These guys were the beginning of it all for me. We're talking about real guitar pioneers. Like, a lot of that surfin' music was just starting up too and I loved that stuff. The Surfari's doing "Wipe-out" . . . Then there was "Pipeline" . . . Then there was Dick Dale. He was the funkiest of those players 'cos most of them were a little stiff when they were playing their melodies, but Dick Dale was looser. His stuff had a real swing to it. Like, on "Let's Go Trippin'" he was all over the place and the beat was real advanced, compared to all the other stuff in that genre.

'Sometimes we'd throw in some funkier, R'n'B-styled stuff as well. I started singing in '64 . . . maybe even '63. First my band was just all instrumental. Then very quickly it became pretty much all vocal. Even before I left Winnipeg in 1965 . . . There were no instrumentals by then. By that time I was experimenting with a different kind of music we'd come up with. It was kinda like "folk-rock" but it wasn't anywhere near as sweet. We took these traditional folk songs – like "Clementine", "She'll Be Coming Round the Mountain When She Comes", "Oh Susannah" . . . Then we'd put them in minor keys, add these weird little harmonies and play them with a surf beat.'

Stephen Stills, a boisterous Southern teenager roughly Young's age, was passing through Canada as one of a staid folk quintet known as the Company. He would later reminisce about his first encounter with the lanky guitarist and his self-designed surf-rock-folk-punk quarter, the Squires:

'They'd just come back from Churchill, Ontario, and Neil had written, I think, his first song, and we had a great time running around in his hearse and drinking good strong Canadian beer and being young and having a good time. Neil was seventeen at the time and I was eighteen and he was playing folk-rock before anybody else. He had his Gretsch, a rock'n'roll band that had just recently turned from playing "Louie Louie" to playing the popular folk songs of the day with electric guitars, drums and bass. It was a funny band 'cos they would go right from "Cotton Fields" to "Farmer John".

'I was trying to set up something for Neil and me, and in the meantime Neil went to Toronto, fell in with this chick, Vicky Taylor I think her name was, who was a folksinger who convinced Neil that he was Bob Dylan. So Neil broke up the band and decided to be Bob Dylan and was playing rhythm guitar, you know. He would just go in and play acoustic guitar in coffee houses. He wanted to be Bob Dylan and I wanted to be the Beatles. We were, as I said, very young.'

Young recalls the elements that prompted him to make his first musical metamorphosis a little differently:

'After I arrived in Toronto I tried to keep my band going and then tried to work with several other bands. But it just never worked out for me there. I could never get anything going in Toronto, never even got one gig with a band. So I moved instead towards acoustic music and immediately became very introspective and musically inward. That's the beginning of that whole side of my music. See, I'd just come from a place called Thunder Bay, which is between Winnipeg and Toronto. The Squires'd done really well there but couldn't get a gig to save our lives in Toronto. Got a manager but even he couldn't find us a gig. All we ever did was practise. So I ended up cruising around by myself on acoustic guitar, playing my songs at coffee houses for a while. I even did some gigs, like in Detroit, just across the border . . . and I was starting to make a living at it. I was by myself, just me and my guitar travelling alone, just showing up at these places. It was quite an experience. The strong image I have now of that period is one of me walking around in the middle of the night in the snow, wondering where to go next. A part of me was thinking, "Wow, this is really out on the edge!" The other part was thinking, "What the fuck do I do now?"

He never stopped moving and there was always a large piece of guitar equipment strapped to his body wherever he roamed. One day in Yorkville, Toronto's very own appointed beatnik strip, a tall, thin eighteen-year-old musician with a bird-like face and extremely long hair named Bruce Palmer saw Young's similarly lanky intense exterior sauntering up the street with a large amplifier thrust upon his shoulders and towering above his head, which was bent down as his eyes silently blistered the pavement in front of him with their determined glare. Palmer was so impressed by this intrepid vision he ran up and introduced himself as a fellow player, inviting him to his apartment for that initiatory jam session.

Palmer knew a guy who owned a local club called the Mynah Bird, and so corralled his former band-mates in the now-defunct Swinging Doors to become the Mynah Birds, so as to capitalize on the connection and gain a bit of patronage on the side. They were an odd group, fronted by a mincing black guy called Ricky James Matthews who excelled in over-the-top Mick Jagger impersonations, while to his left onstage, Young, who'd lately swapped his first Gretsch for an acoustic twelve-string, would look dour and jangle out these country-tinged lead riffs. It was a goofy combination, but it must have worked, as only a matter of weeks after their first gig they were being invited down to cross the border over to Detroit in order to record demos for Tamla-Motown. It was to prove a short but invigorating education for all of them:

'We ended up signed to Motown – we were the first white rock group to be signed on Motown, for Chrissakes – and when we got into the studio, these session guys at Motown would just suddenly turn up and step in for us all the time when a part wasn't being learnt quickly enough. That's how Motown made records! I mean, no one made records by themselves at Motown. Certain people came in and sang right behind you when you were singing your part! Right over your shoulder!! Real loud!!! Plus, they always had their own drummer and the drums were nailed down. I'd never made a record like that before. I was just learning and watching. Whatever they did was fine with me. I just wanted to learn how they made those great records.'

It ended in tears though, and abruptly too, when the Jaggeresque Matthews was suddenly apprehended by the authorities while they were actually laying down tracks in the motor city. It turned out he was a Navy deserter and he had to spend time in jail as a result. As fate would have it, a decade later Matthews would shorten his name to Rick James, affect a distressingly arch funky pimp fop image, connect again with the Motown label and go on to sell millions of records. Neil Young's fortunes meanwhile lay elsewhere.

By the time he was nineteen, Young had experienced almost all the least appealing aspects that life can offer an inexperienced, youthful professional musician. His best friend and partner in the Squires, Ken Koblun, had suffered a nervous breakdown and his lead singer in the Mynah Birds was in jail for draft evasion. His agent was inept and the last manager he'd been involved with had just OD'd, having, unbeknownst to the Mynah Birds, spent all their record advance on heroin. Young was unfit owing to a taxing regime of malnourishment, lousy (sometimes non-existent) accommodation, lack of warmth and sleep, and too much speed. He'd been badly beaten up while hitch-hiking to one gig and had been left unconscious in a ditch miles from nowhere by his attackers. Even his beloved first car, a Buick hearse, had given up the ghost while driving to a gig through a town called Blind River, an incident that would later inspire one of his most popular seventies songs, 'Long May You Run'. Wherever he turned in Canada, doors shut in his face. He'd had a couple of minor run-ins with the police. And so he decided in the late February of 1966 to sell his few worldly belongings and drive down in his second hearse with bassist Palmer and three or four others to connect with Stephen Stills in the promised land of Los Angeles. The images he saw on the long trip were his first real images of America and have remained vivid in his mind ever since:

'The thing I remember most about that trip was the roads. I mean, Route 66 was still open then. It hadn't become a legend. It was still operating as a freeway. There were no inter-states. We went down on Route 66, ploughed our way through the middle of the country. There were six of us in the car and only one of us – a girl called Jeanine – could drive. No one else had a licence. So I was driving all the time 'cos I was worried she couldn't drive. The only time I let her drive was when I was so tired I physically couldn't anymore. Then I'd be laying at the back of the hearse trying to sleep but listening instead obsessively to the transmission [*laughs*].

'I remember going through Missouri and seeing the roads change to this kind of cement with yellow lines from this kind of black tar with white lines. I thought, "Wow! I've never seen a road like that in my life before." Then there were the drive-in restaurants. You'd drive into a town for miles up over these hills in the South-West. Then you'd get to the crest and come over and you could see thirty miles away this little road of lights twinkling for miles 'cos everything else was black. Amazing! It was like, you were on the moon or something. Then you'd get into towns and there'd be all these neon lights and court houses, restaurants, truck-stops, bars, casinos, pinball arcades all flashing madly at you. Amazing! It was a really fantastic experience. I'll never forget it for as long as I live.'

Only a couple of weeks after settling into the Buffalo Springfield and making LA their new home, Bruce Palmer and Neil Young one day found themselves stoned and vacantly standing in a small crowd witnessing a man with a large oval face the colour of raw beetroot demonstrating how a Vegematic could dice up some greens. Palmer duly turned to find his cohort laid out on the ground, his whole body twitching, his eyes glazed and staring vacantly and a thin trail of drool running down the left side of his mouth. Young was in the throes of his first ever epileptic seizure:

'I think it's like anything else . . . psychological is part of it, but only a small aspect of what causes epilepsy. See, epilepsy is a real thing, it gets triggered by real situations. It's all to do with the brain, the firing of electrons in the brain . . . Plus, there's a misbalance in my body . . . from different things that have happened to me . . . I can feel it all the time . . . See, when your brain gets over-taxed by information coming in, it can suddenly turn physical on you. It just happens. Actually, it's funny, because a lot of people – and several guitarists that I really admire – have pointed out to me how my guitar playing sometimes sounds like I'm anticipating one of these fits. I know what they mean. It's real static.'

The condition was to plague his life for the following years. Never knowing when the cursed fits would strike, he was forced to take medication that made him moody, irritable, withdrawn and generally even more dauntingly intense than he was naturally. Of course, he was still fucking himself up as much as he could, smoking dope copiously and taking speed when extra energy and self-confidence were required. Getting high had directly inspired two of his first Springfield songs, 'Flying on the Ground Is Wrong' and 'Burned', both troubled odes to the grief of psychedelic psychosis.

Listening to Young's first releases via the Springfield, you can cut the discomfort and uptightness in his freakish voice with a blunt pocket knife. In songs like 'Out of My Mind',

'Mr Soul' and 'Broken Arrow', he appears to us as a fractured innocent wandering through a Felliniesque fun-house of rock-'n'roll grotesquery like a eunuch in a bordello, simultaneously fascinated by the images he's subjected to but essentially disconnected from all of it:

'There were a lot of problems happening with the Springfield. There were a lot of distractions too. Groupies. Drugs. Shit, every time I'd made a record before, being in the studio it was just me, the group and an engineer. Otherwise the place was empty 'cos there was nothing else happening. We'd only had two or three sessions up till then, but they were always focused on what was going on. And when you walked outside, you could still think about what you were thinking about when you were inside. In LA though, while you were trying to make a record, just anyone was liable to walk into the studio. Some other band recording down the hall would just turn up out of nowhere. You might be intimidated to meet these guys or anxious to meet them but in a studio you just wished they weren't there.

'And then there were all these other people. I'd never seen people like that before. They were always around, giving you grass, trying to sell you hippie clothes . . . I never knew what these people really wanted. And there were so many of 'em! Not to mention all the women . . . all the clubs, places to go, things to do. I remember being haunted suddenly by this whole obsession with "How do I fit in here?" "Do I like this?" And then came the managers. We had these two guys, Green and Stone, and they were real wheeler-dealers, and suddenly it's all a business and you don't know if you're doing the right thing or not. You keep trying not to do anything too stupid but you have no fuckin' clue what you're doing anyway 'cos you're so young. You started out so happy to actually be making a record. But *then* the record doesn't sound like you wanted it to sound and you don't know why. You start thinking, "Why are these other guys involved? They don't know how to get what you want. Who's the boss? Who's gonna say what's really right?"

'I mean, Stills was the boss, more or less. Except, y'know [*smiles*] . . . there were a lot of my songs in there! He had more songs though and therefore did more of his songs live than I did of mine. Jesus, Buffalo Springfield was a great band but the real core of the group was the three Canadians. See, there were three Canadians in the Buffalo Springfield – me, Bruce Palmer and the drummer Dewey Martin – as well as two Americans. And we played in such a way that the three of us were basically huddled together behind while Stills and Furay were always out front. 'Cos we'd get so into the groove of the thing, that's all we really cared about. But when we got into the studio, the groove just wasn't the same. And we couldn't figure out why we couldn't get it. Oh, man, this was *the* major frustration for me as a young musician, it fucked me up so much. See, it took me all the time it took to make all these Buffalo Springfield records and almost all my first album to figure out I had to go back to the way I'd started back in Winnipeg, back in Thunder Bay when I was recorded live, in order to get my sound just right. Buffalo Springfield should have been recorded live – from the very beginning. The vocals always had to be overdubbed. Our producers made us do the new thing in the studio, laying down a track and then singing. That's why the Buffalo Springfield records don't sound right. All the records were great failures as far as I'm concerned.'

It was all up and down, up and down with the Buffalo Springfield. There was Richie Furay, who was basically a sweet guy and a real pro – he had a way of tip-toeing across the stage with feet turned inward which got the girls screaming but the rest . . .! Young was always getting too intense and freaking out about something. And Stills was just this punk blow-hard with an ego the size of Alaska and an offensively belligerent way of taking control of almost any given situation. Some years later he would admit as much to an interviewer: 'You gotta dig that part of my upbringing in the South was very militaristic. I was in this military school and being taught how to be an *officer*. Anyway, a lot of the ways I relate to situations like that are to simply take command. Because someone has to. Because that is the only thing that will work, and of course somebody like Neil or Bruce is instantly going to rebel. So there was chaos.' Then there was Palmer, who was just getting more and more out there, with the dope and all. He even started to resemble one of those large wooden Indians placed in front of saloons for cowboys to strike matches on. In late '67 he'd got busted during a police raid on the Buffalo Springfield's apartment when Eric Clapton happened to be visiting the place. The abrupt arrival of the force's finest through the front door instantly propelled Young into yet another of his epileptic convulsions. In early 1968, Young would suffer an even worse attack while actually playing on stage with the Springfield.

'Looking back on it now, I'm not sure what happened because now, when it happens, I can control it. I don't know whether I just couldn't control it or whether there just weren't too many new things happening to me. Whatever it was, I'd just get this feeling inside of me and I'd just go . . . Bam!'

He left the Springfield for good in May '68. Too many ego stand-offs with Stills. Too many 'weasels in the woodwork'. That's how Young now referred to the group's managers who had them contractually over a barrel, with precious little financial return forthcoming. Elliot Roberts, an ambitious young agent with bohemian leanings, had latched on to Young and was trying to take control of his affairs just as he was leaving the group. It wasn't always easy, as he would later recall in David Crosby's autobiography:

'When David Crosby was telling me about the Springfield breaking up, he said I should definitely get Neil: he was the one. Even though David replaced Neil in the Springfield for about ten minutes at Monterey, Neil was irreplaceable. He brought intensity to the party that no one else could muster because he was so much more serious than anyone else. It was all life and death to Neil. For example, before CSN&Y, on this lousy bus tour with the Byrds, the Turtles and Buffalo Springfield, the last gig the Springfield did together, we checked into a hotel next to a pitch'n'putt golf course, Neil had a fever on the ride down on the bus and I love golf, so after we checked in the guys all went up to their rooms and I went to the golf course to drive a few. When I got back, Neil fired me. I said, "What for?" and he said, "This is serious, man. This ain't no golf match. This ain't no tourney. This ain't no party. This is serious shit. You should have been in your room waiting for us to call, figuring out something, plotting, planning, figuring out my life, figuring out my career, not playing golf." He hired me the next day and then he fired me again later and rehired me; it was that intense.'

Getting his music out and getting it right was all life and death to Neil Young. To look at him, you'd have thought he was just another stumble-bum stoner concerned with nothing more pressing that the rolling of his next doobie, but his mind fixated incessantly on writing more and better songs and pushing his ragged frame and pot-addled consciousness to the very extremities of their capabilities. It's like he'd always had this vision. Now he was having the chance to make it come real.

At the same time, he was supposed to have been 'sweet' on a young folksinger called Robin Lane and had even moved in with her for a time. But, as much as he would moon over her when they were apart and write aching love songs in her image that would end up gracing his first solo album, when they were together he'd somehow more often than not end up reaching out for his guitar instead of reaching out for her. The guy he could best relate to and his closest ally at that time was this funny-looking little mad professor-type called Jack Nitzsche, this obsessive nutcase whose talents as an arranger had further illuminated many of Phil Spector's seminal productions. He'd played piano on several Rolling Stones sessions too, and now he was doing the same, as well as arranging the charts, for Neil Young's first solo sessions. There was a third party along for the ride as well: another crazy man with exquisite taste that Young had met after being knocked out by the car he was driving, called David Briggs. Somehow he'd talked his way into becoming Young's producer. Warner Bros., his new home as a recording artist, had come up with this exciting new improvised sound gizmo and were going to use Young's début album to try it out on the public. One of the first reporters ever to interview Young, a fellow from the LA press, found him sitting on the veranda of his house in Topanga, the one he'd bought with the advance Elliot Roberts had secured from Warners, and described his mood thus:

'He is nervous about the album, as nervous as if it were the first time he'd been in a studio. During the interview he worries about a single, about the sequence of the songs on the album, and about the mix – the relationship of instruments and vocals. He plays it and is alternately proud and fretful, wanting it to be the best he could possibly do, thinking first that it is, then that it isn't, then that it is, and so on.' Twenty-four years later Neil Young would feel more than justified about those initial anxieties:

'Well, the album itself was great. But then they put this new process on the original mixes called CSG and it just fuckin' killed it. CSG was this new-fangled bullshit process that literally squashed the sound so the music sounded the same in mono and stereo. In other words, it just screwed everything up. Anyway the record company decided to try out this piece-of-shit idea on my record, my very first record, so ... [*trails off, eyes blazing*]. Plus it was me and Jack basically, and it was all overdubs. I was still struck trying to see if that bullshit approach would work.'

Elliot Roberts would often shake his head when he got to referring to his client's unnerving predilection for consorting with 'strange impossible' personalities. Nitzsche and Briggs conformed to this description in their own unique ways, but they were more eccentrics than the flat-out crazies and the walking-wounded types that Young seemed particularly drawn to. One of the latter group had to be this soulful loser with the sad junkie eyes called Danny Whitten, whose group, the Rockets, Young had initially infiltrated not long after joining the Buffalo Springfield, mostly in order to get closer to Robin Lane, who'd originally been bass-player Billy Talbot's girlfriend. Of the former group – well, Neil sometimes liked to hang out with Dennis Wilson, the volatile and somewhat confused drummer for the Beach Boys, after they'd spent some time together in early '68 on a package tour. Soon enough, the drummer would invite Young to meet a very special acquaintance of his, a guitar-strumming maniac he referred to only as the 'Wizard' and Young too would briefly fall under Charles Manson's wayward spell:

'I first met Charlie with Dennis Wilson over at Dennis's house. A lot of pretty well-known musicians around LA knew him too, though they'd probably deny it now. But fuck, why deny it? He was potentially a poet, that guy. The girls were around, too. [Linda] Kasabian and the other one [Patricia Krenwinkel] – they were always there. They'd be right there on the couch with me, singing a song. They were *always* around. And Charlie'd talk to me all the time about how he'd been in jail so much that there was no longer any difference between being in or out of jail. He said, "You're in jail, no matter what side of the bars you're on. It's like Hadrian's Wall OK . . . Every wall has two reasons for existing." So, Charlie . . . what side of the fence was he really on? Who knows? He certainly didn't. And that's what a lot of his songs were about. There was a purpose to what he was doing.

'Listen, he was great. He was unreal. He was really, really good. Scary. Put him with a band that was as free as he was

. . . see, that was the problem right there. No one was ever going to catch up with Charlie Manson 'cos he'd make up the songs as he went along. Every song was different. And they were all good. They were all simple . . . He'd just play a couple of chords and keep on going. The words just kept on coming out. Listen, I actually went to Mo Ostin [head of Warner Bros.] and suggested that they sign him. I referred him. I said, "There's this guy, Charlie Manson, he plays these unique songs and he should be on Warner Bros. records." I mean, if he'd had a band like Dylan had on "Subterranean Homesick Blues", then . . . But he was never gonna get that band, because there was just something about him that stopped *anybody* from being around him for long. *I* was always glad to get out because he was too intense. He was one of these guys that wouldn't let you off the hook. I was always thinking, "What's he gonna do next? I'd better get out this guy's way before he explodes." So I did.'

Soon after these encounters had tapered off, Young rather impulsively married a willowy Californian woman with waist-length blonde hair named Susan Acevedo and moved both her and her seven-year-old daughter by a former marriage into his house on stilts, built right on the side of Topanga Canyon and filled with candles, skin rugs, a recording studio sound system, a dog called Winnipeg and half a dozen Persian kittens: 'Well, I thought that would help, I guess,' he would later confide. 'I thought that would ground me out. I've never been what you'd call a run-around kind of guy with the opposite sex. I was looking for some kind of stability, for sure. I was looking to get a grip [on my life].'

At the exact same time, he also created another flat-out rock group for him to front, Crazy Horse, from Danny Whitten, Billy Talbot and Ralph Molina, guitarist, bassist and drummer respectively from the aforementioned Rockets: 'Crazy Horse . . . the original group all came from New York. They used to hang out on street-corners and sing doo-wop songs when they were kids. They were pretty tough guys, as you might well imagine. That's what made them real tough-sounding musicians.'

Billy Talbot – somehow he and Young had made up over the little matter of Robin Lane's romantic loyalties – was like a little fire-cracker, always bursting with a mischievous energy. Molina was more laid back: he preferred to sit and soak things up with more detached eyes. Whitten, the leader, was tough physically but his doped-out, dirty blond-haired exterior housed another of those fatal fragile hearts that had recently been broken – by a sixteen-year-old girl, no less – forcing its owner to feel compelled to sponge up the void with copious shots of heroin:

'Danny Whitten was the leader, and first of all he was a great singer. He kind of reminded me of Richard Manuel of the Band . . . That kind of feel. It was a wonderful voice for me to sing against. *Plus*, he was a great guitar player. And I could play with him and it felt wonderful. Frankly, there are very few people who can really do that for me. But he could. Until his drug problem got the better of him.'

They certainly weren't the greatest musicians in the world but they played in such an instinctive and primordial way that, when enough pot had been communally smoked and the beat had settled down into a thick swampy groove that managed to sound simultaneously plodding and exhilarating well, then, that's when things always started getting good and giddy and Young could feel he was starting to strike at the very mother-lode of his creative abilities.

While Young and David Briggs were putting Crazy Horse through their paces in five freewheeling studio sessions that would result in the album *Everybody Knows This Is Nowhere*, released in mid–'69 only a matter of months after his ill-starred début, his old sparring partner Stephen Stills was finishing off the first album he was making with fellow egomaniac ex-Byrd, David Crosby, and their mellower Mancunian 'soul brother', ex-Hollie, Graham Nash. Maybe it was because the Beatles were winding down for good in 1969 and the whole sprawling youth culture trip was after a new errant band of self-absorbed minstrels to fill the void with more uplifting 'let's keep the faith' musical bromides and more witless radical posturing. Anyway, CS&N and their début release caught on like wildfire during the summer of 1969, by which time Neil Young had been somehow also recruited on to the musical board of directors, making it suddenly CSN&Y:

'Well, Stephen came up to my house and asked me to join the group. I thought about it and said, "Maybe." *Then* they weren't sure they wanted to put my name in with theirs . . . I told them, "No way." So *then*, after my name was included, I thought, "Shit. Well, sure, I'll do this. But only as long as I can do my own thing with Crazy Horse at the same time." So I did both of 'em.

'See, the way I used to work then – this would be the summer of 1969 we're talking about now – I'd usually go in and record with Crazy Horse at Sunset Sound Studios every morning. Then I'd go to CSN&Y rehearsal in the afternoon through to the evening. Then I'd go home, crash out, get up the next morning and do the same routine all over again. That's when "I Believe in You", "O Lonesome Me", "Wondering" . . . a couple of others on *After the Goldrush* – all those songs were conceived there and recorded there. That's where I first cut "Helpless", by the way, and the only reason the Crazy Horse version didn't come out is because the engineer didn't record the perfect take, so . . . bam, that was lost.'

The truth be known, he rarely felt comfortable in the company of the other three. Nash was a sweet guy who wanted to make the best of everything, but Crosby and Stills were already too coked-up all the time (they'd even toyed initially with naming the group 'the Frozen Noses', for God's sake) and the egos and petty irritabilities were already flying around backstage the night of their first gig proper in the windy city of

Chicago. One of them was always picking on the other for copping out in some way. 'You preach one thing in your lyrics but it's another thing in real life' verbal knife-fights were being staged constantly. The second gig they played crystallized their impact and turned them into overnight icons. It was a perform-ance at the Woodstock festival which would have the general public for ever more linking the self-styled 'super-group' and the three-day music and mud-fest together in their collective mind. A year later there was even a three-hour film and CSN&Y's hyperactive hot-shot of a business manager David Geffen had managed to make them the central act of the whole peace-and-love circus even though they'd originally been thirteenth on the bill:

'I would not allow them to use the footage of Crosby, Stills and Nash in the movie unless they used [fellow client] Joni Mitchell's song with CSN&Y singing it as the theme of the movie. That's how that happened. The producers were simply going to give me what I wanted or that was it. And since I represented a lot of important acts on Warner Bros., Atlantic and Elektra, they just weren't going to fuck with me.'

There were two amazing aspects to this coalition. The first was that CNS&Y had actually played so badly and sung so out of tune at Woodstock, they'd had to go back in the studio and overdub new parts for the consequent film sequence and soundtrack album selections of their performance. The second was that, just prior to taking the stage at Woodstock, Neil Young had kicked up a huge fuss about not being filmed or even mentioned at an event that would arguably do more than any other single stroke of luck to catapult both him and his cohorts to the very summit of superstardom:

'Listen, if you look through every frame of the movie, I'm not in the film. I even made 'em change our introduction. If you listen to the introduction by Crosby Stills Nash and Young on the *Woodstock* soundtrack, it's been edited down and juggled around so it sounds like [*funny voice*] "Crosby . . . Stills . . .

Nash . . . [*laughs*]." 'Cos they had to cut my name out. If you listen out for it, it's actually pretty funny. But that's the way it was. Why? Because I didn't want to be filmed, that's why. 'Cos I was playing, that's why. And I didn't want a fuckin' guy standing in front of me with a camera. We were pretty bad at Woodstock. Nothing jelled, not for me anyway. We were riding on our popularity, that's what it was. Just cresting along.'

After a mind-bogglingly successful first CSN&Y tour of America, Young stuck around San Francisco to help the increasingly volatile quartet record their second release, although technically their first as now it was Crosby, Stills, Nash & Young. In the middle of the sessions, Crosby's girlfriend, Christine Hinton, was killed in an automobile accident during the fall of '69 and that sent him spinning off into a drug-sodden void of intense grieving that lent a tragic edge to the endless nerve-frazzling sessions. Nash would find himself bursting into tears from a combination of the frustrations that were keeping all four so distant from each other and the drugs that once seemed to bring them so close together. Stills, after a whole year of cocaine and mass adulation, was becoming more physically aggressive about asserting his musical leadership upon the rest, but only Young was actually coming up with the kind of timeless songs that CSN&Y would quickly need in order to substantiate their ecstatic following. First, he gave them his most sublime meditation on childhood memory, 'Helpless', for the album that became known as *Déjà Vu*; then, spurred by the shootings of four students at Kent State University in May 1970, he pulled together the increasingly disparate elements of the group to record a song written about the incident, entitled 'Ohio', that remains their most incendiary performance. But by this time Graham Nash had run off with a young woman Stephen Stills had had serious romantic designs on, so that was the end of CSN&Y right there for several years.

By that time, though, Young couldn't have cared less. *Everybody Knows This Is Nowhere* was already platinum, and he'd augmented Crazy Horse with Jack Nitzsche's honky-tonk piano playing, so he took off on a tour, recording each date for a projected live album of new songs. The music that was made during these shows, which later resurfaced on bootleg tapes, remains some of the most exciting of Young's whole career, yet Young vetoed the idea of releasing the material and, owing to his alarm at Whitten's deteriorating condition from heroin abuse, went so far as to sack Crazy Horse at the end of the tour, hoping that this would shock the dazed guitarist into quitting the drug. It didn't. Not long after he gave the Horse their marching orders, a song called 'The Needle and the Damage Done' would unflinchingly document the doomed Whitten's slow, sure decline:

'Then it was the end of a great band, that's what it was. See, people always compare Crazy Horse with CSN&Y . . . that's wrong. You should compare Crazy Horse with Buffalo Springfield and, if you do, you'll find that it's like the Beatles and the Stones. That's the difference. But when Danny was gone, Crazy Horse was just like the Stones without Keith Richards. That's the way I looked at it. And it's never been the same since.'

Still, nothing has ever seemed to slow down Young for too long and he quickly rebounded in the early autumn of 1970 with *After the Goldrush*, his third solo album. The title track was a fairly straight depiction of a weird movie script written by the actor Dean Stockwell 'about the day of the great earthquake in Topanga Canyon when a great wave of water flooded the place'. The rest was divided between the Sunset Sound recordings made the previous year with Crazy Horse and a bunch of tracks recorded in his home and produced once again by David Briggs. By the time the record was released Young had left his wife, even though a picture of them together backstage at some gig made up the main photograph for the album packaging. He'd also outgrown the Topanga house he recorded it in and was moving to a 140-acre ranch he'd just bought (with cash) in San Mateo just outside San Francisco.

Whenever he stopped briefly and allowed himself to glance back over the past two years, Young had much to occupy his thoughts. He was aghast at how many of his dearest colleagues were becoming hopeless burn-outs, and it wasn't just Whitten, although he was certainly the furthest gone. Heroin had also infiltrated the CSN&Y camp, and even members of the rhythm section and road crew were falling like flies under its influence. Meanwhile, the omnipresent cocaine seemed to be turning almost everyone Young came into contact with into a twitching wreck. Young liked to use cocaine himself sometimes, but he always made sure he never let the sensation overwhelm him like it evidently had with these other guys. To top it all, one night Young had walked off stage in the fall of '69, having partaken in all these ultra-positive CSN&Y-type vibrations, to be presented with a photograph of some demented-looking hippie stooge that took up almost all of the first page of a prominent daily paper:

'See, when it first came out that there'd been this horrible murder and the guy's name was Charles Manson, I never put it all together with this other guy Charlie that I'd known. Until one day a mutual acquaintance said something that triggered it off. He said, "Y'know, Charles Manson, the mass murderer – that's the Charlie we both used to know." And I thought, "Oh, shit, so *that* was Charlie!" [*Smiles*.]'

Of course, while those he felt the most drawn to were busy losing themselves down their own haphazard highways, Young's road ahead seemed paved with gold and limitless possibilities. But that didn't make him feel any better, either:

'All I knew was that things were happening really fast for me and that I had a lot of music that I had to get out of me. But, all the time, my biggest problem was always in figuring out how in hell to make the fuckin' records sound right! That was really my only concern. I wasn't concerned about my so-called image. For me, an image becomes meaningless inasmuch as it's always temporary. See, I've gone off on that tangent again, because you asked me about the image and all that. I just couldn't relate to all that side of things because, all that time, I was focused on trying to make the music sound half-way decent. I mean, here I was with all this sudden success, all these fuckin' people loving me and looking at me like I'm something special and yet I couldn't really give it to 'em in return! I wasn't making a sound that I enjoyed or that I thought was representative of what I was hearing in my head. I was almost thinking, "Oh man, this is happening too soon for me. Maybe I'm really a hype."'

And then he had to slow right down for most of '71. He'd been lifting heavy slabs of polished walnut in order to decorate a room in his new ranch and the activity had put his back out:

'Well, my spinal column was literally disintegrating and I had to lay in bed for months prior to recording that album. And I'd met an actress named Carrie Snodgrass, who I quickly ended up living with. We had my first son together, a beautiful little boy called Zeke. So those things were very prominent. That was the content, if you like, but the musical feel of *Harvest* had nothing to do with either one of them. Somehow I just wanted to get *really* laid-back. *Harvest* was me saying, "OK, folks, I can do all those other things, play out on the edge, go nuts and do 'Ohio' and 'Southern Man'. OK. Fine. But later for that." I was saying, "OK, let's just get really, really mellow and peaceful. Let's make music that's just as intense as the electric stuff but which comes from a completely different, more loving place."'

Harvest was released in the early months of 1972 and sold up a storm. Everywhere you'd turn that year, Young's baleful little-boy-lost voice riding on a rolling country groove and crooning about searching for a heart of gold – 'And I'm getting old!' – would be assaulting your senses, whether it was leaping from either AM or FM radio or out of your dope dealer's stereo speakers. One such recipient was Bob Dylan, Neil Young's quintessential hero, then in the final years of his self-initiated period of seclusion from a public who still wanted to worship him as a god and a prophet when all he'd really become at that point was a nervous family man and a semi-retired songwriter lost in the unsettling fog of creative inertia. He'd actually tried to deflate his myth by releasing unspeakably bad records like *Self-Portrait* but it somehow only grew bigger, and now he was stuck in Phoenix, Arizona, standing by helplessly as Neil Young stepped into his shadow. Listening to his plaintive Canuck wail that season made Dylan feel extra-spooky:

'The only time it bothered me that someone sounded like me was when I was living in Phoenix, Arizona, in about '72, and the big song at the time was "Heart of Gold". I used to hate it when it came on the radio. I always liked Neil Young, but it bothered me every time I listened to "Heart of Gold". I think it was up at number one for a long time, and I'd say, "Shit, that's me. If it sounds like me, it should as well be me." There I was, stuck out in the desert someplace, having to cool out for a while. New York was a heavy place. Woodstock was worse, people living in trees outside my house, fans trying to batter down my door, cars following me up dark mountain roads. I needed to lay back for a while, forget about things, myself included, and I'd get so far away and turn on the radio and there I am, but it's not me. It seemed to me somebody else had taken my thing and had run away with it, you know, and I never got over it. Maybe tomorrow.'

But while Dylan moped, Young was out and about again, filming his first ambitious under-conceived mess of a film. An obscure autobiographical thing called *Journey through the Past*, clearly inspired by Fellini (Young also claims Godard as a guiding influence in his movie-making), it documented his dreams and more memorable drug reveries (masked horsemen riding along a beach in pursuit of Young was a particularly favoured sequence) and the incredibly stoned pomposity and self-importance of Crosby, Stills and Nash among many other diverse and unconnected themes. What was most surprising about it when you finally saw it was just how little it really told you about Neil Young, apart from the fact that he was hopelessly self-obsessed and smoked far too much pot.

In '73 his back was fully recovered so he returned to the road, but the tour was jinxed even before the first date had been played. Young had gathered together a fine band, including Jack Nitzsche back on the ivories, but during rehearsals he missed Danny Whitten's presence in his music so much he asked him to join the group as second guitarist. Young's offer was to have terminally tragic consequences, for Whitten was in no fit state to play what was required of him. During rehearsals it slowly dawned on Young that continuing drug abuse had finally eaten away all Whitten's natural talent.

'He just couldn't keep up,' Young would later reminisce. 'Once in the middle of one song he'd slip into another and didn't even know it. I tried and tried but he just couldn't do it anymore.' After several days of witnessing this fiasco, Young simply let him go, giving him the air fare back to LA and some extra cash to tide him over. Later that night he received a phone call telling him that Whitten was dead from a self-administered overdose.

There were other problems on the tour itself, including musicians threatening to leave over money and Young losing his voice. He pieced together a live album of new songs from the tour but it sounded nervous and abrasive most of the time, and Young seemed to have suddenly become openly cynical in his lyrics about the freewheeling hippie doctrines he'd once been associated with via CSN&Y's supposed rapport with the counter-culture. 'You can make it on your own time? / Laid-back and laughing? Oh no!' he'd admonished during the album's grand finale. It was just his way of letting the culture know that the upcoming seventies were going to be very tricky indeed, that all that sixties sweet-talk no longer applied to what lay ahead, and that it was time, for him at least, to get to grips with the dark, deadly undertow of the Aquarian age. His next project made the stomach-churning guitar crunch and cloudy sentiments of *Time Fades Away* seem like a romp through the park. Still haunted by Whitten's memory, Young felt compelled to regroup with the remaining members of Crazy Horse and record some kind of tribute to his passing. While sessions were being booked, Young was informed of another drug death close to home:

'Bruce Berry was the brother of Jan Berry of Jan and Dean who did "Surf City" and all those surf hits from the early sixties. He was a roadie for CSN&Y, Stephen's guitar roadie. He was just a really cool guy, always around, part of the scene. Then all of a sudden, he's not right anymore. *Then* he's selling other people's guitars . . . That's when you know there is a major drug problem going down. Guitars disappearing and he's one of the crew and he's telling us all this bullshit . . . Then he died.'

Young quickly pulled together a bunch of bleak, sinister-sounding odes to the on-going drug culture and recorded them in a series of sessions which involved all the musicians drinking and drugging themselves into near-oblivion. There was a ghostly tribute to Berry entitled 'Tonight's the Night', a couple of numbers that referred ironically to Young's own sodden condition ('Borrowed Song', 'Roll Another Number') and, most chilling of all, the matter-of-fact recounting of a mass murder during a drug deal over an electric grave-yard waltz otherwise known as 'Tired Eyes'. Everyone thought he'd taken the incident from some random newspaper report. In fact, the guy who'd done the killing was yet another of Young's strange, impossible running buddies:

'That actually happened to a friend of mine. My friend was the guy who shot the other guys [*laughs*]. He's doing OK now. He's already been to jail and come back. He wasn't gone for that long, either. It was just one of those deals that turned bad. He didn't have any choice really. The lyric is just a straight narrative account of what happened.'

Needless to say, Warner Bros. and Elliot Roberts were more than a little disturbed by Young's 'new direction'. *Time Fades Away* had sold abysmally in relation to the platinum bonanza reaped by its predecessor, *Harvest*, and the *Journey through the Past* movie had not been greeted favourably by either critics or fans. The record label compelled Young to put his uncomfortably raw mix of *Tonight's the Night* – the title he'd chosen for the album he'd fashioned from those raucous sessions – on the back-burner. But Roberts couldn't prevent Young from going out to tour the *Tonight's the Night* material around Europe in a series of breath-taking performances that found the singer-songwriter more determined than ever to destroy all traces of his old 'sensitive' downbeat-guy persona:

'That tour was so much fun. We were just testing the boundaries, seeing how people would react. We were consciously trying to make the whole thing much less serious. I mean, if the audience were serious when they came to those concerts about me being some "rock god" or "prophet" or something, that show would really fuckin' straighten 'em out [*laughs*]! We just wanted to be as sleazy as possible. We were basically saying, "This is total bullshit, you might as well be gambling and eating while you're listening to this music." That was the motto of the show. "Everything's cheaper than it looks . . . Welcome to Miami Beach, everything's cheaper than it looks [*laughs*]."'

Upon his return to the States at the end of 1973, Young secluded himself in his newly purchased Malibu house and continued to preoccupy his mind with gloomy thoughts. He was drying out from a lengthy drink-and-drugs binge precipitated by the *Tonight's the Night* sessions and continued throughout the subsequent tour, but a deeper angst was daily growing from the fact that he was fast finding he had little in common with the woman who'd borne his beloved only child and who was now living back on his San Mateo ranch. So Young did what he did best: he brooded and wrote songs obsessively trying to accurately reflect what was going on in his soul. A number of these ended up on the down-beat *On the Beach* album released in mid-'74. Both the title track and cover shot portray him standing stoned on his beach, staring out at the sea but seeing only his own problems looming back at him, while just beyond the horizon the whole glorious counter-culture he'd once been so taken with was slowly sinking under the weight of its own selfishness and inherent apathy. It's one of his best albums, but it's evidently not one he's particularly comfortable with these days:

'Oh, that was a pretty dark album as well. It was obscure too. I remember writing and recording those songs just before the break-up of my relationship with Carrie . . . Actually it was just at the very beginning of that.'

By the time *On the Beach* was out in the shops, Young was back filling the stadiums, standing tall alongside his old cronies Crosby, Stills and Nash. He travelled separately from the rest of the group, avoiding the bitching and back-biting that still went on between them as much as possible:

'That '74 tour was really the swan-song of Crosby, Stills, Nash and Young for me. I remember when we started the tour and I wanted to play one of my *On the Beach* songs, "Revolution Blues", which I wrote about Charles Manson. And Crosby and the rest . . . Man, they didn't know if they wanted to stand on the same stage as me when I was doin' it! I was goin', "It's just a fuckin' song. What's the big deal? It's about the culture. It's about what's really happening." See, *that's* why I always went for Crazy Horse over CSN&Y. We tried to record a third album live with CSN&Y in '74 . . . but the problem simply was they didn't have enough material to make a third album apart from me. They ended up doing seven of my new songs on that tour and, if we'd released a live album of that tour, there'd have been seven of mine and one each from the other three. They had no more new songs. That's why I wouldn't let them put it out. 'Cos I didn't want it to be the Neil Young show with CS&N in support . . . Fuck that! That's not what I wanted from working with that group, ever.

'Actually, after that tour we tried one more time to record together at the Record Plant in LA. I walked in and . . . almost immediately everybody got too drugged out and they were fighting all the time. So, one time, I was driving to the studio and I just knew it was going to be a drag so I just turned around and went home. And stayed home, as far as that project was concerned.'

By the end of the year, CSN&Y were gone from his life and so was Carrie Snodgrass. Their final parting provoked a period of even darker brooding for Young, who felt particularly guilty about not being able to provide a solid family unit for his young partially crippled son. A collection of songs directly relating to the break-up that he'd composed and recorded under the title of *Homegrown* was deemed too depressing for release, even by Young's standards, so the singer-songwriter retaliated by pressing for the release of *Tonight's the Night* once more. Warner Bros. relented in early 1975, by which time he'd reunited with Crazy Horse, who'd found one 'Poncho' Sampedro to cover for Danny Whitten's old guitar role. The fruits of their jamming throughout the early part of 1975 were streamlined into a vibrant, sometimes even upbeat collection of songs that were recorded and released under the title of *Zuma*. Starting with a spirited version of one of his first ever compositions from back in Thunder Bay, 'Don't Cry No Tears', it continued on by portraying the singer as alternatively a swinging bachelor cautiously up for grabs ('Looking for a Love', 'Barstool Blues') and a tortured soul deeply wounded by the failure of his most recent relationship. There were also a couple of new meaningless rockers, a strange splurge of rock'n'roll spleen entitled 'Stupid Girl' rumoured to be aimed at Young's Canadian singer-songwriting soul sister Joni Mitchell, and a remarkable fantasy about the explorer Cortez recorded in a live take that also managed to capture extracts of his electric guitar playing at its incandescent peak. Yet even in the midst of this moody meditation on the taming of ancient civilizations, he couldn't prevent himself from referring back to his angst over leaving Snodgrass:

'*Zuma*'s a good one. I was a single man again so there was *that* feeling going on. *American Stars 'n' Bars* is like that too. There was certainly cause for a celebration as I had just gotten back with Crazy Horse. Danny's death changed the dynamics of Crazy Horse. But not the overall feeling of what we were about. We still remember, but – it's a band. Especially when I look at Ralph [Molina] and Billy [Talbot], when I'm playing with them. We go back a long way and there's never going to be a replacement for those guys. And when I feel like playing that kind of music, those are the guys I like to play it with. So many rock'n'roll musicians are out there trying to do something unique – the biggest thing in their way is *how much* they know. Crazy Horse is not about technical expertise.'

The whole album was recorded in David Brigg's house in Zuma, California, and one night, while Young and the rest were recording, the producer happened to peer out of his front window and see a suspicious-looking stranger with beard and curly hair in an anonymous-looking van parked directly in his driveway, listening intently to the music being played inside. It turned out to be Bob Dylan, fresh from recording his own raw depiction of a marriage gone sour in the form of his greatest album of the seventies, *Blood on the Tracks*, furtively checking out his nearest rival.

Young toured with the Horse after that, as well as later putting in some time with the Ducks, a tough bar-band managed by a close friend. He released another fairly upbeat collection, *American Stars 'n' Bars*, which further projected his single man status with much rambunctious country-rock and one of his most outstanding meditations on the overwhelming force of romantic infatuation at first bud, 'Like a Hurricane'. During the sessions, he started dating one of his back-up singers, Nicolette Larson, and the two became an item for a while. Young was still with her when he went to Nashville to record an attempted return to the easy listening country-rock format of *Harvest* that he first entitled *Gone with the Wind* before changing it to *Comes a Time*. Every note sounded polished and there wasn't a single decibel of loud electric guitar to be heard in the mix, but there was still a chilly edge to Young's intense romantic advances in 'Look Out for My Love'. The record also contains his most moving rumination on the ties still binding him to Carrie Snodgrass and little Zeke, a piece of country auto-biography every bit as naked and plaintive as any of Hank Williams's finest rolls over the coals of heartache, a song called 'Already One'.

But even before *Comes a Time* was out on sale, Young was finished with being mellow and reflective and back to being bold and abrasive and holding up the rear with Crazy Horse. Young had heard about punk rock, realized quite correctly that it was basically the kind of racket he and Crazy Horse had been making all along and gathered together a clutch of his noisiest rockers. 'Sedam Delivery' and the remarkable 'Powder finger' were two songs he'd first written in the early seventies when punk was still a fifties slang term for a feisty juvenile delin-quent, then tried to get them recorded by Lynyrd Skynyrd, an ill-starred Southern boogie band renowned for putting Young down by name in the lyrics of their biggest hit, 'Sweet Home Alabama'. 'Out of the Blue' – a terse reflection on the fall of Elvis and the rise of Johnny Rotten – forwarded the theory that in rock'n'roll 'it's better to burn out than fade away', senti-ments that would haunt him profoundly in later years. And there were some radiant acoustic songs on board, principally 'The Thrasher', a magnificent testament to Young's thirst for continual change in which his old colleagues Crosby, Stills and

Nash are portrayed as 'Just dead weight to me/Better down the road without that load.'

Rust Never Sleeps, the album that collected together these remarkable songs, proved to be arguably the finest of his career to date and, as it was released in early 1979 and had presaged a number of other records of almost equal merit, most of the prestige rock critics got together and awarded Young the title of 'Artist of the Seventies' in both *Village Voice* and *Rolling Stone*. At almost exactly the same time he'd married a Californian girl called Pegi Morton who'd grown up living in the area next to his ranch and who was already expecting his second child, a little boy they called Ben, who arrived in November 1978. As the final months of those bountiful seventies scurried by, Young should have felt like he was truly on top of the world. But he didn't feel blessed; no, instead, he felt cursed, cursed with a fatal trick-gene that now caused him to be the father of a spastic, quadriplegic, non-oral new-born baby by one woman, when his first child Zeke, by another woman, had been born with slight cerebral palsy.

'It was too big a picture,' Young reminisced to a journalist from the *Village Voice* many years later. 'Too big. Pegi's heart-broken, we're both shocked. I couldn't believe it. There were two different mothers. It couldn't have happened twice. I remember looking at the sky, looking for a sign, wondering, "What the fuck is going on? Why are the kids in this situation? What the hell caused this? What did I do? There must be something wrong with me." So I made up my mind I was gonna take care of Pegi, take care of the kids. We were gonna go on, we weren't gonna be selfish. That's what I was gonna do, and I wasn't going to hurt. And if you shut yourself off and say, "This isn't going to hurt me," you can't shut it down without shutting it down *totally*. I closed myself down so much that I was making it, doing great with *surviving* – but my soul was completely encased. I didn't even consider that I would need a soul to play my music, that when I shut the door on pain, I shut the door on my music. That's what I did. And that's how people get old.'

Young's domestic upheavals in the eighties seeped into his music-making, throwing his music a curve it never got to bounce back from until the very end of the decade. Many of the songs on the unspectacular *Hawks and Doves* are almost private assertions regarding enlarged family responsibility. The dizzyingly brash and repetitive *Reactor* was conceived to accompany a gruelling therapy programme he committed his child to undertaking ('The programme is driving, implacable, repetitive,' he was quoted as saying at the time. 'And so is *Reactor*.') *Reactor*'s failure in the marketplace compelled him to stomp off Reprise records, where he'd remained since 1969 and the release of his first album, signing instead with the Geffen label. This only precipitated further nightmares for Young. His first album for the label – *Trans* – made no sense to anyone. Apart from Young, that is, who'd fashioned an unintelligible sci-fi rock opera about computers directly inspired by his own son's inability to communicate. ('*Trans* is about communication, about not getting through. And that's what my son is. You gotta realize – you can't understand the words on *Trans* and I can't understand my son's words. So *feel that*!')

After that Young just seemed to get weirder and weirder for a time. A subsequent foray into country music was shunned by Geffen, who wanted more rock'n'roll. So Young quite vindictively gave the label *Everybody's Rockin*, a make-weight and generally pointless fifties rockabilly pastiche, before returning to the country field and inhabiting a Reagan-supporting 'good ole boy' cartoon of a persona that would finally cause David Geffen himself to slap him with a three-million-dollar lawsuit for continuing to make 'unrepresentative' music. An album of crusty mainstream Nashville country, *Old Ways*, duly appeared, however, and this coincided with Young – now in his forties – doing a number of interviews in which, betwixt voicing a disturbingly pro-Reagan bias, he stated that playing full-tilt rock'n'roll was pretty much all a thing of the past for him now ('Rock'n'roll is like a drug . . . I don't want to do it all the time 'cos it'll kill me').

However, these sentiments didn't hinder him from next recording a loud electric rock album – *Landing on Water* – which featured several promising songs left still-born by ill-conceived arrangements and production. Sensing this, Young next relocated with Crazy Horse, and a passable album in the seventies vein, *Life*, resulted from the collaboration. Young celebrated the end of his fractious Geffen tenure by touring extensively with Crazy Horse while at the same time filming a documentary of the event. The tour was frustrating for Young however – Crazy Horse bass-player Billy Talbot was suffering from a drinking problem, and as Young would later claim, 'I would do the song, lay it out and they wouldn't be able to remember the arrangement . . . There's gotta be a memory-retention problem.' Consequently there was considerable ugly friction spilling over into the documentary footage which Young edited together, entitling the results *Muddy Track*.

Uglier still was the friction Young next had to face after committing himself to a second album as Crosby, Stills, Nash and Young. It had started with a promise he'd made during a 1984 radio interview, when he'd vowed to record again with Crosby, Stills and Nash if David Crosby succeeded in conquering his now fabled addiction to free-base cocaine. Three years later, Crosby had achieved just that and Young was left with no alternative but to deliver on his word. Suddenly, his former manager and current bitter enemy David Geffen was phoning up Ahmet Ertegun, Atlantic's elegant head man, demanding 50 per cent of the action if the musician he'd just been suing was involved, screaming down the line, 'Crosby, Stills and Nash are *old fat farts*! The only one with any *talent* is Neil Young! I can't believe we're arguing about this!' However, there was a bigger problem looming, as the addiction that almost destroyed Crosby had now turned its grip on

Stephen Stills. By the end of the sessions – which took place in Young's own ranch house studio – Stills was unnerving everybody with his deranged mush-mouthed behaviour. Guns and free-base equipment were often visible around him, but what was even more disturbing was his deluded insistence about having served in Vietnam when everybody around him had to keep reminding him gently that he'd in fact been playing in the Buffalo Springfield at the time he was claiming to have been on special manoeuvres, killing 'gooks'.

Even though during the recording he'd once remarked disgustedly that the album be entitled *Songs for Balding Base-Heads*, Young still tried to make the best of things. But even an emotive ballad he'd written for all the dispossessed families of the Reagan era, 'This Old House', couldn't disguise the fact that, as Geffen had so acidly put it, Young was the only one in the quartet left with any talent now.

The CSN&Y reunion did have one providential aspect though, in that witnessing his old Buffalo Springfield sparring partner in such a wretched condition soon spurred Young on to pen one of his most powerful rockers ever, 'Cocaine Eyes', a withering indictment of drug paralysis that clearly pointed the finger at Stills and his hateful ego. 'Do I think that cocaine destroyed CSN&Y? Absolutely. Cocaine and ego. Shit, all you need is one and if the other comes around, then it's like an explosion happens.'

Perhaps it was because 'Cocaine Eyes' was just too wounding in its portrayal of Stills, but Young, after recording the number as well as four others in a blazing session held in New York's Times Square and using just a bassist, a drummer and his devastating electric guitar-playing, released the results on a limited-edition EP available only in Japan. 'Eldorado' – that was its title – thus enjoyed a somewhat limited exposure, but wherever it got played as an import release it became clear to those among Young's core following that something had come alive again right at the heart of his creative spirit.

He'd been doing his chameleon act in '88, playing a funky old blues guitarist fronting the Bluenotes, a band with a big, brash horn section, and had managed a freak hit of sorts with the anti-'rock-stars-playing-corporate-kiss-arses' invective of 'This Note's for You'. However, even Young himself seemed somewhat nonplussed by its success: 'I remember writing it in my bus, turning to my driver and saying, "Jesus Christ, this must be the most idiotic fucking song I've ever written." I still can't believe that such a dumb little song could have helped resuscitate my career the way it did.'

I'd first met him a year later, in the late autumn of 1989, after he'd compiled and made available an album called *Freedom* containing three 'Eldorado' cuts, a bunch of mellower items from Young's archives and a great surging instant classic called 'Rockin' in the Free World', 'part anthem, part protest song about democracy and what's going on every day in the streets of America' that even managed to connect briefly with a moment of sweeping world change when it became an unofficial soundtrack item for the demolishing of the Berlin Wall. Young was back in the creative vanguard again but he still seemed most taken with dark visions of humanity. He didn't feel so good about all this *glasnost*, for example. 'This is like the Bible,' he muttered gravely at one point, referring to the relaxing of the grip of communism across the East. 'This is a biblical thing that's going down right now, you understand. And I'm just saying here and now that it's . . . all . . . completely out of control . . . The drugs are gonna be all over the streets of Europe. We've got a lot to deal with here, but it's probably . . . too late.' The only other issue that caused him more consternation was the subject of him 'coming back' after his years in the creative wilderness.

When he heard the word 'comeback' associated with his name, his wise old owl's face would turn suddenly gaunt and foreboding. His eyes would snake out and his hands would stab themselves into the ample pockets of an extraordinary calf-length medicine man coat he was wearing, an artefact of clothing so unsettling to the eye it looked as though Young must have won it off some ill-attired Red Indian wino during a friendly card game. Then he would address the topic with a hard bark to his voice:

'All these reviewers writing stuff about my comeback! . . . Listen, I don't have to come back 'cos I've never been gone. They write stuff like, "Oh, this year Neil Young's OK again." Fuck them, I don't need them to tell me if I'm OK or not. As far as I'm concerned, I've *always* been OK! I just can't associate with anyone or anything involved in a comeback right now. Well, sure, I can associate with Bob Dylan and Lou Reed. Both their recent albums are great. But with us three, you've got to understand – it's a big time in our lives right now. We've come through, we've survived intact and we're still creatively focused. But I can't – and I won't – relate myself to the Who or the Stones or the Jefferson Airplane. Not in the nineties! No way. And I used to love all those bands, particularly the Stones. Only somewhere along the line they lost it for me. And then what happened in 1989 with those mega-tours – that is not what I love. That was nothing more than a remembrance, a swansong. The music the Stones and Who play now has got nothing whatsoever to do with rock'n'roll. Spiritually it's all Perry Como.

'But, I never went away. I just did other things. But I didn't go away, OK! I'm not like some sixties band coming back to take advantage of some wave of bullshit nostalgia. I mean, I'm someone who's always tried systematically to destroy the very basis of my record-buying public. My whole career is based on systematic destruction. For years and years! See, that's what keeps me alive. You destroy what you did before and you're free to carry on. So I've been busy destroying all these things.' He starts to laugh now, in that weird ironic croak of his. 'And now . . . Now I'm just fine!'

Later he would talk about this dream he'd just had in which he'd encountered these miraculous songs he'd never heard before and how he was currently obsessed with getting those songs out of his dreams and down on tape, whatever the consequences:

'I feel I'm moving in the flow of something that is easier for me now. My music has taken me to a place now where I'm not fighting things anymore. Through most of the eighties I didn't want my innermost feelings about life and everything to come out. Back then I had a lot of dark thoughts weighing on my mind, tied into experiences that happened in my immediate family. Things happened to me over those years I had no possible reason or way or capacity to expect to explain. At the same time, this inner voice has always dictated exactly what I have to do, but sometimes I'd wake up in the morning and I'd be given my orders, "OK, Neil, today you're going to make this kind of music." And I'd think, "Oh my God . . . OK I want to do this, I have to do this, but not too many people are going to like it!" But I'd still go ahead 'cos I'd want to hear it anyway.'

The following fall he had those songs he'd been dreaming about nailed down, with a rejuvenated Crazy Horse sending the recording console arrows flying into the red each full-moon-lit night the quartet would convene at Young's ranch to play. Released in 1990, when the very idea of rock'n'roll seemed ever so slightly bankrupt and devoid of creative potential, the album really was something to behold. Certainly, there was no one else – young or old – capable of competing with it in terms of sounding so wild, wilful and true. The Horse now swung harder and longer than the Rolling Stones had for eons, but the real breakthrough lay with Young, who fashioned a remarkable collection of songs mostly focused on facing up to the daunting responsibilities of leading a productive and loving life and then scorched them to ribbons with guitar-playing so hyper and abandoned it evoked the sensation of witnessing some buzz-saw-wielding maniac let loose in a rain forest. But there was something else to the feel of *Ragged Glory*, something truly remarkable. For no longer was Young's most physical electric music powered by a spirit of taut anger. It had been replaced by a force somehow guided by a mixture of joy and exhilaration. 'You've got love to burn/You've got to take a chance on love,' Young would admonish on one track, before joining the Horse to lose himself in a throbbing jam every bit as ecstatic and spiritual as one of John Coltrane's classic extrapolations with his own mighty quartet.

'I'm just a part of Crazy Horse. It's never me and Crazy Horse – no matter what it says on the album sleeves – it's Crazy Horse. When there's a guitar solo of mine on a Crazy Horse record, it's not a guitar solo, it's an instrumental. It just doesn't happen without them. You hear me play with other people, my whole psychedelic side just doesn't happen because nobody but Crazy Horse can really bring it out of me.'

I next spoke to Young a year later, after he'd just finished mixing down two CDs' worth of live recordings from the US *Ragged Glory* tour he'd subsequently undertaken with Crazy Horse, a series of dates that had coincided with America beginning its Gulf War against Saddam Hussein. As a result, most of the music had a genuinely cataclysmic edge to it, with Young and his cronies orchestrating long feed-back finales at the end of most selections that sounded like a series of horrendous bombs ripping a large building slowly to its foundations:

'The war, the tour and this record are all one thing in my mind. You can't separate them. The whole thing was a sign of the times and the record is also very much a reflection of the audience we were playing to. Everyone in the States was so emotionally involved in the Gulf War. We could see and hear it every night, on people's faces, on the TV, on the telephone . . . Each night the audience would be full of "Support Our Troops" stickers, yellow ribbons and peace symbols . . . At one show there was a lady there, maybe twenty-five years old, with two kids, and she was crying through the whole show. So something was really happening with her. She'd come just to try and relate to something she could understand. She wanted to make real contact with me and my music. It was this kind of emotional explosiveness that was the real catalyst for the music you hear on *Weld*.'

He also claimed to be almost through working on his next studio release, a tender acoustic foray brought on after Young's hearing had suffered temporary damage as a result of playing at the excessive volumes required for the *Ragged Glory* tour's sonic firestorms.

'I may do a little more work but basically it's finished. See, after completing *Arc*, I didn't want to do any more of that loud stuff. It would have been like flying into the sun. I feel just like a moth sometimes. It's like someone just turned the light bulb off in time. This next one's very, very quiet, so quiet you can really get up close to it. There's nothing angry or violent about this new music. It's about relationships and feelings. There's a lot of love in it. But it's still very focused and intense. It certainly sounds like the sequel to *Harvest*. I have no problem with that, though. I'm not backing away from that side of me anymore.

'It's so obvious this next record is *Harvest 2*. When you hear it you'll think, "Damn he's finally made that follow-up to *Harvest*. All of twenty years later!" [*Laughs*.] "When's the next *Harvest* coming out?" Farmers have been asking me that for years [*laughs*]. "We all need a good bountiful harvest, Neil." Whether it's better or worse is not for me to say. I wouldn't put it out if I didn't like it. But by the time that record hits the streets, I can guarantee you I'll be into something completely different. So it doesn't bother me what people'll say about the record because I'll be preoccupied with the next project. That's the groove I like to be in.'

The last time I saw him, in Paris in the late autumn of 1992, *Harvest Moon* had just hit the shops and was selling up a firestorm of its own. Yet while his new release promoted his soft folky side, a whole new generation had simultaneously started dressing exactly like Neil Young in flannel shirts and rancid old jeans festooned with patches and playing stoned, wilfully eccentric electric rock'n'roll music in bands that seemed mostly to relocate themselves over in Seattle. They called their stuff 'grunge', but it sure sounded like Neil Young to Neil Young. He caught some of these young cats on MTV when he had occasion to watch it and he quietly marvelled at the unavoidable fact that, after thirty years as the most carelessly dressed musician in all of rock'n'roll, his stumble-bum's wardrobe suddenly made him a major fashion symbol for his elder son's own sartorially challenged generation. 'This fashion stuff . . . It's a little too rich for me,' Young remarked drily . 'I only hope they don't take my old flannel shirts after I die and stick 'em behind glass in some Hard Rock Café!'

The day before our encounter he'd been thousands of miles away in New York, mingling with a mostly older generation of music lovers when he'd put in a special appearance at 'Bob-Aid', his own wry term for the Bob Dylan thirtieth anniversary bash that Sony had hosted for the venerable old icon of contemporary song-craft at Madison Square Garden. Old members of the Beatles and the Rolling Stones had been there, dressed in their chic Armani jackets, swapping tales, wizened folkies like Tommy Makem and hardy old survivors like the great Johnny Cash bonded easily, while a small gaggle of newcomers like Seattle's Pearl Jam looked on saucer-eyed, their jaws slack with amazement at being in the same room with so many of their childhood heroes. Dylan himself chose to see the show via a small television located in his touring bus, which was parked just outside the gig itself. At the show's climax he'd sauntered out into the vast hall, lost within the motions of his own mystique and performed two mesmerizing acoustic selections. His performance was one of three musical peaks, it was generally noted. The second involved Lou Reed grappling manfully with the epic but little-known 'Foot of Pride' – even though he'd had to recite most of the lyrics from written prompts laid out on a music stand. The third was Young, who arrived hot on the heels of Sinead O'Connor and her calamitous reception and duly tore the place apart as, with Booker T. & the MGs backing him up, he crashed into gritty extended amp-ups of both 'All Along the Watchtower' and 'Just Like Tom Thumb's Blues':

'I said to Steve Cropper just before we played the first note, "Listen, Steve, we can just do what the hell we want. If we want to play each one for fifteen minutes, we play it for fifteen minutes! I don't have an *arrangement* as such. Whatever happens is cool by me. If I don't sing a verse and start playing a solo, don't worry, it's OK." See, I chose those songs because I could play them exactly the way I'd play a song with Crazy Horse. I was *real* nervous before "Bob-Fest" last night. I mean, a 200-million potential viewing audience – what the fuck! I was *nervous*. Last night in the dressing-room . . . See, when too many people get in the room, I get light-headed. I start feeling like too much is going on. So I go to the bathroom and just sing vocal scales in the shower. It opens up my voice, so I'll give a better performance, and it centres me, just listening to these musical scales resonating. I'm breathing deeply and the whole thing becomes some sort of an Indian trip. But, also, in its finest hour, it's the perfect excuse for leaving any situation around a show. [*Smiles.*]'

As the nineties got under way it became increasingly clear that Dylan, Reed and Young were now well and truly the three leading lights out of their aged but unbroken generation of mythic rockers. Dylan was there because he was Dylan and because he was still out there performing, even though quite frankly most of the time he appeared to be lost in some deep bewildering mental fog that mostly overwhelmed both his creative instincts and his more objective logical faculties. Sometimes it also seemed like he'd become utterly cynical in his rapport with the rest of the world. He'd walk around in public, his face hidden behind a hooded T-shirt and ski-mask. It had always been difficult to pin Dylan down in the sixties and the seventies, but more recently he seemed to become a mystery even to himself. Why, for example, did he keep touring the world over and over again on a never-ending treadmill of dazed one-nighters? 'I've tried to get away from working but I never could,' he'd admitted during the mid-eighties. 'I wouldn't know what else to do. I would be lost.' He complained constantly about how he hated his fans thinking they knew him and treating him 'like their long-lost friend'. He'd long ago separated from his wife Sara and was now rumoured to have a 'long-time companion' called Carole Childs, but there were a lot of other women passing through as well. 'It's lonely where I am,' Dylan had once remarked during his drugged-out dandy phase back in '66. More than twenty-five years later, little appears to have changed.

Reed was another case altogether. Like Dylan, he'd done his great early work in the sixties, although he'd achieved it as composer for the largely under-appreciated Velvet Underground. He actually became successful in the seventies but muddled thinking from drug abuse had propelled him to create an image for himself as some slightly phoney degenerate street reptile. By the end of the seventies – and several frustrating albums later – he married a New York woman, Sylvia Morales, swore off drinking and drugging, and determined to refocus himself creatively. After that he made some fine rejoicings in the early eighties, principally with the splendid *Blue Mask* album and the later, jauntier, *New Sensations*, featuring the fabulously inane hit single 'I Love You Suzanne'. And then, like Young, Reed experienced some kind of creative breakthrough towards the end of the eighties which moved his work on to a whole new plateau. *New York* had some dazzling poetry going for it as Reed stealthily eased himself into the role of Swiftian social critic of all-American heartlessness and bigotry. The follow-up, *Songs for Drella* – a duet with former Velvet Underground eminence John Cale – mourned the passing of mentor Andy Warhol eloquently, and the album after that, *Magic and Loss*, movingly wove its entire theme around the deaths by cancer of two of Reed's dearest friends. Reed still maintains a long-standing reputation for being weird and difficult, particularly with the press, but his often icy exterior had clearly thawed out enough by 1993 to undertake a Velvets reunion tour, summoning performances from his former comrades, each of them now in his or her fifties, that often dwarfed the muffled intensity of the recorded originals.

But let's be honest, Neil Young was currently doing better than both of them because, unlike Dylan, he was still 100 per cent focused on all the creative aspects of his art, and unlike Reed, Young didn't just appeal to the art-rock crowd. He had the old beer-drinking guys with their little grey-haired pig-tails, and the young punkers with their back-to-front baseball caps and 'grunge' fixations. He still had the stoners and the loners, shy young souls who felt unattractive and rootless. But he also now had the families who respected what he'd achieved as a married man who'd committed so much of his energies to rearing his gravely disadvantaged child. Indeed, Young himself had finally come through the darkest of dark tunnels, beaten back all his most hateful impulses and let his heart brim over with the soothing balm of forgiveness: 'Something just opened up inside me,' he'd say softly. 'I don't know what it is but I can feel it every day now. I don't take anything for granted anymore. For example, I've just begun to feel really thankful for all my old bands, be they Crazy Horse, the Stray Gators, the International Harvesters and the Blue Notes, not to mention Crosby, Stills and Nash, for how they've been able to help me. I can just go from one to another and they're quite used to me doing this now. I know of no other musician who's afforded the luxury of such a huge musical support network that will help me do what I feel I have to do. Rather than worrying about moving away and leaving them behind and not knowing how to deal with saying goodbye, I deal with it now. I try to be as understandable and easy-going as possible.'

He'd even written an open letter of a song on *Harvest Moon*, called 'One of These Days', thanking them all for making his music sound so good over the years. Still, Young couldn't help but wonder just how many of his old musical buddies were still receptive enough to be touched by the lyric's sentiments. One of the Blue Notes had just died. Dallas Taylor, CSN&Y's first drummer, was waiting for a liver transplant, because he'd wiped his own one out from too much drink and drugs. There was Stills himself, still floundering around in his own deluded ego-bubble. And then – worst of all – there was the grisly case of Rick James, better known to Young as Ricky James Matthews, the outlandish black Jagger impersonator he'd played with when both were members of the ill-fated Mynah Birds back in 1965. James had finally lost all control from freebasing cocaine constantly and had ended up kidnapping two separate women, raping and torturing them with the aid of his equally demented girlfriend. Young would just shake his head quietly when he pondered the fates of those lost souls, for he knew how closely he had come in the past to getting permanently side-tracked down the same haphazard highway of hedonistic blow-out.

'And I was very lucky indeed to be able to get out of that state too. I don't know what saved me. I think I've just had an uncanny ability to escape. There's no magic to it, but it's like a little light goes on. And when the light goes on, I leave. I just have to get creative about why I'm going. See, I see my best art as one magical accident after another. I try not to edit anything and to record each song real quickly and then move on to the next bunch . . . I don't see change as a curse. It's just part of my make-up. It's the structure. Without change the whole thing will just fall apart. I'm not just talking about rock'n'roll here. I'm talking about my life. I've got to keep moving somewhere. I've written some of my best songs on the move, driving on a long journey, scribbling lyrics on cigarette packets while steering. I like that style, though I tend to get pulled over a lot by traffic cops for driving erratically [*laughs*]. They just pop into my head, these songs and ideas, while I'm driving along, and when I get home I move over to the typewriter and sometimes what comes out is good and sometimes it isn't . . . But it never stops.

'In a sense, it's all about running away. I've been running all my life. Where I'm going . . . Who the fuck knows? But that's not the point. The point is just to see how long you can keep going strong. And right now there is no end. The way I feel now, I can keep going for a long time.'

Kurt Cobain, 1967–1994

On 8 April, 1994, the day that Kurt Cobain's death was duly made known to the world, several of the Nirvana leader's closest peers and kindred spirits found themselves staggering around Paris, trying to promote their latest albums to the French media but getting bombarded instead by insistent queries about the exact nature of their relationships with the recently coma-ridden Cobain. You could see they were sick of hearing the guy's name, of being asked what drugs he was really taking and what his boisterous spouse Courtney Love was really like. Thurston Moore from Sonic Youth – who personally introduced Nirvana both to their current record label Geffen and their management firm Gold Mountain – is a normally garrulous fellow, but whenever he was asked about Cobain's condition, he would grow uncharacteristically subdued: 'It's a sad business what's going on with him right now,' the Sonic Youth guitarist commented cryptically at one point. 'It's too bad as well, 'cos Kurt's a nice guy. You only hope he can come through something like that.'

Only a few streets away from where Moore was holding forth, the humongous Tad Doyle and his group Tad – Seattle-based bosom buddies of Cobain and the rest of Nirvana from the very beginning – weren't feeling much like commenting on their old buddy Kurt either, mainly because Tad had recently been kicked off a Nirvana support slot by Kurt himself after the 300+-lb guitarist referred to Courtney Love in the press as a 'bitch'. 'Sure, I wouldn't have said it if I thought Kurt would react that way,' remarked Doyle slightly tetchily, 'but saying that doesn't alter how I feel about the woman.'

Finally it was up to Soundgarden to really let the spleen roll on the subject of their Seattle rivals: 'Cobain and Vedder – those guys really have a hard time of things,' remarked their guitarist Kim Thayil at one point during the afternoon. 'People follow them around all the time with cameras in their faces and they always want to know what drugs they're taking. Their fame happened overnight, see. One minute they're the guys in the street minding their own business and playing their guitars. The next minute they're older, they're millionaires, and they're on every magazine cover in the world. These two guys, overnight, their lives were shattered. With Soundgarden, we were gradually obliterated. We had our fingers removed one at a time. Cobain and Vedder just had their heads chopped off.'

Two hours after Thayil's remark was made, at almost exactly 7 p.m., he – along with the rest of Soundgarden and Tad – got the news via a transatlantic phone call made to the promoter of the Paris venue they were playing that night. The fame-leeches hadn't chopped Cobain's head off; he'd blown it off himself with a shotgun while all alone, having alienated practically everyone he'd ever been close to. He'd taken a bunch of drugs and written a rambling, rather pathetic suicide note, then purposefully placed his identity card and driver's license on his chest so that whoever found him with his face splashed all over the wall would know instantly who was lying there. This time, quite clearly, Kurt Cobain didn't want any mistakes made about how he was going out.

Coming only a few months after the gifted young actor River Phoenix's equally senseless OD, Kurt Cobain's suicide is likely to be one of those white-hot media enquiries destined to run and run as more sordid tidbits of his singular slacker eccentricities rise to the surface and yet more fair-weather flannel-brained friends 'who knew the real Kurt better than anyone else' spout self-righteous eulogies about the terrible price of fame and how all the media vultures never giving him any peace is what really caused him to pull that fatal trigger.

Cobain himself belly-ached about it to the press almost as ceaselessly as he bemoaned those strangely undiagnosable 'stomach problems' that so cursed his life, but I always saw his griping as a punk-rock pose and essentially a cop-out on his part. I mean, this guy was planning on being a rock star from the age of two. The only thing he ever found halfway motivating was playing guitar, writing songs and singing them in a voice that sounded like one of those chamois-leather cloths used for washing cars being methodically ripped down the middle. In truth, Cobain probably had all his 'major-league rock icon' moves worked out far in advance of the early fall of 1991 when his trio finally got catapulted rudely into the greater public eye. He always professed to hate all the attention with which fame presented him, yet the first thing he did upon going platinum was to marry Courtney Love, a young woman who wantonly draws attention to herself like a magnet sucks up tiny ball bearings.

Throughout Michael Azerrad's excellent biography of Nirvana, *Come As You Are*, Cobain comes across as part likeable sensitive tortured soul and part petulant whining mess. The more you read about him, the more you realize that nothing was ever good enough for this guy. His parents let him down by splitting up when he was eight and he could never forgive them for subsequently making him feel so unwanted and bereft of self-esteem. He was rather a sickly, underdeveloped figure of a young man who got picked on a lot, but the one time he responded to a physical attack he got so caught up in his rage he put his assailant in a hospital with a coma. He clearly felt an overwhelming spiritual kinship with all the outsiders of society, openly fantasizing about being gay even though he was really just another slightly confused hetero-sexual. He'd become a confirmed pothead as early as the age of ten and naturally felt drawn to an older group of local stoner outcasts, at least one of whom robbed chemists from time to time, duly initiating a thirteen-year-old Cobain into the perilous joys of consuming narcotic and opiate medication. He always claimed that the intense stomach pains that blighted his life from his mid-teens to his untimely death came from some unknown source, but the years he spent punishing his intestines with all manners of cheesy pain pills washed down with the most disgusting codeine-infected cough medicines available almost certainly provided the direct reason why his poor old guts ached so viciously. In fact, as far as the drug abuse and overwhelming suicidal impulses starting to engulf him, you could argue that Cobain was a lost and broken soul just before *Nevermind*'s cataclysmic success, if Azerrad's depiction of late 1991 is any indication. Here he was with all this beyond-his-wildest-dreams stuff happening to him, all this vital music pouring out of him, all this new-found acceptance coming his way as well as money and acclaim, and all the guy wanted to do was sleep through the whole experience.

'I would prefer to be in a coma and just be woken up and wheeled out on stage and play and then put back in my own little world,' Cobain is quoted by Azerrad as blithely admitting at one point. 'Everyday simple pleasures that people might have in having conversations or talking about inane things I just find really boring, so I'd rather just be asleep.' Add to this somnambulistic propensity a sudden jolting rise in one's immediate cash flow and the noisy arrival in your day-to-day existence of a woman you see as the love of your life and who loves to get high on dangerous drugs just as much as you do, and you have all the ingredients you could possibly need for impending personal disaster. This word 'tragedy' keeps getting thrown around about the way this guy went out, but how much of a tragedy is it really when someone who so ardently craves to embrace the void twenty-four hours a day finally gets his wish? I still can't get over the fact that here was a man who, when first revived after his last suicide-bid coma in Rome, scribbled 'Fuck you' as his personal message to all those who'd succeeded in pulling him back to life. In 'Smells Like Teen Spirit,' Cobain's text shifts from lines ringing with howling cynicism towards the whole so-called cathartic rock-'n'roll experience he and his group seem by the same token so totally swept up in, until they descend on one word which he concludes the song by screaming over and over again. The word is 'denial', something the singer as a hardened junkie and a hater of life knew far too much about for his frail soul to come to terms with. Even the sketchy details of his final days currently available scream volumes to anyone conversant with the way heroin addiction first breaks its victim's spirit, exiles him from his nearest and dearest, drives him crazy, and then casually snuffs him out, after yet another night of soul-sucking moral conflicts and the black funk of hopelessness which even the most numbing high can't obliterate proves too unendurable to even contemplate. Cobain's denial of his drug addiction had sent him off on the lam from a drug rehab clinic, had apparently destroyed both his group and his marriage, and finally caused him to deny himself his own life.

It remains a heart-rending scenario, however, because the guy was somebody's father, somebody's husband, and somebody's son, and his embracing the void will leave a gaping void in their lives that won't vanish as quickly as all the tawdry headlines. His fans and admirers will continue to play his music, salute his unwashed image whenever it gets aired on TV and quickly start looking around for some new maladjusted-but-charismatic young unwitting voice of a generation on which to hang their hopes and focus all their wild romantic fantasies. Countless articles will appear mourning the death of grunge and tossing in suitable Sid Vicious comparisons, but this is just a sad little tale about a guy who never felt good about being alive, who channelled that screaming unease into a remarkable body of rock'n'roll performances, and who then ended it all by shooting his face off. One can only hope his soul has finally found some sort of rest.

Iggy Pop: The Innocent

This is sublime: to be cruising through Miami's sleek, well-heeled South Beach drag on a warm summer evening with a cool ocean breeze in my face and Iggy Pop – a human blow-torch on stage but pleasantly restrained when driving – behind the wheel of his recent purchase, a huge, orangey-red 1969 Cadillac. Tonight I am the passenger, but we're not visiting any cities' ripped backsides here. Instead, Iggy is playing tour guide to his new home stretch, dutifully pointing out myriad Miami beauty spots and points of local notoriety as we swoosh along highways separating large expanses of glowing, luminous seascape and clean-looking, well-marked roads with names like Ocean Drive and Flamingo Road. So do you get to hang out much with Madonna and Ingrid Casares at their big club, Liquid? 'Nah [dismissive shrug], their shit's too rich for me.' So where exactly did Jim Morrison expose himself when they busted him down here in 1969? 'I honestly don't know,' – for once he seems genuinely taken aback. A moment later, we pass a pristine-looking auditorium named after the corpulent comedian Jackie Gleason. 'Maybe it happened in Jackie's place there,' Iggy offers before diving into a spirited rave on the actor's remarkable, dead-eyed performance as Minnesota Fats in 'The Hustler,' followed by a respectful nod to Don DeLillo's memorable depiction of a drink-addled Gleason during the opening chapters of his labyrinthine *Underworld*.

Iggy first set eyes on Miami when he came here in 1970 after his first group, the Stooges, had splintered apart and a big

New York rock manager named Steve Paul flew him down to work with a 'hot' guitarist of the period named Rick Derringer. 'Me and Derringer never really clicked, but my love of Miami bloomed like a motherfucker. I remember when [David] Bowie's boy Tony DeFries started managing me a couple of years later, one of the first things I told him was, "Hey, you should send me and James Williamson [Stooges guitarist] down to Miami, man. We'll get healthy there. We'll stay straight – honest to God!"' He starts cracking up here. 'Then, a couple of years ago a rich friend of mine needed some cash for some reason. He came and tried to sell me some paintings which I didn't particularly care for. So then I suggested maybe he could sell me one of these "condos" he owns down in Miami.'

The upshot is the modest home he now owns and operates from over in Miami Beach, which we'll be seeing more of in due course. Iggy used to live in a large apartment overlooking Avenue B in New York City, but moved out over a year ago after breaking up with his wife of fourteen years, Suchi. Their divorce has not yet been finalized, but by the end of the year it will be. 'Now, of course, some of everything of mine is also hers,' he tells me. 'She's now as secure as I am. We're both very, very financially secure.'

He claims he and Suchi are still friends: 'I just spoke to her on the phone this evening.' Still, the breakup has clearly been an ordeal. 'It has been a long, arduous, drawn-out process for both parties' is his idea of an understatement here. Like the apartment his ex-wife now owns, Iggy's new album, released next month, is also entitled *Avenue B*. People will call it a divorce album, but it's not about his marriage breaking up so much as it's an unflinching warts-and-all documentation of his life and various affairs since leaving his wife. The way he tells it, he's had a fairly serious thing going with a young, voluptuous-looking Argentinian woman for the past couple of years, but he also admits there's a girlfriend of sorts he sees here in Miami from time to time. 'She's twenty-three – into that whole "dance" scene with the Ecstasy and that Special K shit.' (Iggy quickly adds that he hasn't been tempted to try either drug, but most likely took something like them while in the Stooges.) The album is about these – and presumably other females – trying to ultimately cage him in, but at the end of the day, Iggy pulls the rug from under their crafty monogamous designs and extricates himself to wander freely in his slightly sad, midlife emotional void.

The most 'adult' record of Iggy's career, with only three rockers and loads of confessional crooning over acoustic guitars and cool jazz accompaniment, it's remarkable for several reasons, not least the fact that Iggy is rarely looking to be liked or easily sympathized with here. Instead, he's hellbent on supplying the listener with a raw, uncompromising autobiography of a lonely middle-aged guy dying to be loved but too terrified of getting close to anyone else to make the required leap of faith. In a very real sense, *Avenue B* is a modern musical equivalent of Marlon Brando's performance in Bertolucci's *Last Tango in Paris*; certainly it's a parallel Iggy has already taken into consideration. His eyes light up when I mention it. 'It's funny because that image crossed my mind as well. They're both about this image of a middle-aged man out on his own – who can't relate too well with other people – and who gets involved with a young girl and who ends up blowing his stack? Of course, Marlon died at the end of *Tango*. I don't die at the end of my album. Quite the opposite.

'The overall stance of the record – the concept, I suppose – is that I am categorically not going to be made a slave or a fool of by women. Ever. Even if by so doing I end up doing something immoral or against my destiny. What I'm saying is that ultimately I'm willing to defy my own motherfucking destiny in order to maintain my sense of personal strength and self-respect.'

We pull up to a quiet main street, and he guides me into one of his favourite local eateries – an unpretentious, downmarket Chinese restaurant. The owner and various waiters congregate around Iggy like birds around St Francis of Assisi while he exchanges greetings and brusquely orders a large Oriental chicken dish and some sparkling water. Under the establishment's modest lighting I get my first good look at him close up. He has a full head of chestnut-brown, shoulder-length hair parted precisely at the centre. Not much grey and it doesn't look like a dye-job either. His face and torso – swathed in a black, pin-striped shirt open to his stomach – are tanned so deeply and luxuriously his skin is an even darker brown than his hair.

His face is weathered and lined, tapering into a pointed chin accentuated by his fiery eyes, prominent cheekbones and maniacal grin. His body, with all its myriad exotic contours and tight little muscles, remains as lean and supple as it's ever been. Iggy doesn't work out at a gym – he tried briefly in the mid-eighties but quickly found the experience unappealing. Instead, he commits himself to long, daily 'stretching' exercises. More recently, he's taken to practising half an hour of t'ai chi a day; one of his few real friends in Miami is an old Chinese guy who teaches yoga and other forms of Oriental discipline locally. Iggy's one of his pupils. Self-discipline has been a big issue with him for a long time now.

He doesn't smoke cigarettes currently and sticks to a regime of one glass of wine during his evening meal. He tried having a second one at lunchtime for a while 'but it just blurred my senses too much.' Drugs haven't really played any part in his day-to-day life for fifteen years. Every now and then he finds himself tempted to puff on a marijuana joint, but he finds the chemical generally makes him 'too tentative and paranoid to function properly for any length of time.' Cocaine and heroin haven't re-entered his life in the nineties, though three years ago he had to confront his son Eric and place him in drug rehab for having become addicted to the very same stimulants that had so cursed his father's life during his early years as a musician.

Iggy's often troubled history with his only son plays a central theme in a new documentary on the singer and his thorny past, commissioned by America's 'hot' cable music channel VH-1 partly as a prelude to *Avenue B*'s release. An hour-long, slightly tabloidy creation, the program is still compulsory viewing: first and foremost, for all the Stooges' archival video footage wonderfully woven together and reshown so that younger generations can finally see what all the fuss was about. Also, all the living Stooges members are relocated and interviewed again on camera. Ron Asheton, the original guitarist, currently a beer-drinking gun nut living with his mother in Michigan, looks fat and sounds bitter. His successor, James Williamson, is shown to have morphed from the hollow-cheeked, guitar-strangling reprobate of his youth into a straight, solid-looking, slightly sunburnt fifty-year-old businessman currently heading a computer-software business over in Silicon Valley, California. Drummer Scott Asheton – now living in Florida with his wife and two children – manages to deliver some cool soundbites. 'It was the period when everyone around was telling people to turn on, tune in and drop out,' the drummer nonchalantly explains during the show when asked about the Stooges' 'social context.' 'So that's just exactly what we did.'

Iggy's quotes are invariably the most memorable, though: on occasion they're even genuinely shocking. 'I was shooting up every day and passing out every night, drinking and drugging and screwing and . . . defying,' he proudly blurts out at one point. Meanwhile the Stooges' first manager, Danny Fields, grimly reminisces about having to pull a blood-drenched syringe out of the singer's arm after he'd overdosed on heroin in a toilet just prior to a performance. Ron Asheton remembers Iggy defecating onstage and having sex with sundry females in the audience. Later, Asheton recalls a performance event in Los Angeles during 1974 when the singer begged to be beaten and stabbed repeatedly while onstage, ending the spectacle by being bound inside a gunny sack and dragged into a nearby gutter, where his bleeding, unconscious corpse was left to rot.

For his part, Iggy never backs away from talking candidly about his darkest moments. At one grim juncture, he and his son reminisce about the early eighties when the eleven-year-old Eric spent his days and nights not in school but following his alcoholic father around New York bars watching him drink, snort cocaine and pick up girls night after night. 'He did exactly what I did,' Iggy states unflinchingly. 'I know people are going to find that horrific but, hey, that's who I was!' Still that doesn't mean to say that he likes the finished result. In fact, he can get quite worked up when thinking about how it ultimately misrepresents him as an artist.

'This is the key thing that has always been misunderstood about me. All this fucking crap they say I did in this hour-long TV show – close-up on the blood, close-up on the dick, close-up on the butt, close-up on the profanity – all this terrible shit I supposedly did. I only did it because I believed I was in the right and that I was playing the actual music that was appropriate and good to reflect that time and place and the music that real people who had any real life in 'em wanted to hear. And the only reason my music was fuckin' disseminated was because it contradicted the motherfucking commercial pyramid. Yet things have changed. I've been vindicated. Frankly, throughout my life I've always felt I was completely innocent. I originally wanted to call my last record "Innocent Little Doggie," but I was a little hesitant about making that big a point of it. But, yeah . . . I see myself as a genuine innocent. Always have done.'

Even in the Stooges?

'Yeah. There was something deliberately pristine about us. The music . . .'

I'm not talking about the music. I'm referring to your lifestyle then. That wasn't innocent at all.

'Well, I'm just talking about the music! Music and performance – that's all that's important here. That's all you owe people; that's all that's anybody's business. Everything else is justified by the moral integrity of the finished work.'

Iggy's 'finished work' began appearing in 1969 with the release of the Stooges' self-titled debut album, followed shortly afterwards by 1970's *Funhouse*. In 1972, after all manner of personal grief, Iggy reconvened the Stooges and – augmented by guitarist James Williamson – moved to London, where he recorded *Raw Power*, which David Bowie helped remix. If he'd just made these three records and then crawled off and died – as most business insiders of the time were tartly predicting – his immortality would still have been assured. For the Stooges' recorded music and the legends surrounding their extraordinary live shows were the key ingredient that fuelled the self-destructive ranting spirit of so-called punk rock several years after the group itself had finally self-destructed in 1974.

The music never really sold at the time of its release, though, and things went from bad to worse until Iggy ended up checking himself into a Los Angeles mental institution in the early summer of 1975. ('They ended up diagnosing me a hyper-manic – that's one level below becoming a full-on manic depressive. But they also told me, "Listen, you're really not insane."') David Bowie, himself struggling with grave drug dependency problems at the time, reconnected with Iggy at the mental hospital, and the pair later went on to live in Berlin, record and even tour together. *The Idiot* and *Lust for Life* – the two seventies albums they made together – remain new wave classics, probably as powerful in their way as the Stooges' superhuman recordings.

From then on, Iggy's solo career became something of a hit-and-miss affair. His albums have sometimes been excellent

(1979's *New Values*, 1990's *Brick by Brick*, the forthcoming *Avenue B*) and sometimes they've been a bit lame (1981's *Party*, 1996's *Naughty Little Doggie*). Drinking and drugging caused his live shows to be precarious affairs until 1986 when – clean and sober – he returned to the stage deathly determined to prove himself one of the hardest-working professionals ever to perform in a rock'n'roll context. His still-demented live shows and weighty punk-godfather cred have made him much loved and handsomely rich throughout the nineties. He's like God in heaven to all the nouveau punkers with their piercings, as well as to the sad-eyed stoner alternative rock crowd. Kurt Cobain was so in love with Iggy he wrote one of his very last (unreleased) songs expressly for him. (Iggy – slightly mistrustful of Cobain's widow Courtney Love's 'merry-widow-of-grunge act' – hasn't even bothered to hear the track.) Iggy made a lot of money by having his name and music associated three years ago with the whole *Trainspotting* phenomenon.

Right now in the States, he's riding a new wave of contemporary cool – as the media-ordained spiritual Mac Daddy forefather to Michigan's latest musical hoodlums, the platinum-selling, controversial white boy rappers Eminem and Kid Rock. The accumulating publishing revenue from numerous cover versions of Stooges and solo material over the years, coupled with a massive cash injection from the sale three years ago of no less than three Pop compositions for use in high-profile commercial advertising campaigns, have all conspired, finally, to turn the fifty-two-year-old singer into a millionaire.

Dinner conversation inevitably turns to a discussion of *Velvet Goldmine* – last year's controversial celluloid fantasy about glam rock in early seventies London, starring Ewan McGregor as Kurt Wild, an Iggy ersatz who falls in love with the David Bowie-like Brian Slade. Iggy claims he hasn't seen it yet. 'To tell you the truth, all I thought about when *Velvet*

Goldmine, or any other project pertaining to be about me, rolls along, is "Ah well, there'll be some more people talking about me tomorrow. Maybe they'll be playing more of my old stuff as a direct consequence." That's all I think. Other than that, I do not give a fuck! Someone asked me when *Velvet Goldmine* came out, "Hey, do you know they portray you as gay?" Like I'm supposed to give a shit! [*bursts out laughing*] I couldn't care less.'

So you're saying you have no problem whatsoever with the film portraying you and Bowie screwing each other's brains out?

'That absolutely just strikes me as hilarious. It's fantastic how much work other people do for me. It's incredible! [*screams with laughter*] I didn't even have to lift a finger, and yet I've been given all the benefits of a high-profile homosexual affair. And I didn't even have to bend over for it!'

Bowie and Iggy's relationship has cooled considerably over the years since the late seventies (there was a brief reconciliation in 1986 when they recorded 'Blah Blah Blah' together). When Bowie was celebrating his twenty-five years of success at a special Madison Square Garden concert in 1996, he pointedly chose not to invite his former colleague to share the stage with him. Even if he had, Iggy probably wouldn't have shown up anyway. 'We'd just had enough of each other,' Iggy reminisced to VH-1 recently when asked about Bowie, pinpointing the competitive essence of their relationship. 'It was petty stuff like, "Well, I don't like the way you smoke your cigarette any more!" "Oh yeah, well I don't like your hair!" "Oh yeah, well I don't like your shirt." "Oh yeah, well I don't like your girlfriend!" All just silly musician shit.'

As a result, any thoughts of the pair reuniting in the studio seem very distant and far away at the moment. However, Iggy has seriously considered reuniting the Stooges over the past four years. The singer and the Asheton brothers were set to enter the studios with US mega-producer Rick Rubin in 1996, but Iggy pulled out at the last minute. *Avenue B* was originally promoted as a Stooges album until it became clear that Iggy's new songs were too personal to work as a group project. According to Art Collins, his gently spoken manager of thirteen years, 'Iggy really wants to play with the Stooges again. He just needs the right reason to arrange it. If they were to get elected into the Rock'n'Roll Hall of Fame, that would be perfect. He could play with them one last time.'

But that, according to the singer himself, is unlikely ever to happen. Thrice nominated throughout the nineties, the Stooges have so far failed to make the final cut, even though their music has been so influential on what passes for contemporary rock these days. According to Iggy, 'I've been told, unofficially, by those connected to the powers that be at the Hall of Fame, that "Oh Iggy, if you're a good boy then maybe one day we might condescend to let you enter our illustrious pantheon. But those dreadful Stooges – forget it! They're never getting in!"'

'We played in Cleveland last year with Pearl Jam,' remembers Collins, 'and I took Iggy over to the Rock'n'Roll Hall of Fame because he hadn't actually been inside the place. And they had his first guitar – this weird Hawaiian thing that he'd painted himself – as an exhibit, as well as the original silver evening gloves he wore on stage to hide his track marks during the Stooges. He tried to brush it off by saying it felt corny but nice, but I could see that inwardly he was very excited by being represented there.'

But ultimately being passed over by the Hall of Fame hierarchy is just one more example of Iggy's singular, ongoing dilemma as American rock's ultimate outsider. He's never really had a big hit single in America. His biggest-selling US album, *Brick by Brick*, barely grazed the Top 30. He's always been in strong demand as a live performer, but when in 1996 he signed on as headliner of a travelling alternative rock festival known as ROAR, he found himself often playing to three-quarters-empty stadiums.

By contrast, Iggy Pop has always been way more popular in Europe than in his homeland. Iggy's at a loss to explain exactly why this is, but is clearly rather haunted by the situation. At the same time, it tends to keep him relatively driven and spry, and as such he actually makes out a compelling case for his commercial-outsider status being a genuine blessing in disguise.

'I like to keep my options open. I don't like to get too defined. When one thinks of contemporaries of mine like, say, Alice Cooper – well, if Alice has got to go out to work, he's still always going to have to bring some fake blood and some gallows with him. But I'm in a place now where I can do a whole bunch of different things. I crooned "All the Time in the World" for that David Arnold James Bond tribute (1997's *Shaken And Stirred: The 007 Project*). Just recently, I rapped a bunch of stuff with Death In Vegas (on a track entitled "Aisha," released soon). I've even appeared in an upcoming Chevy Chase film entitled *Snow Day* playing a crusty old geezer who hates modern music and who wants to take everyone back to the era of Perry Como and Al Martino. Probably what I'd like to do next – presuming *Avenue B* pans out OK – is to make a real archaic hard-rock record. Not heavy metal. Not good-time rock'n'roll. Just 110 per cent mean, hard-fucking rock. But at the same time, I've become extremely curious about what I could do being let loose with dance music, so . . .'

The remains of the day are now scarce in the sky by the time we leave the restaurant and drive off towards Iggy's Miami Beach condo. After traversing a number of intersections and side roads we come upon a quiet, sedate street. Iggy pulls up suddenly in front of a highly elaborate Disneyland-styled pirate grotto jutting out from the immediate landscape like some mind-boggling rococo architectural tribute to the spirit of Peter Pan. 'Jesus Christ, Jim,' I mutter. 'You didn't tell me you were living next door to Michael Jackson!'

He just chuckles maniacally and explains that the property belongs to 'this mad old coot' who made his fortune from helping create the Ziegfeld Follies aeons ago and who now lives in this whimsical, opulent fantasy of his own creation. Every now and then, Iggy gets an invitation to party with the old dude. 'He's serious fun,' enthuses the Pop, before letting it be known that Ricky Martin is also alleged to be a close neighbour of his. Four or five doors along from Swashbuckler's Cove stands the modest Spanish-looking condominium Iggy currently calls home. You'd call it 'functional' rather than 'spacious'; 'comfortable' more than 'lavish'. It's full-on dusk by the time we enter the premises and, for whatever reason, Iggy chooses not to turn on any lights. Walking straight into the lounge, one is immediately confronted by a spartanly furnished environment. Several bizarre-looking paintings glare out from the semi-darkness engulfing the walls. They all seem to have rather warped voodoo-ish connotations. One prominent tableau features a huge voodoo priestess staring vacantly – almost sweetly – back at the spectator. Her body is naked and obese and her limbs are all swollen. A similar Mexican-style painting features a demonic-looking female dominatrix grinning gleefully as her male prey – a huge red-horned devil – lays unconscious before her. 'These are some malevolent images you've got plastered on your walls here, Jim,' I remark.

'Malevolent.' He considers the word for a moment and then cackles again. 'Yeah . . . that's as good a word as any to describe the basic vibe of this stuff.'

Before taking me upstairs, he points out a small self-portrait he painted around the mid-eighties, hanging next to the larger dominatrix daub. Entitled *Old Ugly*, it's a gloomy evocation of the drink-and-drug-addled Iggy he was then trying to banish from his day-to-day existence. Turning around I notice a well-stocked bookcase as well as a modest CD collection propped up in some dim corner. (He'll tell me later his current listening runs the gamut from the Chemical Brothers and

Beth Orton to Verdi and good jazz, not forgetting a key influence on *Avenue B* – Frank Sinatra's desolate-sounding *Only the Lonely* album.)

We end up seated out on the first-floor patio, admiring the eerie stillness of the encroaching night. Tomorrow there'll be an intense thunderstorm for hours, accompanied by torrential rain. 'The weather's funny down here,' reckons Iggy. The last time he left and came back, he found his favourite tree ripped out by the roots due to a hurricane that had hit the premises in his absence. Talk turns to family stuff. He is particularly pleased that his son Eric (now thirty) is drug-free and leading a responsible life. Since the mid-nineties rehab episode, Eric has 'grown up a lot . . . gotten married to a teacher . . . went to college. He lives in Phoenix now.'

When Iggy Pop next tours, Eric will be his tour manager. 'People are always saying to him, "Wow, man, it must be weird having to drag your dad out of a mosh pit every night."' Iggy adds that he's excited by the prospect of becoming a grandfather.

His mother Louella died a couple of years ago after a long and painful illness. 'She was a wonderful person. She had a basic good nature, which I feel I've inherited. She was just happy to see people for no particular reason. It was very important to her that there always be a harmonious atmosphere. She was always cool with me. Always kept quiet and kept pushing. Just a typical good mom. Always had a good word for me. She'd give me $25 a week when I was really down and out. Two bucks a day if I was doing OK. She was always out there trying to help and support her son, the struggling musician. She did that forever – right up to when I needed hospitalization in the mid-seventies, and that only happened because she always kept a medical-insurance policy out for me even though I was already an adult. If she hadn't been there for me all those years, I would really have been up shit creek without a paddle.'

Iggy's father is now seventy-eight and retired to Colorado. He and Iggy's mother had always been one of those inseparable couples, so 'when she died it was horrific watching him suffer the way he did. I thought he'd go insane with the grief. But he pulled through. He's really an amazing man.' Though there was much friction in the early days over career and lifestyle choices, Iggy and his father have always been kindred spirits split by different eras and different social circumstances. 'We're both intellectuals, we're both stubborn and we're both naturally reserved. He's a bit of a cowboy but without the horse and the hat. And we're both outsiders.'

Like his father, Iggy tried to banish his natural sense of isolation by committing himself to a loving, monogamous relationship ordained through the holy act of matrimony. For a while there, it seemed to work. But not any more.

Apart from the time you were with Suchi, you've always seemed to me an inherently lonely person. How lonely are you right now?

'I only feel comfortable living alone because I have access pretty much when I want to quality female company – people who are charming, personable and attractive, and who I can be friends with. But if I didn't have that . . . no, I wouldn't be at all comfortable living alone. I'd be going fucking crazy. There are times when there's certain work to be done or certain things you have to figure out for yourself; then it's time to be alone. Generally speaking, over the past few years, it's been that time for me.

'This is where it gets tricky for me. What are gonna be the circumstances of my death? I think a lot about that. Is becoming monogamous the most appropriate and fulfilling thing I can achieve for the future? I have this idea to protect and enhance and nurture one woman and to see her bloom from that, having kids and everything. That is the ideal. Then I look around at other relationships and it's just a mass of human wreckage everywhere.

'Lots of people have the same experience. Millions of people all over the world – they can define their key relationship in just one phrase: "All we do is fight." So at the end of the day, I invariably find myself feeling love for someone I can't possibly live with. And that only feels about one short piss better than just out-and-out losing in love. Frankly, it's not a very satisfactory way to live on a day-to-day basis.'

Prince Is a Champion Too

'Has anyone come along in the nineties that I've found even vaguely threatening on a pure talent level? Surely you jest! There ain't no one out there as good as me. No one even comes close!'

The man has a point of course, for he is the Artist, the miraculous little fellow who sometimes trades under the name of Prince. Throughout the eighties he led the pack with the most audaciously brilliant albums of the decade and an equally potent live show, but during the nineties public interest in him waned dramatically as he appeared to become more and more self-indulgent and foolhardy with his career moves. He flooded the market with albums of largely mediocre material, got into an ugly battle with his old record label, scribbled 'SLAVE' inappropriately on his face, and generally got pigeonholed in the international press for being a self-obsessed control-crazed madman. Not surprisingly, the terms 'media' and 'critics' make the Artist openly seethe. His eyes take on a messianic glint as he ponders their ungodly pronouncements: 'The critics have never given me proper credit for being anything more than a one-dimensional cartoon. I was reading this article on me the other day, and it was just total fiction. They were calling me a control freak. They were calling me paranoid. It's the usual riff with me. "He's flamboyant, he's mad, he's paranoid." It's just bullshit. I am not mad and I am not paranoid, but that's what most people's idea of me is.'

Still, many who were formerly smitten with him now like to give the impression they find Prince and his aliases all a bit ridiculous. This always tends to happen to the real groundbreakers – they get out so far ahead of everyone else that when they suddenly fall behind for whatever reason, critics tend to become extra-vindictive in their evaluations, or else they simply distance themselves by taking cheap shots such as suddenly referring to him as 'The Artist Formerly Known as Talented.' But lack of talent has never been a problem with Prince. On the contrary, he's too talented for his own good and, as a result, has such an exalted sense of his own artistic worth that he's fundamentally unable to comprehend why the rest of the world isn't in a state of unceasing celebration about his amazingly prolific output. Try making gentle suggestions to him about 'editing' his work – stripping the next weighty future 3- or 4-CD package he's got planned down to one red-hot new album – and he looks at you as though you're making crazy talk. It's a look that also screams, that there is no one alive who has the right to even suggest what the Artist does with his own music.

The nineties and he were often on completely different musical wavelengths, he now readily admits: 'During that time that Nirvana and those guys were all over the place, I went into "big band" mode, doing "big band" versions of my songs. If people go left, I'm going right. I've been "dark" already. Check out *Sign o' the Times*. But if you're any kind of artist you realize pretty quickly that it comes down to a choice. You make the wrong choice, then you're going to dim your light and end up casting yourself into darkness. Likewise, I don't get involved with "gangsta" rap.'

Prince sat in a dimly lit hotel room immediately facing me. He looked more Puerto Rican than black, with beige-brown skin, straight black hair parted dead centre and covering both his ears and the back of his neck. He had wide, vulnerable eyes and a Deputy Dawg cartoon character mouth, around which a well-groomed goatee brought his chin to a dagger point. I was probably a foot taller than him, but he still managed to look down on me: his chair was specially elevated, as were his shoes which sported heels that could've measured 6 inches in added height. He still dressed like you'd expect Prince to dress. In a new-age, emerald-green bolero jacket, he resembled a psychedelic leprechaun who'd spent too long under the sun-ray lamp. He rather theatrically kept a large wooden walking stick with him propped against his chin – which he'd sometimes stroke to further underline the wisdom of his words. He was a real piece of work. But fascinating to talk to. Prince often comes across as a new-age nutcase when he gives an interview, but he chose to steer clear of such utterances when we spoke – at least 99 per cent of the time. What I didn't anticipate was just what a stimulating and eloquent conversationalist the man can be. When he was on a verbal roll, Prince talked like he performs – with eye rolls, voice changes and all manner of physical gestures. When the word 'oxymoron' jumped out of his mouth, he looked at me for half a second as if to say 'Can you imagine James Brown saying four-syllable shit like this?'

He readily admits to liking D'Angelo, Me'Shell Ndegéocello, Maxwell, TLC and a number of other contemporary black acts, but had few tender words for anyone else coming up, least of all those who'd covered his own songs. 'On one level, you can't argue with the kind of sales Puff Daddy's been getting. But damn – there's no originality left. You shouldn't be stealing older cats' songs and just pass 'em off as your own. Chaka Khan, she wrote "I'm Every Woman" – that's her song. She don't want Whitney Houston taking it over; she don't want Mary J. Blige messing with her "Sweet Thing". Just like I couldn't stand it when Tom Jones took "Kiss" from me. And I didn't want Ginuwine messing with "When Doves Cry". You can't change my song, man. He didn't even get the groove right.'

The Artist currently has his records released through Arista/ BMG; he and Clive Davis, the label's head, have 'an agreement, not a contract – contracts do not work,' where he keeps his masters and gets to release his weirder projects via the Internet. Also, so obsessed is he with owning his music that he's re-recording all his old Warner Bros. albums anew. 'Well, sometimes it just involves remixing to get a brand new master, not a whole re-recording process. Although I have re-recorded 1999 in its entirety quite recently.' His new mantra – repeated endlessly – is 'You own your masters or your masters own you.' The whole brouhaha with Warner now pains him to look back on and has clearly left him embittered. 'If WB had to try to get me to re-sign by saying, "Hey, we've made so much money off you, let's be fair and revert your old master tapes back to you," I'd probably still be with them. But they didn't, so . . . And I can't help feeling there's a racial discrepancy going on here. Bob Dylan and David Bowie – those cats got theirs back along with their brand-new $80-million contracts. But you look at the terrible struggle the Hendrix family had to put up before they got the right to Jimi's work. Jimi only made three or four records, right – not counting the posthumous stuff – and yet they've generated millions and millions of dollars, mostly all to businessmen who had absolutely nothing to do with the music's creation. Well, I've got at least four times the legacy of Jimi, and I want to own it all before I die.

'The law has never made sense to me. I created it: I own it. That's just a God-given right. "Legal" right is just an oxymoron here. I see Bono trying to get everyone together to wipe the Third World debt. That's cool, that's righteous, but maybe he should also be helping to get all the musicians together so they can form some kind of coalition to control their own music. We need to liberate ourselves first.'

Lest we forget, Prince is still a veritable powerhouse for godly conversion. It's one of the great ironies of the eighties: throughout the decade, everyone dreamt about what an exotic experience it might be, personally encountering the magic of Michael Jackson or the seductive savvy of Prince, never realizing that the reality would probably be closer to finally letting into your living room for a cup of tea that intense little guy who kept filling up your letterbox with pamphlets about giving over your life to our Lord and Saviour Jesus Christ. The way Prince sees it, a human being either dwells in the dark or he/she dwells in the light, and if he feels you're one of the ungodly he doesn't want to have anything to do with you, even if you're a member of his own immediate family. He abhors drug-taking and drinking, and talks about people who haven't yet accepted God into their lives as though he were addressing the handicapped. I asked him at one point if he ever thought of trying to work with Sly Stone, the drug-diminished genius/casualty who many see as Prince's greatest inspiration. His face went through a myriad of expressions – he winced, he smirked, he rolled his eyes. Then he chose his words very, very carefully. 'Wow, that . . . that [*he burst out laughing*] would be . . . too many problems! Oh boy! Me and Sly – that might be interesting. But I'd imagine we'd be on such different wavelengths, spiritually speaking, we'd never really connect musically.' By contrast, Prince now works full-time with Sly's old bass player Larry Graham and never lets the opportunity go by to rave about his talents: 'I've stolen everything Larry Graham's ever done, every note he's ever played,' he enthuses. The other thing Prince loves about Larry is that he's even more of a hard-nosed Christian zealot than he is: 'I don't use curse words around Larry. He won't let me,' Prince notes admiringly.

The Artist now likes to hang out with older cats – guys from his father's generation of musicians. His favorite jam sessions these days include Maceo Parker and Larry, as well as Carlos Santana: Prince has dreamed of playing with these guys since he was a young boy, and now he just calls them up and he's got his dream band. Carlos Santana – whose album *Supernatural*, also on Clive Davis's Arista label, is currently number one in the US – has been publicly making it his mission to try and force the Artist and Michael Jackson to record a duet album together. The Artist grimaces comically when I mention it. It's a look that says 'Never in a million years'. Then he speaks:

'Well, Michael wanted to record with me some years ago, though it never evolved into anything. Frankly, I don't know if it's such a good idea. The way I see it – there's no real point for us to get together.'

The Artist has never had to deal with the kind of media roasting that Jackson experienced in the nineties from being suspected of paedophilia, but he must have gone through hell when the tabloids found out that the first child born to himself and wife Mayte was brain-damaged so severely it had died within a month of its birth. Bearing in mind that this only happened to him two years ago, I ask him if he's ever found himself doubting his faith in the God he sings about so euphorically. His answer is immediate and unblinking: 'Never have I doubted God existed. I always knew there was a God; I've known he existed since the age of five.'

Prince has a lot of vivid memories from when he was five: What he saw and felt during that year has shaped him significantly both as gifted artist and cagey, remote individual. One of his most beautiful recent songs is entitled 'I Love You but I Don't Trust You Anymore.' It's a sad, lonely confession, and I ask him if it's autobiographical. Surprisingly he admits it is. 'The first verse is based on a memory I have from when I was five. My mother came into the house one day with a tag sticking out of her dress because she was wearing it the wrong way round. She'd actually been trying on dresses at a shop and made a simple mistake, but my father thought she'd been fooling around and so he went crazy at her. And I realized then just like I know now that there's love and there's trust, but if you love someone and you don't trust them, basically it's fucked up.'

The Artist's marital status seems to be in a state of some dispute these days. Though he and Mayte are still seen together from time to time – they recently made the cover of *Vogue* smiling happily in each other's embrace – he recently had the marriage annulled. According to a press officer, she has her own house in Spain. He still favours Minneapolis. (Within a year they would break up altogether.) 'The audience – that's my woman now!' the Artist remarks several times during our interview.

Two years ago, in a television interview, he told Oprah Winfrey that therapy had revealed to him that he'd created a whole alternative personality for himself at age five. Many felt the revelation – coupled with the bizarre name changes – was his own way of publicly admitting that he was in some way schizophrenic. When I put it to him, though, he gets kind of offended: 'This is where language imprisons us. I don't believe in schizophrenia. Prince and I are the same person. It's not like I have all these different personalities I have to control. I've never tried to reinvent myself like David Bowie, where one year he was Ziggy Stardust, then the next he was Aladdin Sane. I'm no different from Muhammad Ali. Was Muhammad Ali schizophrenic just because he changed his name from Cassius Clay? Hell no. I'd like to see you ask Ali if he's schizophrenic – he'd probably knock you out faster than he did Joe Bugner!'

One month later, the Artist reverted back to his original name again. It always suited him better anyway. Prince: he's not mad; he's just special.

The Conflicted Cool of Johnny Cash

It's been more than ten years now since reports started surfacing in the international media indicating that broad-shouldered, gravel-voiced country music icon Johnny Cash was not long for this world.

In the eighties, he'd been in and out of hospitals for a variety of problems. He'd had to undergo emergency bypass surgery on his heart and had been plagued with recurring drug dependency problems for much of the decade. But in 1990, an oral surgeon's fumbled operation on the singer's left cheek caused his jawbone to break, leaving Cash with the sensation that someone was continually hammering a nail into his chin twenty-four hours a day. For the next five years, he was in such unbearable pain it seemed only logical that he would develop an addiction to Percodan and other opiate-based medications. Even though he was in his sixties, he never really stopped touring, but everyone who witnessed one of his shows could see he was sometimes struggling just to make it through to the next breath.

The last time he attempted a European tour was in May of 1995: Cash boarded a flight from New York to London, locked himself in the first-class toilet and promptly shot himself up with so many pain pills that he passed out for several hours, slumped awkwardly alongside the metal commode. When he was finally brought back to consciousness, the pilot informed the singer that he would be handed over to the London police for arrest upon arrival at Heathrow Airport. Cash somehow managed to appease the aircraft crew (no police were ultimately summoned) and went on to perform a single show at the Royal Albert Hall that merited a standing ovation before suddenly cancelling the rest of the tour and flying back in order to get enrolled in a California drug-rehabilitation centre.

Then in 1997, he contracted double pneumonia followed by blood poisoning and was left in a coma for ten days and nights. When he awoke from that, the doctors told him he'd also developed Shy-Drager syndrome – a rare, more malevolent form of Parkinson's disease. 'I staggered when I tried to walk. My eyes blinked spasmodically uncontrollably,' he only recently confessed. 'When I stood up from a sitting or lying position, my blood pressure dropped so quickly that I almost blacked out. A couple of times there was no "almost" about it.'

Cash's condition has been somewhat stabilized by taking the appropriate medication, and nowadays he spends most of his time quietly sequestered in his Jamaica estate – a former sugar plantation once owned by the father of the late poet Elizabeth Browning – where the climate is apparently ideal for his ailments. If he stays put down there and doesn't do anything dramatic enough to provoke a further seizure, then it's quite possible that he and his wife June Carter could enjoy at least several more years together in this idyllic setting. But 'staying put' has never been part of Johnny Cash's bottom-line agenda. Last April – presumably against doctor's orders – he turned up at a tribute concert for himself, looking like a Southern Baptist King Lear who'd just quite literally dug himself out of his own coffin. Six months later, he was back in the studio with Rick Rubin, even though the producer already had several hours of perfectly good unreleased Cash performances stocked away in his vault. Cash just couldn't stop working, but time wasn't healing old wounds. He fell victim to yet another bout of pneumonia, which sent him spinning back into the hospital surrounded by evangelical in-laws and well-wishers fervently praying for the Man in Black to pull through just one more time.

Cash's current dilemmas are really nothing new for him. He's been a victim to chronic restlessness and his own deeply self-destructive urges for most of the sixty-seven years he's been prowling the planet. One of seven children born to a poverty-stricken couple, Ray and Carrie Cash, during America's Depression years, 'J.R.' Cash – that's how he was actually christened instead of 'John' – was working in the cotton fields of Dyess, Arkansas, from the age of four. By the time he was eight, his hands had become bloated and slightly deformed from being cut and stung from all the manual labour he'd undertaken. At the age of twelve, he was emotionally devastated when his favourite elder brother Jack died from internal wounding after he'd been cut from mid-torso right down to his upper thigh by a large whirring electrical buzz saw. According to books on the Cash dynasty, Jack had been a paragon of virtue with his heart set on becoming a preacher. J.R. was religious too, but less sweet-natured, more easily lured towards paths of sloth and petty sinfulness. His was a conflicted youth. He found the flat Arkansas landscape stultifyingly depressing during his teens and started to ramble as soon as he was legally able. He loved the country music station, particularly Hank Williams, and had started singing for his mother as a child. Out of sheer boredom, he enlisted in the army and spent three years in Landesberg, Germany, intercepting enemy messages as a radio operator. Apparently, it was a task he excelled at. It was Cash who first alerted American Intelligence in 1953 that Stalin was dead. Off-duty, he'd sometimes end up drunkenly singing on stage at a local club with a bunch of erstwhile army buddies who called themselves 'The Barbarians'.

When he got back to the States, it was 1954. He quickly married a woman he'd been corresponding with throughout his posting in Germany called Vivian Liberto and moved to

Memphis. His younger brother Ray introduced him to two garage mechanics, Marshall Grant and Luther Perkins, and the three men started playing music together. At first, the sound they made was clumsy and stilted. 'I'd never held [a bass] in my hand and didn't even know how to tune it,' bass player Grant later recalled. 'We didn't work to get that boom-chicka-boom sound. That's all we could play.' Guitarist Perkins – a kind of hillbilly prototype Keith Richards – plunked away idiosyncratically whilst Cash's stiff earnest baritone boomed forth, covering up the foreground.

Soon enough, the trio approached Sam Phillips, owner of Sun Records, with the idea of recording at his local studio. Phillips in due course auditioned the group, whose sound he found primitive but interesting. Cash, however, had chosen to perform only religious material at the session, and Phillips – uninterested in hiring any hillbilly gospel singer for his label – suggested he and his cohorts return only after they'd written new songs focused on more secular themes. Cash – already deeply impressed by the tumultuous effect a young Sun-affiliated singer named Elvis Presley was having on the local Memphis scene by blending country and rhythm'n'blues together – needed no further prompting and returned with two self-penned ditties that would quickly go on to become his first single for Phillips – 'Cry Cry Cry' and 'Hey Porter'. Another song he'd recently finished – 'Folsom Prison Blues' – would take up one side of his second single. Based on another song entitled 'Crescent City Blues' (its author Gordon Jenkins successfully sued Cash over the matter in the late sixties), Cash still fleshed it out with some unforgettable images of his own. After all, 'I shot a man in Reno just to watch him die' is as definitive a declaration of the utter banality of evil-doing as one human being has ever expressed it.

Cash's real breakthrough record at Sun, though, was his third single. It started from a backstage conversation between Carl Perkins and Cash on the subject of spousal fidelity. Perkins asked him if he ever fooled around on the road. 'Not me, buddy,' replied Cash. 'I walk the line.' Perkins then urged him to write a song with this title and Cash quickly complied. The music and vocals on 'I Walk the Line' were so primitive and yet so heartfelt they quite literally wobbled under the weight of their own earnestness. The backing group stumbled in and out of a lumbering verse/chorus structure which seemed to change key every time it was played, causing Cash to sing like a seasick man trying to find his bearings during a particularly stormy boat trek. The performance's very artlessness was its saving grace though because it screamed sincerity and also because Cash even with his manly baritone wasn't scared of displaying his 'vulnerable' side to the public, portraying a genuine struggle with moral issues most other entertainers were content to glibly brush aside. And all the tension in his voice told you the struggle was never over and never easy. The conflicted youth had found his new role in life as 'the conflicted man.'

Between 1955 and 1957, Cash's star was on a raging ascendant. Hank Williams was not long dead, and there were many who felt that Cash with his haunted voice and eerie songs was Hank's rockabilly heir apparent. Almost all of his truly timeless songs were written during this period too. But things changed when he got introduced to the pills. 'I took my first amphetamine – a little white Benzedrine tablet scored with a cross – in 1957,' he recalls in his autobiography, 'and I loved it.' So much so that within less than a year, he was taking such vast quantities that 'as soon as I woke up, I started feeling little things in my skin, briers or woodsplinters, itching so badly that I had to keep trying to pluck them out . . . They started to be alive, actually twitching and squirming in my flesh, and that was unbearable. Then I had to take more pills.' He tried to talk to other speed-users about his condition, 'but no one else had the problem for the simple reason that nobody else was taking as many pills as I was.'

Cash spent the next ten years in a continual state of speed psychosis. He left Sam Phillip's Sun stable and signed to Columbia Records in 1958, the same year he moved his family out of Memphis way out west to California. By 1960, he and his wife had brought four daughters into the world, but Cash was the pill-addicted epitome of a dysfunctional dad. His eldest daughter, the singer/songwriter Rosanne Cash, still has fierce memories of her father's dread presence around the house. 'He was always so wired you would almost break down in tears to be in the same room with him. He'd set fires. He seemed so miserable.'

In due course, he accelerated his pill intake even further, getting cross-addicted to barbiturates to calm down from the usual fistloads of amphetamine. He started drinking to excess too before separating from his wife in the early sixties, and moved to Nashville where he ended up sharing a bachelor apartment with another troublemaker and future country music big wheel, Texas-born Waylon Jennings. In his own auto-biography, Jennings vividly recalls Cash's mean, low-down ways rising to the fore during this era. One of the highlights of sharing space with the Man in Black was having to put up with him dementedly hurling a large Bowie knife into the living room wall over and over again at any given time of day or night. 'Me and John were the world champions of pill-taking,' Jennings later wrote. 'I hid my stash in the back of the air conditioner, while John kept his behind the television . . . If we had started combining supplies and sources, we probably would've bottomed out and killed ourselves, feeding each other's habits.' Still, Cash bottomed out enough times during this period to necessitate being incarcerated for brief stretches on seven different occasions. In Nevada, the police found him stark naked and passed out at the wheel of his car. In Mississippi, he was put in jail after being found in a state of total delirium picking daisies on a stranger's front lawn at two in the morning. A few days later, he managed to single-handedly burn down a large forest range (the US government later successfully sued him for many thousands of dollars over the incident). In 1965, he was busted at the El Paso airport for being in possession of 1,000 Dexedrine pills. In 1967, he drove two separate cars off the high cliff at his Tennessee home and crashed them both into the sea. One night at the Grand Ole Opry during the mid-sixties, Cash's speed psychosis became so acute he felt he was hearing voices hissing and cursing at him during a live performance. He retaliated by grabbing the mike stand and smashing sixty footlights as he stormed off stage. Told he would never be invited back by Opry bigwigs, Cash broke down and became so carried away with his grief, he ended up crashing his car into a tree and fracturing two bones in his face.

Miraculously, his career survived all the mayhem. His own songs didn't quite have the power of the Sun-era output, but he managed to score hits with other people's material. One such number, 'Ring of Fire', had lyrics written by June Carter, a young woman Cash had fallen in love with as early as 1961. Carter was part of a country music hierarchy – she was one of the three daughters of A.P. and Maybelle Carter, and had even spent time as a teenager living at the New York apartment of Elia Kazan and his wife and studying at the Actor's Studio. She clearly loved Cash back – they'd been performing together since the early sixties – but refused to marry him until he'd put the substance abuse behind him. In his autobiography, Cash relates a frankly unbelievable tale of being so demented from pills that some time in 1967 he drove to a desert and purposefully lost himself down a deep labyrinthine cave. Instead of dying, though, Cash experienced a vision of God and was so illuminated he managed to somehow find his way out again. At the cave's mouth, he was met by Carter and Cash's mother. They'd somehow sensed he was there – he claims – and arrived bearing food and ointment.

Carter and Cash did marry in late '67 but he wouldn't totally rid his life of the pills until 1970. Sources differ as to whether he was really speeding his brains to buggery or not during the 1968 landmark performance he gave before the inmates of California's Folsom Prison (in his autobiography Cash says he was straight; others are less convinced). It got recorded anyway and – along with its follow-up, a performance recorded at San Quentin Prison the year after – became the best and biggest selling album of his career. Cash is truly in his element in this stark setting, every word he utters resonates deeply. Here is a man who can relate to the prisoner in us all and yet still shine a light into the darkest circumstances to achieve a soul-stirring sense of artistic catharsis.

It's only unfortunate he didn't take this cathartic gift he possessed even further. Instead, he softened everything up, found religion, became pious, well respected, purposely got rid of any dark connotations. Partly it was a reaction to all the years of drug dementia – partly too it was the influence of his status-seeking spouse – but the fact remains that Cash became something of a crashing bore throughout the seventies. He was also drink- and drug-free for virtually the entire decade. I interviewed him in 1973 when he was promoting his own *Heaven's Gate* – a tedious, clumsily pieced-together glorified home movie he'd made about the life of Jesus Christ called *The Gospel Road*, and whenever he answered a question, he seemed like he was reading from a script that had been concocted by a committee of Scripture-quoting Stepford Wives. The location was backstage at the Royal Albert Hall: earlier, as he was poised to enter the building, a deformed figure of uncertain gender had suddenly been held aloft to his immediate right by two mad parents. 'Touch me, Johnny!' the poor creature had pleaded over and over again. Cash had stared down at his own feet as though silently praying the ground beneath him would suddenly open up and eat him alive.

Cash remained one of America's best-loved and most successful entertainers throughout the seventies. It didn't hurt that June Carter was a close blood relative of President Jimmy

Carter. She'd even boast that when Jimmy was struggling alone with particularly troublesome world crises, he'd sometimes call Cash to personally serenade to him. (Can you imagine Tony Blair asking the same favour of Noel Gallagher or Mick Hucknall?)

Ronald Reagan, however, chose not to heed Johnny Cash's advice on foreign policy, or anything else for that matter. The eighties were a cold decade for the Man in Black – an ornery miserable time – and he soon found himself strung out once again on speed and pain pills. In the nineties country music radio wouldn't even play his new recordings, so he found himself improbably endeavouring to appeal to the alternative rock demographic. This had a briefly liberating effect on his fragile muse – *American Recordings*, the stark, gloomy album he made with producer Rick Rubin, was his best, most personal-sounding record since *San Quentin*. Still, there was something forced about Cash being shoe-horned into the world of grunge fashion and MTV sound bites, and he didn't look at all comfortable standing next to all the cute young dudes at the Viper Room just begging to soak up Cash's authenticity and wear it like a rare fur coat at photo ops. But where exactly did he still feel comfortable? Only when he was onstage performing, it seemed. When he connected with other people through his music, only then was all the pain and inner turmoil lifted from his body and soul. But then in October of 1997, Cash dropped his guitar pick in mid-performance, and when he attempted to pick it up, he practically fell over. The audience laughed. 'It ain't funny,' he shot back, before making his first public acknowledgement that he was suffering from Shy-Drager syndrome.

What drives an individual to keep pushing himself as insanely hard as Johnny Cash always has? Clearly he doesn't need the money. Time and time again, he's put his health at risk in order to keep on performing or at least recording music. In an excellent profile on Cash from the mid-nineties featured in a book entitled *In the Country of Country*, author Nicholas Dawidoff makes a forceful case for linking the singer's driven, restless personality with a tormented sense of guilt first brought on when his saintly brother Jack died. June Carter, Rosanne Cash, and even the psychiatrist who treated him for drug addiction in the late 60s are all quoted vigorously backing up this theory. Cash, though, remains unconvinced by the whole 'guilt' trip. The key passage in his recent autobiography comes when he writes about his father and you suddenly feel whole decades of deep-seated unresolved grievances welling up within him. Johnny Cash describes his father as a callous drunk. 'He killed my dog. I was only five. It was plain meanness.' Ray Cash used to beat up his wife too. But most telling is Cash's recognition that 'I inherited my addictive nature from my father. It's his legacy but it's my responsibility. Similarly, I've always found a need to control my restlessness. That I inherited from my father. He was always on to the next job. That desire and need to do something led me to use stimulants and then sedation to make me stop for a while.'

Ultimately you can't come away without being awed by the man. He helped revolutionize popular music in the fifties. He's arguably the most charismatic country singer/songwriter since Hank Williams, whilst his songs and whole rebel stance have been an ever-present, all-nurturing influence on the careers of rock thoroughbreds like Bob Dylan, Neil Young and Bruce Springsteen. As a substance abuser, in his days he could clearly outdo even Hunter S. Thompson, but what was really cool about Cash was that he always knew his hedonistic excesses were anything *but* cool – more a manic manifestation of guilt, weakness and inner conflict. Cash's kudos as an epic pill-head may make him a figure worth venerating amongst the Shaun Ryders of this world, but it's his God-given talent – that cathartic edge as well as an unparalleled ability to *inhabit* any song he chooses to perform – that'll be remembered and cherished with the passing of time.

Plus, as a fully qualified survivor, he's practically without peer. On 1 November, 1999, Johnny Cash left Baptist Hospital in Nashville, Tennessee, having successfully beaten off yet another potentially fatal bout of pneumonia. Death will certainly return, but Cash intends to carry on fighting back as long as possible: 'I go along with Edna St. Vincent Millay's idea that it's okay to go out screaming and scratching and fighting. When death starts beating the door down, you need to be reaching for your shotgun.'

Eminem's Rage in a Cage

American culture has always been deeply haunted by the violence of its desperado origins, but over the past fifteen years or so, the country seems to have become increasingly locked into some unwinnable internal conflict. Listen to its modern music. Step inside their cinemas. You'll get the message fast enough. Americans are angry, goddammit. They love nothing more these days than to see and hear their fellow countryfolk with their eyes and neck muscles bulging out, screaming and cursing, kicking and fighting. It almost doesn't matter who or what they're kicking against. Blind rage alone will suffice. American cinema over the past decade has given rise to a new kind of outsider – cute-looking young leading men driven stark staring psychotic by all that rage seething within. Think Brad Pitt's punch-hungry delirium in *Fight Club* or skinhead Nazi Edward Norton crushing skulls in *American History X*. But this is small beer compared to the way anger has become the all-consuming energy in American contemporary music.

By the end of the eighties, the menacing milieu of rap had given vent to a plethora of pissed-off word-spitting malcontents who went on to sell millions of CDs. To keep in sync, the US rock audience found themselves their own maladjusted Kings of Spleen to venerate. The first was named Axl Rose; he was lead singer of Guns'N'Roses, and between 1988 and 1991 he reigned supreme in terms of record sales and media speculation. Rose was a paranoid schizophrenic redneck youth from Indiana whose childhood had been torn apart by dysfunctional parenting and sexual abuse, and it had left him royally pissed off about everyone or everything he encountered. Through his group's records, he vented his scary-voiced spleen at his parents, the system, the police, ex-girlfriends and women in general; and on one memorable song entitled 'One in a Million', homosexuals and Negroes. 'Niggers and faggots – they make me no sense to me' opined Rose, who went on to portray the African-American population as a nation of gold-chain-wearing thieves, and homosexuals as disease-spreading parasites. Rose's commercial reign was to be significant but short-lived. By the early nineties his mad rage turned on the other members of Guns'N'Roses, whom he alienated one by one before disappearing into a suspended state of Howard Hughes-like invisibility. He'd been displaced as American rock's rage-filled sovereign anyway back in 1991 by doomed wunderkind Kurt Cobain. The Nirvana frontman wasn't some small-minded racist/homophobe, and his hatred of being alive sounded more authentically soul-searing than Rose's self-indulgent Hollywood shit-fits. The colossal rage at the centre of Nirvana's music was at once existential – like Sartre, Cobain clearly subscribed to the theory that 'hell is other people' – and self-flagellating. It's the sound of a man who can't stand being inside his own skin. 'Despite all my rage / I am still just a rat in a cage' sang one of Cobain's disciples, platinum-selling Smashing Pumpkins' Billy Corgan, perfectly defining the sense of rage-warped impotence most young Americans seemed to be experiencing simultaneously. Everywhere you looked in the US alternative rock marketplace of the mid-nineties, you'd bump into seriously pissed-off dudes who just weren't going to take it anymore. Rage Against the Machine raged against 'the system'. Muscle-packed Henry Rollins screamed himself hoarse with spleen. But then the whole alt-rock scene lost its commercial momentum in America, and a new wave of home-grown bands more in tune with rap attitudes, skate-board fashions and hip-hop break-beats came along to fill their space on MTV and the *Billboard* best-seller charts. They had names like Korn and Limp Bizkit, and they played a strange disjointed music that mostly consisted of creepy, moodily paced verses (during which the singer would whine on about his myriad personal problems) that suddenly exploded into barbaric, bludgeoning choruses full of homicidal guitar riffs and bombastic drumming that sound like the sonic equivalent of a bunch of sadistic thugs gleefully beating some hapless victim to death in a back alley. This new breed are the 'mooks' – at least, that's what their 'politically correct' detractors have quickly termed them in various stations of the media. The word came from Scorsese's 'Mean Streets', where it was used to define Robert de Niro's infantile self-destructive Johnny Boy character. And then in 1999 Eminem suddenly shambled onto the scene with his high, creepy voice spitting out poison verse after poison verse, and America found its Supreme Messiah of Mook – its very own poet laureate of the trailer park.

Unless you've been living in a cave over the past twelve months, you'll have noticed that the year 2000 belonged to Eminem – and Eminem alone. Radiohead and U2 were little cult acts compared to his global selling power. 'God sent me here / To annoy the world / And destroy your little four-year-old boy or girl' he bragged, and the world responded with a scary intensity. The year 1999 marked the release of his debut album *The Slim Shady LP*, and during 2000 – flanked by his mentor/producer Dr Dre – he burst like a supernova to become rap's creepy white-boy saviour, a devastating word-smith inwardly tormented enough to fill the charisma void left by the deaths of Tupac Shakur and Notorious B.I.G. Then he and Dre unveiled *The Marshall Mathers LP* and everything fell before him. 'I don't make black music / I don't make white music / I make spite music' he declared during one of his demented rhyme sprees for that record, and upwards of 12 million people responded to that spite like malnourished dogs who'd just been thrown a steak. Suddenly everyone had something to say about Eminem and his ugly mouth. Gay-rights movements hauled him over the coals for promoting and exploiting hostility towards homosexuals. ('Hate fags? The answer's yes.') Domestic-violence help-lines deplored the homicidal fantasies he verbalized about killing his wife whilst their daughter looks on. Women's groups railed against his venomous word spews denigrating 'bitches'. Even America's governing body felt compelled to butt in. Congresswoman Lynne Cheney delivered a blistering tirade to the American Senate last autumn against Eminem's 'Satanic' influence on his audience. 'Wives, nuns, sluts,' she recited. 'Whoever the bitches might be. He will kill them slowly, leaving enough air in their lungs so their screaming will be prolonged. He will paint the forest with their blood.' Cheney even created a new word to define Eminem's utterances: 'viloporn'.

At the same time, the Michigan-born rapper discovered that he had supporters in the strangest places. Britain's *New Musical Express* last December claimed that 2000 would go down in history as 'the year when Eminem, the most artistically grown-up person on the planet became – simultaneously – the toast of the tots, anti-hero to two generations (aged 10 to 40) and the first artist in living memory to cross the rigid authentic pop/rap/rock'n'roll divide to become his very own category. In short, he's the 21st century Elvis.' A month earlier, another Elvis – Elvis Costello – wrote a feature for *Vanity Fair* in which he listed what he considered to be the 500 greatest records ever released. *The Marshall Mathers LP* was one he chose, and he went out of his way to praise the record as 'faster, funnier and more natural than most records.' (Another equally unlikely fan turned out to be the extremely homosexual Elton John, who raved to the press that *The Marshall Mathers LP* was an 'innovative masterpiece.') Meanwhile *Rolling Stone* and *Spin* suddenly saw him as the crossover heir apparent to Kurt Cobain, 'intelligent working-class heroes who found it all too much.' Courtney Love even started talking about him sympathetically: 'Without context Eminem is nothing.'

In this the merry widow of grunge is right. For if you take away the sensation-seeking slasher-film scenarios from his lyrics, what you're left with is the Eminem essence – the tortured terminally pissed-off bleat of the sensitive youth who went through trailer-park hell and who now wants to torment the world the way the world has mostly always tormented him. Anyone who's listened to his debut album will already be acquainted with many intimate details from his past. He was born to a seventeen-year-old mother, Debbie Mathers-Briggs, and her twenty-four-year-old husband Marshall in 1973: the couple performed in a band called Daddy Warbucks, playing Ramada Inns along the Dakota–Montana border. The husband disappeared to California soon after the child's birth, leaving mother and child to drift before eventually settling in the blue-collar projects of Detroit's notorious east side. The child got beaten up savagely throughout his teens; on one occasion he suffered a cerebral hemorrhage and was in and out of consciousness for five days. He became obsessed with rap after being introduced to it at age nine by his closest friend, his uncle Ronnie, who played him an Ice-T album. Ten years later, uncle Ronnie would commit suicide. By this time, Eminem would become embroiled in a volatile needy relationship with his teenage sweetheart Kim. They gave birth to a daughter, Hailie, but often separated for stormy spells. He'd also started developing his rapping skills on Detroit stages as one of many hungry contestants at numerous open-mike MC throw-downs. 'As soon as I grabbed the mike, I'd get booed,' he'd later recall. 'Once motherfuckers heard me rhyme though, they'd shut up.' He helped form a six-piece rap crew incongruously known as the Dirty Dozen. Then in 1996 he released his first album, *Infinite*, on a local Detroit label, but it found the young rapper too caught up in apeing the mannerisms of then popular rappers like Nas and Jay-Z. The record stiffed and he got sacked from his cooking job at Gilbert's Lodge and didn't even have enough money to buy his beloved daughter a Christmas present. Then one fateful night, he was seated on the toilet when divine inspiration struck him: 'Boom – the whole Slim Shady name hit me and right away I thought of all these words to rhyme with it. So I wiped my ass, got up off the pot and went and called everybody I knew.'

Slim Shady, his secret weapon, was a one-man redneck Clockwork Orange who used his diabolical rhyming skills to kick merry hell out of his former tormentors. A demo tape of several Slim Shady performances found its way to Dr Dre, the west coast Phil Spector of hip-hop, and his co-producer Mel-Man in 1997. It was a bad time for the pair: their much-hyped production of the Firm – a rap supergroup involving sex bomb Foxy Brown, Nas and AZ – had just flopped in the marketplace. 'You remember the scene in *Titanic* when they was puttin' the children and the women on the boats and they was tellin' the men they had to wait?' asked Mel-Man last year. 'Luckily a helicopter came and it was Eminem. He dropped a ladder and we climbed up.'

Rap's new saviour meanwhile was keeping his ire stoked up to boiling point. 'After *Infinite*, every rhyme I wrote got angrier and angrier. A lot of it was because of the feedback I got. Motherfuckers was like "You're a white boy, what the fuck are you rapping for? Why don't you go into rock'n'roll?" All that type of shit started pissing me off.' On *The Slim Shady LP* he turned on everyone in his past who'd ever fucked with him. He bad-mouthed his mother for being a mentally unstable drug addict, he luridly depicted the murder and dismemberment of girlfriend Kimberley. He even spat venom at D'Angelo Bailey, the black youth who'd given him his cerebral hemorrhage back in high school. His ravings were delivered in a relentless whine like some malevolent bee endlessly buzzing around its intended victim, whilst Dr Dre worked his creepy magic in the background, locating off-the-wall old soundtrack samples and binding them together with strange loops and herky-jerky break-beats. It caught on straight out of the box, selling millions of copies in a matter of months. And then, in the classic traditions of white-trash America, Eminem suddenly found himself besieged by demented in-laws wanting to share in his new-found wealth. His own mother sued him for 10 million dollars over his accusations of parental neglect and drug abuse on 'Slim Shady'. His grandmother tried to sue him when he attempted to release a song featuring a rap he'd found by his beloved deceased uncle Ronnie. Though his father had never shown any interest in his son before, he suddenly wanted to meet him. (Eminem's rebuttal was short and sharp: 'Fuck that motherfucker, man. Fuck him.') Several half-brothers and sisters showed up in the media. Meanwhile his stormy liaison with Kim suffered further from her mortified reaction to her public murder in front of millions as spelled out on ''97 Bonnie and Clyde.'

Ultimately it's the same old story: young tormented guy makes it big, thinks fame will eradicate all his problems and it only ends up making things worse. 2000's *Marshall Mathers LP* was as intensely autobiographical as its predecessor, but this time he'd left the trailer parks (although the trailer parks will never leave him) to take up residence in MTV Superstar Land. He couldn't stand it there either and vented much spleen at the expense of cohabitants Britney Spears, Christina Aguilera and N'Sync. The long-suffering Kim was once again at the centre of a genuinely shocking murder fantasy. Faggots were often ridiculed. Critics, journalists and rival rappers were all told to go suck his cock. Relatives were – needless to say – held up to further public ridicule. But then amidst all the head-spinning venom appeared 'Stan,' the one song his apologists inevitably end up draping their 'Eminem is a major American artist' theory over.

There's no getting around the fact that 'Stan' is an amazing piece of work. Under a melancholy musical undertow, Eminem tells the gloomy tale of a doomed obsessed fan who copies the rapper's murder fantasy in ''97 Bonnie and Clyde' before committing suicide himself. It's genuinely spellbinding the way he tells the story; he has a magical grasp on contemporary language and a major talent as storyteller and wordsmith. But what makes 'Stan''s grisly scenario work so potently is the way for the first time in his brief career he's so clearly anchored a song with a functioning moral conscience. This is the rapper's key problem with older music lovers. They find 90 per cent of what he has to say distasteful and exploitative, and they have a very valid point. Log onto any Eminem fan's website and you'll be confronted by messages like 'I am a 17-year-old female. I really love Eminem. ALL FAGS MUST DIE. Thank you. Carly' and 'Eminem knows what his fans want to hear. Fags should stay away and live on a leper island.' Dr Dre in particular should be careful about letting his name be linked to such repellent opinions. In 1996 when he was desperately trying to separate himself from the gangster rap milieu of his former home, Death Row Records – a move that almost cost him his life – he became the victim of a smear campaign instigated by label-boss Suge Knight and Tupac Shakur that baldly accused Dre of being gay himself. Still, to Eminem the issue is a pathetically simple one: ' "Faggot" to me means "pussy", "cissy",' he told the *NME* last April. 'If you're a man, be a man – that's what I'm saying. I don't give a shit about "gay". Be gay, take it in the ass, suck dick, do whatever – that's your business. Just don't come near me with that shit.'

Eminem's one admirable personal character trait remains the way he continually obsesses about improving the life of his daughter Hailie. This is clearly the one person in the world he feels unconditional love for. 'That's who I'm doing all this shit for. Hip-hop is in my blood but I'm not going to be young forever. Next in time is my daughter. She's going to be able to go to college and be something that I wasn't. It's about her now. We're put here to make children. That's the reality of it. We're here to reproduce. And I reproduced. So now my life is for her.'

Late last year Eminem was granted joint custody of four-year-old Hailie after divorcing Kim, whom he'd actually married in 1999. Their single year as man and wife had been rife with ugly conflicts. In June 2000 the rapper pistol-whipped a man outside of a Detroit nightclub whom he believed was having an affair with his wife. Earlier the same day, Eminem pulled a gun on Insane Clown Posse associate Douglas Dail at an electronics store in Royal Oak, Michigan. Dail apparently called Eminem 'gay' in front of Kim. Both victims filed complaints with the police. The resulting court cases – still to take place – could find him facing up to nine years behind bars. Then Kim tried to commit suicide after she'd witnessed her husband further insulting her whilst on stage. By the autumn of last year, everyone surrounding the troubled rapper was concerned about what might happen next. Eminem was even bragging to *Vibe* magazine about how he liked to whip out a loaded gun on any over-zealous autograph-seeking fans who happened to cross his path. 'I think he should definitely disappear for a while,' stated his manager Paul Rosenberg last December. 'But having work to do keeps him out of trouble. He gets in more trouble when he's at home trying to be Marshall Mathers and not when he's Eminem.' Even Dr Dre became concerned about his golden white boy: 'Like Tupac Shakur, Eminem has a lot of energy, spirit and talent,' he told *Vibe* last September. 'But you have to be careful. If the energy is not directed in the right place, it's gonna turn into negative energy and that's not good because it can be the end of your career.'

Can Eminem's high-powered homies convince him to open up his heart and accept the healing power of forgiveness into his life so that he can truly save himself? Or do they just think that kind of thinking is strictly for pussies? Time alone will tell. Meanwhile, Eminem and his unquenchable wrath are poised to bring the ruckus to Paris. Expect some serious venom-slinging on the night. Apparently, Eminem hates Europeans even worse than he hates faggots.

Sly Stone's Evil Ways

It is 1978 and I am gamely endeavouring to interview James Brown, the Godfather of soul and funk, in the cramped hallway of the London premises of his record label, Polydor. Lank-haired secretaries regularly slither past us on their way to the Xerox machine, prompting Brown to start flashing his shockingly intense tooth-filled grin and inform every female within range 'I'm single and I like to mingle,' delivered with a whimsical croon to his ragged voice. The Godfather has kind words for everyone today – even the American Mafia: 'I'm sure they're good people and doin' the best job they can,' he remarks about an organization that apparently almost destroyed his profile on American black radio in the early seventies. Only one subject I broach causes him temporarily to banish his beatific smile and furrow his brow as if something deeply distasteful had suddenly entered the conversation. It happens when I ask him – out of the blue – what he really thinks of Sly Stone. 'Well, I ain't gonna say nothing against Sly 'cos I love the man,' are the first words to jump out of his mouth; then he goes silent for about ten seconds and his face becomes clouded with conflicting emotions before he speaks again. 'But he messed up so bad! Man, he was a talented one too, that Sly. Knew him back when he was still a youngster. He had it all going on back then.'

Brown had first met Stone when the latter was a teenager going by his given name of Sylvester Stewart. Stewart had enjoyed success as a musician and disc jockey in the San

Francisco area when he compèred a prestigious Bay Area concert headlined by Brown and his Famous Flames back in 1963. In 1967, Brown went to see the newly formed Sly and the Family Stone perform at a club in Las Vegas and was so impressed he returned the next night, bringing his entire band with him to sit and take notes. Then as the sixties flamed to a close, Brown witnessed Sly Stone suddenly eclipse him in popularity to become – briefly but significantly – Soul Brother No. 1 in the charts and hearts of both black and white America. It did not sit well with him. Then in the seventies Sly Stone promptly destroyed his career and pissed away all his momentum in a frenzy of drug-diminished egomania. Now – looking back on his one-time competitor – Brown the hardy survivor couldn't help but gloat.

'It's sad what happened to the man,' Brown gruffly concluded. 'He sounds like he's gone clear out of control. The talent was there but it's not cutting through anymore. All that success just messed with his mind too much and turned him into a failure.'

For twenty-five years now, Sly Stone has played out the unhappy role of contemporary music's most spectacular burn-out, but it's still not hard to comprehend instantly why he was so omnipotent a superstar between 1969 and 1973. You have only to rent a copy of *Woodstock* and watch him completely upstage everyone else who performed at the fabled three-day event back in August 1969 – including Jimi Hendrix and the Who. Sly practically bursts out of the screen at you. His energy level is supernaturally infectious as he fires up the Family Stone to blast forth a towering inferno of intricately woven funk that is both gospel-joyous and voodoo-demonic in its earthquaking intensity. Better yet, locate a halfway decent 'greatest hits' compilation and marvel at how Stone concocted, orchestrated and fronted his own maverick vision of a multiracial, male-and-female powered pop funk combo that would quickly hold the whole world spellbound and forever change the style and structure of Afro-American music. Everyone from Mick Jagger and Tamla-Motown to Miles Davis wanted to learn from the new master. 'When I first heard Sly,' wrote the jazz legend in his autobiography *Miles*, 'I almost wore out those first two or three records: 'Dance to the Music', 'Stand' and 'Everybody Is a Star'. The shit he was doing was badder than a motherfucker, had all kind of funky new dimensions to its groove. It was with Sly Stone and James Brown in mind that I went into the studio in June 1972 to record "On the Corner".'

Miles and Sly hung out together on any number of occasions. Clive Davis, the head of Columbia Records, even sent the trumpeter to Los Angeles in 1971 to try and help Stone complete his *There Is a Riot Goin' On* album more quickly. 'After he got big he always had strange people hanging around his house and recording sessions. I went to a couple and there was nothing but girls everywhere and coke, bodyguards with guns, looking all evil. I told him I couldn't do nothing with him – told Columbia I couldn't make him record any quicker. We snorted some coke together and that was it.'

Yet Miles still found himself continually drawn to Sly Stone's company like a moth to a flame. Several members of the Family Stone still recall Davis hovering around Sly less as an equal, more like a hanger-on. Rusty Allen, the bass-player who took over from Larry Graham in 1972 after Sly had tried to have the latter killed, recalls an incident that occurred in 1973: 'One night, Miles came to Sly's New York apartment at Central Park West, went into the home studio, got on Sly's organ and started to play these nine-note ethereal crazy chords. Sly was way back in the bedroom and he came out yelling "Who the fuck is doing that on my organ?" He came in and saw who it was. "Miles, get your motherfucking ass out of here," he said. "Don't ever play that voodoo shit here. Get the fuck out of here." Miles left and I said, "Sly, that was Miles Davis you was talking to." "I don't give a fuck," he said. "He shouldn't have been playing that shit on my organ." But Miles didn't care. He was back the next day.'

'Sly had his own way of writing music,' Davis concluded in his autobiography. 'He got his inspiration from the people in his group. That was before Sly got big. Then he wrote a couple of other great things and then he didn't write nothing because the coke fucked him up and he wasn't a trained musician.' He's basically correct in all these views, barring one. Sly Stone *was* a trained musician who could both read and write music. In 1961 Sylvester Stewart had enrolled at Solano Community College specifically to study music theory. A fellow student, David Froelich, remembers him as 'a stand-out because of his extreme interest in the subject. He worked real hard and would stay after class. There was considerable work to be done at home, writing music and so forth. His work was always excellent. He was an A student.'

Earlier in his teens he'd studied trumpet, music theory and composition at Vallejo Junior College. But Sylvester's career in music had begun years before that: 'I think Sly was born with a big voice,' recalls his mother, Alpha (her sister's called Omega). 'When he was about five we went to San Francisco and the bishop put him on the table, so people could see him sing. My kids could always sing. [Eldest Stewart sister] Loretta could always play the piano. They had a group called the Stewart Four – Loretta, Syl, Freddie and Rose – that would perform regularly at various churches.'

By the time he was nine years old, Sylvester had become a proficient guitar player. 'I would see the Stewarts perform on occasion,' remembers Shelby Givens, a long-time family friend. 'In church. It was a family of kids with a lot of musical talent. Sly's guitar and keyboards were always very outstanding. That's how the family made their mark on the gospel scene.'

Alpha and her husband K.C. were from Texas originally. Their first two children, Loretta and Sylvester (known as 'Syl' or 'Sly'), were born down there, the latter on 18 March 1941. Then they uprooted the family and moved to the San Francisco area, settling in Vallejo some forty miles north of the city of brotherly love, where K.C. soon found work as a cleaner of office buildings. Sly was quickly joined by a second sister, Rose, three years his junior, and a brother, Freddie, who was four years younger than him. When not giving birth, Alpha would be devoting her time to attending her local Vallejo place of worship. She and her husband were devout believers in the Church of God in Christ and took great pride in indoctrinating their children and accompanying them to endless church gospel sessions. In 1952, when Sly was just eleven, the Stewart Four recorded and released their first record. 'It was a song that Sly sang lead on called "On the Battlefield"', Freddie recalls. 'I remember driving down to Texas, taking our records down there to sell them. We went to churches and sang down there. We were always in church. If it wasn't with the family, I was singing in the choir.'

Yet there was something already potentially damaging going on behind all these exuberantly youthful shouts of 'Hallelujah!' coming from the Stewart clan, as Shelby Givens observed: 'The most central thing to the whole religious fervour of the Church of God in Christ was the emphasis on the transformation experience that they refer to as the Holy Ghost. That's what made you a full-time member: the ability to speak in tongues. They believed that you could not succeed in the world, because worldliness was seen as something that was a form of departure from God, from righteousness and, by definition, that meant that you were in a sense pretty much doomed. So when people backslid, there was almost a compulsion to take on attributes of worldliness – alcohol, drugs, nightclubbing, dancing, adultery – a whole range of things associated with the unrighteous. You could not have any respectability anywhere in the middle. If you sin, you're going to hell anyway, so you might as well taste it all.'

As soon as he hit his teens, Sly began relentlessly expanding his horizons. His family was not rich, certainly, but neither was it poor and he never had to experience the deprivations of being a ghetto child. He quickly became something of a social chameleon, blending artfully into whatever scene he became attracted to. At sixteen he was given his first car – a light green '53 Chevy – and joined a school gang called the Cherrybusters. But music remained his key interest. John Turk, a childhood friend, had watched Sly perform in church and in 1958 noticed him playing guitar and keyboards in San Francisco clubs with local acts like the Webs and Jimmy Terrell. He got him to join his own band, the Royal Aces. During the same period Sly managed to talk his way into holding down a weekly job as a regular fixture on a San Francisco-based television pop show, *The Dick Stewart Show*. In 1959 he and Freddie recorded a forgettable 'gimmick' record entitled 'The Rat' that Ensign released under the name of the Stewart Brothers. A follow-up, 'Sleep on the Porch', was released a year later to little acclaim. Sly then went solo – he briefly changed his name to Danny Stewart and tried his luck as a gospel-pop crooner, releasing a song entitled 'A Long Time Alone' that enjoyed mild popularity within the Bay Area but not enough to convince him to keep the new name. The same year he reverted to his given name, Sylvester Stewart, and released another single, 'Help Me with My Broken Heart', that also vanished quickly. Then he joined the Viscaynes and recorded a song, 'Yellow Moon', that sold well on the West Coast. One of the musicians backing him up on the recording session was a white saxophone player and future Family Stone member named Jerry Martini.

'The Viscaynes were a Vallejo singing group that was very hip and very unique because it was an integrated band. They had a Filipino. Sly was the Afro. There were girls and boys and all different colours. Sly had a hell of a time back then because he was having an affair with one of the white girls in the band – the most beautiful girl – and they had to keep it secret. He had all this talent and was so far beyond this racial bullshit that was going on back then that it had to affect his psyche. "Yellow Moon" wasn't a hit but it got him the attention of Bob Mitchell and Tom Donahue [San Francisco's two most important disc jockeys of the sixties], who hired him to work at Autumn Records. Then in 1963 he wrote "The Swim" for the black R'n'B singer Bobby Freeman and had his first gold record.'

With the first royalty cheque Sly received from the million sales notched up by 'The Swim', he made a down-payment on a new house for his parents, brothers and sisters. Everyone from back then remembers him as a very focused and responsible young man. According to Carl Scott, who was also employed by Donahue and Mitchell during that period, 'Sly was a rock-'n'roll guy. He was certainly not what we consider to be R'n'B. He had a pop sensibility to him that was always obvious. He was so young and so cool and so nice. He had a Beatle haircut and it was either brown or red or somewhere in between. Tight black pants. Beatle boots. Wore glasses. I used to write his paychecks – he didn't earn a lot but [Donahue and Mitchell] took care of Sly. They knew that Sly was a genius, or could be.'

In 1964 Sly produced records by Gloria Scott & the Tonettes, the Spearmints, San Francisco's Beatle-inspired Beau Brummels and Bobby Freeman as well as 'I Just Learned How to Swim', the first single he released under the name of Sly Stewart. In 1965 he produced the debut sessions for Grace Slick's Great Society and managed to record the first-ever version of 'Somebody to Love', the song that Slick would have a hit with two years later as a member of Jefferson Airplane. He also produced the first demo tape of the Grateful Dead back when they were still known as the Warlocks, as well as singles for local Bay Area bands like the Mojo Men, the Vegetables and Chosen Few. The same year he signed up as a disc jockey for KSOL and quickly became notorious around San Francisco for his slurred hep-cat interjections between records. Veteran West Coast soul radio DJ Johnny Morris worked with Sly on both KSOL and KDIA in the mid-sixties. 'His show opened with [beatnik comedian] Lord Buckley going, "Hey all you cats and kitties." Then a girl's voice would say, "I'm talking about

Sly Stone." He was working seven to midnight, then I'd take over. Billy Preston used to come to the station a lot because Sly collaborated with Billy on one of his albums called *The Wildest Organ*.' After midnight, Sly, often with Preston in tow, would leave the station and journey to North Beach, where he quickly immersed himself in a lifestyle that was diametrically opposed to his clean-living origins. He became infatuated with the world of gangster-owned nightclubs; he wanted to be perceived as something of a bad-ass and started consorting with individuals who were all successful and extremely ruthless career criminals. The most notorious of his new friends was a cut-throat thug named Hamp 'Bubba' Banks, an ex-Marine who ran a hairstyling salon in the Fillmore district that was really just a front for one of San Francisco's largest prostitution rings. Banks taught Sly the rules of pimping and the latter quickly began controlling a number of prostitutes himself. He didn't exactly need the money – he just liked to soak up the feeling of 'street' power it conveyed upon him. 'Every night we were the two players of North Beach,' recalled Banks more than thirty years later. 'We were always the centre of attention. My life is what he was fascinated with. He wanted to be a tough guy and I was that tough guy.'

Sly still found time to perform live in Bay Area clubs. In late 1966 he began Sly and the Stoners with old school friend John Turk and a young female trumpet player and unwed mother named Cynthia Robinson. His brother Freddie meanwhile formed Freddie and the Stone Souls with a skinny teenager named Greg Errico on drums. The two groups then merged into Sly and the Family Stone in early '67, with Sly adding his saxophonist pal Jerry Martini and finally convincing his sister Rose to join on keyboards and backing vocals as well. Sly found the other key ingredient, Larry Graham Jr, playing bass in a jazz club backing up his mother Dell Graham, an accomplished jazz/pop singer/pianist in the Dinah Washington tradition. 'My mother and I didn't have a drummer,' Graham later recalled, 'so I would thump the strings to make up for not having a bass drum and pluck the strings because I didn't have that snare drum backbeat. I didn't think I was developing anything new. It was just out of necessity.'

Sly saw the potential of this novel approach to bass-playing immediately and urged Graham to join his new group. The first time they all rehearsed together, all the parts locked together perfectly. 'Then, after the rehearsal was over,' recalls Cynthia Robinson, 'Larry says, "OK, let's take a vote and see who will be the leader." And Sly simply replied, "There's not going to be any vote. This is my band, I'm the leader of it, and if you don't like that, there's the door." There was no question to anyone who the leader was. It was made very clear to us.' 'If you knew Sly back then,' reflects drummer Greg Errico, 'you knew that he always thought "big", he always thought "different", he always thought "unique". Whatever he was going to do had to reflect that.'

Stone/Stewart was savvy enough to see that the late-sixties music audience was divided into white kids on acid pretending to be hippies and worshipping the Beatles and – across the tracks – black youth grooving to the earthier rhythms of James Brown and Tamla-Motown, and that if he fronted a flamboy-antly dressed, mixed-race, mixed-sex band who excelled at funk but who also had a strong pop sensibility mixed in with a lot of 'love thy neighbour' positivity, then he stood a fighting chance at bridging that great divide and becoming a megastar in the process. That was his basic game-plan, anyway, and it served him well: by 1969 he'd achieved everything he'd origi-nally set out to. Still, it didn't happen overnight; first, they were signed to Epic Records by the label's head man David Kapralik. 'I had, from the get-go, a sense of certainty about him,' remem-bers the diminutive Jewish record executive who also opted to become Sly Stone's manager. 'There was no question that he was a tour de force, an original. After I signed them I said to Sly, "I can help you accomplish your dreams and you will be a star and you will have great power. But only you can decide what you are going to do with that power: either use it in a positive way or use it despotically." '

Sly and the Family Stone's debut album, *A Whole New Thing*, was released in 1967. It was a witty, hip collection of Sly originals, extensively utilizing the talents of his fellow members, but it failed to attract radio play anywhere and sold too few copies to dent even the lower echelons of the album chart. 'I remember Sly and I going to Epic Records,' recalls Jerry Martini, 'and the executives saying to us, "This is what you should listen to." They gave us some shit and Sly threw it down and he looked at me and said, "I'll give them something." And this is when he took off with his formula style. We then recorded a whole album called *Dance to the Music* – it was one long bullshit medley. It was so unhip to us and he hated it.'

However the 'Dance to the Music' single they recorded in early 1968 was the track that broke them into the mainstream of popular music; by the summer of that year, it was a Top 10 hit all over the singles charts of the world. As soon as it charted, the single marked a major change within the group personality of Sly and the Family Stone. On 10 June 1968 the group played two shows at New York's Fillmore East, supporting the Jimi Hendrix Experience. 'That was the turning point right there,' recalls his manager Kapralik. 'Up to that point, each individual member had their star turn. Each member did a solo. At the Fillmore, he decided it was going to be a one-man show and everyone else was going to back him up, and he took away all their solos.'

A key reason for Sly's new egocentric thinking came in the form of a crystalline white powder he had lately become fascinated with inhaling. 'I remember the first time Sly gave me cocaine,' recalls Martini. 'It was at his house at 700 Urbano Street in San Francisco in 1967. It wasn't a big deal to him then but it had become a big deal by the time we played New York.'

Kapralik, in an attempt to further organize the Family Stone's busy schedule, employed a young black woman named Stephani Swanigan to become Sly's 'personal assistant'. She discovered what her main role was going to be the day she first met her new boss in New York during the Fillmore East performances. 'He came to my room and put a couple of large bags of white powder on the table. I asked what it was. He said, "It's pharmaceutical cocaine." He was getting his drugs from a dentist who would give him and anybody in the group as many prescription drugs – cocaine and downers – as they wanted. It got to the point where I'd go myself, get prescriptions for everybody and come back with bottles and bottles of powder and pills.'

He'd soon enough become dependent on constantly sampling the ongoing rush of cocaine because the drug gave him exactly the sensation of ruthless invincibility he as Sly Stone needed to keep his pop-star persona crackling at full force. For a brief while it appeared to serve his music well. After *Dance to the Music* he recorded *Life*, but the album and the single from it of the same name didn't sell as well as their predecessors. No matter: by the end of 1968, he'd achieved his first US No. 1 hit single with the anthemic 'Everyday People', the brilliant follow-up to 'Life'. Then, as 1969 began, he went into the studio to record 'Stand', the feisty hymn to self-assertion he'd always look back on as his finest-ever creation. Stephen Paley, a Columbia Records executive, was present with Sly when he recorded the track. 'After he finished, we drove up to San Francisco to a discotheque and Sly gave a rough acetate of "Stand" to the DJ to play. He watched the audience's reaction and realized there was something missing. The next day he returned to the studio and recorded that funky extension with session musicians and edited it onto the end of the record. He was so together he even wrote out the parts on music paper for the horn players. He took his music very seriously in those days.'

The *Stand* album – with its provocative 'Don't Call Me Nigger, Whitey' and the cataclysmic 'I Want to Take You Higher' (a song that had first gained exposure under the name of 'Advice' on the 1966 Billy Preston *The Wildest Organ in Town* album Sly helped produce) – was all over the US albums Top 20 throughout the summer of '69. In August of that year he decided to release the sunny soul-pop of 'Hot Fun in the Summertime' and that too shot to No. 1, even though the summer was practically over by the time it hit the shops. Woodstock happened that same month and suddenly Sly was the golden funky minstrel-boy of the Aquarian Age, the name on everybody's lips, the superstar who was going to take music out onto the next level – wherever that was. Still, there was no new album to capitalize on the phenomenal success he experienced from being in the movie *Woodstock*. Instead there was just one schizophrenic double A-sided single recorded at the end of the year and released in early 1970. 'Everybody Is a Star' was a sweet soul ballad with lyrics that stressed the power of positive thinking, but its other side, 'Thankyouforlettinmebemyselfagain' was malevolent-sounding and full of murky menace as Sly croaked druggily about fighting with the Devil over a murderous funk riff. It was a brilliant, scary piece of work, but the sinister track also eerily mirrored all the ugly changes too much success and too much cocaine were putting its creator's personality through.

By the end of 1969 Sly Stone had moved from San Francisco to Los Angeles – into a house on Coldwater Canyon full of drugs, guns, dogs, bodyguards and hangers-on. The first call he made once he'd installed himself was to reconnect with his old pimping buddy Hamp Banks, who'd been incarcerated whilst Sly and the Family Stone were getting formed. 'When I got out of jail, Sly got in touch with me and said, "I need you, man,"' recalls Banks. 'When I got to Los Angeles, he was the cocaine king. I saw him walking down Hollywood Boulevard with a violin case and cocaine was just falling out the back of it. Then he got into PCP at Coldwater and he was just out of it. Finished. It was over. He was doing shit you would expect to see in some kind of institution for mentally retarded people. He and Freddie walked around the house all day like zombies. I started sleeping with a pistol. See, I was his personal manager. Sly trusted me. Now he could do what he wanted. He could pass out. Before he would pass out, he'd always say "Where's Hamp?" And if I was in the house, he could do what he wanted.'

Much to the horror of the diminutive David Kapralik, Banks and his hoodlums were suddenly promoted by Sly to business positions involving key aspects of his professional career. It was all starting to fall apart now. Sly wasn't even turning up to his own gigs. His road manager Vernon 'Moose' Constan tried to talk to him about all the grotesque consequences of his super-star whims – riots in auditoriums, fans hospitalized, promoters bankrupted – but he couldn't have cared less. 'He just said to me, "If I worked down at a drugstore and didn't feel like showing up that day, I probably wouldn't even get fired. Here I am this powerful person and I don't have the right to say I don't want to show up." That was his reason for not going to a concert. Another one of his clichés was, "Being sorry is for sorry people," so you would never get that word out of him.'

Group members started to get disgruntled at his self-destructive egomania. Promoters who'd been burned by him swore revenge and muttered darkly about hiring professional hitmen to do the job. Black Panthers began confronting him in a threatening way, suggesting he and his group become advo-cates for their cause. His record-company boss Clive Davis even cut off all his royalties in an attempt to get him to finish a new album. A feverishly paranoid Sly Stone then decided he needed more muscle to solve his dilemmas. According to 'J.B.', a criminal associate of Banks: 'One night me and Sly went to the house of the head of the Long Island Mafia. We went through this tunnel and up to this guy's bedroom. He was a big guy – in his fifties or sixties – and Sly jumps on the bed with this guy and his wife. Then they start negotiating. The next thing, J.R. came into the picture.' J.R. Vatrano became Sly's personal bodyguard. J.R. was truly a gangster. (Another 'gift' from the Mafia to Sly came in the form of Pat Rizzo, an Italo-American sax player who played in the Family Stone horn section between 1971 and 1975. Rizzo is the nephew of the infamous Jilly Rizzo, Frank Sinatra's personal leg-breaker.)

In 1971 Sly moved out of the Coldwater Canyon house and installed himself and his goons at a Bel Air mansion he rented from Mamas and Papas leader John Phillips. 'These people were rough,' Phillips would later recall in his autobiography *Papa John*. 'They laughed at me. There were lots of guns, rifles, machine guns and killer dogs.' In the end, Phillips had to employ a small army of machete-wielding Mexican gardeners to 'persuade' Sly and Co. to honour the original terms of their agreement.

Through the summer and autumn he locked himself away in numerous LA studios, and with a rhythm machine for a drummer and himself playing bass and keyboards, he recorded his long-awaited new album. He practically lived in a huge mobile home he'd park next to whichever studio he was using. It was always party time and though actual Family Stone members are only minimally featured on the finished record, many of his more famous party pals – such as Ike Turner, Herbie Hancock and Bobby Womack – can be heard playing on tracks from the album Sly chose to call *There's a Riot Goin' On*. Womack remembers the sessions as 'very spacey. I'd be sitting in the dark, coked out of my brain, tryin' to sing, staying up four, five, six days. Sly'd be all dressed in red leather, handing out the orders – like "Tiffany, baby. I want you to take Bobby to your room and have sex with him." I forgot where my wife was, where my son was: I was just spaced. I became paranoid of everything. I kept thinking the Feds would bust in on Sly and we'd all be killed.'

There's a Riot Goin' On remains an exceptional album if only for the fact that never has one individual managed to sound so hopelessly drugged up on record and still manage to have a colossal hit with it. Several noted critics wrote admiringly that the album's often soporific groove provided the perfect sonic backdrop to the black struggles of the era, but the only 'riot' going on throughout the record was taking place in its creator's over-stimulated brain-pan. Never has one album sounded so utterly infested with cocaine's disturbing energy. Against all music business logic, *Riot* quickly became his biggest-selling album to date in the States whilst 'Family Affair', its first single, was another rapid-fire No. 1 hit. The added power and prestige only corrupted him further. David Kapralik was now out of the picture, though still suing his former client for $250,000 in personal loans. Drummer Greg Errico quit after Sly called him 'a dog' backstage after a show; he wasn't getting paid, anyway. And Larry Graham was starting to feel increasingly uncomfortable playing in the Family Stone. Sly didn't like him any more. He'd lately been in sour relationship with his sister Rose, and he'd also been having an affair with Freddie's wife. That shit wasn't cool. Worse yet, the motherfucker was blatantly trying to upstage Sly in concert the way he dressed so flamboyantly. There was only one solution in Sly's view – he ordered Hamp Banks to find a hitman to shoot his bass player. Banks quickly imported a hired killer named Eddie Chin. In the ensuing altercation – in the lobby of an LA hotel – one of Graham's henchmen was crippled for life whilst Graham barely escaped with his own life. 'I saved Larry's life,' recalls incoming saxophonist Pat Rizzo. 'I got him and his girlfriend out of the hotel room. I had a rented car outside. They were going to kill Larry. I don't know why.'

Evil followed Sly Stone everywhere after that. He and Banks were invited by then-popular US band Three Dog Night to a private cocaine party at a hotel they were all staying in. Somehow they started a fight. 'Well, it wasn't a fight,' claims

Banks. 'Me and Sly just beat up everyone in the room. Then we got sued.' One evening Freddie Stewart found a stranger lurking by the pool of his brother's Bel Air mansion and promptly karate-kicked him into a coma: it turned out to be the bass player from Redbone. Sly attended a big LA music-awards ceremony in early 1973 and was approached by Karen Carpenter. 'Sly – love you,' chirped the anorexic pop diva. 'Who the fuck is this ugly bitch?' was Sly's riposte. In early 1974 he almost got into a fist-fight with Muhammad Ali on a national televised talk show, *The Mike Douglas Show*. 'Muhammad Ali was putting Sly down,' recalls Jerry Martini. 'He was saying that Sly was a sell-out and an Uncle Tom with everybody watching.' Apparently, the pair had fighting words in the dressing room earlier over their respective girlfriends. Sly's current girl was called Kathy Silva; he'd stolen her from Isaac Hayes and started living with her and her twin sister in a ménage-à-trois scene. Then Kathy got pregnant and Sly contemplated matrimony. Silva became the inspiration for the more tender moments that occur on *Fresh*, Sly Stone's last album of substance, released in 1973. A year later she'd become Mrs Sylvester Stewart at a public wedding/gig performed at Madison Square Garden. The show was a high-profile promotion gambit for *Small Talk*, Sly's 1974 album which featured a cover photo of Sly embracing Silva and their baby son, whom he named Sylvester Bubb Ali Stewart. The album was weak, though – bereft of inspiration – and his marriage even weaker: four months later Silva filed for divorce after Sly's dog Gun had literally bitten off the face of their infant son. 'He ripped off half my baby's skin from his left ear,' recalls Silva. 'At the hospital, he had over 120 stitches from the shoulder up. He was just beginning to talk and he immediately became catatonic.'

Sly tried to continue playing out his despotic role but by the end of 1974 it was all over. Too many cancelled live shows. Too many not-so-earth-shattering new records. Meanwhile, the likes of Stevie Wonder and Marvin Gaye were all kicking his ass as creative black music-makers and stealing his audience. It was all he needed to push him over the edge. One night he walked into LA's Record Plant studios with several of his gun-toting goons in order to 'liberate' some master tapes of recordings he'd made there but hadn't paid for. 'Give me my fuckin' tapes,' he demanded of studio manager Michelle Zarin – but she, like increasingly more people, was no longer so easy to intimidate. 'Go ahead, motherfucker, shoot me,' she remembers taunting Stone that night. 'He finally takes me into another room and says, "Don't embarrass me, please just give me the tapes." And when I tell him he has already ruined his career enough, he says, "Shit." Then he just walks back to the other room and tell the flunkies, "Okay, guys, let's get out of here." Just before leaving he turns back to me and says, "It's tough being me sometimes, but I've got to be Sly to the end of the line."'

Ever since that incident, Sly has stayed resolutely true to his word. He still released albums occasionally. *High on You* in 1975 and *Heard Ya Missed Me, Well I'm Back* in 1978 were his final releases for Epic, but both sold weakly and garnered mediocre reviews. His funk no longer defined the cutting edge of black music. Sly then signed with Warner Bros and released *Back on the Right Track* in 1979 followed three years later by his final release, *Ain't but One Way*. 'Sly didn't finish either record himself,' claims Bob Merlis, Warner's PR director during that epoch. 'He worked on them for a while, then disappeared and we had to bring other people in to complete the tracks. Sly just wasn't physically around.'

Sly's all-purpose invisibility in the late 1970s was prompted by several causes. 'He moved into an out-of-the-way run-down apartment, rode around in a second-hand Mustang,' claims his brother Freddie. 'The glamour didn't mean anything anymore.' Partly, he was hiding from old gangster running-buddies who felt Sly had somehow sold them short. But most of all he was devoting his every waking moment to a new pursuit: freebasing cocaine. Then the drug busts started piling up. He'd been popped several times for drugs and guns in the early seventies but back then he still had his superstar prestige and thug enforcers to deflect the consequences and keep him out of serious grief. Now it was different and he was more vulnerable. In October 1979 a judge placed him on a 'drug diversion programme' after his arrest in West Hollywood for cocaine possession. In August 1981 he and George Clinton of Parliament-Funkadelic were arrested on an LA freeway for freebasing cocaine in a moving vehicle. Eleven months later, in July '82, he got busted again for cocaine possession at the Westwood Plaza hotel in LA. In 1983 police arrested him for stealing a diamond ring from the patron of a gay discotheque somewhere in Florida; the same year police broke down the door of a room in the Ramada Airport hotel in Fort Myers, Florida, and found Sly Stone and a girlfriend unconscious, surrounded by three propane tanks, a torch and a razor-blade with white powder still on it. Sly admitted he'd been freebasing, 'but it's all gone'. Then he fell back into his deep, deep slumber.

In January 1984 Sylvester Stewart was sentenced to incarceration in a Florida drug detox centre for six months. The stay seemed to stimulate a positive upswing in his personality. 'Once he got involved, he set an example to everyone,' remembers Richard Sapp, the clinic's co-director. 'He contributed to group meetings and even assisted other clients. He spent time with those who had severe emotional problems to liven up their day.' But that all changed when he got released in the summer of '84 to perform selected concert dates with Bobby Womack. A&M toyed with the idea of signing Sly up in the mid-eighties. 'Sly can make music history again,' grandly predicted label vice-president John McClain. Yet he too had his doubts about whether such a resurrection would genuinely benefit the man. 'Right now Sly's humble, but give him a hit record and MTV exposure and all his old gangster cronies would come out of the woodwork to suck his blood again. I could be doing him more harm than good.'

Negotiations between Sly and A&M broke down after McClain read an interview with the former in *Spin* magazine in 1985. Sly had begun the interview by driving his inquisitor to a roughneck Los Angeles suburb and initiating a drug deal in a nearby car park. In 1986 he was arrested twice – for cocaine possession in December and non-payment of child support to Kathy Silva a month earlier. In 1987 he was busted five times for cocaine and spent most of the year in LA County Jail. In November '89 he was sentenced to fifty-five more days in jail on outstanding fugitive charges: this was his last-known run-in with American law enforcement agencies.

In the nineties he made just one public appearance. On 23 January 1993 he and the Family Stone were inducted into the Rock'n'Roll Hall of Fame. He arrived late, having been waylaid by an argument with a girlfriend who'd stolen all his clothes. Dressed in a woman's blue leatherette jumpsuit and sporting a cheap wig, Sly looked out of it, barely exchanged a word with former band mates and left as soon as he'd picked up his award.

Nowadays he is said to be living 'quietly' in a West Hollywood apartment. In 1997 he invited a fan named John Dakss to his place to install the Internet on his home computer. Sly even played him some new material. 'Nothing has changed,' marvelled Dakss. 'All his talent is still there.'

Meanwhile his old nemesis Larry Graham had started working with Prince and building a powerful and popular live act based on the old Family Stone hit repertoire. In 1997 he did a world tour with Cynthia Robinson, Jerry Martini and Rose Stewart playing by his side and screaming their old parts on 'Everyday People' and 'I Wanna Take You Higher'. Once, I interviewed Prince and asked him if he'd ever consider 'rescuing' Sly Stone the way he'd done with his old bass player's career. He just laughed and made a cryptic comment about how 'it wouldn't be wise to get involved with someone whose lifestyle got too in the way of his music'.

Meanwhile, back in Vallejo, Alpha Stewart still goes to church daily and prays for her wayward eldest son's deliverance from ongoing spiritual bankruptcy. She and her late husband finally rescued Freddie in the mid-eighties after his cocaine addiction had put him in the nut house. Now he is the pastor of a Vallejo church with a day job driving a bus for disabled school children. But can God still reach out to Sly Stone? Former colleagues think otherwise. According to Rusty Allen, 'I remember once Sly saying to one of the band, "I believe I have done too much evil in this world and God will never take me back."'

'It's a sad business,' concludes Freddie Stewart about the brother he rarely sees these days. 'He knows what he didn't do. He knows what we all wish he had done. I know he wishes he could have done better. By me and by a lot of other people. I believe he thinks about it all the time.'

A Portrait of Serge Gainsbourg

Throughout my career as a music journalist, I've often found myself sharing the same orbit as some of the more maladjusted talents of the late twentieth century, but nothing could have prepared me for the time I spent with Serge Gainsbourg, the louche, turtle-eyed genius of *la chanson française*, little more than two years before his death. In early December 1988 I was invited to be a judge at a week-long festival being held in Val d'Isère – a small village on the snowy, mountainous borderline between France and Switzerland where holidaymakers generally go to ski. Upon my arrival I discovered that Gainsbourg was also a judge: in fact, he was the head of the voting jury which also consisted of Julian Temple and a bunch of French video directors. I already knew who he was – up to a point. As a teenager, I'd seen him act in a couple of films – he'd reminded me then of a shorter, Russian-Jewish version of the dandy theatre critic Kenneth Tynan – and of course I was well acquainted with 'Je t'aime moi non plus', the erotically charged record he made with Jane Birkin that had been a UK No. 1 back in 1969 even though the song had been banned on the radio. I was aware he was a well-loved figure in France but was still taken aback by the reactions of his fellow country-folk gathered at this snow-capped outpost, all of whom seemed to regard him as their very own homegrown Bob Dylan – an untouchable and utterly unique cultural deity.

On the first evening, everyone gathered together at the local cinema to hear Gainsbourg give a speech that would kick off the whole event. We sat there patiently waiting until the air was suddenly rent with horrible screaming sounds followed by a cacophony of Gallic swearing. The owner of the cinema had just informed Gainsbourg in the lobby that he was entering a no-smoking zone and the great man had thrown a royal fit. Five minutes later he entered the room, his face lost in a dense fog of cigarette smoke – the owner was carrying a huge ashtray and stood next to him like his eunuch flunky catching the ash as it fell – and stumbled to the podium. He looked absolutely terrible – his face and body utterly polluted from alcohol abuse, his eyes ugly unfocused slits, his voice a sneerful rasping whisper. He began to tell an obscene story involving Brigitte Bardot and a champagne bottle but he was too drunk to remember the ending so he staggered offstage, literally collapsing into a nearby seat. Everyone else gave him a standing ovation but I just sat there, stunned. I'd never seen anything quite like this: a beloved icon who'd lost all self-control and who was making an ignominious public spectacle of himself over and over again and yet his public wasn't repelled in the least. On the contrary, they couldn't seem to get enough of watching his continued self-abasement.

These days, you read a lot about Serge Gainsbourg – the genius, the subversive, the playboy lover – but the Serge Gainsbourg I had the misfortune to encounter was a raging alcoholic above all else. Alcoholism clouded his moods, actions and work to such an intense degree towards the end of his life that he became another person altogether: 'Gainsbarre', he called his alcoholic alter-ego – a dissolute, disgusting, death-fixated individual perilously close to clinical insanity.

I wish I could tell you I enjoyed at least one meaningful conversation with him during that week but I'd be lying if I did. A couple of times communication was attempted but I could never understand one slurred syllable of what was coming out of his mouth. He preferred the company of his many French admirers anyway. They'd buy him drinks at the hotel bar and listen enraptured to his drunken reminiscences. Their adulation seemed to provide him with a comfort zone he could temporarily lose himself in, somewhere to escape from the looming darkness of oncoming death. He knew he was going to die soon – there was absolutely no doubt about this. One of the other judges had a hotel room directly adjacent to his suite and told us that every night he'd be awoken at around 3 a.m. by the sound of Gainsbourg screaming 'I'm going blind', over and over again.

Still – to his credit – he always maintained a solid work ethic whatever his personal condition and seemed to take his duties as a judge seriously. He attended all the screenings, anyway, even though I can still recall his sonorous snoring throughout a Pet Shop Boys film we both had to endure. The festival ended with the French preview of *Imagine*, the John Lennon documentary. When the film climaxed with the ex-Beatle's death scene – blood-stained glasses crashing to the Manhattan pavement – Gainsbourg bellowed like a wounded animal and had to be physically escorted out of the viewing theatre. Watching another icon's anguished passing was evidently far too close to home for him to tolerate.

As fate would have it, I met the woman who is now my wife on the last night of the film festival. A month later I moved to Paris. As time passed I began to attain a greater understanding of Gainsbourg's true worth as a ground-breaking artist. I came to appreciate his extraordinary gift for elegant, lyrical wordplay and saw him as the direct, though more gleefully perverse, heir to Cole Porter in terms of shaping an inspired lyric. I admired his ruthless need for self-transformation and his daringly eclectic taste in musical arrangements but remained somewhat wary of his 'provocateur' side, which usually became ignited when too much liquor was coursing through his bloodstream.

These days, people talk about the televised incident from the eighties when a drunken Gainsbourg informed Whitney

Houston that he wanted to 'fuck' her – like it was some sort of epiphany. Watch the thing again, however, and it just looks sordid and silly. No one comes out looking good: neither the haughty, flustered Houston not the slobbering, barely coherent 'Gainsbarre'. Meanwhile, the French talk-show compère looks on impotently as though a rhinoceros had just stampeded into the studio. A far more powerful and pertinent example of the delinquent Gainsbarre's penchant to disgust whenever a camera was focused in front of him occurred not long before his death when he appeared on yet another talk show alongside Catherine Ringer, the gifted singer in Rita Mitsouko, a popular French duo of the time. Before becoming a successful professional musician, Ringer had appeared in several porn films and, for some mad reason, this did not sit well with Gainsbourg at all. 'You're nothing but a filthy whore,' he suddenly spat out at her. 'A filthy, fucking whore.' Ringer wasted no time in giving back as good as she got: 'Look at you, you're just a bitter old alcoholic,' she scolded back. 'I used to admire you but these days you've become a disgusting old parasite.' Finally, someone in France had the temerity to challenge the country's crumbling deity in public. It was great television.

Fifteen years after Serge Gainsbourg's death, the alcoholism factor is starting to be subtly air-brushed out of the portrait of the man that is being handed down to the ages. A recent two-hour TV homage to him brought forth a cavalcade of UK and French musicians – many of whom had participated in the newly available *Citizen Gainsbourg* tribute album – to sing his songs and talk about his life and influence in interview snippets. Everyone spoke glowingly of Gainsbourg's unique aesthetic sensibility but no one dared even to broach the subject of what he really became at the end of his life. Like magpies, the Brit rock young bucks hear something alluringly exotic and suave in this crazy French guy's music and want to appropriate it into their own work. Good luck to them – Gainsbourg himself would have been utterly delighted – but there remains the sense that they're still too young and wet behind the ears to have got the full measure of his often depraved but always profoundly human artistic vision.

Phil Spector's Long Fall from Grace

Cast your eyes along a gallery of photographs taken of the mega-producer/rock'n'roll legend Phil Spector throughout the past forty years and soon enough you'll find yourself entering a bizarre world of celebrity wig-wearing that would make even Elton John blush. Spector's mercurial rise as teen pop's very own Richard Wagner at the beginning of the sixties coincided with him also losing his hair at an equally dramatic speed. He correctly deduced that a balding pate would hinder his progress as omnipotent tycoon of teen and promptly filled several closets of his various residences with every style of hairpiece he could get his hands on. The wigs were short haired and well groomed in the mid-1960s when he was riding the big waves of success with the Ronettes and Righteous Brothers, but after his 'retirement' in 1966 they – like their owner – got stranger and stranger. There's a photo of him with his arm round John Lennon in the early seventies in which he's sporting a giant ginger Afro wig with a huge beard to match it, looking like a drunken Scottish fisherman who's just spent two years living in a cave. In 1978 he was photographed at a backstage encounter with Blondie under a thick black-fringed helmet of someone's else hair – his weak chin prickly with a small goatee – doing an unconvincing job of masquerading as the dark prince of Hollywood. As recently as 2005 in *Vanity Fair* he demonstrated once again that he had no shame where rugs were concerned. The result of his first major photo session for many long years found him squinting myopically into the camera, his beady eyes hidden by shades and his wizened tiny face framed by a hideous-looking mullet wig that made him look like Mr Magoo reincarnated as a drowned rat.

In a business where physical attractiveness is paramount, Phil Spector never made it on his looks. He grew up short and wimpy-looking with asthma and a possessive, controlling, French-born mother named Bertha whose mischievous, darting eyes he inherited. Spector was born Harvey Phillip Spector on 26 December 1940 in Brooklyn, where his father Benjamin, a Russian Jewish immigrant, had secured a union job as an iron-worker which helped pay for their modest brick house at 1024 Manor Avenue. Ben Spector was broad-shouldered and well loved within his community. Relatives say that it was his side of the family that possessed the genes of musical talent his son would inherit. But there were always dark shadows lurking in the corners of the Spector household. Spector Sr was a chronic manic depressive who found himself increasingly unable to cope with solving the family's ongoing financial difficulties. Early on 20 April 1949 he left his house to drive to work, parked several blocks away in front of a deserted building at 1042 Myrtle Avenue, methodically attached one end of a water hose to his car's exhaust pipe, put the other end through a crack in the front window and choked himself to death on the deadly fumes in full view of passers-by on a sunny spring morning. Ben Spector's suicide was something his relatives could never bring themselves to address publicly; his children were told that he'd died in some unexplained accident but the legacy they inherited told them otherwise. Phil Spector would spend his whole life battling with feelings of inadequacy, manic depression and suicidal impulses. His older sister Shirley spent most of her adult life in a series of mental hospitals; her brother would always pay the fees.

Life became almost unbearable for Phil Spector as he entered his teens. He'd worshipped his father and now he had nothing but unexplained darkness to relate to. His asthma attacks grew more oppressive than ever. His mother and sister wouldn't stop fussing over him, being over-protective, always telling him what to wear and how to behave. And the nights were the worst of all. He'd fall asleep and start dreaming that he was in the process of being strangled, choked to death – all his twitchy child energy being barbarically squeezed out of his tiny body.

In an attempt to start afresh, Bertha Spector moved the family to Los Angeles – to modest digs in West Hollywood – and started work as a seamstress four years after her husband's inexplicable death. Sister Shirley – tall, blonde and extremely aggressive – started hustling for work as a model whilst Phil hid away in his room, toying with his one treasured possession: an acoustic guitar a relative had given him. His dreams disturbed him so much that he never slept at night; he'd just sit there in the pitch black playing his guitar until daybreak. By day he attended school – first Laurel Elementary School, then the John Burroughs Junior High and finally, in 1954, Fairfax High. He was an excellent scholar but not well liked by most of his peers, who found him creepy and singularly unattractive. His first real friend in Los Angeles was a brawny, athletic youth named Marshall Lieb who was physically the polar opposite of Spector. 'At school, Phil always had this chip on his shoulder. Someone would say something to him and he'd insult them right back. This would instigate a fight and I'd have to go and bail him out. He had a way about his answers that antagonized people. I was really his first bodyguard when you think about it.'

Lieb and Spector's friendship was actually based on a mutual high regard for popular music. By his mid-teens Spector had become a music fanatic – a proficient guitar player and a world-class authority on both white rock'n'roll and black rhythm'n'blues, both of which he listened to voraciously on the radio. For his fifteenth birthday Bertha and Shirley took him to a Hollywood nightclub to watch Ella Fitzgerald perform and Phil Spector became smitten with the guitarist in Fitzgerald's backing orchestra – a well-respected West Coast jazz player named Barney Kessel. Eleven months after the performance the jazz monthly *Downbeat* published a letter in its November 1956 issue from Spector raving about Kessel, 'who in my opinion holds the title of world's greatest guitarist'.

Sensing her son's obsessive zeal, Bertha Spector went so far as to personally contact Kessel by phone and request an audience with the musician. Kessel – who'd seen the *Downbeat* letter – agreed. At a coffee shop called Dupars on Vine Street in Hollywood, Spector sat furtively, watching as his mother explained to Kessel that her son dreamt of being a jazz guitarist. Still she was worried: was there a solid wage to be earned from following such a dream? Kessel understood her concerns:

> I remember telling her that if he had talent, I thought it was a wise move to direct it more into the pop field. Because there were so many great jazz artists who weren't able to make a living anymore from playing jazz. You couldn't go out and play jazz on the road anymore; it was all rock'n'roll. I said that he should get into the pop field and write songs, get involved in publishing and maybe work as an apprentice in a record company, to find out how to mix sessions and get involved in the multi-dimensionality of the whole thing.

This is precisely what Phil Spector wasted no time in doing. He and Lieb started up a band in Fairfax High which specialized in doo-wop and Everly Brothers covers. They played live locally and Spector always did a solo spot, which consisted of him tearing through Lonnie Donegan's skiffle classic 'Rock Island Line', replete with guitar solos. At age sixteen, Spector and Lieb even managed to appear on a late-night TV talent show titled *Rocket to Stardom*. They performed the Moonglows' 'In the Still of the Night' as a vocal duo and ended up winning the night's competition.

Spector graduated from Fairfax High in June '57. In the fall, he and Lieb enrolled at Los Angeles City College. Because of his mother, he'd become fluent in French and considered work as a translator before opting for a course as a court reporter. Spector practised his typing skills by transcribing all the dialogue from Dick Clark's *American Bandstand* TV show onto his stenotype machine every afternoon. He did professional work as a court reporter during this time, transcribing the much-publicized court trial of Cheryl Crane, Lana Turner's daughter, who was accused of murdering Turner's gangster boyfriend John Stompanato. But music remained his key priority. He'd started turning up at local LA recording studios unannounced – full of questions for the long-suffering engineers present about the use of various knobs on the recording console and the effectiveness of the primitive echo chambers that had been rigged up to provide greater sonic depth and atmosphere for recorded sound. Spector's favourite studio set-up was at Gold Star: it boasted two echo chambers. There was a middle-aged guy named Stan Ross who engineered there and who didn't mind Spector poking his nose in and watching sessions. He wouldn't give the teenager any free recording time, however, and so Phil Spector financed his first-ever studio session with $40 collected via $10 donations apiece from Bertha Spector, Marsha Lieb, Harvey Goldstein (a school friend) and Annette Kleinbard, a friend of Donna Kass, his first girlfriend. Kleinbard ended up singing on the two-hour session, with Spector, Lieb and Goldstein harmonizing behind her.

Spector had produced and played everything and had even written the featured song – a forgettable piece of pop fluff entitled 'Don't You Worry, My Little Pet'. He took the finished demo to Lew Bedell, a local figure who, with Herb Newsome, owned Era Records – one of numerous minor LA-based record labels then sprouting up. Bedell signed it up and paid for an extra session to record a B-side. Spector called his group the Teddy Bears after the song 'Teddy Bear' recorded by his hero

Elvis Presley but failed to complete a second session for the recording of the B-side – another Spector original 'Wonderful Lovable You' – successfully. At a third Gold Star session he managed an acceptable take of the song but was more excited by a third self-penned number, 'To Know Him Is to Love Him', which he managed to record in just half an hour at the tail-end of the session. The song was built around Kleinbard's chaste girlie voice. (For Marshall Lieb, ' "To Know Him" was the first girl ballad of its time. There was no innocent white-female-type voice on songs like that.') A session drummer who went on to be surf icon Sandy 'Let There Be Drums' Nelson tapped away timidly in the background.

But it was Spector to whom the achievement belonged. He'd written the song, having taken the title from the inscription on his father's headstone in the Brooklyn cemetery: 'To Have Known Him Was to Have Loved Him'. On the surface, it seemed like just another mushy teenage love ditty but the record possessed hidden depths in the form of an eerie, melancholy edge to its overall impact that was partly created by Spector playing an acceptable take over the studio loud-speakers whilst simultaneously recording additional backing on a second tape deck. To Marshall Lieb, who'd played sorcerer's apprentice to Spector's obsessive early experiments with tape recording, 'We were working on the transparency of music: that was the Teddy Bears' sound. You had a lot of air moving around, notes being played in the air but not directly into the mikes. Then, when we sent it all into the echo chamber, this air effect is what was heard – all the notes jumbled and fuzzy. This is what we recorded: not the notes; the chamber.'

On 1 August 1958, 500 copies of the Teddy Bears' first single were cautiously pressed and sent out to radio stations. After one month nothing had happened to the 'Little Pet' A-side, but then the 'To Know Him Is to Love Him' B-side started picking up radio airplay, first around LA, then in North Dakota, before exploding across the Midwest thanks to heavy rotation in

Minneapolis. Dick Clark heard the song and had the group perform it on *American Bandstand* in October. By the end of November it had rocketed to No. 1 in all the US pop charts.

The success of his record caused an eighteen-year-old Phil Spector to undergo a sudden, drastic personality change. In the eyes of his record boss, Lew Bedell, 'Before his song was a hit, Phil was so polite and obsequious I figured he was half-Japanese. Then, after it was a hit, he walks in and it's, "Hey, Lew baby, we're doing good." He starts calling Herb "Hey, you!". The kid became so fuckin' haughty.' Spector had his own reasons for patronizing the likes of Bedell; he's always maintained the latter screwed him out of some $20,000 in Teddy Bears' royalties. But other members of the Teddy Bears – who received practically nothing from their million-selling hit – tend to point an accusing finger at Spector and his scary sister Shirley, who'd loudly appointed herself the group's manager as soon as the record started selling, when talk turns to where the money really ended up. Spector then moved the group to the more prosperous Imperial Records, home to Ricky Nelson and Fats Domino. (As the performers were all minors, Lew Bedell's signed contracts meant little in court so Spector left him dangling without a second thought.) But things didn't go so well at Imperial. Two follow-up singles flopped ignominiously and when Spector started producing a Teddy Bears album, the label heads chafed at his costly and unorthodox recording methods and replaced him as producer mid-way through the project with a company man named Jimmy Haskell ('I did the songs that sound like they were hurried,' explained Haskell thirty years on in reference to the finished product *The Teddy Bears Sing!*).

By the end of 1959 the group was pretty much finished. Annette Kleinbard had been in a major auto accident that had almost stripped her nose from her face. Spector was unmoved. 'His comment,' she later recalled, 'was, "Too bad she didn't die." I was devastated by that.' Marshall Lieb was suddenly feeling an overwhelming urge to distance himself from his old school friend. 'Phillip was more familiar with the business and he was quickly becoming what he later became: an arch-deceiver of people. I just said, "Phillip, if you make a promise, you better keep it." And of course he didn't. He never paid me a royalty.'

Spector was too busy plotting his next move to waste time with basic moral issues like loyalty and sharing. He understood from the outset that in entering the music industry he was swimming with sharks and so developed a killer instinct in business that ultimately made him seem like the biggest shark of all. Because he was young, Jewish, a great 'schmoozer' and the recent creator of a No. 1 hit, record company bosses from coast to coast courted him, paid him large salaries to produce and A&R for them and then reacted in horror as their beloved boy very cooly and calculatedly fucked them over in some deeply significant way. After exiting brusquely from Imperial Records (he fobbed them off with a couple of instrumental tracks for singles credited to 'Phil Harvey'), he cultivated a close relationship with Lester Sill, a powerful West Coast music-business figure who'd lately bankrolled guitarist Duane Eddy's hit instrumental recordings with producer Lee Hazlewood. Hazlewood quickly came to hate and resent Spector's pushy style, but the older Sill consistently treated him like a favoured son, signed him up as a songwriter and record producer and immediately financed recordings in Los Angeles with the Spector Three, a surrogate Teddy Bears, and a black singer named Kell Osbourne.

Some years earlier, Sill had 'discovered' a pair of LA kids who'd also attended Spector's old Fairfax High – Jerry Leiber and Mike Stoller – and who had gone on to great success in New York, producing and composing for the like of the Coasters, the Drifters and even Elvis Presley. Sill started taking the nineteen-year-old Spector with him to the Big Apple whenever he had business to attend to there. 'He saw all the activity going on,' reminisced Sill many years later, 'because the rock-'n'roll business was really New York – the Brill Building, 1650 Broadway, Leiber and Stoller. Phil knew it, he saw it and he was so bright about how the business worked. By then of course, Spector had a certain amount of notoriety.'

Spector began pushing to relocate in New York under the aegis of Leiber and Stoller. Sill phoned them up one day and told the pair, 'He's strange, this kid – but you won't believe how talented he is.' By the end of May 1960 Spector had moved to the East Coast and was sleeping on the couch Leiber and Stoller kept in their small Broadway office building. He began by playing guitar on a number of sessions – that's Spector playing the jazzy guitar solo at the end of the Drifters' evergreen 'On Broadway', for example. In September he produced a teen-pop rendition of the old folk standard 'Corrina, Corrina' for a young country crooner named Ray Peterson and scored himself a second Top 10 hit. The month after, 'Spanish Harlem', a song he'd co-written for Ben E. King was recorded: it became another major Top 10 hit. Spector often told people he'd actually produced the session, a claim that greatly annoyed Leiber and Stoller – who'd produced the record themselves – as well as vocalist King, whose memory of Spector's participation was less grandiose: 'I seem to recall him leaning against a wall or something.' Spector's real contribution to the song had come from creating the three-note riff played on a vibraphone that made up the record's signature motif. He'd actually created the riff with considerable help from a young New York songwriter named Beverley Ross, but when it came time for giving out credits and record royalties, Ross's name was mysteriously deleted from the project. 'It always seemed to me that Phil's basic nature was not to have any conscience,' she would later remark. 'He didn't want to feel anything for anybody.'

At the outset of 1961 he snubbed Leiber and Stoller and went to work for Atlantic Records in New York, a career move that deeply offended the label's head producer Jerry Wexler. There he produced sessions for Billy Storm, blues diva Ruth Brown, a teen combo called the Castle Kings, Laverne Baker and a group called the Top Notes, who made the first-ever recorded version of 'Twist and Shout'. Then, six months into his contract, Spector simply decided he'd spent long enough with the label and left his office, never to return. A day after this abrupt departure, Jerry Wexler – purple with rage – put in a call to Lester Sill which began with the words: 'That son of a bitch Spector owes me 10,000 dollars!' But Phil Spector was too busy to dwell on his debts. He produced a single for Gene Pitney next – a fabulous piece of epic pop foolishness entitled 'Every Breath I Take' which bizarrely failed to sell in big numbers. The aching tenor behind such immortal tracks as '24 Hours from Tulsa' and 'Town Without Pity' would in due time recall the twenty-year-old Spector as someone who 'understood the big picture of the whole thing and what he wanted to do in the business. He talked fast like a machine gun and he dropped a line on me that floored me. He said, "My sister's in an asylum – and she's the sane one in the family!"' He'd struck out lucky in February though with a fellow named Curtis Lee, who sang on a boisterous R'n'B party record, 'Pretty Little Angel Eyes', that rose to No. 1 in the US charts. Then a record he'd produced for Lester Sill that summer back in LA, 'I Love How You Love Me' – the second single of the Paris Sisters, a white girl trio that subverted the Teddy Bears' old 'transparency of sound' techniques into a more daringly sensual floating dimension – exploded up the chart. Spector seized this moment to set his master-plan into operation. By now he knew how the business worked. For Spector, it was full of talentless greedy cheapskates all grasping for 100 per cent contractual ownership of anything they could get their oily hands on. They felt no inspired affinity to popular music and most weren't even astute business brains. Spector, by contrast, knew he had both qualities in abundance. Indeed, he was a real musical visionary – the Richard Wagner of advanced rhythm'n'blues, no less – and had proven time and time again to his paymasters he understood how to pull together a hit record. Yet he was still being constrained in the recording studio. The sessions were too short; the number of musicians called too few. He was looking for something grandiose and magical and knew the only way to achieve his goals was to start his own record label and become completely autonomous.

When the Paris Sisters' record had taken off in the autumn of 1961, Lee Hazlewood had become so incensed by Spector's golden touch he broke off all business ties with his (former) partner Lester Sill. Spector immediately suggested he and Sill form their own label and Sill quickly agreed. They called it Philles, because their first names were Phil and Les. Spector continued doing freelance sessions – he even produced a Connie Francis record during this time – but Philles was his focus and when he began auditioning a New York girl quartet called the Crystals for the song publishers Hill & Range, he liked what he heard so much he simply stole them for his own label. 'There's No Other Like My Baby' – a song written by Leroy Bates, one of the Crystal's boyfriends (although Spector, as would from now on be his custom, took a co-composer's credit) – was recorded in a New York studio, Mira Sound, with only a handful of session players.

There was no 'wall of sound' yet – the budget wouldn't permit it – but Spector still managed to create a mesmerizing piece of music that soon enough made its way into the national Top 20. Typically, he still managed to piss off a lot of people in the process. The Crystals themselves thought he was too weird and didn't react well to the constant rehearsal sessions he kept putting them through. And John Bienstock, the head of Hill & Range, had steam coming out of his ears whenever Spector's name was mentioned: 'The Crystals were our artists. He was merely supposed to produce them for us and he just stole them right from under our noses. But he showed no remorse whatsoever: just like the typical piece of shit he was. He was talented but he was a piece of shit.'

Next Spector recorded the Crystals on a superb song he'd found from young songwriting duo Barry Mann and Cynthia Weil called 'Uptown'. Recorded in New York, Spector made sure that this time Mira Sound was filled with session players – banks of brooding violinists and cellists, fellows plunking away at mandolins whilst numerous percussionists were put to work playing gypsy castanets. Spector played guitar and controlled every aspect of the session. A young songwriter named Gerry Goffin was present at the recording and asked Spector at one point who had actually written the song. 'I did,' Spector answered without blinking. 'I never understood why he told lies like that. Maybe he thought he could make it his if he said it was,' Goffin admitted later. 'Uptown' made the Top 10 in the early summer of 1962. Spector then produced a follow-up, 'He Hit Me (and It Felt Like a Kiss)', a creepy song about domestic violence written by Goffin and his partner Carole King that unsurprisingly failed to attract radio airplay. Sensing his mercurial rise might suddenly be eclipsed by a flop record, Spector recalled the record from its distributors and focused instead on a song he'd stolen whilst working as an A&R man for Liberty Records in early '62 – a number entitled 'He's a Rebel' written by Gene Pitney. Spector immediately booked a session at LA's Gold Star – he didn't like the New York studios because the musicians union there wouldn't allow over-dubbing to take place – but the Crystals refused to fly out, leaving Spector to angrily coerce an LA black session group called the Blossoms and their main singer Darlene Wright (whose surname Spector would change to Love) to do all the vocal work. The session, which featured a younger arranger named Jack Nitzsche, two guitarists, two bass-players, drummer Hal Blaine, pianist Al Delory and sax player Steve Douglas – a school friend of Spector's – marked the true beginning of Spector's golden age of wide-screen sound. As soon as the perfect take had occurred, Spector brought the musicians in to hear a play-back. 'It just sounded like a roar,' recalled Douglas. 'We just looked at each other as if to say "How can he hear anything?" We all knew we were listening to something different. I remember how excited Phil was: he was glowing. Phil was so happy with the band and especially with Hal Blaine. He just fell in love with Hal.'

Spector had finally found the magic sound he'd been fantasizing about ever since he was a frightened child strumming his guitar alone in the dark. This had much to do with being surrounded by the right assistants, particularly the eccentric Nitzsche, players like Blaine and a long-suffering engineer Larry Levine. But not all his co-workers were in awe of what was happening. One of the guitarists at the 'Rebel' sessions was a well-respected jazz player named Howard Roberts whose fingers were literally bleeding from all the effort Spector demanded of him. Roberts had been Spector's guitar teacher when the latter was in his early teens. Now Spector was the teacher, but in the process Roberts felt the youth had become poisoned by his power: 'Suddenly, he was aloof, very distant: there was no more closeness. Phil slipped into the Never-Never Land of Hollywood success and really strange weirdness and I never saw him again after that. Even when I was seeing him, I couldn't see him.'

At the end of 1962 Phil Spector could savour the triumph of 'He's a Rebel' having made No. 1 in September of that year, followed two months later by a bizarre, echo-drenched funk version he'd concocted at Gold Star of the old Walt Disney nonsense song 'Zip-a-Dee-Doo-Dah' rocketing into the Top 10. He'd used his favourite male session singer – a black guy named Bobby Sheen whose muscular falsetto voice can be heard doing back-ups on numerous Spector classics – for the session, rechristening him Bobby Sox and the Blue Jeans. In the final week of December, the Crystals – even though it was Darlene Love singing again, not the Crystals themselves – peaked at No. 11

with the joyful follow-up to 'Rebel', 'He's Sure the Boy I Love'. The following year, 1963, would be even better. Spector was now twenty-two. He put away the crazy attire he'd been wearing to get himself noticed around New York – the capes, the galoshes, the creepy little goatee – and dressed in stylish shark-skin suits. He got married to a California girl – a beautiful Kim Novak lookalike named Annette Merar who'd sung in his Spector Three outfit. For a while there, it was true love, just like the gooey lyrics to the songs he produced said it would be. Spector even had 'Phil and Annette' cut into the run-off groove of his many vinyl releases throughout 1963. But there was always an erotically charged shadow hanging over the Spectors' short-lived marital bliss and her name was Veronica 'Ronnie' Bennett. Born in Manhattan's Upper West Side, Veronica, her sister Estelle and a younger cousin Nedra Talley began their musical career as the Darling Sisters, before becoming featured dancers at New York's Peppermint Lounge nightclub under the supervision of the deeply corrupt but highly powerful disc jockey known as Murray the K.

Then they signed to Don Kirschner's Dimension label as Ronnie and the Relatives and released a couple of forgettable singles. Gerry Goffin had been originally brought in to produce them but had backed off after several rehearsals. 'I remember trying to get them to sing harmonies and they seemed pretty terrible. I turned 'em down because I couldn't stand Ronnie's voice.' Spector, though, was dazzled when he first encountered the trio in early 1962. He immediately saw great commercial potential in Ronnie Bennett's pouty sex-doll singing voice. He was also consumed with desire for her. Danny Davis, Spector's right-hand man at Philles, recalls his young boss 'definitely threw himself at Ronnie. I remember him telling me at the outset he was crazy about her because she was great sexually. He was very enamoured of that, and I know for a fact they were doing ménage-à-trois scenes.' Whilst his young wife was sitting alone in their New York apartment, Spector was trysting endlessly with his new protégée Bennett in rehearsal rooms and other people's offices. It was all bound to end in an ugly mess. But that's how Spector mostly conducted himself with the people who came into his orbit. Success brought power and power brought a craving for more power. Spector became a total control freak. He viciously cut himself off from his business partners at Philles. He suddenly refused to pay his old mentor Lester Sill any money for his considerable services. Instead he recorded a grotesque-sounding instrumental, titled 'Do the Screw', pressed one vinyl copy and sent it to Sill. It was Phil's own sadistic way of saying 'Fuck you, old buddy.'

Nobody fucked with Phil Spector in 1963. If anyone tried, one of his bodyguards would break their nose or fracture their arm. Spector would enter clubs surrounded by muscle-men and soon enough there'd be a disturbance – someone getting their jaw broken by Phil's goons. Sometimes these people merited their punishment. On other occasions Spector's paranoia would cause completely innocent people to get viciously pulverized. Spector knew what it felt like to be physically humiliated. Either in school or during his early years snaking up the music industry, he'd been beaten up in a public urinal and pissed on by his assailants. Now it was payback time.

He was surrounded by yes men now. An ambitious young promo guy and would-be songwriter named Sonny Bono became his long-suffering flunky for $175 a week. Bono was there cheer-leading at every session in 1963. 'I was blown away by what he did in the studio. He did everything the opposite of what you were supposed to do. Everybody wanted a clean sound and then he comes along with this enormous muddy sound, getting bigger and bigger every time. He was hard to communicate with, though. Phil was sometimes open, sometimes introverted and you didn't know whether you said something wrong or not. Conversation didn't flow with him; it was never comfortable to hang out with him.' In the studio, during playbacks, Spector would always ask Bono the same question:

'Sonny – is it dumb enough?' Sonny would answer: 'Man, that sure is dumb enough.' Then Spector would correct him: 'No, Sonny – that's gold. That's solid gold coming out of that speaker.'

In March he produced 'Da Doo Ron Ron', the nursery-rhyme pop extravaganza that skipped into the Top 3 the following month for the Crystals. Three months later, he created the mighty 'Then He Kissed Me' for them and that made the Top 10 also. He even let the real Crystals back into the studio to record these two singles. He made some fiery gospel-pop singles with the formidable Darlene Love also, but these only made the lower end of the Top 40 and Spector didn't like to be associated with mediocre chart positions. Still, 1963 was his most successful year because it was the year he presented the Ronettes to the world via 'Be My Baby' and its equally stupendous follow-up, 'Baby I Love You'. For any young person in the summer of 1963, hearing the sexually unbridled Wagnerian mega-pomp of 'Be My Baby' for the first time was a life-shaking experience. A young Californian song-writer, Brian Wilson, was driving down an LA freeway when the song burst out of his car radio and he almost crashed the vehicle, so amazed was he by the audacious brilliance of the record. Wilson – who'd started having success with his own group the Beach Boys – hurried home and composed a song specifically to present the Ronettes as a follow-up to 'Be My Baby'. The song was entitled 'Don't Worry Baby' and Wilson timidly walked in on a Gold Star session to personally present it to Spector. Spector thought it had merit but refused to record it because he didn't own any of the publishing.

The truth was, Spector didn't want any other young success-ful guys being around his girls, the Ronettes. He made this abundantly clear to the Rolling Stones' flamboyant manager Andrew Loog Oldham – a self-styled UK Spector wannabe – when the Ronettes were booked to share a short UK package tour with the quintet from Dartford. Spector became close to

Oldham – they took drugs together in January 1964, both behaved outrageously, both employed thuggish bodyguards – and actually produced the sessions that resulted in the Stones' 'Not Fade Away' and 'Little by Little' recordings. He tried, unsuccessfully, to get them signed to Philles in America.

But the Stones themselves weren't as enamoured of him as their manager was. Defying Spector's hands-off edict, Keith Richards immediately began an affair with Ronnie Bennett during the month-long tour whilst Mick Jagger was successfully romancing her sister Estelle. The pair would continue their romances with the Bennett sisters whenever they arrived in New York in the early sixties. 'Phil must have known,' Keith Richards would remark to me many years later. 'I can remember attending one of his sessions and he was looking at me like daggers. But I wasn't going to lose any sleep over that. I always thought he was overrated, anyway. At the sessions I saw, it always seemed to me Jack Nitzsche was doing all the real work. He was the one doing the actual arrangements, he was the one in charge of placing the musicians physically so they'd get that perfect blend on tape.'

Spector loved England – the people were so genteel, they understood 'art' and, most importantly, they called him a 'genius' in their newspapers. Still the British invasion spearheaded by the Stones and the Beatles in the opening months of 1964 would mean the end of Spector and his whole way of controlling pop music. For all his revolutionary zeal, Phil Spector was strictly old school – a 1950s leftover spiritually caught between the innocent yearning of doo-wop and corny Christmas songs and the self-conscious bohemianism of the jazz hipster. As soon as the sixties began creating its own brand of hipness, he was lost. Suddenly everyone else was becoming hip, everyone believed they had their own creative ideas and everyone was growing their hair and taking strange mind-altering drugs. He could no longer control the situation: it had all become too anarchic.

He still made great records in 1964, including the Ronettes' 'Do I Love You' and 'Walking in the Rain', but oddly they didn't crack the Top 20 and even Sonny Bono told him to his face that his sound was getting old. He tried to get out of the rut by injecting new talent into his studio set-up. He found a white duo who called themselves the Righteous Brothers and who sounded just like two black guys. In October 1964 he recorded 'You've Lost that Lovin' Feelin'', with the pair, aided by a new arranger, Gene Page, and a roomful of players including Little Richard's original drummer Earl Palmer and Spector's hero Barney Kessel. Kessel recalls Spector 'working on the track like he was going to invade Moscow'. His endeavour paid off: the record hit the No. 1 position in the second week of February 1965. It was to be his last moment of pure pop omnipotence. 'I remember we were in the studio with the Ronettes cutting "Born to Be Together" [in December 1964],' Jack Nitzsche once recalled, 'and during the playback, Phil stood next to me and said, "It's all over. It's over. It's just not there anymore." The enthusiasm was gone.' Spector continued to make phenomenal music in '65 but most of the songs he finished – such as Darlene Love's dazzling 'A Long Way to Be Happy' and the Ronettes' rhapsodic 'Paradise' – went unreleased. He had further hits with the Righteous Brothers – 'Just Once in My Life', 'Unchained Melody' and 'Ebb Tide' – but the duo resented being perceived as Spector puppets and suddenly walked out on their Philles contract to make records for another label. When Spector heard the news, his assistant Danny Davis had to phone Spector's New York-based psychiatrist Dr Kaplan to get him to talk his patient out of jumping from the window of his LA office.

By 1966 things were falling apart. Spector's old groups were all in disarray or in conflict with their producer over unpaid royalties. His coterie of songwriters were all pissed off at him for adding his name to their credits. More crucially, Spector had fucked over too many important business connections on his way up. Now he appeared to be commencing his decline and all the knives were coming out for retribution. Confused, depressed and extremely paranoid, Spector rallied himself one final time in a concerted effort to reassert his former omnipotence on pop music. He picked a hot R'n'B live act that was having difficulty selling records: Ike and Tina Turner. He made sure the trigger-tempered Ike was never present in the studio – according to Danny Davis, 'Phil was scared to death of Ike.' It was his wife he wanted to record.

On 7 March 1966 in Gold Star studios, surrounded by the biggest contingent of session players Spector had ever assembled in one room, including four guitars, four basses, three keyboard players, two drummers and an army of brass players, Tina Turner ripped her larynx apart to do justice to the whirlwind of sound she was hearing in her headphones. You can hear the results on 'River Deep, Mountain High' – it's like being in the eye of a musical hurricane. It was Spector's most elaborate, most spectacular creation ever and it sold well in England but failed miserably in America, a fact that tormented Spector so fiercely he chose the moment to declare he was resigning from the pop pantheon.

'America didn't reject "River Deep" because it was a bad record,' claims Marshall Lieb. 'They rejected it because the business had a vendetta against Phil. It was very tough for him to get it played on the radio because of the way he'd treated a lot of the programme directors.'

Spector entered his retirement period at the age of merely twenty-five. He was now divorced from his first wife and living with Ronnie Bennett in a big rented mansion in Beverly Hills. He was a very rich and influential man, but his early success and insecurities as a child had caused him to stay locked in a perpetually juvenile and neurotic mind-set. All the people who know him say the same thing. He was still a boy. Only now, with too much idle time on his hands, he was a lost boy. He became infatuated with the doomed junkie comedian Lenny

Bruce. He worked on a film project with Dennis Hopper and even talked briefly about producing an album of Allen Ginsberg reciting his poetry. But Phil Spector was not temperamentally suited to the utopian drugginess of the late sixties. He despised hippies, and LSD terrified him even more than Ike Turner. 'He put himself under the influence of LSD once – prescribed by Dr Kaplan – and he told me that when he was under he saw his father commit suicide,' recalls Danny Davis. 'Phil always said he hated his father for what he did, for taking the easy way out. The acid went right to the heart of that hatred, to the pain, and it horrified him. That's why he was against LSD: it made him confront what he didn't want to.'

In 1969 he made a cautious comeback of sorts. He appeared in the opening sequence of *Easy Rider* playing a cocaine dealer and released a song called 'Black Pearl' that he'd co-written and produced for a black quintet, Sonny Charles and the Checkmates. It was a good record but it sounded more Motown than Wall of Sound: a bit of an anti-climax. Then John Lennon called him over to London to produce 'Instant Karma' for his Plastic Ono Band. Spector did an excellent job of maximizing the sound in the studio for the ex-Beatle and his session pals and Lennon next asked him to 'salvage' the Beatles' cursed *Let It Be* tape odyssey. Many Beatles fans find Spector's resulting 'production' of the *Let It Be* album distasteful, but the producer had a thankless task to begin with, sitting through hours of painfully mediocre music to extract something releasable. The critics beat up Spector mercilessly when the album came out in 1970, but this didn't stop both Lennon and George Harrison from employing him to produce their first post-Beatles solo albums released later that year.

The former took a week to record in the autumn of 1970 and Spector did a remarkable job in capturing the stripped-back raw aching essence of John Lennon's primal-scream masterpiece *Plastic Ono Band*. By contrast, Harrison's hefty triple album entitled *All Things Must Pass* took a frustrating five months to finish. The mystic Beatle soon realized working with Spector 'was more trouble than it was worth. On *All Things Must Pass* Phil came in and we did half of the backing tracks. But he was going through a bad time with his drinking and it made him ill, so he had to leave.

'I literally used to have to go and break into the hotel to get him. I'd go along the roof and climb in the window, yelling, "Come on! We're supposed to be making a record!" He'd say "Oh! OK." And then he used to have eighteen cherry brandies before he could get himself down in the studio.' Harrison and Spector then tried to record some new tracks with Ronnie Bennett, who'd married Phil in 1967 and was now Ronnie Spector. A so-so single called 'Try Some, Buy Some' was eventually released but – according to Harrison – 'Phil didn't have enough energy to sustain an album with Ronnie. . . He kept falling over and breaking his wrists and ankles. The guy who was his helper was having heart attacks.'

Phil and Ronnie's marriage was no happy-ever-after production, either. She first tried to divorce him less than a year after their wedding; he coerced her into staying and once again she'd be locked up in the big LA mansion with nothing but alcohol and pills for company. This developed into a pattern throughout the following years. Two children were adopted by the couple but it didn't bring them closer. Finally, in 1973 Ronnie Spector walked out on her husband for the last time. During one of the many ugly child-custody hearings, Phil chose to bring along his old pal John Lennon to the courtroom for support. Lennon and Spector had gone platinum together in 1971 with *Imagine* but had been rightly slammed for 1972's *Some Time in New York*. Now it was late 1973 and the pair were reunited in drunken desperate sessions for an album of rock'n'roll oldies Lennon wanted to release. The ex-Beatle had just left Yoko Ono and was behaving like a self-destructive maniac. Mac Rebennack, aka Dr John, played on one session, along with guitarists Danny Kortchmar and Jesse Ed Davis.

'The night before, John [Lennon] had bitten Danny on the end of his nose and fractured Jesse Ed Davis's wrist,' recalled Rebennack. 'Phil Spector kept trying to hide a bottle of booze John had brought with him. When John finally found the bottle, the session ended.' Yet even the hard-nut Lennon was left deeply shocked and saddened by Spector's behaviour in court. As soon as his wife entered, Spector started spitting out torrents of obscenities in her direction. The judge found him in contempt. Spector didn't even notice Lennon quickly leave the courtroom by himself. They never saw or spoke to each other again.

'Phil was a very normal person at the beginning of his career,' Ronnie Spector would later state in a reflective moment. 'But as time went on, they started writing about him being a genius and then he said, "Yeah, I'm a genius." Then they'd say he was a mad genius. So he became the mad genius. That sort of destroyed him because he became a replica of everything he read about himself.'

The rest of the seventies were as sad as they were mad for Spector. His drinking grew out of control and he and his goons started waving guns around everywhere they went. He produced records for Dion, Cher and Harry Nilsson, but the wall of sound he conjured up sounded old and bereft of joy: a hollow ghost.

Leonard Cohen got talked into making a record with him in 1978 – *Death of a Ladies' Man* – and found himself practically mixed out of the finished product. 'Phil couldn't resist annihilating me,' he mused at the time. 'I don't think he can tolerate any other shadows in his own darkness.' Two years later, he produced the Ramones. It was not a marriage made in heaven. Joey Ramone recalled: 'He kept a prostitute in the studio. But not for sex. He'd just go over and totally insult her for forty-five minutes: just total verbal abuse.' Most concur with Johnny Ramone's verdict: 'He was just a sad little man with lifts in his shoes, waving his gun and wearing his wig. Not a nice guy.'

The eighties passed in a drunken blur. Things got so desperate he even considered producing La Toya Jackson. At some point in the decade – the details are sketchy – he apparently married his former secretary Janis Savala, who bore him twins – Nicole and Phillip Jr. The nineties were kinder to him, in so far as finally he started receiving industry awards and his Philles output was re-released on CD. He supposedly cleaned up his alcohol problem but was hit hard when his son Phillip suddenly died in 1993 at the age of ten.

As the new millennium started up, he could sometimes be sighted sporting a ludicrous Louis XIV wig at A-list LA parties, swanning around vacantly, surrounded by a fawning mob of similarly geriatric admirers. Nancy Sinatra briefly became his consort whilst his daughter Nicole successfully coerced him into producing a young Brit-rock quartet called Starsailor over in England. The sessions gave birth to two singularly unspectacular tracks and the group went on to make a series of derogatory remarks about Spector's work with them to the world's press. According to them, he'd been out of it all the time and simply couldn't come to terms with new digital technology. Spector then gave an interview of his own to a journalist for a UK daily and spoke at surprising length about his ongoing battles with depression and insanity. The many anti-depressants he admitted taking daily, though, weren't enough to keep him on a straight-and-narrow path. One night, at an upmarket Hollywood restaurant named Dan Tana's, he began hitting the booze again after several years of blessed abstinence and the old demons were suddenly back inside his brain – more vile and vicious than ever. Later that evening he drunkenly coerced a waitress named Lana Clarkson to accompany him back to his princely mansion. At around 3 a.m., Clarkson was shot point-blank in the face. Spector – the only other person in the house – claims it was a suicide. His chauffeur, who was lurking outside the building, claims otherwise. As I write this, a murder trial is forthcoming but Spector has already been arraigned. Perhaps recognizing that this would be one of his last moments as the spotlight kid, he chose his most bizarre wig to wear in court: a voluminous grey monstrosity that made him look like Mozart's senile grandfather.

Since the sixties, Phil Spector's life has been likened many times to that of the self-deluded Hollywood has-been who was the central character in Billy Wilder's *Sunset Boulevard*. Now he has literally become Norma Desmond.

The music he created remains timeless, but the era of contrived innocence it evokes so grandly is long gone, never to be reclaimed. Worse still, he was overtaken by his pupils, specifically Brian Wilson, who took the sonic dynamics of Spector's Wall of Sound and refashioned them into a more benign-sounding and lustrous sheen for his Beach Boys recordings. Wilson's sound 'was all about love', reckoned another famous LA producer, Terry Melcher, before his death, 'but Phil's was just about "anger"'. That's an over-simplification, of course, but still somehow it makes sense. The anger created the mighty wall of sound but it also sowed the seeds for his downfall: he could never rise above it and his soul became increasingly tainted as a result. His numerous former co-workers meanwhile will surely be watching Spector's upcoming court dates amid a cacophony of mixed emotions. Not long before his own death, George Harrison perhaps spoke most eloquently about the bitter-sweet 'strange love' that still bonds the infuriating producer to his former charges:

'Phil – if you're reading this – I still think you're one of the greatest. There's nobody who's come close to some of his productions for sheer excitement. He should be doing stuff right now. But not with me!'

Self-destruction in Rock and Elsewhere

The Franz Ferdinand boys asked me to write a piece about 'self-destruction and its place in rock' and that immediately set me to thinking: what do they mean exactly when they invoke the phrase 'self-destruction'? Terms need to be defined. Everybody has a shadow self to contend with but most manage to contain it effectively as they settle into their regimented routines of daily living. Rock stars, by contrast, are often actively encouraged to cultivate their darker qualities and that's where the trouble usually starts. 'Cocaine and ego,' Neil Young once reliably informed me. 'You put the two together and it's like an explosion going off.' And explosions inevitably cause casualties. A familiar downward spiral is once more set in motion. But is this authentic self-destructive behaviour unravelling itself or just plain old bad luck?

We first need to step back through the mists of time in order to come up with a credible answer. The fifties are suddenly alive once more with pompadoured young men sneering and crooning lasciviously about racing with the Devil. Gene Vincent was probably that era's finest example of a complete lunatic let loose to entertain the masses. In a recent biography about the notorious manager Pete Grant, the urchin-faced hill-billy singer is remembered beating up his wife, breaking a leg and falling offstage drunk in the middle of his opening song – all in the space of a single day. But Vincent at least had an excuse. His foot had been badly injured whilst in the army and he was in constant pain so he took too many pills and drank far too much. Authentically self-destructive or just plain unlucky? I lean towards the latter. Jerry Lee Lewis is a more interesting case. Nick Tosches' *Hellfire* documents some hair-raisingly self-destructive episodes that have dotted the Killer's career like confetti at a high-society wedding. Lewis's problems were stimulated by his gargantuan appetite for pills and liquor but were rooted more in his boundless arrogance. By the same token, this arrogance has also managed to sustain him and keep him bouncing back – against all odds, he's now the last of the Sun originals left standing. Johnny Cash spent his entire musical career trying to keep his self-destructive instincts at bay – often without success. And Elvis Presley exhibited all the classic symptoms of those driven to self-destruction by too much fame and medication: short attention span, an ego-centric, chronically addictive personality, bad taste in friends and horrendous eating habits. He was also stupid. He may have been the King, but dying on the toilet is scarcely the most regal way to exit this planet.

The sixties brought new drugs and with them new ways to fry the senses to ever-diminishing degrees. Still the questions linger. Was Syd Barrett being self-destructive when he ceaselessly bathed his cerebral faculties in LSD or was he just using himself as a human chemistry experiment in order to create suitably other-worldly music for mass enjoyment? Were Jimi Hendrix and Janis Joplin truly self-destructive or simply pampered drug-gies whose charmed lives were cut short in one fatal moment of over-indulgence? The Doors' Jim Morrison certainly had his share of personal demons driving him on to assume the mantle of loose-cannon tormentor of the Love Generation. 'He was a thoroughly unpleasant guy,' David Crosby recently opined. 'If there were flower children, Jim was a mushroom child. Keep him in the dark and feed him shit.' Morrison took perverse delight in starting riots at Doors concerts and also enjoyed falling out of windows and tumbling several storeys to the cold, hard ground. Still, the self-destructive aesthetic he adhered to was mostly ripped off from the traditional alcoholic bravado of American literature's macho brawlers such as Ernest Hemingway and Norman Mailer.

It took a wayward disciple of Morrison – a crazy-eyed Michigan youth known as Iggy Pop – to more fully exploit the allure of self-destructive behaviour in rock's gladiatorial arena of the senses. As lead singer of the Stooges, Iggy often maimed himself, cut himself with broken glass and poured burning candle wax over his torso in mid-performance. In 1974 he was beaten, whipped and stabbed during a show in Los Angeles and then left unconscious and bleeding in the street bound up inside a gunny sack. Whilst the now hale and healthy Pop admits that drug abuse often fogged his thinking in those days, he's still adamant that his trail of destruction was there for a higher purpose. 'All this terrible self-destructive shit I supposedly did,' he claimed five years ago, 'I only did it because I believed I was in the right and that I was playing the music that real people with real lives wanted to hear. Frankly, throughout my life, I've always felt I was completely innocent. I see myself as a genuine innocent. Always have done.'

Innocent or otherwise, Iggy Pop arrived just in time to celebrate the end of the sixties and help initiate the world into the uncertain, solipsistic seventies. Essentially a cynical rebuttal of the previous decade's utopian pretensions, the seventies were soon awash with pale anorexic rock stars struggling to survive in the face of ever-growing drug-dependency issues. Keith Richards of the Rolling Stones was the most notorious excessive of that epoch, certainly, and even came close to serving jail time in Toronto because of his addiction to narcotics. But Richards was never authentically self-destructive; he just adored getting high. Like the keyboard player in Spinal Tap, his philosophy of life was the simple and succinct 'have a good time all the time'. 'Pain – who needs it?' was another of his favoured utterances.

In this respect, at least, the man sometimes known as 'the Human Riff' has always been markedly different from that other key figure of seventies self-immolation: Sid Vicious. I had the dubious pleasure of knowing Vicious and can verify that indeed he was one of the most self-destructive individuals to ever walk the face of this planet. He was also clueless, devoid of a fully formed personality and a borderline psychopath. When Malcolm McLaren invited him to join the Sex Pistols, it was like giving a retarded teenager a gun and involving him in a high-stakes bank robbery. There were bound to be bloody victims. Vicious soon demonstrated he had no musical talent whatsoever, but that has never mattered to his followers who wrong-headedly perceive his thirst for pain and mayhem-making as the definitive badge of punk purity. His notoriety ultimately meant that being a deranged exhibitionist became a greater guarantee of rock-star success than being a gifted musician. Pop culture would never be the same again.

Nowadays we can all too readily see the legacy of Sid suspended like a diseased shadow over the world of contemporary entertainment. His spirit lives on in the mindless thuggery of *Jackass*, the drunken loutishness of Liam Gallagher and the egocentric posturing of celebrity unfit-mother Courtney Love. Her late husband Kurt Cobain, of course, took self-destructing in public to a whole new level in the nineties. Blowing your face off when you're right at the top of your game: it's got to be a hard act for other self-destructive music-makers to beat. Still, Michael Jackson may yet do it. Is he self-destructive or just insanely self-deluded? Probably both.

Watching the latest breed – from Pete Doherty to Whitney Houston – slowly disintegrate before our very eyes surely indicates one thing. Self-destructing – in rock, in public, in fact anywhere – is not good for the human spirit, not to mention the lungs, liver and kidneys. Artistically, it's best approached the way David Bowie did it in the mid-1970s. His cocaine addiction turned him into a withered stick-insect figure of a man but also inspired the best music of his entire career. Then he sorted himself out and became the golden-haired survivor we know and love today. That's the trick, of course: to 'destroy' yourself but somehow 'redeem' yourself artistically in the process and become stronger and wiser as a result. It's a fool's dream but it won't stop younger minds from being seduced down that path again and again. What's the alternative? A long life and a world full of moderate musos like Belle and Sebastian.

ff

Faber and Faber – a home for writers

Faber and Faber is one of the great independent publishing houses in London. We were established in 1929 by Geoffrey Faber and our first editor was T. S. Eliot. We are proud to publish prize-winning fiction and non-fiction, as well as an unrivalled list of modern poets and playwrights. Among our list of writers we have five Booker Prize winners and eleven Nobel Laureates, and we continue to seek out the most exciting and innovative writers at work today.

www.faber.co.uk – a home for readers

The Faber website is a place where you will find all the latest news on our writers and events. You can listen to podcasts, preview new books, read specially commissioned articles and access reading guides, as well as entering competitions and enjoying a whole range of offers and exclusives. You can also browse the list of Faber Finds, an exciting new project where reader recommendations are helping to bring a wealth of lost classics back into print using the latest on-demand technology.